W9-CDV-093

The Gift of Love

The Gift of Love

Augustine, Jean-Luc Marion, and the Trinity

Andrew Staron

Fortress Press
Minneapolis

THE GIFT OF LOVE

Augustine, Jean-Luc Marion, and the Triinity

Cover design: Alisha Lofgren

Hardcover ISBN: 978-1-5064-2340-1

Paperback ISBN: 978-1-5064-1670-0

eBook ISBN: 978-1-5064-1671-7

The paper used in this publication meets the minimum requirements of American National Standard for Information Sciences — Permanence of Paper for Printed Library Materials, ANSI Z329.48-1984.

Manufactured in the U.S.A.

This book was produced using Pressbooks.com, and PDF rendering was done by PrinceXML.

To AJ, Lucia, and Felicity—
Gifts initiating my love.

Satisfy your demand for reason always but remember that charity is beyond reason, and that God can be known through charity.

—Flannery O'Connor, letter to Alfred Corn, June 16, 1962

Contents

Acknowledgments

> If theology cannot teach and lead us—and all the disciplines and their practitioners—by being itself the art of charity, then it is not worth doing. Theology, more than any other, is a creditory discipline: after all, we are all debtors, and our one task is to bring credit to the faith that teaches us that in theology, as in life, you are only as good as what you give away.
>
> —Pete Candler, "On Credit and Debt in Theology"

It was a conversation with Thomas Schärtl over coffee many years ago that first got me thinking along the lines that would open to the possibility of this book. Challenging encouragement would then come from Brian Johnstone, CSsR, Tarmo Toom, and Chad Pecknold. Before this, though, it was attentive inspiration from Theresa Sanders, Frank Ambrosio, Vince Miller, Julia Lamm, and Tom King, SJ, that put me in a position to even begin to look for what I hope to have glimpsed here. And it is Bill Loewe who deserves credit for whatever theological precision I might have and for a significant part of the tenacity-born-of-hope that brought this to completion.

The generosity of Jeffrey Kosky showed me—a complete stranger to him—the truth of Candler's words above. Jean-Luc Marion, beyond his obvious contribution to this work in providing a significant part of its foundation and approach, encouraged me to look to *De Trinitate* to further understand the gift. Jim Sabak, OFM, and Stuart Squires offered the consolation that comes from a shared endeavor. John Slattery offered me a much needed critical eye. Regis Armstrong, OFM Cap., fought fights I could not fight to bring me to a place where I could publish this book.

Doug and Therese Swinehart have never hesitated in their faith in my work. My brother, Jeff, inspires my persistence and devotion. My parents, Ray and Gina, urged me to seek God in a dedication to the church and family and taught this dedication by example. My colleagues at Wheeling Jesuit University, especially Dan O'Hare and Darin McGinnis, have given me a place where I love to work and write—a gift indeed. Jessica Wrobleski's generous friendship and support—both spiritual and practical—has opened space for the art of charity.

My children, AJ, Lucia, and Felicity, continue to be the gifts that quicken my love. And my wife, Andrea, gives me the particular incarnation that allows it all to make sense.

Introduction

"To say and mean 'God,'" writes David Tracy, "is what must drive all theology, whenever, wherever and whoever speaks."[1] But as driving theology, to so *say* and *mean* rouses and draws not a disciplined, abstract, faith-seeking understanding but theologians. God is neither said nor meant by "theology," as such, but by particular women and men who find themselves in the middle of life's way, responding to this restless drive that is itself a response to an always already given gift. Whenever and wherever we say "God," we hope to mean not the idea, image, or model of God, but *God*—we hope to mean the God who creates, saves, and sustains us—to mean the God who loves us first.[2] Because in saying "God" we hope to actually mean God, no theologian speculating amidst the heights of the discipline's discourse can long ignore the question of *how* we say and mean God—*how* we name that which is beyond every name. Therefore, no theologian, Jean-Luc Marion relatedly observes, "can remove himself from the question of the names of God" and each must face the difficulty of "naming the unnameable, and naming it *as such*."[3] Ever before us are both the question of how we name God and the impossibility of our doing so

1. David Tracy, "God, Dialogue and Solidarity: A Theologian's Refrain," *The Christian Century* 107 (October 10, 1990): 904.
2. By using the first person plural throughout part 1, I hope it might serve as a reminder that as a reader of *De Trinitate*, I assume the posture of membership in both the human species created by God and the community to which Augustine wrote (i.e., the church). Augustine writes not so much to *me* as an individual but to *me* as part of a *we*.
3. Jean-Luc Marion, *In The Self's Place: The Approach of Saint Augustine*, trans. Jeffrey L. Kosky (Stanford, CA: Stanford University Press, 2012), 289.

sufficiently, each standing upon the further and fundamental question of how we call upon God by that impossible name. For theology does not name God so as to identify God, to proclaim *this* or *that* as God, to put God "on the table," so to speak. Rather, theology's reason is the naming of God so we might then call upon God by a name that opens us to be saved, healed, and made new.

But the inquiry into this *how*—to understand how we might begin to relate the name of God and our calling upon God by name—requires that we "search for and test the right example, the best test case of the phenomenon we seek to understand."[4] And it is fitting that with the doubled question of the name of God and the calling upon God by name ever before us, we turn for the right example to the name revealed in the New Testament, the mysterious Trinitarian name by which the Christian church has long called and called upon the one God of Jesus Christ: the Father, Son, and Holy Spirit.[5]

Augustine's *De Trinitate* stands as a, if not *the*, paradigmatic Western theological exploration of this Trinitarian name (a name that seemed to have become, by the twentieth century, irrelevant both to the majority of theology and to the experience of the faithful[6]), in large part because of the author's theological authority, but also in part because of its having been misunderstood. Rather than directly engaged, Augustine's argument was reduced to an abstract and clear "exposition of the relations of God *in se*,"[7] and therefore, "a curious kind of intellectual luxury"[8] that paradoxically secured this influence

4. David Tracy, *Plurality and Ambiguity: Hermeneutics, Religion, Hope* (Chicago: University of Chicago Press, 1987), 11.
5. Matthew 28:19, referenced by Augustine as he begins his closing prayer in *De Trinitate* 15.51.
6. "The neo-scholastic dogmatic structure made the tract on the Trinity impermeable to other relevant themes (such a soteriology) and, most unfortunate of all, presented a trinitarian theology disconnected from the revelation and the experience of Father, Son, and Spirit in salvation history. Trinitarian theology became a purely speculative endeavor, of interest to precious few, unintelligible to the vast majority. Hence the misleading commonplace that 'We cannot explain anything about the doctrine of the Trinity since it is a mystery.' (God is mystery, to be sure; the doctrine is complex but not the same as the Mystery.) And so, generations of Christians were taught virtually nothing about this central truth of the Christian faith, except that it was enshrouded in mystery and in any case had no bearing on living out one's faith." Catherine Mowry LaCugna, introduction to *The Trinity*, by Karl Rahner (New York: Crossroad, 1997), x.
7. Catherine Mowry LaCugna, *God for Us: The Trinity and Christian Life* (New York: HarperCollins, 1991), 81.

through minimizing the need to closely read the original text. But with its "exceptionally nuanced fusion of theology and anthropology,"[9] *De Trinitate* offers to its readers more than what this reductionist interpretation allows. Delicately walking along the edge of reason, attentive both to predicative possibility and to the hermeneutical significance of love, Augustine presents an approach to the Trinity that is intimately intertwined with the conversion of our own memory, understanding, and love of God. *De Trinitate* suggests that we advance to the Trinity that God is (and not just to any trinity) via the promise and limits of the idea of the Trinity, always aware that the "sign systems we create are no better than the love in which they were ultimately begotten."[10] The predicative exhaustion of these systems serves as a sign of the efficacy of the gift of love. For although unaided reason cannot traverse the unknown path from our idea of the Trinity to the Trinity that God is, what is impossible for us is not impossible for God (or, at least, that is the hope of Augustine and of the Christian faith).[11]

Praised and proclaimed by the scriptures,[12] love is, for Augustine, the way by which we might investigate further, and on a higher plane, the irrepressible Trinitarian name of God.[13] But to proclaim that the God of Jesus Christ is not only a God of love but the God who is love (following the scriptures generally and, more particularly, the Johannine assertion: God is love[14]) is nothing if not commonplace and often risks (if not outright succumbs to) banality. Mitigating this risk requires attention to an interrelated pair of fundamental questions each inviting both philosophical rigor and theological focus. First, what is

8. Edmund Hill, OP, introduction to *The Trinity*, by Augustine, The Works of St. Augustine: A Translation of the 21st Century, vol. 3, no. 9 (Hyde Park, NY: New City Press, 1991), 19.
9. Rowan Williams, "*Sapientia* and the Trinity: Reflections on the *De Trinitate*," in *Collectanea Augustiniana: Mélanges T.J. van Bavel*, ed. B. Bruning, M. Lamberigts, J. van Houtem (Leuven: Leuven University Press, 1990), 332.
10. John C. Cavadini, "The Quest for Truth in Augustine's *De Trinitate*," *Theological Studies* 58, no. 3 (1997): 436.
11. Matthew 19:26; Mark 10:27; Luke 1:37.
12. Augustine, *De Trinitate*, 8.14. Unless stated otherwise, all English translations throughout are from Augustine, *The Trinity*, trans. Edmund Hill, OP, ed. John E. Rotelle, The Works of St. Augustine: A Translation of the 21st Century, vol. 3, no. 9 (Hyde Park, NY: New City Press, 1991).
13. Ibid.
14. 1 John 4:8.

this Trinitarian gift of love? Second, how does it impact our approach to God? It will be my argument that these two questions cannot be engaged separately because our possible response to the first question manifests itself almost entirely within our response to the second and because the response to "how?" demands the particularity of the response to "what?" (Moreover, let us remember that in the case of the God who is love, asking "what is this gift?" is really a matter of asking "who is this gift?"). To say and mean the Trinitarian name of God through the love of God (in both subjective and objective senses of the genitive), is not simply a matter of discovering the correct theological vocabulary and grammar. An understanding of how we say and mean this name is not therefore simply a matter of calling God by a particular name, nor of a deep philosophical understanding of what such a name might mean about God, but is always also an attempt to call upon God by name in response to the gift of love already given to us by God. To come to know God through love—the path Augustine offers—invites reading *De Trinitate* in a way open to love and its impact upon us. It invites reading with a mind and heart open to the transformation necessary to receive the vision of God. In this way, *De Trinitate* is not only an investigation into the theological and philosophical particulars about the name of God but one that takes seriously that the naming of God is the naming not of an object external to me (grand though it might be) but of the one who is "both sought in order to be found and found in order to be sought."[15] Consequently, while it is the Trinitarian name of the Christian God that is my ultimate concern, it is this gift of love—what it is and how it turns us to remember, understand, and love the Trinity—that is the primary focus of this book.

If love is where we are to look to come to know the limits of our idea of God, to open to the Trinity that God is, and to know ourselves as made to the image of God, then it is only appropriate that we come to remember love, understand it, and even to love it. Jean-Luc Marion's phenomenology of love promises to ground this Trinitarian speculation in the givenness of love, offering a way by which we might

15. Augustine, *De Trinitate*, 15.2.

unite the deepest mystery of the Christian faith—the mystery of God that comes to us in Jesus Christ and the Holy Spirit—with its phenomenological impact upon us. Marion's phenomenology of saturation and excess renders his philosophy of love a promising criterion by which we might begin to speak to the interrelated mysteries of the Trinitarian life of God and our participation in, and transformation by, that life. When this reception of the gift of love is applied to Augustine's theology—and particularly his assertion that the image of God is visible in the mind's remembering, understanding, and loving not itself but God—we might discover both a glimpse of divine love and a demonstration of a union of the theological endeavor with the deepening of our love of God, itself a response to our being loved first. Marion's insight into his own interpretation of *Confessions*, offered in *In the Self's Place*, holds true for this study of *De Trinitate* as well: "the outcome would be at best approximate: somewhat ignorant and surely incomplete, but above all falling incommensurably short of the terrifying gravity of the project undertaken by Augustine—of his advance toward God, more exactly of his harsh discovery that in fact God always advances from all eternity toward me."[16] We always arrive late to this love that is always already given to us. We are always responding to what has already been given. The God who loves us in advance of our response, loves us so we might respond, so we might, too, become lovers. Therefore, along with *De Trinitate*, Marion's work will serve as the second exemplary proposal through which we will seek deeper understanding of this name and of calling upon God by this name. It is my hope that the convergence of Augustine and Marion will illuminate new interpretations of the divine life given in and through this love, and our related naming of, and participation in, this love.

In effecting such a convergence, I hope to read *De Trinitate* in a space focused less upon a theological parsing of the doctrine of the Trinity and more upon how we might come to know and love God through an always insufficient doctrine. If, for Augustine, to call God by name is always already to call upon God, to enter into the space

16. Marion, *In the Self's Place*, xv.

of God's own graced offer and to respond to what arrives in advance of our first thought and first desire, then an approach to the name of God should profit from not only a detailed description of this place but from an invitation into this place itself. And understanding this place of response to that which is given to us might very well help us understand what is given—and perhaps even help us become willing to receive it. Joseph S. O'Leary observes that Marion's writings "do not fuss about ontological claims of classical dogma"—like, for instance, the relationship between the divine substance and the persons of the Father, Son, and Holy Spirit—"but initiate the reader into a space, an enveloping event, something like Teilhard's *milieu divin.* In this space it makes little sense to define ontological foundations. Rather, one discerns its dimensions from within the space itself."[17] It is as this enveloping event that Marion's work holds so much promise for Trinitarian theology. Marion's analysis of this place of loving response invites us to find it within ourselves, an inward turn that corresponds well with Augustine's own interior way.[18] But Marion's work offers a description of this place wherein we might glimpse both a deeper vision of love (offered to us on its own terms) and a fuller understanding of *how* we receive this vision.

In this way, the turn to Jean-Luc Marion's phenomenology of the gift and the rigorous erotic reduction is in continuity with the claims and demands of the ancient text—claims and demands that have ourselves as their intended target. Tracy notes that "hermeneutically the reception of Augustine, *pace* all pure historicists, is sometimes as important for understanding Augustine well as are readings determined solely by Augustine's historical context."[19] This does not only mean that each reader is a part of the reading and interpreting but also that Augustine himself was not only interested in imparting

17. Joseph S. O'Leary, "The Gift: A Trojan Horse in the Citadel of Phenomenology?," in *Givenness and God: Questions of Jean-Luc Marion*, ed. Ian Leask and Eoin Cassidy (New York: Fordham University Press, 2005), 136.
18. See Augustine, *De Trinitate*, 8.1.
19. David Tracy, "Augustine's Christomorphic Theocentrism," in *Orthodox Readings of Augustine*, ed. George E. Demacopoulos and Aristotle Papanikolaou (Crestwood, NY: St. Vladimir's Seminary Press, 2008), 269.

knowledge but also in transforming his readers through their response to his words. For we intend a Trinitarian God not generally but particularly; we intend not the idea of God (however inescapable and necessary such a sign is for us) but God. In our intending God, comparatives surpass the superlatives,[20] leading us not to an unsurpassed abstract idea but to the God who comes to us through the gift of love. In receiving what Augustine offers in *De Trinitate*, we receive his approach to saying and meaning the God who is revealed and offered through, with, and in Jesus Christ. This means that the name of God is inescapably part of our naming God as the one who comes to save us.

To approach *De Trinitate* through love—and particularly through love understood in light of Marion's phenomenology—is certainly to risk an approach without certainty. For if nothing else, to approach through love means that we can only hope to begin to grasp the reality of this approach if we risk ourselves in sympathy and openness; we cannot be intellectually honest to the subject matter of love while remaining detached. It also means that there is no neutral place from which we might analyze what is given, as if it were not given to us but simply there—generally, abstractly, and without intention. But it is also a risk because, although consistent with Augustine's approach, it is not the only possible path by which we might interpret the text. If Augustine intended an unambiguous singular point of departure from which we might begin an explanation of his Trinitarian thought, it is well hidden beneath the at times quite distinct books of the text (differing to such an extent that any presentation of *De Trinitate* inevitably includes a theory by which these fifteen books are grouped, related, and prioritized). What is true of Augustine's thought in general hold true for *De Trinitate*: "Studying the texts of Augustine is indeed like getting to know an ancient, crowded, labyrinthine city," resulting in a "never-completed understanding"[21] not only of a specific text but also of any single rich and complex idea. It is difficult to know where we are in

20. Marion, *In the Self's Place*, 98.
21. Tracy, "Augustine's Christomorphic Theocentrism," 263.

his thought and how one intriguing section of text relates to what we read yesterday, last week, or years ago. When adding to Augustine's vast literary corpus (or even to the vastness of *De Trinitate*) the varying and always increasing amount of secondary literature (among which, I suppose, this book might now be counted), we can be left without a clear way of approach, without a firm foundation upon which to anchor a first step.

No less do other, more standard interpretive warnings remain true here, too. For inescapable as these hermeneutical choices are, they always demand caution, lest we find in the text the confirmation of what we already have in mind—a discovery of our own idols masked by the words of the Doctor of Grace. James J. O'Donnell warns readers of Augustine:

> If repeatedly we feel on reading stories of his life that we understand the issues, concerns, and attitudes he and his contemporaries shared, that's *not* because we have seen and understood them and made a serious historical attempt to compare them to our own, but because they (and their modern translators) use names and labels that elide the gaps that separate us and make their issues and their affiliations seem relevant.[22]

It is *De Trinitate* that we long to understand; we do not want to reduce it to a text about our own issues and concerns. We therefore are right to struggle with its terminology and methodology, prescinding as far as possible from imposing upon it antecedent definition, and to allow the text to speak for itself. At the same time, we cannot hope to read *De Trinitate* as if it can, in fact, speak for itself, as if its words and concepts could mean anything to us without our understanding them within our own contexts. We cannot presume to begin from where Augustine himself began (the date, place, and context of the composition of the text). Nor can we presume to begin from a place of neutrality, where the words (translated or not) of the text have no cultural or personal accent and where we might enter into the world of the text unencumbered by antecedent definition. Nor could we hope to begin to understand anything (let alone something as extensive and

22. James J. O'Donnell, *Augustine: A New Biography* (New York: HarperCollins, 2005), 174.

theologically symphonic as *De Trinitate*) without understanding it as related to our prior, and developing, understanding. We can only come to know this text—as with any text—through our own context, try as we might to conform our context to that of the author. We cannot learn anything without signs signifying something new, Augustine teaches, even if it is also the case that signs cannot teach us anything we do not already know.[23]

While inescapably of concern in all readings of any text, this hermeneutical elision has taken a common form in contemporary—particularly following strains of thought roughly categorized as postmodern—readings of Augustine. Lieven Boeve observes that it is far too easy, for the "postmodern Augustine has merely become a double of the postmodern decentering of the subject, marketed as the structure of religious desire" where "recontextualization here equals accommodation."[24] He encourages theologians to instead attempt to maintain a balance between the tendency to "lift Augustine's thinking out of its historical context, and forget about the historical-contextual dynamics of his searching and thinking" and systematic theology's double insistence that the Christian theological truth claim "does not allow itself to be reduced to a kind of particular filling in or exemplification of a more original religious structure" as well as that "radical historical-contextual consciousness should not necessarily lead to radical historicism."[25] The challenge of a postmodern reading of Augustine is the challenge of postmodernity in general and the challenge addressed by this book: how might I allow the other to speak to me, to remain other, yet at the same time to traverse the distance between us so as to make possible an encounter? Theologically speaking, this challenge may be rephrased: how might we read *De Trinitate* so as to both genuinely read *De Trinitate* (and not find therein

23. Augustine, *The Teacher*, in *"Against the Academicians" and "The Teacher,"* trans. Peter King (Indianapolis: Hackett, 1995). All English translations of *De Magistro* throughout are from this version.

24. Lieven Boeve, "Retrieving Augustine Today: Between Neo-Augustinianist Essentialism and Radical Hermeneutics?," in *Augustine and Postmodern Thought: A New Alliance Against Modernity?*, ed. Lieven Boeve, M. Lamberigts, Maarten Wisse (Walpole, MA: Peeters, 2009), 15.

25. Ibid., 17.

only what we already know or think we know) and read it in a manner that might allow it to impact us, to shape us, to interpret us?[26] How might we, therefore, read *De Trinitate* while remaining on guard against our own sophistries that scorn the starting place of our faith in God[27] (which is the text's own starting place) and deepen of our understanding of our encounter with that very God (which is Augustine's goal in the text)?

I purpose to follow Marion's experiment in *In the Self's Place*, wherein he interprets the *Confessions* "according to the terms of a phenomenology of givenness,"[28] and turn Marion's phenomenology of saturation, gift, and love toward a theological interpretation of *De Trinitate*. But where *In the Self's Place* (and Marion's project in general) is characterized by a marking of the limits of metaphysics, this book neither takes up that work expressly nor seeks, as its end, to criticize it. It is my hope instead to offer a phenomenological theology in which the promises and limitations of Trinitarian theology, read in light of Marion's philosophy, can illuminate the rationality of this transformative encounter with God's gift of love. Ultimately, my question is this: how might this phenomenology of love serve a theological investigation into the self-revelation of the Trinitarian God, such that this revelation might be rendered incarnate in our lives, particularly in our love through, with, and in which we embrace the God whose inexpressible reality can only be seen as inexpressible?[29]

Part 1 of this book concerns *De Trinitate* itself and offers a reading of the text with the gift of love ever in mind. It begins with a study of Augustine's philosophy of language and the impact of love on interpretation, understanding, and belief. The preponderant concern of part 1 is then an exposition of *De Trinitate* read through the animating interest in the gift of love. Part 2 presents Marion's interrelated phenomenology of excess, his philosophy of the gift, and the erotic reduction. I will focus my examination on Marion's

26. See Marion, *In the Self's Place*, 12.
27. Augustine, *De Trinitate*, 1.1.
28. Marion, *In the Self's Place*, 10.
29. See Augustine, *De Trinitate*, 1.3.

phenomenology of the gift and its theological implications. Thus, I lean heavily on his explorations of the phenomenology of love, givenness, and the gift; his more theologically oriented books; and, of course, his study of Augustine's *Confessions, In the Self's Place.* It should be clear at the outset that I am not, therefore, explicitly interested in his extensive work on René Descartes, his study of Husserl or Heidegger, or on phenomenology as such.

Together, Marion's concepts of love, givenness, and gift offer a promising convergence with Augustine's own understanding of the gift of love and its significance to Trinitarian naming. Part 3 is the site of that convergence, wherein Marion's work can serve a reading of *De Trinitate* in two ways. First, with the risk of idolatry in mind, Marion's study of the saturated phenomenon—in particular the icon—divests the *ego* of its self-groundedness, inviting instead a subjectivity that is first and foremost responsive to givenness and to the antecedent gift of love. Such a reading of subjectivity can sharpen Augustine's understanding of the human being as made to the image of God, defined by a gift that always already precedes me and that which gives myself to me. Second, although the exercise of marking possible impossibility leaves phenomenological reason gasping for breath as it tries to outrun its own horizon, such impossibility does not frustrate theology if the discipline is defined not by its ability to name God exhaustively—to present God here within my present horizon—but as reflection upon my formation and movement toward God.

Therefore, this engagement of *De Trinitate* will not be a search for a model of divine life through the interrelatedness of the mind's memory, understanding, and will. Rather, this particular reading of *De Trinitate*, which is not intended to be exhaustive of the text or of Augustine's ideas, will focus on two intimately interrelated aspects of the text. First, it will attempt to draw from the bishop's words an understanding of the gift of love. This name particularly signifies the Holy Spirit but also the Trinitarian life of God. Second, this name will be brought to bear on those who confess it as a name of God, examining how the gift of love orients us and forms us. And while Augustine considers this formation within the context of understanding, it is important to remember that understanding and love can be reduced to neither separate functions of the human mind nor independent actions on the part of two of the divine three. This book undertakes this study of the gift of love by means of a journey through the pages of *De Trinitate*.

Augustine wrote *De Trinitate* in service of the salvation of souls, and the conversion effecting salvation is dependent upon God's antecedent gift of love, a gift that coincides with the life of God and the unity of the Father and Son in the Spirit. Therefore, the emphasis of this study of the text will fall on the *gift* language of books 5–7, the dynamic of *love* that begins in book 8, and the Spirit's role in transforming human beings into the fullness of the image of the Trinitarian God. It is my intention not to argue that there is no other significant theological content within the text, but to articulate a central dynamic of the text, one that has points of connection and comparison with the work of Jean-Luc Marion. Such an approach is certainly not without its assumptions, blind spots, and dangers. The sixteen-hundred-year history of interpretations of the work of the Bishop of Hippo warns against trust in any naïve claim at a possible objective reading of the text—that is, engaging the text itself, without time, space, and one's own subjectivity playing inescapable roles in the reading. Texts do not simply speak for themselves. "To understand," David Tracy reminds his own readers again and again, "is to interpret."[30] And interpretation of a text of the complexity, significance, and subject matter of *De Trinitate* requires of its reader continuous hermeneutical decisions, each shaped by the reader's fundamental concerns and questions. Therefore, a guiding hermeneutic concerned with the nature and effect of the gift of love is not without its weaknesses. However, such a hermeneutic is rendered relatively adequate and trustworthy as internally consistent with *De Trinitate* itself as a significant concern of the text and as an emphasis active elsewhere in the Augustine's vast corpus.

While the language of *gift* and *love* is more prevalent in some parts of

30. Tracy, *Plurality and Ambiguity*, 9.

the *De Trinitate* than in others, the entire text figures in this progressive transformation wrought by the gift of love, pedagogically revealed not as a "school of loquacious chattering"[31] but as a gradual teaching through a definite order directed at the salvation of the reader's soul,[32] while at the same time intellectually defending the rationality of that teaching. While emphasis is not only unavoidable but itself the very method of interpretation, it is valuable to illuminate the text as a whole, if only from a particular perspective.

Finally, I would like to acknowledge my late arrival to Augustine, *De Trinitate*, and to Marion. This book adds to the already countless analyses of Augustine's thought, itself of immeasurable influence upon the whole the Christianity. Moreover, I have arrived late in applying Marion's thought to Augustine directly, such an application having already been undertaken by others.[33] But especially, this book arrives after Marion himself has published his own interpretation of Augustine's *Confessions*, *In the Self's Place*.[34] Furthermore, I recognize that to a significant extent, mine is another work in a tradition that has been followed many times before in the sixteen hundred or so years since *De Trinitate*'s composition. Anything I have to offer here is at best a modest and momentary glimpse of a hope. Indeed, "all of our accomplishments are few. All of our accomplishments are minor: my scribblings, his book, the best lines of the best living poets. We embroider away at our tiny tatters of insight as though the world hung on them, when it is chiefly we ourselves who hang on them."[35] But because we ourselves do hang on them for the deepening of our knowledge of God, any new glimpse (however fleeting, however limited) we may offer of our approach to God is not one to be received

31. Augustine, *Confessions*, trans. Henry Chadwick (New York: Oxford University Press, 2008), 8.5.10. All English translations throughout are from this version.
32. Paul R. Kolbet, *Augustine and the Cure of Souls: Revising a Classical Ideal* (Notre Dame: University of Notre Dame Press, 2010), 96.
33. See, for example, Kyle Philip Hubbard, "'Who Then Are You, My God?': Augustine of Hippo and Jean-Luc Marion on the Nature and Possibility of Loving God" (PhD diss., Fordham University, 2009).
34. *Au lieu de soi* was originally published in 2008, its English translation in 2012.
35. Cristina Nehring, "Loving a Child on the Fringe," *Slate*, November 28, 2012, http://tinyurl.com/h22btex.

lightly—not because of what we offer but precisely because of what is offered to us. We cannot hope to arrive at this approach except as those arriving late, always responding to those who themselves began in response. I take up my place of response to a tradition rooted in the revelation of God's name, a tradition that was given to me so generously by those who, themselves, had received it. To name the Father, Son, and Spirit "the God of love" is to call upon God, to call as one arriving late, panting for what we have already breathed, hungering for what we have already tasted, and yearning for the embrace already given.[36]

36. Augustine, *Confessions*, 10.27.38.

PART I

A Reading of *De Trinitate*

1

Language and Conversion Within the Limits of *De Trinitate*

Human beings must . . . be told how to love.

—Augustine, *De Doctrina Christiana*, 1.54

As he begins the work, Augustine presents his *De Trinitate* as a response to the cry of the Psalmist, "Seek his face always,"[1] through a pursuit of "the unity of the three, of Father and Son and Holy Spirit"[2]—an endeavor, he warns, in which no "mistake is more dangerous, or the search more laborious, or the discovery more advantageous."[3] Having struggled with his own conception of God for years[4] and all too aware of the difficulty of the text to come, the Bishop of Hippo invites his reader along the path of charity, in hope that this "gentle authority"

1. Augustine, *De Trinitate*, 1.5, citing Psalm 105:4.
2. Ibid., "ubi quaeritur *unitas* trinitatis, patris et filii et spiritus sancti."
3. Ibid., "quia neque periculosius alicubi erratur, nec laboriosius aliquid quaeritur, nec fructuosius aliquid inuenitur."
4. See, for example: "By now my evil and wicked youth was dead. I was becoming a grown man. But the older I became, the more shameful it was that I retained so much vanity as to be unable to think any substance possible other than that which the eyes normally perceive." Augustine, *Confessions*, 7.1.1.

might lead both author and reader to a deeper understanding of the Trinitarian mystery.[5] The progressive structure of the text itself conforms to Augustine's general rhetorical and dialectical concerns, which, in turn, conform to his pedagogical *telos*. He intended for his reader a lengthy but focused journey through this tightly unified text;[6] a journey that would, he hoped, prove transformative of the reader's understanding of God, certainly, but even more so of the reader's love of God, each being necessary for the other.

How *De Trinitate* Fails

Augustine's thought rests upon a mutually supportive coherence of theology and rhetoric. While such a coherence may be susceptible to charges of tautology, Augustine's faith in God as creator and end of a good creation—underlying the bishop's most celebrated words, "You have made us for yourself, and our heart is restless until it rests in you"[7]—both permits and demands such internalized implications. Operating with a theological anthropology wherein understanding and love cannot be separated, for all one may attempt to distinguish between them,[8] book 8—and indeed much of *De Trinitate* itself—rotates

5. Augustine, *De Trinitate*, 1.6.
6. That sections of *De Trinitate* were pirated and distributed before Augustine could complete the text complicates the use of the earlier stolen sections but does not in any way discount their use or reveal them to be successive drafts by which Augustine attempted various methods for attaining an image of God. See: "So carefully he had conceived the progressive and pedagogical character of this enquiry, that access to an unfinished version of it, however sizable, could have exposed the reader to a dangerous misunderstanding." Luigi Gioia, OSB, *The Theological Epistemology of Augustine's* De Trinitate (Oxford: Oxford University Press, 2008), 2. David Foster argues that these prologues are therefore a key to understanding Augustine's final thoughts on these first books and the means for tying the text together as a coherent whole: "If I had been able to keep my plans, the contents would indeed have been much the same, but their expression would have been much less knotty and much more lucid, as far as the difficulty of elucidating such deep matters and our own capacities would allow," Augustine writes in *De Trinitate*'s "Prefatory letter" to Aurelius, Bishop of Carthage. He continues, "Some people have the first four books, or rather five, without their prologues, and the twelfth without its considerable concluding section." David Foster, OSB, "Augustine's *De Trinitate*: Some Methodological Enquiries," *The Downside Review* 124, no. 437 (2006): 259.
7. Augustine, *Confessions*, 1.1.1.
8. Lewis Ayres warns against seeing this unity as a theological end in itself rather than in service of the search for God: "Presentations of Augustine's Trinitarian theology as dependent upon and finding its highpoint in an account of the necessary relationship between love and knowledge in the mind are mistaken in according this language such an all-encompassing role. . . . Thus the fact of the human search for God presupposes an interplay between desire and knowledge, the former

around this particular unity. Just as Augustine's concept of love requires an object, and therefore some understanding of that object, so too does understanding of the object per se require a loving openness to it and a proper valuation of it. This legitimizes an emphasis on the conversion of the reader's love to a love for God. The human being is made to desire God—and this is true whether or not we are aware of this intended end of our created desire or have inhibited our love from reaching for this end. Of course, precisely how the relationship of understanding and love within the human being relates to God requires all of *De Trinitate* to explore, and even there, such an exploration can only be done incompletely.

Not only is Augustine's theology rhetorical in form but his rhetoric is theologically conditioned. Whether conceived as psychagogic, pedagogical, or a pastoral function of the role of bishop, Augustine's understanding of rhetoric is not only the result of an anthropology rooted in desire but is also soteriological in its trajectory. That is, the salvific transformation of human love as the central dynamic of the human being itself is the necessary and sufficient condition justifying the linguistic appeal to human desire.[9]

At its heart, *De Trinitate* is not an elaborate study of church dogma,[10] a protracted intellectual exercise,[11] or an establishment of juridical (or ecclesiastical) standards for theological speculation,[12] although it can, in some manner, direct its readers in their investigation into each of these matters. Instead, as Chad Pecknold argues, the Trinity—or

shaped by the latter." Lewis Ayres, *Augustine and the Trinity* (New York: Cambridge University Press, 2010), 322.

9. See Paul Kolbet: "Rhetorical theory is so internalized by Augustine that it not only expresses his theological visions, but also informs it. Moreover, even as it is employed, rhetoric itself is revised and infused with theological content. The deep philosophical link between language, vulnerability, and desire is one of Augustine's chief insights." Kolbet, *Augustine and the Cure*, 11.
10. John C. Cavadini, "The Structure and Intention of Augustine's *De Trinitate*," *Augustinian Studies* 23 (1992): 104.
11. Ibid., 105.
12. C. C. Pecknold, "How Augustine Used the Trinity: Functionalism and the Development of Doctrine," *Anglican Theological Review* 85 (2003): 136. In fact, Pecknold sees Augustine's foray into non-regulatory Trinitarian speculation as a decisive innovation of his text: "I contend that Augustine has ventured to employ the already formalized doctrine for purposes other than previously conceived. Augustine is the first to use the Trinity to perform functions in theology other than regulative." Ibid.

at the very least, theological speculation and dogma about the Trinity—functions most importantly not to regulate theology but to bring about the conversion of *De Trinitate*'s readers. Lewis Ayres, too, concludes that "Augustine is not exploring how the Trinity may be known independently of [Christ's] revealing and drawing, but showing how that revealing leads us to read anew God's creation with the eyes and terms of faith, and showing us how that drawing pulls us into a fuller life within the intelligible order."[13] "The conversion is the point,"[14] Pecknold writes, and the so-called analogies—lover/beloved/love and the inward turn to human memory, understanding, and will—are "tools that perform upon the reader a process of spiritual conversion."[15] Both the analogies in creation and the theological speculation itself serve the salvation of the soul. By way of his ambitious plan "to train the reader, *in the things that have been made* (Rom 1:20)," Augustine hopes that both he and his reader, "getting to know him by whom they were made," will come "eventually to his image."[16]

And yet even as the final book concludes, this arrival is deferred. The Trinity does not yet appear to readers in divine glory. Facing this deferred arrival—this as of yet non-thing—with prayer, Augustine pleads to God, "Let me remember you, let me understand you, let me love you. Increase these things in me until you refashion me entirely."[17] Would this have been an attempt to make the interlocutor in question accessibly concrete and to reify the text's potential signification into substantial actuality, then the reader of *De Trinitate* would be forced to conclude that the theological display, impressive though it may be, is little more than the hollow noise of vanity, unable to grasp the mysterious God who does not "condescend to be possessed together with falsehood."[18] This, however, is not Augustine's intention;

13. Ayres, *Augustine and the Trinity*, 318.
14. Pecknold, "How Augustine Used the Trinity," 138.
15. Ibid., 139.
16. Augustine, *De Trinitate*, 15.1: "Volentes in rebus quae factae sunt ad cognoscendum eum a quo factae sunt exercere lectorem quod est homo in eo quo ceteris animaibus antecellit."
17. Ibid., 15.51.
18. Augustine, *Confessions*, 10.41.66.

in his theology of the Trinity, he does not presume to present the Trinity to his reader.

John Cavadini, in search of the theological significance of such a display of accepted "failure" (that is, the failure to present the Trinity or even a compelling model of the Trinity), acknowledges: "Pointing out how difficult it is to 'see' and 'fully know' the substance of God, and that faith is necessary if we are to 'see the ineffable ineffably,' Augustine goes on to state that his treatise will serve to point out precisely this."[19] Contrary to the claims of his critics, Augustine is not imposing upon God a model based on an inadequate understanding of the human mind[20]—or, to the degree that he is, the inadequacy is recognized and brought to serve the bishop's actual purpose.

That an inadequate approach produces inadequate results can, but does not necessarily, frustrate the movement of conversion. That looking for an opening to the Trinity in that which is made in its image—the human mind—cannot but lead to poor Trinitarian models does not mean that the search itself need be abandoned. Cavadini continues, "But we have also discovered that to continue the purely introspective Neoplatonic ascent is to continue a process which has not only failed but *cannot but fail*, for the more we persist in contemplating a disfigured image as though it were not disfigured, as though it were, so to speak, an accurate image of God, the more we persist in furthering the disfigurement."[21] Our intellectual vision, and particularly our contemplation of God, is not only limited but also distorted by sin, rendering our approach prey to a twisted and self-serving will. Any relatively adequate understanding of the Trinitarian God—a, if not *the*, goal of theology—requires of us a healing and transformation of our will, opening us to relationship with God. By means of the turn away

19. Cavadini, "Structure and Intention," 107.

20. *Pace* Karl Rahner: "That is where, in fact, the difficulties of the classic psychological speculations about the Trinity set in. They have no evident model *from* human psychology *for* the doctrine of the Trinity (a model known already before the doctrine of the Trinity). . . . Rather it postulates *from* the doctrine of the Trinity a model of human knowledge and love, which either remains questionable, or about which it is not clear that it can be more than a *model* of human knowledge precisely as *finite*. And this model it applies again to God." Karl Rahner, *The Trinity*, trans. Joseph Donceel (New York: Crossroad, 2005), 101–2.

21. Cavadini, "Structure and Intention," 108.

from the revelation of the scriptures and the philosophical rules of Trinitarian predication, and a turn inward toward his deepest part (described by Edmund Hill as the movement of a patristic Alice through the Neoplatonic looking glass[22]), this intellectual inadequacy and weakness of will can be made to further conversion in being quickened by love.

In inviting his readers to locate, understand, and love that which is signified by the text, while at the same time demonstrating the impossibility of doing precisely that, Augustine attempts to persuade his readers of our total dependency on the transforming power of God's gift of love and affirm that this impossible signification is transcended in the incarnate person of Jesus Christ, understood in light of the Holy Spirit. Cavadini concludes:

> But what it is important to note here is not simply that we have a new "way" for completing an ascent which remains definitively Neoplatonic in its goal, but that the goal—*noesis* itself—has acquired a new character. Our contemplative regard is pushed outward, from the consideration of a static metaphysical self essentially disconnected from the uncomfortable realm of the bodily and historically contingent—that realm which defines our ontological distance from God—to that very realm itself and to the blood, irreducibly contingent and irreducibly historical, which for Augustine became its central node.[23]

The contemplative inwardness having turned to Christ inexorably moves us to *irreducibly contingent blood*—both that which was shed in love upon the cross and that for which it was shed. This is an intellectual conversion, to be sure, but one marked by the priority placed upon one's concrete loving relationship with God and with neighbor—that is, a conversion to, and by, love.

The reader who begins *De Trinitate* in expectation of unearthing within the human mind a veracious model of the triune God will leave disappointed at best—and potentially woefully misdirected—if he or she does not attend to the hermeneutic of love. Augustine orients his reader to conversion to love, by love. The inadequacy of our own

22. Edmund Hill, "Introductory Essay on Book VIII," in Augustine, *The Trinity*, 237.
23. Cavadini, "Structure and Intention," 109.

attempts to attain this end—a result of both our created finitude and our fallen nature, to be sure, but perhaps better put, a result of how we hope to come to know the mystery of God—has a pedagogical role. For what it is we were created to know cannot be learned as pure data, delivered to our unconverted understanding to be seen directly with the mind's eye. Rather, as Peter Burnell observes, this limit "implies that we were created such that the humility that accords with our nature must be learned."[24] What it is we seek to know—the Trinitarian God of love—comes to us only in and through our transformation. "Where this supreme Reality is concerned, therefore, our cognition is an act of loving," he continues, "The deepest knowledge, then, is charity."[25]

Rhetoric, Pedagogy, and the Conversion of the Soul

Before that day in a Milanese garden when Augustine took and read Paul's letter to the Christian community in Rome (or so his own narrative goes), his professional training and practice had been primarily focused upon rhetoric. This appreciation for, and application of, the power of beautiful and persuasive language would mark Augustine's work as bishop and would continue to be part of his later theological works. *De Trinitate* is no exception to this. Its structure is consistent with the subject of Augustine's schooling and teaching even as the bishop transforms classical rhetoric by exceeding it. A text easily and often dismissed as obtuse, as "an intractable mass of speculation floating oddly aloof from foundation in any particular context,"[26] *De Trinitate* has a form that fully serves its Trinitarian content; a content that, in turn, cannot be separated from its status as a linguistic (and conceptual) presentation of the nature of the triune God. An engagement with *De Trinitate*, therefore, requires an understanding of the rhetorical and pedagogical features of Augustine's thought and his philosophy of language. Where its detractors read its speculative

24. Peter Burnell, *The Augustinian Person* (Washington, DC: Catholic University of America Press, 2005), 92.
25. Ibid., 100.
26. Cavadini, "Structure and Intention," 103.

theology as a foundation for the so-called Western or Latin model of Trinity, "understood to be the exposition of the relations of God *in se*, with scarce reference to God's acts in salvation history,"[27] *De Trinitate* has been more recently interpreted as fundamentally focused on the transformative and salvific heart of Trinitarian theology. Therefore, to understand *De Trinitate*, we must first explore the relationship among language, knowledge, and love—a relationship effectively structuring Augustine's understanding of the Trinity itself and illuminating the reader's way of proceeding toward knowledge of the triune God.

Roughly four years after having been ordained, Augustine was consecrated bishop, assuming pastoral responsibility for the Christians of the North African maritime city of Hippo Regius, putting an end to a personal dream that had been dying since he was compelled into the priesthood: living a life of contemplation removed from the concerns of the world. His first biographer, Possidius, tells us that the tears Augustine generously shed the day of his ordination had been ascribed by many "to wounded pride and by way of consolation told him that while he was worthy of greater honor the office of presbyter was but little inferior to the bishopric."[28] However, having intentionally avoided visiting cities in need of episcopal leadership in fear he would be seized and forced to serve, Augustine was mourning not the insignificance of his new position, but the death of the contemplative life he had desired to live,[29] smothered as he now would be beneath the precarious responsibilities of his office and ashamed that he had "once thought ill of clergymen and their congregations."[30] Although he had long since abandoned his determination to achieve political and oratorical success, he had remained hopeful that a contemplative life might yet be possible, a life in which he and his close companions and

27. LaCugna, *God for Us*, 81. To be fair to LaCugna, she does recognize that those aspects of *De Trinitate* that would prove most influential do not exhaust the text. In fact, she interprets Augustine as concerned for salvation but only the salvation of the individual soul. However, in her reading, this is accomplished only through his disregarding the incarnation.

28. Possidius, *Sancti Augustini vita scripta a Possidio episcope*, trans. Herbert T. Weiskotten (Princeton: Princeton University Press, 1919), ch. 4.

29. Ibid.; see also Garry Wills, *Saint Augustine* (New York: Viking, 1999), 67.

30. Peter Brown, *Augustine of Hippo: A Biography*, rev. ed. (Berkeley: University of California Press, 2000), 132.

students would retreat from the world and focus on an ideal of the Christian life centered on prayer and intellectual speculation. Such a life would be transformed beneath the enormous pressures of his new position, forcing Augustine to reconsider both what type of life ought to be the Christian's goal and the way of achieving that end.[31]

While responsibilities for his flock required the new bishop to transform his earlier way of life, he did not completely abandon it. Indeed, he had already taken to revise his previous classical rhetorical ideal to be of service to his Christian students. This revision would simply have to be taken a step further; it would now be directed toward shaping a rhetoric designed to appeal to the Christians of Hippo. However, while a study of the rhetoric Augustine employs in his sermons—in those words directed at the Christians of little or no formal philosophical education, the many who occupied the nave of his church—is indeed a worthy endeavor, our focus on *De Trinitate* concerns us with a form of rhetoric directed not at the masses but at the educated few.[32] This rhetoric was not, unlike that of his sermons, "made deliberately artless"[33] to appeal to the uneducated mind, but instead reveals Augustine's high intellectual expectations for his readers.

Before his conversion, Augustine was both talented enough and strategically positioned to achieve not a small amount of success in a Roman culture that revered a gifted rhetor's artistic brilliance in

31. "Augustine, indeed, had decided that he would never reach the fulfillment that he first thought was promised to him by a Christian Platonism: he would never impose a victory of mind over body in himself, he would never achieve the wrapt contemplation of the ideal philosopher. It is the most drastic change that a man may have to accept: it involved nothing less than the surrender of the bright future he thought he had gained at Cassiciacum." P. Brown, *Augustine of Hippo*, 140. See also John Burnaby, *Amor Dei: A Study of the Religion of St. Augustine* (Eugene, OR: Wipf & Stock, 2007), 50.

32. "So whoever reads this and says, 'This is not well said, because I do not understand it,' is criticizing my statement, not the faith; and perhaps it could have been said more clearly—though no one has ever expressed himself well enough to be understood by everybody on everything. . . . But if the person who complains that he has not understood this book has never been able to understand anyone else's painstaking and penetrating investigations of such subjects, he should set about improving himself with serious study, instead of trying to silence me with querulous abuse." Augustine, *De Trinitate*, 1.5. For an excellent study of the development and its homiletic form of Augustine's rhetoric, see Kolbet's *Augustine and the Cure of Souls*.

33. Frederik van der Meer, *Augustine the Bishop: The Life and Work of a Father of the Church*, trans. Brian Battershaw and G. R. Lamb (New York: Sheed & Ward, 1961), 418.

shaping the stories and ideas that would define a people and an empire. At its worst, "the speech of such a rhetor," Paul Kolbet writes, "would provide the audience with an image of themselves—not as they were in fact but as they wanted to believe they were,"[34] perpetuating the prejudices and misconceptions already dominant in a society. However, the Socratic ideal of uniting rhetoric and philosophy—bequeathed to Augustine through an education shaped, however subtly at times, by Aristotle and Ciceronian Stoicism—orients him toward employing persuasive language not merely for praise but "in a manner that overcomes the audience members' resistance so that they actually become receptive to hearing the truth about themselves."[35] A rhetoric designated psychagogic by contemporary scholars of the classical period,[36] this practice accepts the affect as inescapably part of the human condition and, as such, recognizes the need for engaging the emotional facet of human experience as part of the formation of one's rational, ethical, and religious capacities. It was this psychagogic rhetoric, esteemed in both Neoplatonic and Stoic pedagogy, that would provide the foundation for Augustine's own rhetoric as "self-consciously, language ordained toward action"[37] and toward the interrelated intellectual and religious conversions of his listeners and readers. Reason cannot be liberated from the affect, and the attempt to do so betrays the very nature of human reason.

Human emotions—and in particular the decisive desirous capacity of the human being (i.e., the will[38])—cannot simply be contained and controlled by a dominating intellective reason. Such a competitive dualism is foreign to Augustine's conception of the human being. For the bishop is not beholden to a faculty psychology that "compels one to a choice between the primacy of the intellectual faculty and that of the will,"[39] but understands that our knowledge of a thing cannot be

34. Kolbet, *Cure of Souls*, 67.
35. Ibid., 23.
36. Ibid., 7.
37. Michael J. Scanlon, "Augustine and Theology as Rhetoric," *Augustinian Studies* 25 (1994): 38.
38. The will as necessarily oriented desire as a decisive feature of Augustine's *voluntas* is discussed later in this chapter.
39. Frederick Lawrence, "*Cor ad cor loquitur*: Augustine's Influence on Heidegger and Lonergan,"

separated from our experience—whether physical or affective—of that thing.[40] Our subjectivity is at play in all our knowledge. Moreover, such an experience is always an experience not only of the thing, per se, but also of our valuation of it. The value we ascribe to a thing—that is, the manner and degree with which we love it—is a decisive aspect of our understanding of it. Therefore, the scale of value active in our experience is a constituent part of the processes of our coming to know a thing. Rhetoric's power is introduced precisely on such values impacting our loves and concerns.

Neither necessarily good or evil in itself, rhetoric is a tool in the hands of an orator, directed and manipulated in a manner reflective of the desire of a speaker who recognizes the affect effects significant influence on human rationality. The persuasive power of the language employed does not, in and of itself, intrinsically lead to abuse and deception. In fact, the appropriateness of language is not tied to the object of the discourse so much as to the desired transformation of the audience—it appeals to the mind to elicit conversion. The "style suitable for moving minds to action,"[41] no more adulterates the truth than it legitimates the lie. Augustine, having been overwhelmed by Cicero's rhetorical appeal to truth in the *Hortensius*, recognized that such persuasive words "can do more than make lies sound like truth. They are also means for making truth sound like truth—the only means, on many occasions, that are available."[42] In contrast to an impoverished rhetoric concerned with the mere sale of words and in an appeal to the audience's pride and self-esteem,[43] Augustine sought to use the power of such language to articulate a "non-conventionally determined scale of valuation,"[44] dependent not upon the fashions of

(paper presented at "Augustine: Theological and Philosophical Conversations—A Conference Honoring David Tracy," University of Chicago Divinity School, Chicago, May 4–6, 2008).

40. "But the apparent cleavages and inconsistencies in Augustine's doctrines which critics have been at such pains to lay bare, will often disappear if we are careful not to divide what he never thought of dividing, and still more if we remember the character of his thought—digressive and radiating rather than synthetic or linear." Burnaby, *Amor Dei*, 78–79.

41. Augustine, *On Christian Teaching*, trans. R. P. H. Green (New York: Oxford University Press, 2008), 4.104, p. 125. All English translations of *De Doctrina Christiana* throughout are from this version.

42. Thomas Cole, *The Origins of Rhetoric in Ancient Greece* (Baltimore: Johns Hopkins University Press, 1991), 140.

43. Augustine, *Confessions*, 9.5.13.

the society or the individual, but upon a reasoned reflection on truth. For Augustine, the exercise of rhetoric has as its only justifiable end in making truth so attractive to the soul that its attainment becomes the occupation of the will now on fire with desire for it.[45]

This recognition of desire's association with the attainment of truth, central to Augustine's later rhetorical practice, was certainly already present in his thought during his time at Cassiciacum, when the newly baptized teacher sought to integrate the faith he now embraced with the pedagogical rhetoric always precariously open for abuse. Kolbet reasons that against both the tyranny of imposed doctrinarism[46] and the great debates of the skeptics, which for all their impressive verbosity provided students with no way to confidently proceed, Augustine the teacher concluded that "if truth were to refrain from coercion, it had to make itself desirable enough to be freely chosen."[47] Not a mere object to be handed from teacher to student, truth required of its suitor a willingness to be transformed by the encounter with it and therefore, of its teacher, the skill to adorn it alluringly. "Despite Augustine's misgiving about the abuse of rhetoric in its service of evil," Jeff B. Pool writes, "he understood quite well the necessity of *persuasion* in the exercise of love toward neighbor, which the method of teaching serves."[48] Ernest Fortin notes, significantly, that the rhetoric by the

44. Kolbet, *Cure of Souls*, 201.
45. Ernest Fortin draws attention to the fact that the young Augustine's desire for truth was enkindled by his encounter with Cicero's *Hortensius* and not by the reading of the scriptures. Eventually, as articulated in *On Christian Teaching*, Augustine will come to understand truth as inseparable from God's love, rendering his later understanding of truth more relational (and more linguistically situated), and hence more biblical than Stoic: "As employed by the sacred writers, 'truth' is more apt to mean something like fidelity or trustworthiness. To say that God is true is to proclaim that he is utterly reliable, that he does not renege on his promises, or, as we still say, that his is 'true' to his word, as opposed to Satan, the 'father of lies' (John 8:44) or the most untrustworthy of beings." Ernest L. Fortin, "Augustine and the Hermeneutics of Love: Some Preliminary Considerations," in *Augustine Today*, ed. Richard John Neuhaus (Grand Rapids: Eerdmans, 1993), 38.
46. How Augustine's reliance of the persuasive beauty of truth compares—or conflicts—with his later reasoning behind the use of force against the Donatists is indeed a difficult question. If one is not to simply abandon the search for continuity and defer to a theory of "three Augustines" in which the temporally last is a significant departure from his earlier selves, one would do well to investigate both Augustine's conception of the communal significance of *caritas* and his articulation of the profound depth of human sin.
47. Kolbet, *Cure of Souls*, 91.
48. Jeff B. Pool, "No Entrance into Truth Except through Love: Contributions from Augustine of Hippo to a Contemporary Christian Hermeneutic of Love," *Review and Expositor* 101, no. 4 (2004): 652.

Christian serves a different purpose from the great speeches of the Ciceronian orator. Not strictly persuasion, per se, but *teaching* is the goal of the Christian, and the Christian does not just teach anything at all but imparts the doctrine of the faith. The Christian orator offers a teaching grounded in the trustworthiness of God.[49] And while "adapting his discourse, in a way, to his students' taste and enriching it so that it was sweet placed Augustine's practice at Cassiciacum uncomfortably close to that of his former school of rhetoric in Milan,"[50] the possibility that seductive and playful words might be abused did not extinguish his hope that human desire might also suggest a truth beyond oratorical flare and that his audience might be converted to embrace this truth.

Such a conclusion is certainly not incidental to Augustine's personal spiritual and theological pilgrimage any more than is the more explicitly autobiographical *Confessions*.[51] Aware that with his education and his intelligence, he occupied a place of intellectual privilege within the vast borders of the Roman Empire, Augustine struggled with his own inability to adequately understand and embrace the truth he sought.[52] At one point, he had excitedly imagined "that through such

49. Fortin, "Augustine and the Hermeneutics," 43.
50. Kolbet, *Cure of Souls*, 95.
51. For good reason, *Confessions* stands as an indispensable aid to reading the rest of Augustine's corpus. "I find it . . . important, time after time in reading Augustine, to remind myself that nothing Augustine writes is intelligible apart from his own experience of God, not only in the pages of scripture, but also in his own life. If we take the trouble to think our way into Augustine's most fundamental religious awe, we will often see a consistency and a clarity in his thought that would otherwise elude us." James J. O'Donnell, "Augustine's Idea of God," *Augustinian Studies* 25 (1994): 28.
52. The interpretation of Augustine's own understanding of whether or not we can attain this truth remains contestable. Robert Barron argues against the Derridean undecidability that has shaped much contemporary Augustine scholarship: "At the end of his questioning, Augustine found a truth in which he could rest, a truth that, he was convinced, had set him free. And this was none other than the conviction that ultimate reality is the Trinitarian God revealed in the life, death, and resurrection of Jesus Christ." Robert E. Barron, "Augustine's Questions: Why the Augustinian Theology of God Matter Today," *Logos* 10, no. 4 (2007): 35. John Caputo and Michael Scanlon, certainly among those influenced by Derrida, are hesitant to grant Augustine's heart rest (although even for them, *grace* seems to have brought Augustine peace): "Perhaps more than any other theologian, Augustine viewed authentic Christianity as 'an aporia of the impossible.' The *Doctor Gratiae* attributed the actual possibility of passing through the impossible path to the Gift, his favorite name for the Spirit as God's Self-donation. Through the Gift he did what he knew he could not do—he did the truth which is the only path to God." John D. Caputo and Michael J. Scanlon, eds., introduction to *God, the Gift, and Postmodernism* (Bloomington: Indiana University Press, 1999), 11–12. Fortin importantly adds to the discussion a recognition that the biblical notion of *truth* differs from that of Cicero's *Hortensius*, the text that would first draw Augustine toward

spiritual exercises the souls of at least a few capable of benefitting from them could attain in microcosm the stability, solidity, and wholeness of the cosmos itself."[53] And, perhaps, having immodestly believed himself to be among the spiritually advanced few, Augustine had to come to terms with the feebleness of his desire for the truth that would bring peace. His confrontation not only with the limitations of language but also with his understanding and love suggests a horizon that would continue to stretch beyond Augustine's reach, always reminding him of both his finitude and his failing and always inviting his desire. Augustine's philosophy of language, an understanding that informs his rhetorical approach to a theology that has its only authentic end in salvation, dynamically embraces both reflection on the limitations of signification and the relationship of language to a knowledge born of love.

The Hermeneutic of Love

> Little by little, I began to be aware where I was and wanted to manifest my wishes to those who could fulfill them as I could not. For my desires were internal; adults were external to me and had no means of entering into my soul. So I threw my limbs about and uttered sounds, signs resembling my wishes, the small number of signs of which I was capable but such signs as lay in my power to use: for there was no real resemblance.[54]

So Augustine presents the frustrations of his infant self, a child crying aloud in deficient signification, flailing to generate in his listeners an intelligible connection between his signs and the object of his desire. However, like the self recounted, the Augustine narrating his youth would be ever immersed in the limitations of language, eventually recognizing the interpretive and theological significance of the

truth: "As employed by the sacred writers, 'truth' is more apt to mean something like fidelity or trustworthiness. To say that God is true is to proclaim that he is utterly reliable, that he does not renege on his promises, or, as we still say, that he is 'true' to his word, as opposed to Satan, the 'father of lies' (John 8:44) or the most untrustworthy of beings." Fortin, "Augustine and the Hermeneutics," 38. This notion of truth, dependent on relationship, hints at Augustine's eventual recognition of the interrelatedness of love and truth. As will be evident later in these pages, where one comes down on this question significantly shapes one's understanding of the (im)possibility of the gift of love, on both the human side and that of the divine.

53. Kolbet, *Cure of Souls*, 100.

54. Augustine, *Confessions*, 1.8.

positive and transformative capacity of such a limitation, rendering it an "antidote, rather than a catalyst, for sin."[55] Against such a breach in signification, between the sign (*signum*) and the thing (*res*) intended by signification, Augustine offers a response grounded in both reason and hope: a responsive love, conditioned by the love of God, makes an otherwise vain signification possible.

The basic level of the linguistic mediation of meaning, while important enough for Augustine to dedicate his *De Dialectica* to, is not of primary theological concern. The ambiguities of language as a system of linguistic signs—the lack of clarity between possible interpretations of a single word or phrase—can, for the most part, be resolved by the use of context. Referring to the ambiguity resulting from general lexical or syntactical interpretation (classically speaking, those aspects of writing that fall under the category *scriptum*[56]), Augustine argues that words are given significant context when spoken or written, in which "an ambiguous word 'becomes clear by a statement in which it occurs.' . . . Augustine believes that the meaning of ambiguous words becomes unambiguously manifest in their context."[57] Words do not carry with them their own contextless, nonconventional meaning, so that a simple and direct encounter with new words might result in new knowledge. Even the recognition of a word as something with potential signifying intentionality behind it is a convention that is learned. The meaning ascribed to signs is derived from the "effects on the mind from each individual's agreement with a particular convention."[58] Agreement to convention, not anything intrinsic to the nature of the signs, grants signs their meaning. Further complicating this is the fact that *signa* themselves exist already only in reference to other *signa*—words are clarified by words that, themselves, reference further words.

However helpful such knowledge might be—and it ought not be

55. David Dawson, "Sign Theory, Allegorical Reading and the Motions of the Soul in *De doctrina christiana*," in *De doctrina christiana: A Classic of Western Culture*, ed. Duane W. H. Arnold and Pamela Bright (Notre Dame: University of Notre Dame Press, 1995), 131.
56. Tarmo Toom, "Augustine on Ambiguity," *Augustinian Studies* 38 (2007): 408.
57. Ibid., 415.
58. Augustine, *De Doctrina*, 2.94.

begrudged what it is for what it is not—the entire text's meaning is further deferred as a consequence of the ambiguities surrounding the author's intention.[59] This real and inescapable interpretive problem resides where the reader inquires after the philosophical or theological meaning of a text, in which discovering the author's intention is complicated by the necessary corresponding experience on the part of the reader. Regarding the unknown or unclear *res*, precision in *scriptum* does not sufficiently orchestrate the movement from sign to thing. The resulting obscurity—which is not simply an ambiguous lack of clarification between possible interpretations but an indetermination of the thing itself that is to be interpreted[60]—is of particular importance when discussing the interpretation of the sacred scriptures, whose ultimate object is God. Taking up the general question of language in *De Magistro* and the particular question of scriptural interpretation in *De Doctrina Christiana*, Augustine wrestles with a "deep and persistent concern regarding the insufficiency of language."[61] In the former, he articulates this insufficiency as a tension between two truths: nothing can be taught without signs while conversely nothing can be learned through signs.[62]

Signs—things attributed signifying power by convention—are necessary for the possibility of the communication of meaning. Directing one's attention to a thing, referencing this particular thing, and subsequently explaining the meaning of this thing requires the signifying capacity of language. Augustine is clear: nothing is taught without signs.[63] Katherine Rudolph summarizes Augustine's conclusion:

> This is another way of saying that naming, as a linguistic procedure, and names, as grammatical place-holders, only subsist within a general economy of signs, an economy that is internally differential and relational. This signified, like the sign itself, is never directly present; it is

59. Toom, "Augustine on Ambiguity," 408.
60. Ibid., 411.
61. James K. A. Smith, "Between Predication and Silence: Augustine on How (Not) to Speak of God," *The Heythrop Journal* 41, no. 1 (January 2000): 66.
62. Ibid., 71.
63. Augustine, *The Teacher*, 10.31.

> never self-sufficient, for it is structured by its reference/relation to other concepts; it acquires a positive status only within a differential medium. In other words, language never escapes analogy; in order for an object to appear at all, it always and only appears "as something," and never "as such." This amounts to saying that the limits of signification *are* the limits of knowledge.[64]

The process of learning anything new requires, seemingly by the very definition of learning, that something with which we are unfamiliar be made known to us. However, Augustine argues with his dialogue partner, his son Adeodatus, that without a reference already internal to us, a word can tell us nothing of what we do not know. This tension between attempted signification and the intended signified thing illuminates the apparently nonnegotiable distance between our signs—as they are known to us—and what they signify. James K. A. Smith observes that such a distance does, in fact, inform us of one thing—that language manifests the confidence that there is something, incomprehensible perhaps, beyond our linguistic signs. Words function with an apophatic referentially, directing us beyond themselves through their own insignificance while at the same time signifying that insignificance by pointing beyond themselves.[65] Nevertheless, this intractable tension between the *signum* and the *res*—between the word signifying and the thing (perhaps) signified—remains part of Augustine's investigation: "we must have some pre-understanding of the subject-matter in order to interpret the 'signs' in texts correctly."[66] Any remotely accurate understanding of a sign's meaning requires that one have some experience of the thing (perhaps) signified. "Therefore," he writes, "a sign is learned

64. Katherine Rudolph, "Augustine's Picture of Language," *Augustinian Studies* 36, no. 2 (2005): 338–39.
65. J. Smith, "Between Predication and Silence," 72. Relatedly, Jacques Derrida proposes an understanding of apophatic theology as hyper-cataphasia in disguise. He argues that the goal of apophatic theology is not the reduction of all theological language to silence. Rather than simply annulling affirmative divine predication, apophatic theology—by its very nature as theology—denies in order to makes God's presence hyper-present. See Jacques Derrida, "How to Avoid Speaking: Denials," trans. Ken Friedan, in *Derrida and Negative Theology*, ed. Harold Coward and Toby Foshay (Albany: State University of New York Press, 1992) and Jacques Derrida, *On the Name*, ed. Thomas Dutoit (Stanford, CA: Stanford University Press, 1995).
66. David Tracy, "Charity, Obscurity, Clarity: Augustine's Search for a True Rhetoric," in *Morphologies of Faith: Essays in Religion and Culture in Honor of Nathan A. Scott, Jr.*, ed. Mary Gerhart and Anthony C. Yu (Atlanta, GA: Scholars Press, 1990): 133.

when the thing is known, rather than the thing being learned when the sign is given."[67] Augustine is aware that, despite his own extensive knowledge and his facility with persuasive language, he cannot teach his son anything that is completely foreign to the latter's young mind. "If Adeodatus was to have access to truth itself rather than to signs about the truth," Kolbet concludes, "it would not be because someone else was ever able to communicate truth directly to him. No human teacher, not even his adept father, would be able through words or other forms of signification to exhibit truth to him as a kind of commodity."[68] Not a process of purely cool intellective procurement, learning requires experience.

De Doctrina Christiana engages this same problem in a different manner. Where Augustine composed the older *De Magistro* while still expecting permanent retirement to a Christian monastic community, he wrote *De Doctrina* after assuming the heavy robes of the bishopric, in an endeavor to provide his readers with a structure by which they might properly interpret the scriptures. That we can learn nothing from signs indicates a difficulty in the reading of the scriptures as well. The sacred texts being, after all, *linguistic* texts situates them as apparently impotent textual signs, composed of lexical signs, telling us only what we already know and certainly unable to give us an understanding of that which remains both the ultimate end of the canonical books and incomprehensibly more than we can ever experience: God. Hence, book 1 of *De Doctrina* is concerned with that which is to be signified. Only after this *res* is discussed—significantly in the context of love—does Augustine delve into the method of signification in books 2 and 3. Book 4 considers the method of teaching what one has discovered in one's reading of the scriptures, with particular emphasis on the responsibility of the teacher to make the signified *caritas* accessible to the given audience by prayerful example and obedient participation in the teaching of the love that they themselves received. This modification of the structure of *De Magistro*,

67. Augustine, *The Teacher*, 10.33.
68. Kolbet, *Cure of Souls*, 111.

in which the conversation first takes up the question of the method of signification before the question of its possibility, suggests a change in Augustine's emphasis between his time in Cassiciacum and in Hippo. While the philosophy of signification is still part of his thought, he grants increasing significance to that which is signified in the scriptures. That God is signified—and that love is revealed to be a constituting element of all signification in light of the proper end of all of creation is in God—shapes the method of signification itself.

As both authorial intention and ultimate context direct the reader to God, the reader of the sacred scriptures is required to search the texts for some directive as to how one might discern what one ought to know about this holiest of mysteries. For Augustine, this guidance comes only from the revelation of what one is to know—the love of God.[69] The apostles' experience of the revelation of God is given linguistic shape in the New Testament, forming a community for whom this experience is mediated through word and sacrament. Understanding the scriptures requires of the reader some understanding of what the scriptures signify—but, living centuries after Jesus Christ walked the earth, Augustine's audience could only uncover this signification through reading the scriptures and participating in the sacramental community shaped by them. An understanding of love is not simply the result of reading about it or hearing it preached. Understanding love requires one actually love and be loved, and this loving relationality is the end of the scriptures themselves.

De Doctrina, a text concerned with both the question of interpretation and that of the presentation of what is learned, begins in book 1 with an intriguing statement that hints at the unity of love and knowledge that will invite much attention in the pages to follow: "For all the things which do not give out when given away are not properly possessed when they are possessed but not given away."[70] This claim

69. Tarmo Toom notes that Augustine's theological conviction that each scriptural text is double authored (by a human author and by God) "relativized the hermeneutical importance of the human authorial intent" and promoted instead an "Intentionalism with a capital 'I,' which prioritized the divine intention(s)." Tarmo Toom, "Was Augustine an Intentionalist? Authorial Intention in Augustine's Hermeneutics," *Studia Patristica* 54 (2012): 8–9.

70. Augustine, *De Doctrina*, 1.2.

is significant. The things about which Augustine writes—things that are not decreased when given away—can only be properly understood when they are taught, generously, beyond the structures of the interchange of money or honor for words. Knowledge of any *res* must be shared with others so that it might be properly understood by the possessor. The requirements of being part of a community—whether intellectual, contemplative, or ecclesial—are not limited to the exclusively ethical, cultural, or societal spheres but, in some manner, shape the mind's understanding of the thing in question (in this case the scriptural text). When considering those signs that (perhaps) direct us to things that "do not give out when given away," gratuity is not simply a moral command or ethical injunction but actually sharpens and assists the very interpretation of the *res* in question.[71] The truth of this reality is such that our possession of it—whatever nuances may be necessary to clarify such "possession"—is only possible in our loving participation in the community, beyond any strictly obligatory structural participation. Tracy observes that such *caritas* is transformative, not simply confrontational,[72] and a functioning hermeneutic—textual or more broadly interpretive—is, according to Rowan Williams, "a *process*—not a triumphant moment of penetration and mastery, but an extended play of invitation and exploration (the resonances of these metaphors are deliberate, and not wholly absent from Augustine's vocabulary)."[73] The sexual metaphors appropriately hint that supple cooperation of interpretive play, not technical mastery, is descriptive of Augustine's method. Moreover, such language hinders the simplistic reduction of Augustine's thought to hostility between faith and knowledge, between Christianity and the philosophies of the world. There remains—here, at least—some intercourse between Athens and Jerusalem.

While the syntactic ambiguity often can be minimized through

71. "Where this supreme Reality is concerned, therefore, our cognition is an act of loving. . . . The deepest knowledge, then, is charity." Burnell, *The Augustinian Person*, 100.
72. Tracy, "Charity, Obscurity, Clarity," 135.
73. Rowan Williams, "Language, Reality and Desire in Augustine's *De Doctrina*," *Journal of Literature and Theology* 3 (July 1989): 142.

contextual clarification,[74] the scriptures' spiritual context and their status as the word of God renders ultimate clarification—despite Augustine's acknowledgment of the significance of human authorial action—deferred, perhaps eschatologically so. Thus, without ever abandoning the real interpretive progress possible through proximate context,[75] Augustine is unwavering in his insistence upon the assured obscurity of the scriptural text, upon our inability to know precisely *what* is to be understood. Such an insistence grows from the *regula fidei*, the rule of faith that guides his hermeneutics: "Namely, if an interpretation promotes *caritas*, the requirement of the twofold first commandment (Mark 12:28–31; Gal 5:14), an interpreter has understood the Scriptures correctly."[76]

Pool argues that the structure of the rule outlined by Augustine is, itself, structured upon the two-fold scriptural command to love:

> However much the entire *De Doctrina Christiana* (most obviously, Book IV of course) formally relies upon Cicero's rhetorical theology, Augustine nevertheless discerned the theological basis for this formal account of the hermeneutical task in the twofold commandment to love itself. In other words, the necessity for the formal character of the twofold hermeneutic arises from the mandate of the twofold command to love God and neighbor.[77]

Augustine's hermeneutic, informed as it is by classical sources, is essentially tied to the words of Jesus Christ and to the interpretative method Christ himself offers in the Gospels:

74. Toom, "Augustine on Ambiguity," 415.
75. Toom notes that maintaining the significance of the concrete text serves as an important guide for the interpreter who "when trying to follow authorial intention, is tempted to disregard the *scriptum*." Ibid., 423. Augustine recognizes that, along with the rule, "which warns us not to pursue a figurative (that is, metaphorical) expression as if it were literal, we must add a further one: not to accept a literal one as if it were figurative." Augustine, *De Doctrina*, 3.33. We do well to follow, and not dictate, the course of the text.
76. Toom, "Augustine on Ambiguity," 429. Augustine writes: "The chief purpose of all that we have been saying in our discussion of things is to make it understood that the fulfillment and end of the law [cf. Rom 13:10; 1 Tim 1:5] and all the divine scriptures is to love the thing which must be enjoyed and the thing which together with us can enjoy that thing. . . . So anyone who thinks that he has understood the divine scriptures or any part of them, but cannot by his understanding build up this double Love of God and neighbor, has not yet succeed in understanding them." Augustine, *De Doctrina*, 1.84–86.
77. Pool, "No Entrance into Truth," 645.

> "Teacher, which commandment in the law is the greatest?" He said to him, "You shall love the Lord, your God, with all your heart, with all your soul, and with all your mind. This is the greatest and the first commandment. The second is like it: You shall love your neighbor as yourself. The whole law and the prophets depend on these two commandments."[78]

This rule, derived from the scriptures and interpretive of the same, encourages an approach to the truth of the scriptures that is not—or at least, not simply—a process of gathering "spiritual data" and reference points for factual knowledge but recognizes that what the scriptures are about, in a direct sense, is nothing less than a revelation of the love of God and a narrative of the transformative effect of that revelation on human beings.

A reading of Luke Ferretter's study of Augustine's Trinitarian language offers another insight into Augustine's thought, albeit *pace* Ferretter. Ferretter argues that Augustine maintains: "a metaphysics of inner light in which knowledge is as unaffected by words as the soul is by the body."[79] This illumination, which resonates in, but is not univocal with, *De Trinitate*'s inward method structuring its second half, sublates the limited relationship of sign and signified by the light of Christ's presence in the mental life. To illuminate the thing in question, we must consult the "truth that presides within over the mind itself," because "He who is consulted, He Who is said to *dwell in the inner man*, does teach: Christ—that is, *the unchangeable power and everlasting wisdom of God*."[80] However, this assertion overstates the distinction between inner light and outer words as a separation, contradicting as it does Augustine's christological understanding of language and knowledge. The dualism Ferretter tries to establish between knowledge and words is not as dichotomous for Augustine as it may appear. Augustine's autobiography and his account of knowledge significantly complicate Ferretter's account of "a metaphysics of inner light in which knowledge is as unaffected by words as the soul is by the body."[81]

78. Matthew 22:36–40 NAB.
79. Luke Ferretter, "The Trace of the Trinity: Christ and Difference in Saint Augustine's Theory of Language," *Literature and Theology* 12, no. 3 (1998): 256.
80. Augustine, *The Teacher*, 11.38.

While it is certainly possible to see in the immaterial soul's distinction from the affective tumult of the bodily passions an analogy for a knowledge that is not solely dependent upon a linguistic structure, Ferretter's analogy is revealing (albeit negatively) beyond this limited comparison. A "metaphysics of inner light" cannot simply exist with the necessary signifiers bracketed and deemed incidental to knowledge. For as much as signs alone remain impotent to signify, so any knowledge of things in themselves still requires signification. For Augustine, meaning cannot exist unmoored from language and abstracted from creation. *Confessions* narrates the story of one whose soul is in constant disquiet. Significantly, it is not the bodily influence on the soul that threatens Augustine most dramatically. It is not his unruled bodily desires, as such, that keep him restless and without peace, though they certainly are a contributing factor. Kolbet observes, "As a bishop, Augustine continued to believe that passion and sin often go hand in hand whenever the soul's non-rational, lower faculties failed to follow its higher ones. He, nevertheless, came to identify the soul's sin less with a loss of self-control than with its active grasping to impose an order of its own making upon itself or others."[82] The folly lies in the imposition of an alien order upon that which derives its being from a source far beyond our own intellect and will. Neither strictly an intellective error nor that of untamed bodily passion, Augustine is concerned with the human being's approach to understanding creation. "As unaffected" therefore cannot simply mean, "not affected," and this analogy requires a further look. It is not passion or emotion themselves, but the imposition of an alien order upon the interpretation of creation as a whole and particularly and significantly upon the scriptures—both of which have God as their true author—that signals the involvement of sin. Sin is not principally found in the passions but in the fact of their being insufficiently or inappropriately ordered (and therefore controlled).[83]

81. Ferretter, "Trace of the Trinity," 256.

82. Kolbet, *Cure of Souls*, 129.

83. This remains a crucial difference between Augustine and the various philosophies that maintain a dualism that makes possible a fundamental conflict between body and soul. "Augustine was intent

To praise the calm of the soul's "inner light" amidst the turmoil of incomplete knowledge or bodily passion is to maintain the Stoic principles that Augustine recognizes as inadequate for both the understanding of the human being and of the human being's proper moral and intellective engagement with the world. Not only is such a lack of affect essentially impossible but it disallows both desire's constitutive role in shaping the human being and that its incomplete nature might serve to quicken love for God and neighbor. Moreover, the relationship between the inner light and the language of a community and a tradition hints that meaning itself is inextricably tied to that love. Linguistic structure alone does not simply confer meaning abstracted from the human engagement with one's community. However, while taking into account the external cultural and religious linguistic structures that provide the individual with the means to engage questions of meaning, Augustine invites his readers not to a passive participation in these structures but to a recognition of the significance of the individual's loving interaction with those structures. While always grounded in language, Augustine's vision is of a love with hermeneutic priority over language even as it remains understandable and presently meaningful only in light of language.

The interpretive process of the scriptures, and by analogy of creation, does not necessitate either a conquest or a renunciation of the passions or of love itself. Love cannot be dismissed as an extrinsic impairment to interpretation and consequent understanding of the sacred scriptures. In turn, the difficulty of interpretation, rather than hindering the process, actually prepares the reader's heart to fruitfully and inseparably participate in the mind's activity. That ambiguity and obscurity of the scriptural texts serve to "conquer our pride by hard work" is a component of the texts' actual purpose[84] and, furthermore, has a positive function in frustrating our attempts to impose

on preserving or restoring human wholeness by directing all of the individual's activities to the goal or goals to which they are intrinsically ordered." Fortin, "Augustine and the Hermeneutics," 51. For Augustine, there is no possible control abstracted from the end to which the passions are ordered.

84. Tracy, "Charity, Obscurity, and Clarity," 138.

interpretive meaning upon them. For Augustine, this ostensible lack of clarity inspires in the reader an increased desire for truth itself—and particularly for a truth that can be attained not through intellectual or moral conquest but through the generosity of God. We can never achieve, through our own considerable efforts, the position of hermeneutical clarity but are only granted fragments of vision as part of our ongoing conversion. Therefore, "For Augustine the rule of truth or faith is never truly internalized. Because we only truly attend to the rule of faith insofar as we grasp the movement that is participation in Christ, the rule is internalized only in the sense that we internalize a movement towards the goal, we internalize the transference that Christ effects."[85] The presence of Christ with us, only present as process—as conversion—both gives wisdom to us and invites further love. Ferretter writes that the inner light is the presence of Christ,[86] and "*Christ's presence is different.*"[87] Always present as invitation, never to be equated directly with human reason, Christ draws us through love. Our love is ever in formation, seeing indistinctly and knowing partially, in hopes that as the perfect comes, the partial will pass away, that we might know fully, as we are fully known.[88]

The meaning of the scriptures is bound to the economy of God's salvific work in and through Christ and the Spirit, by the quickening of *caritas* through the words of the sacred texts. Pecknold writes, "Augustine wants to shape reading practices because he wants the Word of God to transform the way readers live and practise their faith—change the way people read, and you change the way they love."[89] Love is the meaning of the scriptures, a meaning that is transformative. All other meanings, valid though they may be, are proximate and imperfect. The *res* of ultimate significance to Augustine, to which the *signa* of both scriptures and creation point (albeit at times

85. Lewis Ayres, "Augustine on the Rule of Faith: Rhetoric, Christology, and the Foundation of Christian Thinking," *Augustinian Studies* 36 (2005): 48–49.
86. Ferretter, "Trace of the Trinity," 262.
87. Ibid., 263; emphasis in original.
88. 1 Corinthians 13:9–12.
89. C. C. Pecknold, *Transforming Postliberal Theology: George Lindbeck, Pragmatism and Scripture* (New York: T&T Clark, 2005), 51.

obscurely and ambiguously, and always eschatologically deferred) is the final loving enjoyment of God.

Ordered Love

It is not coincidental that Augustine's introduction of *signa* and *res* in *De Doctrina Christiana* is immediately followed by a parallel discussion of the tension between *uti* and *frui*—the love of something for the sake of something else (i.e., use) and the love of something for its own sake (i.e., enjoyment).[90] A theoretical complement to the rhetorically performative *Confessions*,[91] *De Doctrina* "articulates the central theological vision (viz. *caritas*) that pervades Augustine's entire thought through all its remarkable twists and turns, its revisions, intensifications, exaggerations, and retractions."[92] That Augustine's most self-consciously hermeneutical work is concerned with the question of love—and particularly with the manner in which different things ought to be loved—is consistent with his assessment that proper understanding of the judgment of things is dependent upon a proper valuation of them. Ordered knowledge requires an ordered love and, conversely, a "perversion of love is also a perversion of vision."[93] Thus, I, in all my subjectivity, am an inexorable part of my knowing and therefore what I value and how I value it shapes what I know and how I know it.[94] For the Bishop of Hippo, this self that knows, it needs to be stated, is far from a modern *cogito* whose thinking implies mastery and control of the object of thought. Indeed, the interpretive centrality of love—expressed in the ordered relationship of *frui* and *uti*—in this

90. Augustine, *De Doctrina*, 1.4–96.
91. Tracy, "Charity, Obscurity, Clarity," 128.
92. Ibid., 127.
93. Michael Hanby, *Augustine and Modernity* (New York: Routledge, 2003), 38.
94. This insight is foundational, too, to the work of Bernard J. F. Lonergan, whose second of two great works—*Method in Theology* (New York: Seabury, 1972)—presents knowledge as significantly shaped by the religious conversion of falling in love in an unrestricted manner. Interestingly, and I suspect not coincidentally, Lonergan noted to some of his former students (at the very least to Fred Lawrence and Joseph A. Komonchak) that as he aged he was finding himself much more Augustinian that he used to be. This can be seen in the increased significance of the "religious conversion"—that is being in love in an unrestricted fashion—in *Method* over love's place in his earlier text, *Insight: A Study of Human Understanding* (Toronto: University of Toronto Press, 1992; originally published 1957 by Philosophical Library). His later articulation of love assumes a role that saturates, and more effectively directs, cognitive operations.

process of valuation privileges an orientation of all knowledge to God and not to the self.

This relational quality of language is ultimately dependent upon the relationship of all of creation to its Creator, who imbues creation with meaning in the act of creating itself. The interpretation of *signa* and the knowledge born of the (possible) signification of *res*—without proper contextualization of both *signa* and *res* as part of the goodness of God's creation (while, of course, recognizing the quasi-creative participation of human beings)—undermines the radicality of the rational endeavor, resulting in attenuated understanding. However, that love ultimately conditions the meaning of things—that creation *qua* creation demands an expressly theological hermeneutic—can threaten to bathe all notions of meaning with such a blinding light of love that crucial (or even just pedestrian) distinctions among things can be lost in the intensity of such resplendence. That all is ultimately illuminated by divine love does not require that such love be the only factor to consider. Nor might we simply draw clear distinctions between the empirical knowledge of bodily realities and the knowledge by which we know ourselves and spiritual truth. The distinction of *scientia* (commonly translated "knowledge") and *sapientia* (commonly translated "wisdom") in Augustine's thought need not be rendered as separation, nor ought *scientia* ever abdicate its proper role in the process of human reasoning, its administration of daily affairs:

> And now with the Lord's assistance let us carry on with the consideration we have embarked upon of that part of reason to which knowledge belongs, that is to say, the knowledge of changeable and temporal things that is needed for the conduct of the business of this life. . . . With bodily sensation, after all, bodily things are sensed; but eternal, unchangeable and spiritual things are understood with the reasoning of wisdom. But the appetite is very close to the reasoning of knowledge, seeing that it is the function of this knowledge to reason about the bodily things that are perceived by bodily sensation. If it does this well, it does it in order to refer them to the highest good as their end; if badly, in order to enjoy them as goods of a sort it can take its ease in with an illusory happiness. So this channel of the mind is busy reasoning in a lively fashion about temporal and bodily things in its task of activity, and along comes that carnal or animal sense with a tempting suggestion for self-enjoyment, that is, for

> enjoying something as one's very own private good and not as a public or common good which is what the unchangeable good is.[95]

Significant, if subtle, is Augustine's implication that, although it is easily seduced by the finite happiness it discovers, the process of everyday human knowing is not, itself, to blame for human sin. Rather, it is deficiency in wisdom's ordering of reason to its ultimate end that fails to recognize knowledge for what it precisely is.

Wisdom's governance of interpretation does not imply impotence on the part of *scientia*. While recognizing (and for now bracketing) the unique nonempirical foundation of knowledge of spiritual reality, we might still acknowledge a vital relationship between knowledge of creation and the proper love of it—which is ultimately dependent upon one's knowledge of, that is relationship with, God. Gioia summarizes the epistemological process of Augustine's concept of *scientia*:

> In the case of knowledge of temporal or bodily realities, the process might be described as follows: something is recorded by our sensorial activity; this sensation awakens in us a desire to know its cause and to appreciate its value; this desire drives us to turn the sight of our mind to the reasons and standards so that they might enable us to define and to evaluate the object known; at this point, if this definition or evaluation pleases us to the point of converging our initial eagerness into full-blown love, we conceive a word (knowledge with love); this love, however, will not be satisfied until it is united to the thing known or possesses it (*copulatio*); only then the word is not only "conceived," but really "born."[96]

Love, for Augustine, is always love *of something* and is always drawing the lover *toward something*.[97] Never an immovable, self-contained, and self-sufficient substance, love, to be at all, requires a beloved person or thing for its genesis. Thus *sapientia*—this knowledge born of love—is both bound to, although not limited to, *scientia* for its instantiation and "fulfils a discriminating role in our dealings with temporal things."[98]

95. Augustine, *De Trinitate*, 12.17.
96. Gioia, *Theological Epistemology*, 202.
97. "Yet all love hath a power of its own, nor can love in the soul of the love be idle; it must needs draw it on." Augustine, *Expositions on the Book of Psalms* (London: F.&J. Rivington, 1853), 122.1. Love is always actively leading the lover on, either to heaven or the abyss. Although, to be sure, only the love of God (in both senses of the genitive) deserves to be called "love." If not ultimately directed to God, love for anything is properly *cupiditas* rather than *caritas*.

However, like many distinctions in Augustine's thought, the difference between *scientia* and *sapientia* is both unquestionably evident and ambiguously drawn. Gioia observes, "In Augustine's treatment of the relation of science and wisdom, it is very difficult to distinguish that which applies to epistemology as such and that which specifically applies to knowledge of God, undoubtedly because he himself was unwilling to draw such a distinction."[99] This apparent unwillingness on the part of the Bishop of Hippo is, in itself, significantly consistent with the theological structure of both knowledge and hermeneutics thus far established. For any so-called knowledge, if lacking an engagement and valuation by wisdom, remains the very knowledge Augustine so often criticized and against which Augustine begins *De Trinitate*, warning his readers: "My pen is on the watch against the sophistries of those who scorn the starting-point of faith, and allow themselves to be deceived through an unreasonable and misguided love of reason."[100] This reason is misguided not in its chosen engagement with either bodily or spiritual reality but in its presumption to measure, rather than be measured by, the structure of wisdom born of the love of God.

The resonances of sin have both epistemological and hermeneutical tones, here echoing together in (dis)harmony. While accepting a certain limitation of human knowledge and recognizing the inherent complexity of the acquisition of any knowledge through signification (a difficulty certainly amplified in spiritual matters), any relatively accurate assessment of reality is corrupted by the insufficiency—intentional or no—of contextualization. While ostensibly a question regarding the analytical, critical, and synthesizing performance of the human mind, an assessment of creation, absent the relating of this reality to God, constitutes the sinful presumption of pride. However different in content, this intellectual error is at the same time a spiritual transgression. The line demarcating the border between human limitations that are the result of our finite created nature—that is, of not being God—and the perversion of human nature as a result

98. Gioia, *Theological Epistemology*, 223.
99. Ibid.
100. Augustine, *De Trinitate*, 1.1

of sin is firm, even while its incarnate reality remains unclear. Augustine's conviction regarding the goodness of creation—a goodness that is proportional to its being—eliminates the possibility that sin might directly result from such created finitude. Much to the contrary of his cultured despisers, Augustine locates the empty perversion of sin neither in the passions nor the physical human body. While Augustine grants that, "something about the corruption of the body distorts our desires,"[101] the origin of this ever-deepening corruption is in our will. We do not desire the proper object with the appropriate ordered love. We suffer from internal conflict of desire. Bodily disobedience is a manifestation of our conflicted desires (and, indeed, furthers the conflict) and masks this conflict as its source. Peter Burnell writes, "What we experience as if it were a disobedience of the body to the soul (first moral weakness, finally death) is in fact an internal disobedience in the soul. This real disorder gives us the illusion that the trouble emerges along a line of division between soul and body."[102] In perhaps sin's most insidious perversion, the refusal of a loving relationship with God and with neighbor is masked as a consequence of created finitude, as though we were created by God so that we might not embrace such love. The veils that "hang at the entrances to the schools of literature"—schools so attractive to the young Augustine, while so vehemently attacked by the adult—signifying not "the prestige of the élite teaching so much as the covering up of error,"[103] hid teaching that was erroneous not because it did not fully understand God but because it deemed such spiritual contextualization irrelevant. It was the lack of *caritas* governing knowledge, not the lack of particular knowledge per se, that Augustine deemed so dangerously distorting. Augustine does not condemn *scientia* itself but only—yet aggressively—the presumption of its sufficiency.

Augustine's understanding of the insufficiency of *scientia* without *sapientia* is evident in his interpretive method in the reading of the sacred scriptures. In taking up the particular question of the scriptures

101. Burnell, *Exercises in Religious Understanding*, 33.
102. Ibid., 34.
103. Augustine, *Confessions*, 1.13.

in *De Doctrina*, Augustine is privileging the text above creation not in its derivation of its meaning from God but that it stands as a paradigmatic example of God's meaning-giving activity in all of creation.[104] The hermeneutic Augustine presents in *De Doctrina* can serve as the cornerstone for a larger interpretive framework that is present, among other places, in *De Trinitate*.

The proper ordering of our loves is seen, too, in the relationship between enjoyment and use. *Frui*—the love that enjoys its object as an end in itself—is properly directed only to God. All else—even, although with some important distinctive qualifications, other people[105]—is meant to be used as a means to enjoy God. In the end, to be human is to have one's end in the peace of God's love and attempting to end in anything else betrays one's humanity and results in unquelled restlessness. The directional quality of Augustine's conception of love as the "weight" of the soul, as that which ultimately directs the soul to its resting place,[106] precludes the possibility that a soul might

104. Cf. "Christian culture had inherited a veritable cult of the word from its Hebrew ancestry. That cult turned into adoration at the beginning of John's Gospel: *In principio erat Verbum*. Had not God created the world by his Word? And had he not revealed himself through that same Word? Scripture and cosmos supported each other in giving meaning to reality. Nature also can be read as a book, but only by means of a code provided in *the* book. The Bible alone, Emile Mâle wrote, discloses the harmony that God has established between the soul and the universe. 'Some people read books in order to find God. Yet there is a great book, the very appearance of created things. Look above you; look below you! Note it; read it! God, whom you wish to find, never wrote that book with ink. Instead, He set before your eyes the things He had made.' This wrote Augustine." Louis K. Dupré, *Passage to Modernity: An Essay in the Hermeneutics of Nature and Culture* (New Haven: Yale University Press, 1993), 102.

105. For a discussion of the unique status of such use-love of other people, see Tarcisius J. van Bavel, "The Double Face of Love in Augustine," *Augustinian Studies* 17 (1986): 169–81, and Burnaby, *Amor Dei*, 104–10. "A means which can be loved is not *only* a means. The keyword is *referre ad Deum*, 'relation to God', and the distinction of *uti* and *frui* is merged in the 'order of love.'" Burnaby, *Amor Dei*, 106. Fortin contributes an important addendum to this discussion, illuminating that this distinction can take our created finitude into account and protect the individual from the possible abuses of the command to love: "Properly understood, the distinction between 'enjoyment' (*frui*) and 'use' (*uti*) directs our attention to one of the most problematic features of the New Testament teaching on love, to say nothing of the modern account of love and friendship as 'I-Thou' relationships. It is characteristic of the New Testament commandment of universal love that it ignores all the limitations that nature imposes in us in this matter. One is summoned to love others without discrimination and independently of their personal merits or qualities. But this could amount to little more than a tyranny of every individual over every other individual. The pitfall is avoided only if the love that unites human beings has its ground in the one good that can be shared by all of them without partition or diminution, namely, God himself." Fortin, "Augustine and the Hermeneutics," 48.

106. "The weight's movement is not necessarily downwards, but to its appropriate position: fire tends to move upwards, a stone downwards. They are acted upon by their respective weights they seek their own place. . . . Things which are not in their intended position are restless. Once they are in

successfully serve two masters and have two absolute desires. Conflicting desires tear the soul asunder, leaving one desire ultimately victorious in the devastated wake. In the end, we each love someone or something more than all else and cling fast to it even while abandoning or sacrificing each other beloved thing. This use-love for creation, though certainly positioned for possible self-serving manipulation, serves to dignify and protect the whole of creation as not only *res* but as *signum*, as that which has the potential to direct our vision to God. Interpreting Augustine as tyrannically rejecting the good of creation in favor of a so-called purely spiritual good grossly misreads the author who cried to God:

> And see, you were within and I was in the external world and sought you there, in my unlovely state I plunged into those lovely created things which you made. You were with me, and I was not with you. The lovely things kept me far from you, though if they did not have their existence in you, they had no existence at all.[107]

To be sure, as for Augustine, "human bodily corruption that is not the original cause of sin nevertheless causes actual sin in us,"[108] his appreciation of bodily goodness is more often drowned out by his indictment of the manifestations of the lust to dominate (*libido dominandi*)—most notably for him in various forms of pride and in sexual desire.[109] However, in whatever ways Neoplatonic body/soul dualism remained a structural part of his thought and permitted him to "see that the mental power by which [he] formed images does not occupy any space, though it could not form them unless it were some great thing,"[110] Augustine's rejection of Manichaeism confirmed the goodness of the finite created world. His appreciation of creation results in not "a flight from the temporal, but a proper referral of the temporal to its eternal origin and end."[111] The interpretive key lies

their ordered position, they are at rest. My weight is my love [*pondus meum amor meus*]. Wherever I am carried, my love is carrying me." Augustine, *Confessions*, 13.9.10.

107. Ibid., 10.27.38.
108. Burnell, *Exercises in Religious Understanding*, 180.
109. See, for example, Augustine, *Confessions*, 2.1.1–3, 3.1.1.
110. Augustine, *Confessions*, 7.2.
111. Hanby, *Augustine and Modernity*, 58. See also Burnaby: "The apparent approval of Porphyry's

first in Augustine's understanding of the will as responsive to God's antecedent love, which thereby defines our desire as a directed response to a love already given. A competing conception of the will as a morally and theologically neutral force by which I achieve my desired end, threatens to reduce *uti* to the quality of being manipulatable, as a means by which I achieve an end determined by my own autonomous choice. The second part of Augustine's understanding of the will is the coextensive nature of this desirous love and of *being* itself.

In his work delineating not only the lack of genealogical relationship between Augustinian inwardness and the so-called modern self ("the arbiter and source of value in the world,"[112] "simultaneously mastering the universe and draining it of any intrinsic meaning"[113]) but also the intrinsic antagonism between them, Michael Hanby emphasizes the bishop's understanding of the will as precisely that which liberates Augustine's concept of love from mere erotic self-gratification or the lust for domination. Radically christological (and therefore inescapably Trinitarian), Augustine's conception of the human being emerges from the two-fold single action of God's creative and salvific love, eliciting our desire through the prior beautiful gift of love in the person of Jesus Christ. What a human being *is*, is unintelligible outside of Jesus Christ—outside of Christ's gift of the Trinitarian delight between the Father and the Son. There is no "natural" human being to consider separate from God.[114] In the human being so conceived as created to the

maxim—'Flee from all that is bodily'—is one of the errors in the Dialogues which are noted in the *Retractations*. The Neo-Platonic attitude to the body became untenable for Augustine when he discovered that the Catholic faith in the Word made flesh was more than the acceptance of a divinely-authorized teaching and example." Burnaby, *Amor Dei*, 69.

112. R. Williams, "*Sapientia* and the Trinity," 317.

113. Hanby, *Augustine and Modernity*, 6.

114. Henri de Lubac famously takes up the question of nature and the possibility of an understanding of particularly human nature outside of an expressly christological/theological framework in *Surnaturel. Études historiques* (Paris: Aubier, 1946) and more extensively in *Le Mystère du surnaturel* (Paris: Aubier, 1965). Dupré, in agreement with de Lubac's suspicion of this heuristic category, notes that the conception of nature outside of its being ordered toward God is a distinctively modern idea, one that had no bearing on the great minds of the Patristics: "Theologians did not begin to treat the concept of *pure nature* as a concrete independent reality until the sixteenth century. Despite its philosophical appearance, this concept was deeply rooted in late nominalist theology. . . . Once the idea of an independent, quasi-autonomous order of nature gained a foothold in Catholic theology, it spread to all schools except the Augustinian." Dupré, *Passage to Modernity*, 178.

image of the Trinitarian God of love, Augustine conflates *esse* (being) and *dilectio* (love as regard, delight),[115] and renders possible "no sheer *being*, no existence deprived of all form, no mere quantum, to which the transcendentals good, beautiful, and true are simple accidental qualifications."[116] *Voluntas* is, for Augustine, the responsive desire for God that intimately constitutes us as human beings.

In Hanby's reading, there is absolutely no possibility that Augustine's conception of *voluntas* can be understood either as the "immanent causal force" of human agency[117] or as the neutral faculty adjudicating among alternative desires.[118] The former assumes either (1) a conflict between an agent God's imposition of divine "will" through the efficient causality of grace upon human beings rendered objects buffeted by whims of a voluntaristic deity or (2) human beings as righteous antagonists whose being is only assured to the degree by which they negate the tyrannical will of God. The latter posits the will as prior to love—an antecedent will, such as it is, that, without external influence, decides to prioritize one thing over others.[119] Such a choice—unaffected by love—assumes a faculty of the will operating without any discernable reason for choosing one alternative over another but maintains the virtue of such a choice as the foundation for an equally specious understanding of human freedom.[120] Although proximate ends can contextualize the choice, providing directive clarity amidst ambiguity, discerning those ends and one's ultimate *telos* while liberated from love's discriminating esteem renders the

115. Hanby, *Augustine and Modernity*, 74.
116. Ibid., 83.
117. Ibid., 82–90; quote from p. 82.
118. Ibid., 90–105.
119. Hanby sees these differing conceptions of the will as the heart of the Pelagian controversy, in which Augustine attempts to maintain a Christocentric concept of human beings in which our being itself is rendered intelligible only in light of its willing to be with God. Here, Hanby borrows from James Wetzel who, confirming Étienne Gilson, concludes that, "the concept of the will as 'power of choice' is a Pelagian 'fiction' and counters that 'there is no *faculty* of will, distinct from desire, which we use to determine out actions.'" Ibid., 92.
120. When venturing into the political arena, as Augustine does in *City of God*, the tones of freedom resonate differently. Without making a political assertion, I suggest only that part of the theological confusion regarding human freedom is a result of an imposition of the terms of the political relationship between the individual and the state upon the religious relationship between the created and the Creator. Where the relationship of believer and church falls is an additionally complicated question.

antecedent will both all-powerful and without preference. Such choice, "with its resultant notion of 'freedom,' drives a wedge between the act and its motive and institutes a motiveless choosing of motives in the breach."[121] Here, the will is declared free by rendering motive unintelligible. Rather than freedom, this unintelligible motivation indicates an inability to properly value, and thus order, those goods that we encounter—it indicates a weakness in love. Articulating this Augustinian principle, Hanby concludes, "Choice between alternatives is not a sign of the will's freedom to choose but its bondage to an internal division of desire."[122]

This imprisonment manifests itself intellectually as well, both as negating the presence of a comprehensive guide in textual interpretation and in the great marketplace of contrasting and conflicting ideas, in which it remained to Augustine to discern credible authority: "Among so many dissentient voices each one professed to be able to hand [truth] to me."[123] Here, he found himself confronted by "an inextricable thicket"[124] in which the promises lavished by the maze of philosophies concealed the absence of a method by which to discern among them. "This error," Kolbet writes, "leaves one with what Augustine calls, 'your reason,' and by that he is not referring to the universal reason that orders the universe, but a purported rationality that amounts to nothing more than a particular social construct."[125] Seeking to be free of external influence and the power of love, the all-powerful but motiveless will adapts to the whims of convention, even while we loudly assert our independence.

121. Hanby, *Augustine and Modernity*, 102.
122. Ibid., 93. See also Augustine's *City of God* on the freedom of the blessed: "Now the fact that they will be unable to delight in sin does not entail that they will have no free will. In fact, the will will be free in that it is freed from a delight in sin and immovably fixed in a delight in not sinning. The first freedom of will, given to man when he was created upright at the beginning, was the ability not to sin, combined with the possibility of sinning. But this last freedom will be more potent, for it will bring the impossibility of sinning; yet this also will be a result of God's gift, not of some inherent quality of nature." Augustine, *The City of God*, trans. Henry Bettenson (New York: Penguin, 1972), 22.30, p. 1088–89. All English translations throughout are from this version.
123. Augustine, *The Usefulness of Belief*, in *Augustine: Earlier Writings*, trans. John H. S. Burleigh (Philadelphia: Westminster Press, 1953), 8.20, p. 307. All English translations throughout are from this version.
124. Ibid.
125. Kolbet, *Cure of Souls*, 124.

Augustine's concept of the will harbors no such pretense of autonomy and freedom from one's love. Rather than an unaffected neutral faculty of choice, the Augustinian will is inexorably desirous.[126] It is the means by which one's loves are incarnated in the world and made into action, not merely as the mechanism of efficient causality but as *dilectio*—a love that discerns, discriminates, and cherishes—that which "makes thinking a coherent activity, an act from which we can rationally *go on*."[127] Thus, our action and choices are intelligible only as manifestations of our loves—of those things willingly desired by the concomitant fact that we love them. Such desire is excited by goodness and beauty—by those qualities in creation reflective of the Creator.

It is the incarnation of the Word of God, the act truly and fully infusing creation with the presence of the Creator, in which the unity of signification and the (perhaps) signified thing is rendered possible through the proper valuing of all loved things, ordered to be used for our final enjoyment of the vision of God. Such a Word excites and transforms our love. "As beauty [of the incarnate Word] it has a certain splendor which delights us and thus moves us to the love of love itself," Hanby writes. "In so doing, it draws us into its ambit. In other words, Christ's exemplary function is *rhetorical*; he is the sign of signs, the *plenitudo* and *finis* of all signs, whose purpose is to delight and captivate our love."[128] This responsive love, transformed by the presence of the incarnate Word, establishes a proper relationship with creation and Creator—that is, with the source, sustenance, and *telos* of creation *qua* creation. The ordering of desire illuminates our being—both that of the self and of the *res* (perhaps) signified—by rendering it what it essentially is, by valuing it as an expression of the goodness and love of God.

Thus, Augustine defends scriptural "'obscurity' as an intellectual

126. "The hypothesis Augustine favors is that souls, having all been created at the initial foundation, become successively embodied in the course of the administration, but become so neither in conscious obedience to divine orders nor in a spontaneous, intentional act by each (though Augustine discusses both these possibilities), but by a natural willingness utterly intrinsic to every human soul, 'because for this the soul is made' [*Literal Commentary on Genesis* 7.27.38]; this, then, is what a human soul duly does, in order to be a human being." Burnell, *The Augustinian Person*, 25.
127. R. Williams, "*Sapientia* and the Trinity," 329.
128. Hanby, *Augustine and Modernity*, 61.

value . . . in *both* the literal and spiritual senses,"[129] not as a means of ensuring a dispassionate indeterminacy, withholding judgment on the text's *truth*, but as a veiled part of the text's seduction. Obscure scriptures—which have the same lack of clarity as all of creation—when understood as a gift of God, excites *caritas.* Inviting readers into a deeper engagement with the text, with themselves, and ultimately with God, scriptural obscurity fulfills its primary purpose if it quickens the desire for knowing God. Thus, while the *signa* cannot, in the end, teach what it is for us to know, the discovery of *truth*—textual or otherwise—is made possible if the means to that discovery are already present within us. *Caritas* becomes both the means and the end of scriptural hermeneutics—and indeed, of interpreting the meaning of all of creation.

Uti, when conditioned by a love whose direction is responsive to God's sending of the Son in the person of Jesus Christ, precludes the reduction of that which I love to a mere means to my own self-sufficient satisfaction. Augustine does not intend *use* neutrally, as a practical or technical act, but as an already-orientated response to an *a priori* act on the part of God. And while I may certainly attempt to enjoy those created good things that I ought to lovingly use, that is, venture to make proximate ends ultimate, this results not in a peaceful completion of the erotic self but in its imperfection. It is this "abridgment of the self,"[130] and not a disparagement of the created world, that Augustine seeks to contest in his distinction between *frui* and *uti.* Williams notes that for the human being, created for no final end but rest in God, "the language of *uti* is designed to warn against an attitude towards any finite person or object that terminates their meaning in their capacity to satisfy my desire, that treats them as the end of desire, conceiving my meaning in terms of them and theirs in terms of me."[131] The hermeneutical significance of this ordered love—that I do not read the scriptural signs (or any signs, for that matter) in terms of *what I want them to mean* but in terms of *what*

129. Tracy, "Charity, Obscurity, Clarity," 129.
130. Kolbet, *Cure of Souls*, 106.
131. R. Williams, "Language, Reality, and Desire," 140.

they mean in relation to God—is found in the application of the *frui/uti* relationship to that of the *signa/res.*

Caritas "awakens in us a love for its beauty that is so powerful that it revises our relationship to everything else."[132] In concluding *City of God*, Augustine even suggests that in the fullness of *caritas*, seen and received in the beatific vision, "God will be known to us and visible to us in the sense that he will be spiritually perceived in one another, perceived by each in himself; he will be seen in the new heaven and the new earth, in the whole creation as it then will be."[133] To see God through God's relation to all things—and to be related to God through our relationship with all things—is a possible implication of seeing all things as related to God.

Augustine's hermeneutic of love requires that the interpretation of one's life be governed by the rules of that faith as instantiated precisely through the turning of one's love to the incarnation of the Word. This hermeneutic might be tentatively summarized in three parts: (1) the theological contextualization of signification, (2) the part love plays in this signification, and (3) the transformation that love effects within us.

First, Augustine's hermeneutic is inescapably theological, in that, at its root, the only knowledge to actually qualify as such is dependent upon an understanding of a thing's proper value and therefore an understanding of its relationship with its Creator. What something is and how it ought to be valued are inseparable, if distinct, questions whose relationship begins to illuminate a proper Augustinian understanding of language, thought, and love. Rowan Williams observes, "In the sense that no worldly *res* is securely settled as a fixed object 'meaning' itself, or tied in a fixed designation, that no worldly state of affairs can be allowed to terminate human desire, that all that is present to us in and as language is potentially *signum* in respect of the unrepresentable God . . ."[134] The fluidity with which Augustine moves between *signum* and *res*—in that not only can things both stand

132. Kolbet, *Cure of Souls*, 154.
133. Augustine, *City of God*, 22.29.
134. R. Williams, "Language, Reality, and Desire," 145.

as themselves in a limited sense and signify something else, which "are at the same time signs of other things"[135]—is justified by his belief that all the things of creation can serve as *signa* precisely as created, that is, as given being and meaning by God.[136] Regarding even the meaning of a *res* itself, "at the most basic level, it appears that intelligibility and signification are 'built in' to the meaning of creaturehood."[137]

Second, the orientation of *uti* to *frui*—whereby all created good might direct toward the enjoyment of the Good who is God—suffers from a similar challenge of that of *signa* to *res*, as they both appear to be lacking the means by which such a bond may be forged whose foundation is rooted deeper than that of mere convention. But where signification is insufficient, *caritas*, if incarnated in life and therefore transformative by its presence, can provide the contextualization for the discovery of "the true meaning (and thereby the true arguments) from the new 'classics'—the scriptures."[138] Love, Augustine proposes, makes possible the interpretation of the scriptures through their proper orientation to God—a turning that not only is effected by love but that has love as its goal as well. The hermeneutic efficacy of this love—and its significance in the process of all understanding—is absolutely dependent upon faith in the God of love as Creator, as both beginning and end of human life and meaning. Should this be neglected or disregarded, Augustine's theological construct—Trinitarian, christological, and anthropological as it is—would collapse beneath its unfounded faith that all being originates in the love of God.

135. Augustine, *De Doctrina*, 1.5.

136. The implications of the orientation of everything to God, overlooking the possibility or significance of natural and theologically-neutral ends—even if only as a conceptual tool—stand out most insightfully in Karl Rahner's critique of Henri de Lubac's *Surnaturel.* While agreeing with de Lubac in part, Rahner highlights the risk of a theology that so unites nature and grace that their distinction is lost in the process. As this question pertains to Augustine, de Lubac responds (with the help of Jacques Maritain): "Despite all that has been said to the contrary, we must certainly maintain that 'St. Augustine taught as clearly as possible the ontological value of the distinction between nature and grace.' . . . The definitely and intrinsically supernatural character of divine adoption is one of the fundamental elements in his teaching; it is expressed there so clearly, and so insistently, that we should be astonished to find that it has not always been recognized. . . . If there is a lack in Augustine's teaching, it does not consist in an insufficient stress on 'deification,' not in any confusion between natural and supernatural orders." Henri de Lubac, *The Mystery of the Supernatural*, trans Rosemary Sheed (New York: Herder & Herder, 1967), 20–21.

137. Hanby, *Augustine and Modernity*, 34.

138. Tracy, "Charity, Obscurity, Clarity," 135.

This knowledge, grounded in *scientia* yet contextualized, valued, and understood through *sapientia,* makes eschatologically deferred meaning truly present—albeit fragmentally—in the very process of its deferral. The orientation of everything to God permits no final judgment of meaning while at the same time confessing that final meaning only in God. Most clearly revealed in the life and cross of the incarnate Word, this always present yet always to come love of God "represents the absence and deferral that is basic to *signum* as such, and represents also, crucially, the fact that absence and deferral are the means whereby God engages our desire so that it is freed from its own pull towards finishing, towards presence and possession."[139] The infinitely deep and often obscure mystery—the trace of Creator in creation and the hint of love that is to come—is intended to drawn us through, not from, the beauty and goodness that we do see towards a vision of what we long to see.

Third, as referential of relationship with God, ultimate meaning—while necessarily mediated through language—cannot be simply conventional, conditioned by a cultural-linguistic structure that shapes human reason. Nor can it be found in the isolated experience of the individual human person, navigating their way through determinations of meaning and value on the sheer causal force of a neutral will. Requiring that which is outside of cultural, societal, or personal convention, the vision of truth—as with any learning at all—is only possible where new language and ideas are brought to bear on one's thought. But that which is new is only learned by eyes already trained to see it, by a mind already taught to understand it, and by a heart already desirous of it. Not so much a way out of this *aporia* as an end that illuminates a way of proceeding in its midst, love serves Augustine as the necessary governing criterion of any interpretation of creation or understanding of God. A life lived in faith in this love frames the meaning of the language of the scriptures and the book of creation itself. "Certain things cannot be understood unless we are prepared to incarnate them," David Burrell writes. "The language

139. R. Williams, "Language, Reality, and Desire," 148.

model allows this point to be made quite precisely: The rules of inference which govern a particular language must become the rules of one's life if he is to use that language with confidence and alacrity."[140] Even marred by sin, Rowan Williams notes, "the dimmest human self-awareness, far short of *sapientia*, acts out of a buried and inarticulate connectedness with eternal knowledge and love."[141] The desire for God, even if not faithfully embraced, inescapably marks the desire to know as, ultimately, the desire to know God and therefore to love God. The remainder of part 1 will attempt to read *De Trinitate* with this interpretive structure in mind, always attentive to the question of the signification of the *res* that is nothing less than the Trinitarian God of love revealed in the gift of love.

140. David B. Burrell, CSC, *Exercises in Religious Understanding* (Notre Dame: University of Notre Dame Press, 1974), 25.
141. R. Williams, "*Sapientia* and the Trinity," 321.

2

Books 1–4: The Revelation of God in Salvation History

Whoever does not give God, gives too little.

—Joseph Cardinal Ratzinger,
homily for the Funeral Mass for Fr. Luigi Giussani

Arising from christological roots and "designed to preserve faith in Christ, the Son of God, and to direct the Christian hope toward full salvation in the divine fellowship,"[1] the doctrine of the Trinity was forged by the blows struck in the heat of contentious intellectual and ecclesiastical negotiations about the language with which we might talk about, and more importantly address, God. Speculation about the nature of the God and the Nicene priority placed on the same substance of the Father, Son, and Spirit has its historical roots in practical and polemical formulations intended to respond to threats against both the full divinity of Jesus Christ and the irreducibility of the Son to the Father (and only secondarily to analogous threats against the Holy

1. Jürgen Moltmann, *The Trinity and the Kingdom: The Doctrine of God* (San Francisco: Harper & Row, 1981), 129.

Spirit). The first four books of *De Trinitate* follow in this inherited polemic against both Monarchian modalism and Arian subordinationism, and defend the trustworthiness of the Nicene interpretation of the scriptures by which Jesus Christ (and concomitantly the Holy Spirit) might be understood both as distinct from, yet one with, the Father.[2]

In turning to the scriptures, contextualizing the equality and irreducibility of the divine persons by the missions of the Son and Spirit, Augustine initiates a delicately but firmly balanced defense of the scriptures as revelatory of God. The divine missions mediate between humanity and divinity, offering to the former not information about God but the true presence of God in and through creation. The witness the scriptures bear to the incarnation of the Son and the sending of the Spirit reveals something true about who God is. Therefore, even as Augustine engaged in the polemical battles of his time, he sought to illuminate this primary witness. Lewis Ayres notes that although *De Trinitate* shares the same general line of argumentation with the bishop's actual debate with Arians, his approach in books 1–4 is "primarily literary" and "treats heretical positions as also constant possibilities for the Catholic mind."[3] That is not to say that the polemical battles were not part of *De Trinitate*'s context but that Augustine was less concerned with responding to a particular subordinationist claim and more with a "common failure to understand what it means for Christ to have been a visible revelation of the invisible."[4] From the beginning, *De Trinitate* shows its author to be concerned with securing the veracity of this missional mediation of

2. In *Augustine and the Trinity*, Lewis Ayres extensively chronicles the anti-Monarchian rhythm of much of Augustine's early thought, concluding that the very theology often attributed to him (the reduction of the Trinitarian relations to the single substance of a divine mind) expressly contradicts the irreducibility of the divine persons in his thought. For his is not a theology, shaped though it was by Neoplatonism, that supposes a God beyond the Trinity, a unity beyond the divine persons, a divine mind drawing all distinction into itself like a theological black hole. *Augustine and the Trinity* unearths Augustine's sources and while acknowledging that Augustine was, in one sense, a Platonist, his adoption of the doctrines of that tradition was done for Christian theological purposes, countering Manichean, Sceptic, and Monarchian thought and supporting, although somewhat idiosyncratically, the formulation of Nicaea.
3. Ayres, *Augustine and the Trinity*, 172.
4. Ibid., 173.

God and the inseparable operations of the Father, Son, and Holy Spirit. We can trust in revelation because—and only because—the activity of the Son and Spirit is nothing less than the activity of the one God. After briefly contextualizing the pro-Nicene tradition Augustine inherited, this chapter will focus primarily (1) on how Augustine defends Christ's mediation (through the Spirit) of the invisible God and (2) on the place of love in our understanding of this mediation.

Augustine's Polemics

Books 1–4 open *De Trinitate* in response to Arian subordination. *Arianism* was for Augustine an umbrella signifier for a varied and disparate collection of theological movements or conventions that, for one reason or another, held to the inequality of the Father and the Son.[5] It appeared on the historical and ecclesiastical scene in the ante-Nicene period, taking its name from the theology of a Alexandrian priest, Arius (ca. 256–336 CE), who, "ventured to put forward a one-sided solution to the half-measures"[6] of the implicit but unclarified subordinationist tradition present in the church.[7]

This subordinationist tradition arose in response to varying forms of modalism maintaining that the mission of the Son and Spirit were modes of the Father's own self-manifestation and not signs of a triune God, and offered instead an emphasis on the distinction of the Father and Son and on the irreducibility of the Son and Spirit to the Father. The challenge that faced the ante-Nicene church was, in part, a matter of understanding divine mediation. In defending both Christ's role as mediator and his distinction from the transcendent God, many of the theologians of this period (significantly Justin, Tertullian, and Origen) emphasized the work of the Son/Logos/Christ in the theophany stories

5. For more on the distinctions among the variety of theological traditions that might fall under the heading of "Arian," see Michel René Barnes, "The Arians of Book V, and the Genre of *De Trinitate*," *Journal of Theological Studies* 44, no. 1 (1993): 185–95; Michel René Barnes, "*De Trinitate* VI and VII: Augustine and the Limits of Nicene Orthodoxy," *Augustinian Studies* 38, no. 1 (2007): 189–202. See also Alois Grillmeier, SJ, "Arius and Arianism," part 2, chap. 2 in *Christ in the Christian Tradition: Vol 1, From the Apostolic Age to Chalcedon (451)*, trans. John Bowden (Atlanta, GA: John Knox Press, 1975).
6. Grillmeier, *Christ in the Christian Tradition*, 219.
7. Ibid., 224.

of the patriarchs, prophets, and philosophers. They "seized upon this belief in their Christological polemics, seeing in the theophanies proof of the Son's distinctive identity and activity before the incarnation,"—and the separation between visibility and invisibility led to a subordination of visible Son to invisible Father.[8]

Following and furthering the path laid out against modalism by the early Christian apologists and by Origen, Arius writes against the eradication of the distinction between God and Christ:

> So there are three subsisting realities (*hupostaseis*); but God, being the cause of all things, is without beginning and supremely unique (*monōtatos*), while the Son, timelessly (*achronōs*) begotten by the Father, created and established before all ages, did not exist prior to his begetting, but was timelessly begotten before all things; he alone was given existence [directly] by the Father. For he is not eternal or co-eternal or equally self-sufficient (*sunagennētos*) with the Father, nor does he have his being alongside the Father, [in virtue] as some say, [of] his relation with him (*ta pros ti*), thus postulating two self-sufficient first principles. But it is God [only], as monad and first principle of all things, who exists in this way before all things. That is what he exists before the Son (*pro tou huiou*) . . .[9]

Arius and his followers sought to maintain the fullness of God's divinity by advocating for a mediator between God and creation—a mediator of the highest rank in all creation, but part of creation, nonetheless—who might allow the perfect, timeless, impassible divine monad to interact with the imperfect, temporal, suffering creation. Arius's "particular understanding of monotheism"[10] allows for the divine monad to be equated with "the first and only *arche*, or the first hypostasis in the triad. All duality is excluded from this monad."[11] That which is God—the divine substance—must be understood singularly as the Father.

8. Kari Kloos, "Seeing the Invisible God: Augustine's Reconfiguration of Theophany Narrative Exegesis," *Augustinian Studies* 36 (2005): 398.
9. From the statement of faith of Arius and his Alexandrian supporters (from Opitz, U.6 = de syn.16, Epiphanius, haer. 69.7), from Rowan Williams, *Arius: Heresy and Tradition*, rev. ed. (Grand Rapids: Eerdmans, 2001), 271.
10. Grillmeier, *Christ in the Christian Tradition*, 222.
11. Ibid., 227.

In contrast to this, the Nicene Creed attests to Christ's full divinity and his distinction from the Father, asserted over and against any notions of subordination or modalism. The creedal *homoousios* is a fortification against all possibilities of subordination, particularly in its Arian form in which the Son is created by the Father and therefore not truly God as the Father is God (and therefore not God). Such theology, if extended into the decisive realm of soteriology, both threatens the possibility of human salvation—as a creature cannot save a fallen creation—and calls into question the liturgical worship of Jesus Christ as an idolatrous worship of one who is other than the true God. Locating the unity of all three divine persons in one divine substance—rather than, for instance, finding the source of divine unity in the person of the Father—is a conceptual barricade against a subordination that disunites the Son from the fullness of the one God. Augustine's primary interests throughout the first four books is to follow the catholic tradition and secure the irreducibility of the divine persons to a divine singularity,[12] thereby maintaining both the full divinity and the irreducible distinction of the Son and Spirit and thereby defending the doctrinal formulation of the Trinity.

Augustine's stated concern in *De Trinitate* is to respond to the questions and worries of those people for whom this rule of Christian faith might prove a stumbling block in light of the language of the scriptures. These people, "when they hear that the Father is God and the Son is God and the Holy Spirit is God, and yet this threesome is not three gods but one God . . . wonder how they are to understand this, especially when it is said that the trinity works inseparably in everything that God works."[13] Augustine is concerned not only with

12. Notable among Augustine's critics is Karl Rahner, who sees his own work on the Trinity as a corrective step to the "Augustinian-Western conception" of "a Trinity which is absolutely locked within itself—one which is not, in its reality, open to anything distinct from it; one, further, from which we are excluded, of which we happen to know something only through a strange paradox" (Rahner, *The Trinity*, 18), which is the result of beginning "with the one God, the one divine essence as a whole, and only *afterwards* does it see God as three persons." Ibid., 17. However, Rahner seems to be more concerned with the scholastic separation of the studies of the one God and the triune God, most notably in Thomas Aquinas. Rahner's critique is not so much of Augustine but of what he understands to be the Augustinian Trinitarian tradition.

13. Augustine, *De Trinitate*, 1.8.

what the text says, or even with establishing a continuity of the Testaments against Manicheism,[14] but also with how the text, precisely as revelation, aids its reader in salvation—his exegesis serves his soteriology. The real possibility of human salvation is a governing component of the tempestuous debates of the Patristic-era church, and Christ's nature and relationship to God is the point around which most of the ink—and blood—was shed. In light of this soteriological consideration, Augustine occupies himself with a study of the scriptures focused on constructing a response to the subordinationist claim that, as Christ himself attests, "The Father is greater than I," the Son is "less than" God the Father. And while such attestation does not preclude a privileged status, either as created or adopted by God as "Son," it does necessitate that the Son not be fully God, "for every substance that is not God is a creature and that is not a creature is God. And if the Son is not of the same substance as the Father he is a made substance; if he is a made substance then not all things were made through him."[15]

The Mediation of the Son and Holy Spirit

Throughout much of books 1–4, Augustine endeavors to articulate a relationship of created mediation with that of the revelatory mediation of the Son and Spirit, wherein both creation is not disparaged and the Trinity of irreducible persons works in all things inseparably.[16] The stakes of proper delineation of this relationship are high, for it permits the theological articulation of both the Trinity and Trinitarian activity in creation while at the same time attempts to ensure that the one whom Christians worship and entrust with salvation is, in fact, God.[17] At the heart of this articulation of mediation lies Augustine's proposal about how we ought to interpret scriptural language about the incarnate Son and the implications of the interpretation upon our

14. Kloos, "Seeing the Invisible God," 408.
15. Augustine, *De Trinitate*, 1.9.
16. Ibid., 1.8.
17. This concern is expressively presented throughout *Confessions*, although perhaps most memorably in and around the question: "What do I love when I love my God?" Augustine, *Confessions*, 10.7.11.

understanding of God—the bishop is wrestling with the question of how God reveals Godself to us. Augustine defends revelatory mediation through his canonical rule explaining the apparent scriptural tension between the Son's subordination to the Father and the Son's equality with the Father. He distinguishes words spoken of the Son in the form of God from those spoken of the Son in the form of the servant. Of christological significance, certainly, this interpretive rule also contains within it intriguing potential for a theological understanding of love. Relying on the christological hymn in what is now chapter 2 of the letter to the Philippians, the bishop writes:

> For he did not so take the form of a servant that he lost the form of God in which he was equal to the Father. So if the form of the servant was taken on in such a way that the form of God was not lost—since it is the same only begotten Son of the Father who is both in the form of a servant and in the form of God, equal to the Father in the form of God, in the form of servant the mediator of God and men the man Christ Jesus—who can fail to see that in the form of God he too is greater than himself and in the form of a servant he is less than himself?[18]

Writing approximately one half century before the institution of the christological language of Chalcedon, Augustine theologically engages the paradoxical mediation of Christ by establishing an exegetical rule[19] and (beyond that and because of it) by beginning his argument that what it is we are given to see in the revelation of the Son is the mystery of who God is.

Perhaps we may here detect a hint of what is to come. Augustine presents the relationship of Father and Son such that the Son's taking on the form of a servant neither separates the divine persons,

18. Augustine, *De Trinitate*, 1.14.

19. E.g., "There are then some statements of scripture about the Father and the Son which indicate their unity and equality of substance. . . . And there are others which mark the Son as the lesser because of the form of a servant, that is because of the created and changeable human substance he took." Augustine, *De Trinitate*, 2.3. Also, "Stay within this rule: whenever you read in the authoritative words of God a passage in which it seems that the Son is shown to be less than the Father, interpret it as spoken in the form of the servant, in which the Son is truly less than the Father, or as spoken not to show that one is greater or less than the other, but to show that one has his origin from the other." Augustine, *Answer to Maximus*, in *Arianism and Other Heresies*, trans. Roland J. Teske, ed. John E. Rotelle, OSA, The Works of St. Augustine: A Translation for the 21st Century, vol. 1, no. 18 (Hyde Park, NY: New City Press, 1995), 2.14.8. All English translations throughout are from this version.

subordinating the Son to the Father, nor secures the true divinity of Christ by rendering it the incarnation of a singular Monarchian God. In a particular point about divinity, Augustine indicates that it is within the power of God to remain God even in becoming a servant. Not simply antithetical to divinity (as we might suspect Augustine would understand the absurd proposition of God's taking the [un]form of evil), there is herein a redoubled revelation of who God is. This "emptying" is not only coherent with God's being but in some way reveals it. In presenting the missions of the Son and Spirit as revelatory of who God is, Augustine signals that the unity of the Trinity is revealed in the inseparability of divine activity in salvation history:

> So too the trinity together produced both the Father's voice and the Son's flesh and the Holy Spirit's dove, though each of these single things has reference to a single person. Well, at least the example helps us to see how this three, inseparable in itself, is manifested separately through visible creatures, and how the three are inseparable at work in each of the things which are mentioned as having the proper function of manifesting the Father or the Son or the Holy Spirit.[20]

Taking the form of a servant, properly attributed to the Son, is at the same time the revelatory work of the Trinitarian God. Therefore who God is, is to be discerned through the mission of the Son and, we shall see, the Spirit, too. Being servant is not simply an ostensible conflict with divinity that must be overcome through creative exegesis but illuminates who God actually is.

This is the foundation upon which Augustine distinguishes between the missions of the Son and Spirit in the incarnation and on Pentecost on one hand and the theophanies of the Old Testament and the work of angels on the other. The visions of God received by the patriarchs and prophets (and one might imagine, any vision received since the apostolic age) "were produced through the changeable creation subject to the changeless God, and they did not manifest God as he is in himself, but in a symbolic manner as times and circumstances required."[21] Augustine is modest in what he believes we can ascertain

20. Augustine, *De Trinitate*, 4.30.

about the specifics of God's activity in the Old Testament. Discerning which divine person acted in which narrative is less important to him than the fact *that* God acted. Furthermore, as he is interested in the distinction between such theophanies and the sending of the Son and Spirit in the New Testament, he shifts his line of questioning from *whether* the Son and Spirit were sent in the Old Testament to *why* they were sent in the New.[22] The former theophanies only hint at what the latter missions actually manifest: God. Where in the theophanies, God made use of creation, the sending of the Son in the New Testament is an act of true revelation in which God was flesh.[23] And Augustine endeavors to articulate what they reveal through another interpretive rule: the missions of the Son and Spirit as being sent from the Father are "intended to show not that one person is less than the other, but only that one is from the other."[24] Being "from"—as the Nicene language describes the eternal generation of the Son—does not necessitate being "less than."

However, Augustine's defense of the Nicene formulation is not an end in itself but a means for further entering into the mystery of the Trinity. Not merely a defensive formulation against the implication that "being from" necessitates inequality, the creed allows us to see the missions into salvation history as revelatory of something of who God is. In fact, that revelation seems to be constitutive of their mission: "And just as being born means for the Son his being from the Father, so his being sent means his being known to be from him. And just as for the Holy Spirit his being the gift of God means his proceeding from the Father, so his being sent means his being known to proceed from him."[25] What the Son and Spirit reveal is their eternal generation and procession—that is, the very life of the Trinity itself. "In reality," Gioia summarizes, "Augustine is simply saying that revelation of the Trinity

21. Ibid., 2.32.
22. Kloos, "Seeing the Invisible God," 414.
23. Augustine does hesitate to ascribe to the appearances of Spirit such direct revelation, equating, for example, the tongues of fire from Acts 2:3 more closely with the burning bush from Exodus than with the incarnate Son. Augustine, *De Trinitate*, 2.11. The Spirit's role in revelation is not so much to show itself but to reveal the revelation of the Son.
24. Augustine, *De Trinitate*, 2.3.
25. Ibid., 4.29.

only occurred with the Incarnation and Pentecost."[26] The missions then, are God's being present to God's own people and making that presence known. God is the one who is present in the forms of servant and gift, and being servant and gift is revelatory of who God is.

Receiving this Mediation

Seeing this revelation, however, requires a hermeneutic of love. In book 4, Augustine submits charity as an interpretive concern, warning his reader that further progress requires one be "roused by the warmth of the Holy Spirit," and love God.[27] The one who does so, Augustine continues, "has taken a look at himself in God's light, and discovered himself, and realized that his own sickness cannot be compounded with God's cleanness. . . . Well, such a man, poor and grieving in this way, is not *puffed up* by *knowledge* because he is *built up* by *charity* (1 Cor. 8:1)."[28] It is only in charity that this revelation of God's salvific presence in, through, and to the world can actually occur—revelation requires a receiver, and reception is tied to charity.[29] While the Son is eternally begotten and the Spirit eternally proceeding, being sent in the incarnation and on Pentecost means that they are known by someone in time.[30] But as mediated in time, the "words Father and Son and Holy Spirit are separated and cannot be said together, and if you write them down each name has its own separate space."[31] The signification of the eternal Trinity in (always temporally situated) language is crippled not only by the challenges of relating *signa* and *res* but moreover by the eternity of the *res* in question. The missional mediation of the divine Trinity is challenged by the incongruence of the temporal reception of that which is eternal. Augustine suggests

26. Gioia, *Theological Epistemology*, 29.
27. Augustine, *De Trinitate*, 4.1.
28. Ibid.
29. One might contrast this with Augustine's naming of the Spirit as "gift" in book 5. There, he maintains that such a name can be eternally predicated of God—that is, the Spirit is eternally "gift," and therefore is "gift" *before* (whatever that might mean) there was a creation to be given to, because it is givable. If the Spirit is properly named "gift" eternally, that is, even without being given (ibid., 5.16), can God be called "revelatory" eternally without revealing to someone?
30. Ibid., 4.28; the Son and the Spirit being *eternally from* the Father is a matter for book 5.
31. Ibid., 4.30.

that love reconciles this incongruence because it opens us to the very nature of the eternal Trinitarian God of love.

In beginning an ontological exploration that will take on thicker significance as *De Trinitate* continues, Augustine locates the source of Trinitarian unity not exclusively in the shared divine nature or essence but also in the unity of love between the Father and the Son. The bishop writes:

> But he is declaring his divinity, consubstantial with the Father—as he says elsewhere, *I and the Father are one* (Jn 10:30)—in his own proper way, that is, in the consubstantial equality of the same substance, and he wants his disciples to be one in him, because they cannot be one in themselves, split as they are from each other by clashing wills and desires, and the uncleanness of their sins; so they are cleansed by the mediator that they may be one in him, not only by virtue of the same nature whereby all of them from the ranks of mortal men are made equal to the angels, but even more by virtue of one and the same wholly harmonious will reaching out in concert to the same ultimate happiness, and fused somehow into one spirit in the furnace of charity. This is what he means when he says *That they may be one as we are one* (Jn 17:22)—that just as the Father and Son are one not only by equality of substance but also by identity of will, so these men, for whom the Son is mediator with God, might be one not only by being of the same nature, but also by being bound in the fellowship of the same love.[32]

There are at least four points within this selection of significance to the question of the gift of love. First, it is important to acknowledge that, for Augustine, the Trinitarian persons do, in fact, have the same nature. Whether this leads to a Trinity in which the distinction among the persons proves to be nothing more than a complicated linguistic or theological masque, betraying a Monarchian modalism (of which Augustine and defenders of the *homoousian* have long been accused) that is the very antithesis of Augustine's intent is left to be seen. It would be a significant failure, indeed, if Augustine's treatise resulted in little more than a nuanced defense of the anti-Nicene presentation of the divine persons as a modalistic manifestation of God. Such modalism would render the missions of the Son and Spirit as an inauthentic

32. Ibid., 4.12.

presentation of the divine (and therefore could not be said to be revelation as such).[33]

Second, the Son's revelatory mission is ordered toward the unification of human loves, bringing to broken and conflict-ridden humanity a participation in the life of God. In this way, it is salvific in its aim and offering a unity with God born of charity.

Third, Augustine presents this love as at least as significant of a unifying factor as a shared nature. Neither for God nor for human beings does a unity of nature have the final word—love's significance demands that it be taken into account. However, the strict dichotomy animating the oft-asked question of whether Augustine's theology of the Trinity is grounded in "relational love" or "substantial nature" is not Augustine's (and it reveals more about contemporary assumptions than it does about Augustine's thought). He here talks about both an equality of substance and a shared loved, without anxiously striving to ground one in the other.

Finally, the salvific unification is possible only through being one in Christ. What is inadequately achieved through philosophy or the human will is made possible when suffused with, and transformed by, divine charity. Significantly, the Son can mediate God's unity to creation not because this gift is simply dependent upon a unity of natures (although this becomes doctrinally significant to the Chalcedonian formulation two decades after Augustine's death) but because love traverses distinction while maintaining it, joining Father and Son and Spirit, humanity and divinity, and human person with human person. Gioia writes:

> In fact, Christ is mediator not only, nor primordially, because of the hypostatic union. . . . On the contrary, Christ's role of mediation . . . consists in the fact that *the union of will* between the Son and the Father 'becomes'—thanks to both the descendent movement of the Incarnation and the ascending movement of the sacrifice—the union of the will of Christ with the Father and, in Christ of the whole *redempta ciuitas.*[34]

33. While *De Trinitate* has often been read as doing just this, Ayres wisely cautions, "Whatever may or may not be the errors of a metaphysics' drawn from Augustine, this is not what Augustine himself does with his insight." Ayres, *Augustine and the Trinity*, 207.

34. Gioia, *Theological Epistemology*, 91.

What is primarily a consequence of the tension between reducing neither divine persons to the divine nature nor divine unity to persons in relation, Augustine's theology seems to maintain both a unity of essence/nature/substance and a unity of love—albeit this "both/and" sits amidst tension born of ambiguity and limit.

In what will take on further significance to Augustine's overall theological project, Christ's mediation of this love is not uniformly articulated in the gospels: at times they speak of the Son in the form of God and at other times in the form of the servant. Maintaining that *mission* reveals "being from" and not subordination, Augustine distinguishes between the unified work of the always invisible Father and Son and the making visible of the Son in the person of Christ. That Father, Son, and Spirit operate inseparably means that the Son, in being sent in the form of the servant, is also operative in this sending in the form of God; at the same time, the Son is distinguished from the Father as being eternally begotten, as the Father (as the one origin) eternally begets the Son.[35] This invisible/visible distinction is analogous to that of God/servant inasmuch as both pairs are concerned with *how* the incarnate Son effects the mediation of God to and through creation. "As it is, the form of the servant was so taken on that the form of God remained immutable, and thus it is plain that what was seen in the Son was the work of Father and Son who remain unseen," the bishop writes. "That is that the Son was sent to be visible by the invisible Father together with the invisible Son."[36] While the Father is always invisible, God the Son is invisible as God and visible as servant.

Reading this against the argument of Augustine's Arian opponents can throw into relief the stakes of this use of the invisible/visible distinction. Invisibility being properly predicated of the true God only, the Arians reason that it ought to be understood as a marker of divinity. That the Son is visible means he cannot be God. Therefore for the Arians, Barnes writes, "the Son's role as revealer of the Father means that the Son cannot be God as the Father is God. The very

35. Augustine, *De Trinitate*, 5.1.
36. Ibid., 2.9.

attributes which constitute, as it were, the Son's capacity to reveal are judged as decisive indications of the Son's inferior status to the Father who is revealed by the Son—the Father who is the 'one true God.'"[37] A traditional weapon used against modalism, the visibility of the Son proved to be a weakness against the Arian tradition, and the differentiation in predication when speaking of the Son and the Father became a defense for the Arian position.[38]

What then does it mean to say that the invisible Son is visible? Indeed, what does it mean to say, with all pro-Nicenes, "true God from true God"? Acknowledging that as both created and fallen, our minds cannot grasp that which is eternal but instead remain fixated on the material and temporal, Augustine concludes that, "we could only be purified for adaptation to eternal things by temporal means,"[39] thus necessitating a true mediator between that eternal and temporal. Edmund Hill notes that Augustine is more occupied with this hermeneutical question of Christ's mediation than with redemption or salvation. That is not to say that *De Trinitate* is not oriented toward soteriology but that Christ saves through ordering our understanding

37. Michel René Barnes, "The Visible Christ and the Invisible Trinity: Mt. 5:8 in Augustine's Trinitarian Theology of 400," *Modern Theology* 19, no. 3 (July 2003): 330.
38. Ibid. The type of subordination propounded by the "Arians" of Augustine's era shapes particular circumstances surrounding the composition of *De Trinitate* and illuminates the nuances of Augustine's own polemic. Noting that Augustine carefully distinguishes between the doctrines held by Arius and those by his theological descendants, the Arians, and the Eunomians, Barnes highlights Augustine's engagement with 1 Corinthians 1:24 ("Christ the power and wisdom of God") and argues that, as books 6 and 7 are an extended exegesis of this passage, understanding the use made of this biblical statement by Augustine's opponents is necessary for understanding this central part of *De Trinitate*. Barnes emphasizes that fundamental to the anti-Nicene position is the belief that, "the title 'Power'—like other titles applied to the Son—is attributed only equivocally. When Scripture says that the Son is the 'power of God' Scripture does not mean that the Son is the very power God has as an existent, God's own power, but that the Son is one of many instrumental powers that serve as God's agents." Barnes, "*De Trinitate* VI and VII," 193. The interpretive framework used by Augustine's opponents, the Arian Latin Homoeans, leads to a reading of 1 Corinthians 1:24 in which the Son is the Father's power in the sense that the Son participates in the power of the Father, the Son being a derivative image of what the Father is and not equal with the Father. Against this, Barnes distinguishes between what he calls "the Neo-Nicene position," in which "the Son is identified with the very power that God the Father has as an existent: the Son is *the* power of God" (Barnes, "*De Trinitate* VI and VII," 195), and what he calls "the Pro-Nicene position," in which "there is one divine power that the Father and Son both share, that is, the Father and the Son have the same power (and therefore the same nature)." Barnes, "*De Trinitate* VI and VII," 196. In books 6 and 7, Augustine distances himself from the Neo-Nicene interpretive framework and moves toward that of the Pro-Nicene, although Barnes asserts that Augustine never fully and clearly embraces the direct relationship between power and nature.
39. Augustine, *De Trinitate*, 4.24.

and love of the world to the love and understanding of God. It is for this reason that Augustine notes the difference between the mediation of Christ and that of the devil.[40] The devil tempts through a promised mediation that ultimately "does not draw one to higher things, but rather blocks the way to them by inspiriting men with proud and hence malignant desires,"[41] while "in fact giving them only addiction and ruin; and then he easily persuades the proud to despise and scoff at the death of Christ."[42] Thinking that they are correct in denying the true divinity of the visible, and crucified, Christ, the proud remain satisfied with "their own imaginings," rather than the truth of God.[43] The devil's mediation is false because it stands between human beings and that which is not God. Creation, ordered to nothing but itself, does not save. Despite promises to the contrary, the devil mediates *nothing* to us and conforms us to *nothing.*

The mediation of Christ therefore reorders us to interpret—to see—creation as signs directing our vision to God. Emphasizing Augustine's epistemological description of knowing as a kind of vision,[44] Barnes illuminates the bishop's response through a focus on book 1 and its eschatological deferral of the realization of the promised visible and temporal mediation of the invisible and eternal God. Whether sensual or intellectual, such an epistemology reveals knowledge (*scientia*) to be "very much in the realm of direct experience."[45] In contrast, the wisdom of faith by which we might come to know God (*sapientia*) is dependent upon the "disposition of our will"[46]—that is, the purity of our heart and the dedication of our love. Christ's sonship—his being from the Father as God from God—is revealed not by sight but in faith working through love. Barnes argues that for Augustine, "the Son *is not* a revelation of the divine in any direct, available-to-the-senses, way; the Son *is not* divinity-insofar-as-

40. Edmund Hill, "Introductory Essay on Book IV," in Augustine, *The Trinity*, 148–49.
41. Augustine, *De Trinitate*, 4.15.
42. Ibid., 4.18.
43. Ibid., 4.1; see also Augustine, *City of God*, 8.19–22.
44. Barnes, "Visible Christ," 331.
45. Ibid., 343.
46. Ibid.

it-may-be-perceived; the Son, as divine, *is not* the occasion of human faith (the Son, as human, is)."[47] The form of the servant serves as the sign of the invisible Trinitarian God, the vision of whom is eschatologically deferred. The Son as God, inseparably operating with the Father, sends the Son as servant, whose visibility—only when seen with the proper disposition of faith and love—signifies the invisible *res*—that is, the Son as eternally begotten of the Father as God from God.

But the christological focus of these three points overlooks the Holy Spirit's part in the mediation. Throughout most of books 1–4, Augustine is occupied with the relationship of the Father and Son first, and only as a second step does he include reflection on the Spirit. This unbalanced emphasis is certainly not unique to Augustine, and it can be found in the development of the Nicene Creed itself, to which the lines about the Holy Spirit were added only as a result of the Council of Constantinople in 381. Although mentioned throughout, it is not until the end of book 4 that the Holy Spirit receives sustained attention by the bishop. Here, Augustine names the Holy Spirit "gift," a name that carries with it a reference to being from the Father.[48] Gioia writes, "The Gospel of John explains that the Holy Spirit is said to be given (*datus*) or sent only after [Christ's] resurrection, because only then that gift (*datio, donatio*: here is the origin of the notion of Holy Spirit as *donum*, 'gift') or mission was going to have a new characteristic, a new property."[49] Our naming the Spirit "gift" is our acknowledgment of the Spirit's true divinity: "And just as for the Holy Spirit his being the gift of God means his proceeding from the Father, so his being sent means his being known to proceed from him."[50] The new characteristic

47. Ibid., 335.
48. Augustine's elaboration on the name "gift" in book 5 will occupy much of my attention in the next chapter. This naming was not an innovation of Augustine's, following as he does both the scriptural precedent (Acts 8:19–20) and that of Hilary of Poitiers (*On the Trinity*, 2.29–55), the latter, Hill notes, "is the only work of his predecessors that Augustine actually quotes by name" in *De Trinitate*, 6.11. Hill, *The Trinity*, 49.
49. Gioia, *Theological Epistemology*, 115.
50. Augustine, *De Trinitate*, 4.29. Jaroslav Pelikan writes: "The tragedy of Augustine's own admitted ignorance of the Greek Trinitarian tradition is perhaps nowhere more in evidence than in his not having formulated a 'canonical rule' about the Holy Spirit to correspond to that about the Son; for such a 'rule' would have been obliged to make a sharp distinction between economic 'sending

manifest in the double sending of the Spirit—Augustine recognizes both Christ's breathing on the Apostles (John 20:19–23) and the appearance of the tongues of fire (Acts 2:1–4) as this sending—is the revelation of Christ's sonship. Revelation requires one to whom this sonship is revealed, and such a disclosure necessarily means recognizing the invisible God through the visible Christ. It is by the Holy Spirit that people come to believe in Christ as Son—that is, as the visible incarnation of the Son eternally begotten of the Father. In making possible our understanding of Christ's mediation, the Spirit effects revelation.

This understanding of mediation has at least three tentative implications for Augustine's presentation of the gift of love. First, the interpretive significance of love, discussed in chapter 1, finds footing in Augustine's explicitly Trinitarian thought and in the contemplation of God. Knowing God in and through Christ—understanding what is signified by the incarnate sign—requires the proper orientation of love.

[*pempein*]' and eternal 'proceeding [*ekporeuesthai*],' a distinction analogous, though by no means identical, to that between the eternal relation of Father and Son in the Trinity and the temporal event of the Incarnation." Jaroslav Pelikan, "*Canonica regula*: The Trinitarian Hermeneutics of Augustine," in *Collectanea Augustiniana, Augustine: "Second Founder of the Faith,"* ed. Joseph C. Schnaubelt, OSA, and Frederick Van Fleteren (New York: Peter Lang, 1990), 333–34. One ought to note at least three things about Pelikan's argument. First, while Barnes ("Rereading Augustine's Theology of the Trinity," in *The Trinity: An Interdisciplinary Symposium on the Trinity*, ed. Stephen T. Davis, Daniel Kendall, SJ, and Gerald O'Collins, SJ [Oxford: Oxford University Press, 1999], 152n11) cautions against crediting the argument that Augustine was familiar with Greek theology—as was proffered by Irénée Chevalier, *S. Augustin et la pensée grecque: les relations trinitaires* (Fribourg: Librairie de l'Université, 1940)—Hill follows Chevalier and posits that Augustine "had read the relevant writings of Gregory Nazianzen and Didymus the Blind, possibly also of Basil the Great and Epiphanius of Salamis. In any case he had a general knowledge of the kind of problems, largely linguistic and metaphysical, that engaged their attention." Hill, *The Trinity*, 38. Second, Augustine does clearly apply his "second" canonical rule to the Spirit—that being "from God" refers to the Spirit's being sent and does not necessitate subordination. Third, Ayres argues that the distinction between the form of servant and the form of God is not merely an exegetical tool, designed for a proper understanding of the ostensibly contradicting language of the scriptures. He writes against Pelikan, "It is a rule which Augustine presents as implying and revealing a comprehensive conception of what it means to read Scripture at this point in the life of faith, at a point when we should seek to see what is said and done in *forma servi* as a drawing of our desires and intellects toward the *forma Dei* that will remain hidden until the *eschaton*." Ayres, *Augustine and the Trinity*, 146–47. If I read these arguments correctly, maintaining such a sharp distinction between the economic sending and the eternal begetting/proceeding can mislead a reading of *De Trinitate*, which is less concerned with who or what God is and is more ordered to a conversion of the mind and heart toward a contemplative love of God. While Augustine was aware of such a conceptual distinction, he alternated between speaking of the Spirit as proceeding from just the Father and as proceeding from the Father and the Son (*filioque*), never sacrificing one way of speaking about the Spirit to the overemphasis on the other.

This assertion, which will continue through the rest of *De Trinitate*, and resolutely in book 8, is both hermeneutical and christological in nature, a fact that will be significant to understanding Augustine's pneumatology.

Second, "God from God" is not only an assertion of the equality of the Father and Son and an elaboration of their shared nature (though it is that) but also a statement of faith in the trustworthiness of the revelation of the Trinitarian God through the incarnation of the invisible Son in the visible Jesus Christ. Christ's being true mediator requires both that who he is be a visible (i.e., accessible and intelligible) reality and that he somehow renders visible the invisible Son and therefore the Son as eternally begotten of the Father.

Third, as God's presence with us (Christ as Immanuel) is mediated through love, the improper orientation of such love threatens to render the form of the servant as an idol. Augustine notes, almost in passing, the significance of the ascension as a guide to interpreting the mediation of Christ. "So it was necessary," Augustine writes, "for the form of a servant to be removed from their sight, since as long as they could observe it they would think that Christ was this only which they had before their eyes."[51] Concerned that his disciples might come to cling to that which can be seen and touched, Christ's departure serves to order the loves of his disciples toward the Father by revealing himself as Son. Rendering himself absent is, itself, a sign relativizing the perceived ultimacy of his created flesh. The absence reveals the form of the servant to have been a mediator, bringing believers to the Father through the Son: "His ascension to the Father signified his being seen in his equality with the Father, that being the ultimate vision which suffices us."[52] Christ reveals the invisible God without ever making God visible as part of creation.

As he concludes book 4, Augustine's theology proves, yet again, to be something other than the caricature often drawn of it.[53] While never

51. Augustine, *De Trinitate*, 1.18.
52. Ibid.
53. Cf. Colin Gunton's concluding critique of Augustine: "The only conclusion can be that, in some sense or other, it is divine substance and not the Father that is the basis for the being of God,

wavering from asserting the inseparability of operation in God,[54] Augustine also maintains the traditional Trinitarian *taxis*—Father, Son, and Holy Spirit—and the Father's proper status as the eternal origin of the Son and the Spirit. Augustine's pneumatology is stubbornly scriptural and consequently he famously maintains that the Spirit proceeds from the Father and from the Son, as described in the Gospel of John.[55] But in doing so, he also affirms that, as the Son's eternal origin is in the Father, "so the Spirit who proceeds from the Father and the Son is traced back, on both counts, to him of whom the Son is born."[56]

Challenged in often conflicting manners by ideas of both Arianism and modalism, Augustine begins *De Trinitate* with a crucial exploration of the scriptures and the God revealed therein. The heart of the bishop's response attends to the unity of action of the divine persons rather than the crafting a more expressly ontologically based defense of the Son's equality with the Father. Augustine's primary concern is securing the veracity of the salvific mediation of God as attested to in the scriptures. The following chapter will focus upon the language and concepts that Augustine brings to bear on this mediation, straining as he does to offer a rational way that we might understand what, in fact, is revealed therein. The reading of the remainder of *De Trinitate* will then concern the question of how this gift if mediated to us as, and through, love.

and therefore, a fortiori, of everything else." Colin E. Gunton, *The Promise of Trinitarian Theology* (Edinburgh: T&T Clark, 1991), 54.

54. "I will say . . . with absolute confidence that Father and Son and Holy Spirit, God the creator, of one and the same substance, the almighty three, act inseparably." Augustine, *De Trinitate*, 4.30.
55. Ibid., 4.29.
56. Ibid.; see also ibid., 2.2, 4.32, and 15.47–48.

3

Books 5–7: Naming God

> The process we are seeking to characterize is one in which we are brought to a point where to *go on speaking* at all requires a shift of expectation, away from the assumption that there will be a point of descriptive closure, some expression or formulation that is definitively adequate to what is in view. This happens when a descriptive account which is correct and sustainable as far as it goes leaves out of consideration what we most want to talk about.
>
> —Rowan Williams[1]

Concluding book 4, the bishop writes of the books to follow, "we shall see with the Lord's help what sort of subtle crafty arguments the heretics bring forward and how they can be demolished."[2] With a focus and methodology significantly influenced by the theological controversies with the Homoeans (Arians), these next three books, which according to Hill form "a distinct unit,"[3] engage the question of speaking about God as Trinity, of how we might name the one God of Jesus Christ as "Father, Son, and Holy Spirit." But although we would do well to read these books within their polemical context (as,

1. *The Edge of Words: God and the Habits of Language* (New York: Bloomsbury, 2014), 8–9.
2. Augustine, *De Trinitate*, 4.32.
3. Edmund Hill, "Forward to Books V, VI, and VII," in Augustine, *The Trinity*, 186.

for instance, Gioia rightly encourages readers of *De Trinitate* to do[4]), these controversies do not exhaust the content or the overall aim of these books. In contrast to Gioia's moderate dismissal of Augustine's argument as a polemical detour misleading readers into an ontological mire governed by philosophical categories, Michel René Barnes suggests that these books reveal a profoundly theological concern for the vulnerability of Nicene theology and provide insight into the constructive work accomplished in *De Trinitate*.[5] The Trinitarian relationship between the relational and the substantial predication taken up by the bishop, although itself following the specific line of argumentation of his opponents, is of significant importance to the overall construction of his argument—particularly as it helps mark the limits of philosophical language and open to the formation of the reader's memory, understanding, and love to the image of God in books 8–15.

This chapter is concerned with Augustine's discussion of substantive and relational predication of God in books 5–7. After briefly touching upon what it might mean to name God, it explores Augustine's philosophical and linguistic rules of Trinitarian predication. It concludes with a study of the relationship of the Spirit's gift of love and the language with which we address God. Finally, as primary focus in this chapter is Augustine's discussion on the proper naming of the Trinitarian persons, and particularly the naming of the Holy Spirit as "gift," those aspects of the text that do not aid in the examination of this denomination are left alone, not because they have no implications in the development of the text as a whole but in favor of committed attention to the question at hand.

The Limits and Necessity of Naming

> From now on I will be attempting to say things that cannot altogether be said as they are thought by a man—or at least as they are thought by me. In any case, when we think about God the trinity we are aware that our

4. Gioia's focus on this is situated primarily in chapter 7, "Trinity and Ontology," of his *Theological Epistemology*.
5. Barnes, "*De Trinitate* VI and VII," 202.

> thoughts are quite inadequate to their object, and incapable of grasping him as he is. . . . Now since we ought to think about the Lord our God always, and can never think about him as he deserves [*digne*]; since at all time we should be praising him and blessing him, and yet no words of ours are capable of expressing him, I begin by asking him to help me understand and explain what I have in mind and to pardon any blunders I may make.[6]

So the Doctor of Grace begins book 5. As we have established, Augustine is acutely aware of both the necessity and limitation of language. While language is the means by which we come to knowledge of a thing, it is also haunted by a disconcerting *perhaps*; the fullness of the correlation of *signum* and *res*, while reasoned for and hoped for, is never a settled certainty. Here both language and thought interrelatedly fail to grasp their object because of their natural limitations, the distortions resulting from human sinfulness, and the ineffable mystery of the divine life. Moreover, and perhaps primarily, that theology gropes in the dark for ever more (relatively) accurate language about God is the direct result of the theological dynamics governing how we come to grow in understanding and love of God.

Yet this insecure signification does not lead Augustine directly into pious silence but serves ever more to shape his understanding of both the end of such an attempt and, by extension, the nature of theology itself. For grope in the dark theology does, situated as it is for Augustine as a response to the command to "think about the Lord our God always," all the while reminding us that we "can never think about him as he deserves." It is not, then, simply the infinite mystery of God that makes the acquisition of enough knowledge about God impossible (although it is certainly that); it is not only the result of the imbalance of finitude and infinitude that ties the investigative hands of theology and restricts its reach. That we do not think of God as God deserves indicates the relational structure of the theological endeavor—that there is a sort of obligation, by our being created and saved, to grow in our understanding of our Creator and Savior. For the weakness and shallowness of our theology relative to its object is not

6. Augustine, *De Trinitate*, 5.1.

an offense to God insofar as it marks an authentic attempt to grow in relationship with God. For Augustine continues, "Yet for all that there is no effrontery in burning to know, out of faithful piety, the divine and inexpressible truth that is above us, provided the mind is fired by the grace of our creator and savior, and not inflated by arrogant confidence in its own powers."[7]

While Hill is correct in reminding his readers, "It is well to bear in mind that in these books he is not so much talking about God the Trinity, as talking about how to talk about God the Trinity,"[8] and Roland J. Teske beneficially distinguishes among gradations of linguistic and conceptual truth when he maintains, "In order to understand what Augustine is saying in book 5, it is necessary to bear in mind his distinction between speech about God, thought about God, and the being of God,"[9] it is inescapably speech about God that informs our thought about God. Speech and thought about God can serve as a means of conversion, of transforming our thoughts and actions in a deepening of love. While we can, and should, maintain a distinction between our idea of the Trinity and the Trinity that God is, it is decisively the latter that is of Augustine's final concern in *De Trinitate.* Although the text itself is occupied with language about the former, it is an occupation in service of the latter. Herein lies a significant difficulty. Augustine distinguishes between the linguistic predication of God and God in Godself—again recognizing the inability of both linguistic and conceptual signs themselves to effect signification. However, perhaps only barring extraordinary divine intervention, it is only through such woefully inadequate signs that we come to know God. And yet we are not abandoned to a futile faith, for God does still speak to us in grace, effecting signification in revelation, mediated though it may be. While Augustine and Karl Rahner are certainly not of like minds on many theological questions (and it may be difficult to

7. Ibid., 5.2.
8. Hill, *The Trinity*, 186.
9. Roland J. Teske, SJ, "Properties of God and the Predicaments in *De Trinitate* 5," in *To Know God and the Soul: Essays on the Thought of Saint Augustine* (Washington, DC: Catholic University of America Press, 2008), 95.

reconcile the two even in the anthropological context of the following quotation), it does not seem out of the question that the bishop would agree with Rahner's words: "In the first place, revelation is revelation for salvation, and therefore, theology is essentially theology for salvation."[10] Language and thought shape and quicken our love not of words or ideas about God but of the being of God—that is, of God in Godself.

Theology's end is to deepen our love of God and to open us to salvation in transforming our words and thoughts about God into ever less inadequate signs signifying God, allowing the reader to be "at least piously on his guard against thinking about [God] anything he is not."[11] Books 5–7, although occupied as they are with the controversies of the time and configured as they are around the loosely philosophical terminology of *substantia*, *essentia*, and *persona*, are intimately part of the trajectory of the text, focused as they are on naming the source of our salvation in a manner that tempers our pride and fires our love.

Substance, Relation, and the Substance of the Argument

Standing against both the Homoean (Arian) and Monarchian threats of subordination and the Sabellian reduction of divine personhood to an aspect of a more fundamental divinity, Augustine strains to maintain both the equality of the divine persons and their irreducibility. The bishop engages the Arian belief concerning the "emphasis on *Unbegotten* as the primary characteristic of divinity"[12] and the subsequent problem of substantial predication resulting from this. In partial agreement with his opponents, Augustine grants that nothing said of God can be said accidentally—that is, ascribing to God an attribute that in some manner modifies the substance of God. There are no such accidents in God. God is not logically first divine and then subsequently good, immutable, powerful, or any number of characteristics predicated of God. His Homoean opponents conclude

10. Karl Rahner, "Theology and Anthropology," in *The Word in History: The St. Xavier Symposium*, ed. T. Patrick Burke (New York: Sheed & Ward, 1966), 9.
11. Augustine, *De Trinitate*, 5.2.
12. Barnes, "Arians of Book V," 190.

from this: "Therefore the Father is unbegotten substance-wise, and the Son is begotten substance-wise. But being unbegotten is different from being begotten; therefore the Father's substance is different from the Son's."[13] However, Augustine argues that substantial predication cannot alone explain all the scriptural references to the relationship of the Father and the Son. He reads Christ's statement that "I and the Father are one"[14] as either speaking of a shared substance or inviting another form of divine predication. He concludes that as nothing said of God is predicated accidentally, either everything said of God is said substantially (in which case the Arians would be correct in their understanding of the Son) or there are exceptions by which something is predicated of God neither accidentally nor substantially, but by means of a third way. But before exploring this alternative, it would serve to consider Augustine's understanding of substance—a concept that impacts both the question of predication and the relationships of the divine persons.

The divine simplicity crucial to Augustine's theology requires that all divine attributes, whether power or wisdom or goodness, be substantially, rather than accidentally, predicated and not be a result of the dynamic relationships among the divine persons. Although the Son can be said to be the power and wisdom of God, each term is univocally predicated of each divine person (as each person is God without remainder). The Son is not the Father's power or wisdom all by himself. And while the theological significance of this will be part of analysis and formulations later in later chapters, here it is important to observe Augustine's location within the midst of post-Nicene controversy, his loyalty to the conciliar formulation endorsing an understanding of the Son as of the same substance as the Father, and his awareness of the danger of the Arian interpretation and the need for further explication of Trinitarian language. Ayres observes

13. Augustine, *De Trinitate*, 5.4.

14. John 10:30, referenced in *De Trinitate*, 5.4. How to interpret this unity was at the heart of the issue. If, for instance, Augustine's dichotomous paths exhaust the possible interpretations, then he has clearly won the argument. But it remains possible, at least logically, to understand this unity as one of will and obedience and thereby not rule out the Arian understanding of the Son.

that "Augustine seems to have understood himself as inheriting a developing tradition,"[15] one that both encouraged and bounded his constructive thought.[16] Maintaining the theological integrity of the Niceno-Constantinopolitan formulation against the insights of his opponents required Augustine to say a great deal more about the Trinity than was articulated at the councils—he needed to consider not only the Trinitarian name of God but *how* this name relates to our calling upon the Trinity by this name.

It is the challenge of how to say more that leads Augustine to articulate the relationship between language about the one divine substance and that about the three divine persons and specifically explore the name "gift." Augustine begins his response writing:

> There is at least no doubt that God is a substance, or perhaps a better word would be being; at any rate what the Greeks call *ousia*. Just as we get the word "wisdom" from "wise," and "knowledge" from "know," so we have the word "being" from "be." And who can more be than he that said to his servant, *I am who I am*, and, *Tell the sons of Israel, He who is sent me to you* (Ex 3:14)? . . . Anything that changes does not keep its being, and anything that can change even though it does not, is able to not be what it was; and this only that which not only does not but also absolutely cannot change deserves without qualification to be said really and truly to be.[17]

Here Augustine once again stands at the ambiguous edge of (possible) signification. For though he grounds the identification of God with substance/being in both scriptural authority and reason, he concludes by suggesting that "to be" ought only to be used to describe God, a move by which Augustine quietly introduces his readers to the heart of the rest of his treatise—the relationship of human being to that of the divine. If *being* is only truly said of God, by what experience can we understand the meaning of this word? If our own changeable being is self-contradictory and thus hardly being at all, can we progress linguistically or conceptually from such an impoverished being as our own to that of God? Can we, by any means, come to a greater

15. Ayres, *Augustine and the Trinity*, 43.
16. Ibid., 38.
17. Augustine, *De Trinitate*, 5.3.

understanding of what it means to say that God alone *is*, an elaboration of the name of God given to Moses in Exodus 3:14?

Roland J. Teske examines a form of this question in his study "Augustine's Use of *Substantia* in Speaking about God."[18] Against precisely the accusation that "Augustine's use of 'substance' in speaking about God is devoid of sense," he argues that "it should also be possible within the limits of philosophy to argue the opposite case or at least to reexamine the issue to see whether the case of the intelligibility of what Augustine says is indeed in the dire straits in which it has been said to be."[19] Drawing on Aristotle, Teske distinguishes between two senses of the word, both used by Augustine, so as to bring a precision to the bishop's words that he, himself, never seemed to feel the need to do (despite the fact that the bishop's rhetorical training would have made him familiar with such distinctions). The first is the signification of "an individual thing,"[20] of anything that is itself and not something else, as each particular person, animal, or object is itself and not other people, animals, or things. The second sense of the word signifies "not an individual thing, but the nature of an individual thing, that which is signified by predication to substance."[21] That is, there is the individual substance that includes unique and contingent attributes (those very things that make it individual) and then there is the substance of what it is—its nature—that receive the attributes. There is Augustine—in all his particularity—and then there is human nature that receives the particular attributes to make the individual possible. Augustine notes the challenge for Latin speakers in translating the Greek "one essence, three substances" (*mia ousia, treis hupostaseis*), into a Latin language that customarily held *essentia* and *substantia* to be synonyms. Hence, the justification for the traditional use of *persona* as a translation for *hupostaseis*. While Augustine prefers the term *essentia* to *substantia* for

18. Roland J. Teske, SJ, "Augustine's Use of *Substantia* in Speaking About God," in *To Know God and the Soul*; see also, William P. Alston, "Substance and the Trinity," in Davis, Kendall, and O'Collins, *The Trinity*, 179–201.
19. Teske, "Augustine's Use of *Substantia*," 113.
20. Ibid., 118.
21. Ibid., 119.

its etymological connection to *being*, he moves freely between these words as a translation for the Greek *ousia*.[22] However, helpful as Teske's presentation can be, it should be attenuated by Ayres's cautious reminder that the lack of a clear definition of substance ought to be taken seriously as a point in itself and not simply as an absence of what supposedly ought to be there. Augustine did not clearly define his term and that is significant, particularly in light of his preference for *essentia* over *substantia*.[23] The philosophical nuances, beneficial though they may be in explicating ways forward, are not Augustine's final concern and he clearly does not treat them as such.[24]

Augustine's argument continues in light of the conceptual inflexibility of substance language before the scriptural demands of predication. That nothing can be predicated of God accidentally does not necessitate that the only possible divine predication is substantial. "Some things," the bishop writes, "are said with reference to something else, like Father with reference to Son and Son with reference to Father."[25] Beginning from Christ's assertion in the scriptures that he is one with the Father, Augustine reasons that if nothing may be said of God accidentally, and the unity of Father and Son must be substantial, then there must be other means of accounting for the distinction between that signified by the name "Father" and that by the name "Son." Indeed, Augustine here maintains both the Nicene rejection of Monarchian subordinationism (by arguing for substantial unity) and of all forms of modalism (which Nicaea did not reject with sufficient clarity). For he does not allow the names "Father" and "Son" to be understood as merely a linguistic distinction, something to be maintained as a tradition or convenience of speech but having no bearing on the being of God. If accidental predication is cripplingly misleading when speaking of the divine and substantial predication is insufficient to account for the demands of the scriptures,

22. Augustine, *De Trinitate*, 7.7; see also Teske, "Augustine's Use of *Substantia*," 117.
23. Ayres, *Augustine and the Trinity*, 200–201.
24. Augustine, *De Trinitate*, 5.9–10.
25. Ibid., 5.6.

Augustine suggests that "Father" and "Son" be categorized as what can be described as eternally requisite relational predication.

Neither accidental—it is an element of Christian faith that the Son's sonship has its origin not in a temporal event but is, in the Nicene creedal language, "eternally begotten"—nor substantial—as "neither is said with reference to itself but only with reference to the other"[26]—this third category of predication allows "Father" and "Son" to be references to the relationship each has with the other. The Father is not Father without Son; the Son is not Son without Father. The structure and effects of this argument allow Augustine to articulate further rules about theological language:

> The chief point then that we must maintain is that whatever that supreme and divine majesty is called with reference to itself is said substance-wise; whatever it is called with reference to another is said not substance- but relationship-wise; and that such is the force of the expression "of the same substance' in Father and Son and Holy Spirit, that whatever is said with reference to self about each of them is to be taken as adding up in all three to a singular and not to a plural.[27]

Acknowledging that the addition of the Holy Spirit may significantly transform this predicative structure, we may tentatively summarize four rules of Trinitarian language.

First, nothing may be predicated accidentally of God. Any such predication that adopts an accidental idiom common to the description of creation when articulating theological truth about God ought to be understood as referring to the substance of God. For example, a reference to a *just* person is an accidental reference. Justice (or goodness, power, wisdom, etc.) when predicated of God is not an attribute of God but refers to the substance of God. God does not have or acquire justice, rather, God *is* justice.

Second, all substantial predication of God speaks of God's substance. God's power refers to God's substance, not to a particular Trinitarian

26. Ibid.

27. Ibid., 5.9. Ayres argues against the belief that Augustine received this formulation from the Greeks and suggests that this innovation is Augustine's own. Despite its similarities to the work of Gregory Nazianzen, "Augustine's argument appears to have proceeded independently of Greek sources at this point." Ayres, *Augustine and the Trinity*, 213.

person. As Barnes illustrates, to say that Christ is the power of God is not to say that Christ is the fullness of God's power and that God's power is contained in Christ. Power is substantially predicated. Father, Son, and Spirit: each is power by virtue of each being God. But neither is it appropriate to speak of three powers or three Gods. Substantive predication is singular.[28] This distinction will become all the more important when engaging Augustine's approach to the Trinity through memory, understanding, and will. The reader of Augustine would do well to keep in mind that a simple transposition of Father/memory, Son/understanding, and Spirit/will stands, at the very least, against his regulatory linguistic and conceptual predicative structure.

Third, however, following revelation, it can be fitting to apply specific terms as proper to one of the divine persons in particular—a personal or hypostatic predication. Certainly, this is the case in the names "Father," "Son," and "Holy Spirit," each uniquely predicated of one of the three divine persons. There are some terms, that while proper to the Father, Son, or Spirit, can also be said of the others—that is, can be said substantially of God.[29] Moreover, other terms, when applied to the divine persons, direct us to the missions of the Son and Spirit. The Son is the wisdom of the Father in a manner that neither subordinates the Son as a property of the Father's, nor "depersonalizes" the Father as though the fullness of the Father's wisdom existed only relationally to the Father, but instead as wisdom *from* wisdom.[30]

Fourth, relational predication, when speaking of God, is never contingent. While I become a husband when I marry and become a father when my child is born, the Father and the Son are eternally

28. However, even the term "singular" can be problematic, insofar as it is established through a system of quantitative comparison. In a sense, God is not "one," if by "one" we understand it as the basic numerical unit. God is no more one than two, three, or four. There does not simply happen to be one God as opposed to two. If by "singular," however, we are trying to describe the divine as unique and undivided, the term is significantly less inadequate.

29. See, for examples, the name of the Holy Spirit (Augustine, *De Trinitate*, 5.12) and the application of the term "origin" (ibid., 5.14). Complicating matters further, Augustine had to makes sense of a Latin text that describes the Son (rather than the more typically so described Father) as *principium* (John 8:25).

30. Augustine, *De Trinitate*, 7.2–3.

Father and Son. Moreover, the Father is Father only in relationship with the Son, and the Son is Son only in relationship with the Father. "Father," requires Son; "Son" requires Father—and both names refer to a relationship, rather than a substance. But what is this thing that *is* only in relation to something, this divine person of whom Augustine writes, "Yet when you ask, 'Three what?' human speech labors under a great dearth of words. So we say three persons, not in order to say that precisely, but in order not to be reduced to silence"?[31]

Richard Cross offers a valuable insight into this question in his examination of "what Augustine professes not to understand" in using the term *persona*.[32] Cross states his understanding of the problem: while the divine persons are *named* relationally, they themselves—that is, the divine persons, as such—in *being* truly God cannot *be* relations but must *be substance*. Augustine writes:

> Of course, if it is the same for God to be as to subsist, then it ought not to be said that there are three substances any more than it is said that there are three beings. It is because it is the same for God to be as to be wise that we do not say three wisdoms any more than we say three beings. So too, because it is the same for him to be God as to be, it is impious to talk about three beings as about three Gods. But if it is one thing for God to be, another for him to subsist, as it is one thing for him to be, another for him to be Father or be Lord, then substance will no longer be substance because it will be relationship. That he is, is said of God with reference to himself; that he is Father is said with reference to Son, and that he is Lord is said with reference to the creation that serves him; so on this supposition, he subsists by way of relationship, just as he begets by way of relationship and lords it by way of relationship. For just as the name being is derived from to be, so we get substance from subsist. But it is ridiculous that substance should be predicated by way of relationship; every single thing that is, after all, subsists with reference to itself. How much more God, if indeed it is proper to talk about God subsisting?[33]

Father, Son, and Holy Spirit, though named relationally, are called "persons" with reference to themselves.[34] And everything said of the

31. Ibid., 5.10.
32. Richard Cross, "*Quid Tres?* On What Precisely Augustine Professes Not to Understand in *De Trinitate* 5 and 7," *Harvard Theological Review* 100, no. 2 (2007): 215–32.
33. Augustine, *De Trinitate*, 7.9.
34. Ibid., 7.11.

persons with reference to themselves is understood because it is referenced substantially, to be predicated of the divine substance. That there are three persons and that each person is God means that each person is substance and yet there is one God. Cross's crisp analysis of the structure of Augustine's argument—summarized here in three points significant to our overall focus—both serves to clarify the text in question and augment the tension between language and God so important to our reading of *De Trinitate.*

First, Augustine explores the terms "essence" and "person," seeking to discern how these words fit into a structure of genus and species in a manner that might be advantageously applied to the Trinity. The terms are both commonly and appropriately applied to the divine persons, signifying by the like usage, a *res* (a something) common to the Father, Son, and Holy Spirit (although not something independent and other than them). But what interests Augustine is to explore how we might understand the contours of this commonality. After all, if person is a substance and there are three divine persons, how do we not conclude, against orthodoxy, three substances in the Trinity?

By way of trying to clarify the complexities of Augustine's argument against a simple categorization of essence as genus and person as species, Cross distinguishes between what he calls "generic commonality" and "indivisible commonality." The first delineates a shared genus among species or a shared species among individuals, as "animal" is shared among a horse, sheep, and cow or "man" is shared among Abraham, Isaac, and Jacob. In each case, however, we have a commonality that is divided among the three, allowing us to transpose the numerical count of the more specific nouns to the more general; if there are a horse, sheep, and cow and Abraham, Isaac, and Jacob, then there are three animals and three men. However, it cannot be said that as there are three divine persons, there are three Gods. The "indivisible commonality" (relatively) appropriate to the Trinity maintains "the commonality of something identical in the things that share it."[35] The divine essence is not divisible either into parts—each divine person

35. Cross, "*Quid Tres?,*" 227.

having one-third of the essence—nor is it a genus in which each person shares a common divine nature as three people share human nature. Likewise, Augustine is hesitant about the analogy of common matter: that we may say three statues made of gold, three statues, one gold. Although each is made of gold generically common to each, the three statues cannot be said to be made of the *same* gold but simply of the same type of matter. While we may speak of *the* divine essence, we may not speak of *a* divine essence generically common to each divine person.

As he understands a foundational characteristic of both genus and species to be their divisibility and the divine essence cannot be divided, "Augustine will eventually draw the conclusion that the divine essence is common to the persons, but *not* in the divisible way that a genus or species is common to three individuals or particulars."[36] Augustine concludes that the divine essence is neither genus nor species.

Second, although Augustine establishes relational predication in book 5, arguing that the proper names Father, Son, and Holy Spirit—and a specific few other words as well—are said relationally, "it seems that 'person' should be a non-relational predicate" since "being a person entails subsisting."[37] Save for that which is said of their relationships, anything said of the divine persons, as true God, is said substantially. "Person" signifies a substance, not a relationship (or better, a substance defined through its relationship with substance). In a passage that would be particularly vexing to anyone trying to "redeem" Augustinian thought through a social Trinitarian definition of personhood as relation, Augustine maintains that "every being that is called something by way of relationship is also something besides the relationship."[38] Although anything said of the Father, Son, and Holy Spirit is said relationally, the term "person" itself references not a relationship but the substance of each person—that is, the divine substance. Each person is truly God.

While recognizing that Augustine's theology protects against a form

36. Ibid., 225.
37. Ibid., 218.
38. Augustine, *De Trinitate*, 7.2.

of subordination among the divine persons—a focus of Nicene theological tradition—contemporary critics of the bishop often draw attention to what seems to be sacrificed in the name of such security.[39] In Augustine's approach, the Father, Son, and Holy Spirit, while distinct divine persons, are each identical with the divine substance, rendering each person no less "God" than the others. However, although such a structure defends against subordination, the high cost of the particular form of fortification threatens to render such a victory merely a Pyrrhic one. The critics of Augustine and his theological descendants argue that the cost of this structure of equality is nothing less than the Christian understanding of God as precisely Trinitarian. That is, the identity of persons and substance (rather than allowing persons to be identified as relationships) effectively prohibits any real and concrete Trinitarian personhood (that is, personhood understood in an individualized modern sense), "reduced" (so to speak) as they are to the substance. However, it is precisely this identification and Augustine's refusal to say that persons are relations that secures their irreducibility and guards against Sabellianism, here threatening to render the Father, Son, and Spirit as manifestations of a more fundamental "relationality" of God. That the Trinitarian persons are in relation is one thing. But to say that the persons themselves *are* relations is to take the language further than Augustine allows.

Third, Augustine concludes that "person," itself a substance, is a genus, or grouping, divided into three, but he remains unsure as to what these three are—that is, "what *species* are the three persons?"[40] According to Cross, the bishop is "hesitant to use a merely generic word ('person') in the absence of a species word."[41] A divine person is

39. See, for a variety of approaches (not all critical of Augustine's work in itself, but of patterns whose roots are often attributed to Augustine): Jürgen Moltmann, *History and the Triune God: Contributions to Trinitarian Theology* (New York: Crossroad, 1991); Moltmann, *Trinity and the Kingdom*; LaCugna, *God for Us*; Cornelius Plantinga Jr., "Social Trinity and Tritheism" and David Brown, "Trinitarian Personhood and Individuality," both in *Trinity, Incarnation, and Atonement: Philosophical and Theological Essays*, ed. Ronald Jay Feenstra and Cornelius Plantinga Jr. (Notre Dame: University of Notre Dame Press, 1989), 21–47 and 48–78, respectively; and John D. Zizioulas *Being as Communion: Studies in Personhood and the Church* (Crestwood, NY: St. Vladimir's Seminary Press, 1997).

40. Cross, "*Quid Tres?*" 229.

41. Ibid.

a genus without species, this lack rendering the genus itself an empty category, as we are unable to define what the persons have in common that makes them each a divine person—that is, what this personhood is.[42] Ayres notes that "we are unable to understand the character of a divine person in the abstract."[43] There is no such thing as abstract "divine personhood," only the Father, Son, and Spirit naming the divine persons whose substance is God. The fact that the scriptures remain silent on this matter significantly increases Augustine's hesitancy. "Crucially," Gioia observes in kind, "whenever Scripture resorts to the plural openly, it uses or implies relative names, like Father and Son. What Scripture never does is to use one common name—like person or *ὑπόστασις*—to designate 'what is three' in God."[44] Augustine asks, "Three *what*?" without an answer. This is what Cross concludes that Augustine finds impossible to comprehend.

It is precisely the conceptual distance between person—a substance and genus—and the proper names for the divine persons—Father, Son, and Holy Spirit, predicated relationally—that Augustine does not overcome. The concept of the person is never smoothly aligned with the proper name. The name Father is predicated relationally, signifying relationship with the Son and marking the distinction between them. As Father and Son both share fully in the identical and indivisible divine essence, their proper names mark only the predicative relationship they share and nothing substantial nor anything held in common. The line between these two linguistic and conceptual ways of proceeding is measured by the distance between the indivisibly common substance of the divine persons—that of whom we can say divine person—and the relational difference among them marked by their proper names. The divine substance is the one substance of the three substantial divine persons. Augustine is at the same time trying to express both the unity of God illustrated in the

42. This is not only rhetorical bewilderment but speaks to the heart of Trinitarian mystery, *pace* John Behr, "Calling Upon God as Father: Augustine and the Legacy of Nicaea," in Demacopoulos and Papanikolaou, *Orthodox Readings of Augustine*, 153n2.

43. Lewis Ayres, "*Sempiterne Spiritus Donum*: Augustine's Pneumatology and the Metaphysics of Spirit," in Demacopoulos and Papanikolaou, *Orthodox Readings of Augustine*, 151.

44. Gioia, *Theological Epistemology*, 155.

essence of the divine persons as divine—for it is precisely the adjective that controls the noun here—and the relational distinction entailed in naming God "Father, Son, and Spirit."

The Trinitarian name of God speaks to the Christian faith in the true mediation of the divine in and through the missions of the Son and Spirit, as Augustine presented in books 1 to 4. The Son and Spirit are "God *from* God." God reveals that God gives God. The Christian concept of God is both driven and bounded by the Trinitarian name. This name evokes and calls to God and regulates our understanding and worship. The central question with which the bishop wrestles is how this name forms our concept of God of whom the scriptures proclaim: "Hear, O Israel! The Lord is our God, the Lord alone! Therefore, you shall love the Lord, your God, with all your heart, and with all your soul, and with all your strength. Take to heart these words which I enjoin on you today."[45] And contrary to those voices proclaiming Augustine's subservience to substance and those attempting to rehabilitate him through a substance that is the relations of the persons,[46] the Doctor of Grace, always aware of the harrowing limits of human signification, concludes book 7 not with the victorious charge of one form of predication, nor a reconciliation of the tension, but by reminding his reader that where understanding fails, faith opens us to a wisdom nourished by our formation toward the image of God.[47] What Augustine does not say and establish can be more informative than what he does, in fact, say.

Naming God through the Gift of Love

The relational predication of books 5–7 is an enterprise born of the eternal relationship of the Father and the Son, allowing Augustine to avoid the snares of Arian inequality while remaining faithful to the witness of the scriptures. The tradition Augustine inherited regarding this witness, however, insists that the Holy Spirit needs be taken into

45. Deuteronomy 6:4–6 NAB.
46. For example, Sarah Heaner Lancaster, "Three-Personed Substance: The Relational Essence of the Triune God in Augustine's *De Trinitate*," *Thomist* 60, no. 1 (1996): 123–40.
47. Augustine, *De Trinitate*, 7.12.

account as well,[48] an insistence that proves to be a wrinkle in the bishop's philosophical and theological canvas. That Augustine is first concerned with articulating the relationship between Father and Son and does not significantly extend "the principle of consubstantiality to the Holy Spirit" until later, Gioia reads as a conformation of "the fact that Augustine is not driven here by a systematic ambition" but is occupied with responding to particular arguments of his Arian opponents.[49] But this is hardly the only possible interpretation of Augustine's method (i.e., working out this question in regards to the Father and the Son first, while only subsequently applying his conclusions to the Holy Spirit). This pattern is consistent throughout much of the controversies of the early centuries of Christianity. However, while many patristic and conciliar texts—including *De Trinitate*—were composed *in tempore belli*,[50] the assertion that such a context renders them merely polemical assumes that the reason why the controversies take place can be separated from what the combatants believe about God and the church and from what would become the canon of faith. Although these three books are significantly shaped by the Arian argument, they need not be dismissed as only polemics, as though controversy could be independent of structures of understanding and the content of belief.

One difficulty facing Augustine is that the name "Holy Spirit" does not participate in the same rules of relational predication as do "Father" and "Son." That these rules were built around the relationship of the Father and Son, and that the very names themselves are relational because they function analogously to human paternity

48. See, for example, Niceta of Remesiana's *De Spiritus sancti potentia*, probably written in the late fourth century. Niceta writes, "If, along with the Father and the Son, [the Holy Spirit] gives me remission of my sins, and gives me grace and eternal life, I should indeed be ungrateful if I refused to glorify Him along with the Father and the Son. On the other hand, if He is not to be adored with the Father and the Son, He is not to be confessed according to the word of the Lord and the tradition of the Apostle—if faith is to be more than half-hearted [1 Pet 1:12]. Who, then, can keep me from worshipping Him? I am commanded to believe in Him; I shall pay Him due honor with all my heart." Niceta of Remesiana, "The Power of the Holy Spirit," in *Writings; Commonitories; Grace and Free Will*, trans. Gerald G. Walsh, The Fathers of the Church: A New Translation 7 (New York: Fathers of the Church, 1949), sec. 18.

49. Gioia, *Theological Epistemology*, 152.

50. David Anderson, introduction to *On the Holy Spirit*, by St. Basil the Great (Crestwood, NY: St. Vladimir's Seminary Press, 2001), 7.

and filiation, burdens the transfer of relational predication to the Spirit and even threatens to destabilize the structure Augustine constructs to this point. While God in essence can be properly called both *holy* and *spirit*, these words are distinctively used in relational predication, naming the third person of the Trinity with particular attributes appropriate for descriptive substantive predication. But because of this equivocality of language, and because "Holy Spirit" lacks the explicit inherent relationality of "Father" and "Son," Augustine suggests that, following the scriptures, the Spirit be called "the gift of God."[51]

Gioia stresses the importance of recognizing the source for the name, arguing that it is misleading to interpret Augustine's use of it as primarily a polemical device and only secondarily because the employment of this name has scriptural warrants. Rather, the name of the Spirit is a further elaboration of the love that comes from God, who is love. An "outcome of [Augustine's] lengthy treatment of the issue of the sending of the Son and the Holy Spirit in Books 1 to 4 is that everything which 'comes from God' for our salvation is God's own very presence through the Son and the Holy Spirit."[52] The Holy Spirit is God's giving God. That the name "gift" resonates scripturally while at the same time fits Augustine's philosophically articulated presentation of the Trinity is unsurprising in light of the bishop's demonstrated confidence that true philosophy coincides with a faithful interpretation of the scriptures.

The name "gift," proceeding from the Father[53] and of the Son,[54] suggests a relationality that "Holy Spirit" does not; the Father and Son become the givers of the gift rather than simply sharing in the descriptive nature of the name "Holy Spirit." Therefore, there are two related but distinct lines of relation in Augustine's language. First, there are the Father and Son, whose very names imply relationship, and the Holy Spirit here is grafted on as what they have in common. Looking at what they have in common, the second line of relation is

51. Augustine, *De Trinitate*, 5.12.
52. Gioia, *Theological Epistemology*, 137.
53. John 15:26.
54. Romans 8:9.

that of Gift and Giver (Father and Son giving together). It is worth noting that Augustine himself does not strictly follow his own relational predication, often using "Father" and "Son" with "gift," or using "Holy Spirit" when discussing its being gift, lending to his writing not an insignificant amount of ambiguity. Ayres defends this ambiguity not as a lack of precision, per se, but the result of a redoubled approach to speaking toward God.[55] That these two methods do not coalesce is the result of Augustine using precisely two linguistic and conceptual approaches to the same ultimate reality, not because of some obstructive inconsistency in thought. Nevertheless, precisely because the Spirit is the gift of both Father and Son, it is understood as "a kind of inexpressible communion or fellowship of the Father and Son,"[56] underlining the name "Holy Spirit" as also a description of what the Father and Son have in common.

At first, Augustine discusses the Father and Son only as givers of the gift to creation and not to each other. The Father and Son are both givers of the gift to us. Augustine is not yet implying that the Spirit is the eternal exchange of love between the Father and Son, binding them in divine fellowship not reducible to substance.[57] In respect to creation, it is perhaps better to speak not of two givers but of one. "Creator" is a name proper to God—therefore to Father, Son, and Holy Spirit—in relation to creation: "And so when we call both the Father origin and the Son origin, we are not saying two origins of creation, because

55. Ayres, *Augustine and the Trinity*, 247.
56. Augustine, *De Trinitate*, 5.12.
57. Such a declaration first appears in *De Trinitate*, 6.7. Ayres (*Augustine and the Trinity*, 88) observes that the Spirit being the mutual love of the Father and Son is present in Augustine's earlier work (e.g., *De fide et symbolo* in 393). It is therefore interesting to note that although Augustine does not begin with the Spirit as mutual love in the earlier part of *De Trinitate*, it is not something that he had to discover in the course of writing the treatise but rather something to which he returned (and furthered) as needed. Augustine remarks, "Some have ventured to believe of the Holy Spirit that he constitutes the very communion between the Father and the Son, which I may thus describe as the Godhead, and which the Greeks call the *Θεότητα*. This means, therefore, that, because the Father is God and the Son is God, the divinity itself is equal to the Father, that is, the divinity by which they are joined to each other, both the Father by begetting the Son and the Son by being united to the Father, by whom the Son has been begotten. This divinity, which they also interpret as the mutual love and charity of each to the other, they say is called the Holy Spirit." Augustine, *Faith and the Creed*, trans. Michael G. Campbell, in *On Christian Belief*, ed. Boniface Ramsey, The Works of St. Augustine: A Translation for the 21st Century, vol. 1, no. 18 (Hyde Park, NY: New City Press, 2005), 9.19. All English translations throughout are from this version.

Father and Son are together one origin with reference to creation, just as they are one creator, one God."[58] Moreover, against all blunt critiques to the contrary,[59] the bishop continues to say that the Father is named origin of all things not only in reference to all creation but also in reference to the begetting of the Son and the procession of the Spirit.[60] When speaking of the divine persons, it is to be understood that what is meant by the name "Father" or "giver" is that the Father is the one timeless origin of the Trinity.[61] In giving the Spirit to creation, the Father is the origin of the gift and of the Son's giving. When speaking of God's relation to creation, Father, Son, and Holy Spirit are to be understood as origin, because the Son and the Spirit are God from God, the single origin of creation. Augustine argues that "gift" ought to be understood in a like manner; the Father and Son are the one origin of the Spirit, and "with reference to creation Father, and Son, and Holy Spirit are one origin, just as they are one creator and one lord."[62]

Further complicating the matter, Augustine moves more deeply into this naming, aware that "gift" can imply that it is necessary for God to create so that God may be truly God. If the Spirit is best named "gift"—one given to creation—than the very essence of the Spirit seems to be dependent on its being given to creation, thus necessitating a receiver of the gift. Augustine does not here see fit to establish this gift

58. Augustine, *De Trinitate*, 5.14.

59. See, for example, "Related to this is Augustine's emphasis on the unity of the divine substance as prior to the plurality of persons. If divine substance rather than the person of the Father is made the highest ontological principle—the substratum of divinity and the ultimate source of all that exists—then God and everything else is, finally, *im*personal. The metaphysical revolution of the Cappadocian doctrine of the Trinity had been to see that the highest principle is *hypostasis* not *ousia*, person not substance: the *hypostasis* of the Father, Unoriginate yet Origin of all, even Origin of the Son and Spirit. As we shall see in later chapters the consequences of Augustine's digression from the Cappadocian ontology of the Trinity were mere than merely doctrinal. The changed metaphysical options for the theology of God changed politics, anthropology, and society as well." LaCugna, *God for Us*, 101.

60. Augustine, *De Trinitate*, 5.14–15. For a helpful analysis of Augustine's understanding of the Father as origin of the Son and Spirit and the challenges that poses to the use of the word "God," see John Behr, "Calling upon God."

61. Cf.: "Augustine insists . . . on the absolute simultaneity of the Trinitarian relations, in a way which makes it impossible to accept any crude account of the Father's priority, or even any model of the trinity in which the Father as prime 'possessor' of the divine essence distributes it to others." R. Williams, "*Sapientia* and the Trinity," 328. Williams importantly notes that there can be no temporal element nor substantial possession involved in the Trinitarian generation and procession. That being said, Augustine does recognize the Father as the "origin" of the Trinity.

62. Augustine, *De Trinitate*, 5.15.

as the eternal exchange of love between Father and Son, a move that would seem to resolve his dilemma. Instead, Augustine distinguishes between the Spirit as gift (*donum*) and donation (*donatum*), arguing that the Spirit's eternal procession is *as givable*, not *as that which has been given*. Strikingly, this method of clarification serves to present God not as dependent upon creation but as eternally open to creation—as eternally open to giving love to that which is not God. Moreover, continuing his insistence that substance of God is not relational, he states that any change in the Spirit's being eternal gift and its being given takes place on the part of those who receive the gift and not on the part of the gift.[63] Again, because Father, Son, and Gift are names marking Trinitarian relationships and the actions of God with respect to creation are done inseparably, the one God undergoes no change in bringing about salvation through giving the gift of love.

There is something in some measure unsatisfactory with the fine lines Augustine draws around the use of the name "gift": the necessity of relational predication; the inadequacy of the name "Holy Spirit" in such predication; the gift as given together by the Father and Son, thus forcing two lines of relational predication together; the gift as eternally givable and not eternally given. Juggling these affirmations, Augustine strains to articulate the substantial unity and the relationality of God in a reasonable manner. It seems that his successes are more dependent on the constant juggling than on the smooth correspondence of these affirmations. The path of discovery trod by the bishop is not yet the map of Thomas Aquinas, providing us with a bird's eye view of the theological path and a clear sense of the surrounding topography. With an ad hoc exploration that forces him to confront both peaks and valleys as he comes to them, laboring to remain consistent with what he has said, with orthodox thought, and with where he desires to go, Augustine requires further elaboration of this gift as a name signifying the relational references within the Trinity.

This he attempts in book 6, investigating, among other things, the nature of this gift as love, with love seeming to reference both the

63. Ibid., 5.17.

substance of God and particularly the Holy Spirit. Augustine writes: "So the Holy Spirit is something common to Father and Son, whatever it is, or is their very commonness or communion, consubstantial and coeternal. Call this friendship, if it helps, but a better word for it is charity. And this too is substance because God is substance, and *God is charity* (1 John 4:8, 16)."[64] In one sense, this is simply another manifestation of the challenges of Trinitarian predication Augustine confronts earlier in his treatise. God is wise, Christ is the wisdom of the Father, and yet this necessitates neither that the Father is wise only through the Son, nor that the Son is the locus of wisdom in God—representing one of the faculties of the divine mind. Divine simplicity requires that names that one can predicate of God can be predicated of each of the divine persons without sacrificing the unity of God—and yet there are not three gods but one God. That being said, love occupies a unique place in the names and substantial descriptions of God because of the statement of identity in the first letter of John ("God is love"[65]), which echoes the identity structure of the divine name in Exodus (more ambiguously, "I am who am"[66]). God's identification with love stands, along with the name of Exodus 3:14, uniquely among the divine names, at the very least insofar as Augustine understood scriptural revelation.

This love is proper to the Spirit, as wisdom is to the Son, and serves as the unity of the Father and Son as mutual givers of the gift to creation while at the same time is the divine substance, both challenging a clear understanding of love and rendering imprecise Augustine's rules of Trinitarian predication. The unity of Father and Son as relational is their (acting together) giving the gift of love. Whereas the equality of the Father and Son as both wholly the divine substance renders them both God, who is love. Regarding the former, Augustine writes:

64. Ibid.
65. 1 John 4:8, 16.
66. Exodus 3:14.

> For whether he is the unity of both the others or their holiness or their charity, whether he is their unity because their charity, and their charity because their holiness, it is clear that he is not one of the two, since he is that by which the two are joined each to the other, by which the begotten is loved by the one who begets him and in turn loves the begetter. Thus *They keep unity of the Spirit in the bond of peace* (Eph 4:3), not in virtue of participation but of their own very being, not by gift of some superior, but by their own gift.[67]

Clearly, the gift of love that is the Holy Spirit is the unity of Father and Son, here also a mutual gift of begetter and begotten, of Father and Son, to one another.[68] Not only are the Father and Son united as the one giver of the gift to creation, but the Father loves the only-begotten Son, who returns that love to the Father in a bond of love. Augustine discusses this bond in a manner distinct from that of substance, while at the same time offering a sign that this unity of love is at least as true of God as the unity of substance—a further signification of what it means to assert that God is love.

The gift of love strains Augustine's predicative structure; readers are invited to interpret this gift as indicative of the bishop's "real concerns, that is a 'knowledge' which does not aim at systematization, but coincides with the desire to enjoy [*frui*] the gift of divine life revealed through the mystery of the Trinity."[69] That the articulation of the gift of love resists the structures Augustine so carefully built only serves to present love all the more distinctly against a philosophical and linguistic background, "already problematic in the case of the relation between the Father and Son," now "virtually meaningless for the Holy Spirit."[70] Gioia stresses that the foundation for naming the

67. Augustine, *De Trinitate*, 6.7.
68. David Coffey criticizes Augustine for naming the Spirit as the mutual love of the Father and Son without the requisite scriptural support. Whether or not Coffey's claim is warranted, and to what extent and in what manner such a critique is of concern, is of less significance here than the fact that Coffey's article serves to firmly defend the assertion that Augustine does eventually grant this mutuality of gift to the Father and Son, leading to what Coffey calls an "imprecision" in the language distinguishing between the eternal divine relationships and the gift of love given to creation. David Coffey, "The Holy Spirit as the Mutual Love of the Father and the Son," *Theological Studies* 51, no. 2 (1990): 193–229. What Coffey sees as fundamentally problematic is here taken as a sign of the richness of Augustine's understanding of love and the limitation of theological language.
69. Gioia, *Theological Epistemology*, 166.
70. Ibid., 153.

Spirit the gift of love is revelation, not so-called ontology. "Thus, love does not have anything to do with the alleged explanatory role of an ontological category," Gioia writes, "but draws its epistemological unique role from its wholly theological nature."[71] Augustine's use of love is first and foremost a theological testament to Christ's saving actions and an application of the first letter of John, rather than of an abstract philosophical category.[72] Love, for Augustine, is defined in light of the revelation of the Trinity.

Ayres observes that while Augustine's pneumatologic sources are difficult to definitively discern, an analysis of some of the bishop's earliest work reveals both "echoes of pro-Nicene pneumatology"[73] and the absence of a definitive link to non-Christian Platonism.[74] There is more operative in Augustine's thought—particularly in his reflection on the Spirit—than simply a translation of philosophical categories into the language of Christian revelation. Ayres argues that in the case of Augustine:

> Reticence to use those terminologies may also reflect a belief that the philosophical questions they always beg may be circumvented, or at least better approached, by means of other summary styles. The prevalence of these traditions should warn us that attempts to summarize Latin tradition by an etymological focus on a particular term—such as the oft-repeated claim that *persona* originally means "mask," an etymology which is then taken to reveal something essential about Latin tradition—have little cogency.[75]

This better approach to language and thought about the Trinitarian God is never a complete rejection of philosophical terms and questions

71. Ibid., 166.
72. See also David Tracy's gloss on this question: "The truest naming of God for Augustine, however, is not Exodus 3.14, nor the Plotinian the One or the Good. For Augustine, God reveals Godself through Christ in both creation and redemption. As Love, God is the Trinity of the loving, interrelated divine persons of Father, Son, Holy Spirit. To so name God (and therefore, the Real) occurred to Augustine not principally through personal mystical experience (with Monica) but through faith in the revelation of Jesus Christ. One can, I believe, reformulate Augustine's point this way: only by naming Jesus of Nazareth (i.e., the Jesus whose words, actions, and sufferings are narrated in the gospels) the Christ can we name God." Tracy, "Augustine's Christomorphic Theocentrism," 272–73.
73. Ayres, *Augustine and the Trinity*, 36.
74. Ibid., 39.
75. Ibid., 77.

but is instead a contextualization of them within the frame of Christian revelation. However, that this revealed love is something new and that theology need not be beholden to possibly ossifying philosophical categories do not alone simply unfetter the gift of love from philosophy. Preoccupation with being, even as only that from which love must be liberated, itself threatens further entrapment by defining the field and goal through which revelation can be discussed. And while Gioia perhaps is overenthusiastic in restricting these books as polemics, his reason for doing so—the observation that philosophical categories break when applied to God[76]—can be all the more illuminative when we examine the details of this rupture.

The personal relations of the divine Trinity are not simply relations in general, they are not philosophical categories to be independently established and then applied to God. Rather, they are marked particularly by the gift of love both between the Father and the Son and given by the Father through the Son to creation—they are the prototype, not type. We may therefore tentatively conclude three layers of identification of God and love, each standing firmly on its own while at the same time relying on the one love to carry each. First, the Holy Spirit may be personally (or hypostatically) named the gift of love. This gift is given by the Father and Son together for the sanctification of creation and serves as the unity of the Father in Son as the giver in that they both give this gift to creation.[77] Second, this gift of love is the mutual love of the Father and Son for one another, a love that unites them in a bond of peace and not in virtue of their identification with the divine substance. Third, God (here not any of the divine persons specifically) is identified with love in 1 John, a passage Augustine takes quite seriously as a statement of direct identity. That God *is* love and *gives* love both continues Augustine's rule of faith (that the Holy Spirit is God from God) and adds a further nuance to the Spirit. Although

76. Gioia, *Theological Epistemology*, 150.

77. Cf. "But Augustine here is pressing on into territory for which no maps were (or are) available, and it is significant that apart from . . . one text in *De trinitate* 5 Augustine never again speaks in this manner of Father and Son as the one *principium* of the Spirit. Instead, we see him develop the formulae . . . stating that the Father gives it to the Son and to the Spirit that the Spirit proceeds also from the Son." Ayres, *Augustine and the Trinity*, 265.

in the first two points, the Spirit seems passive in its giving, that the Spirit, too, is true God renders this giving as active—the Spirit is both giver and gift. Moreover, although the Spirit's apparent passivity has been cause for much concern in some contemporary theology,[78] it is far from clear, save when operating with an overly anthropomorphized understanding of divine personhood, that such a criticism is a clear and relevant trump card to play against Augustine's articulation.

The unity of will of Father and Son through the gift of the Spirit serves along with substantial or ontological unity as the unity of the Trinity—and both of these articulations of the one unity of God are ultimately revelations of love.[79] This means that love is that which determines both the divine relations and the divine substance, while at the same time being reducible to neither. This does not lessen the tension between the theological articulations of relation and substance. Of a distinction to be "diligently looked into and not casually taken for granted," Augustine concludes, "What is meant is that while in that supremely simple nature substance is not one thing and charity another, but substance is charity and charity is substance, whether in the Father or in the Son or in the Holy Spirit, yet all the same the Holy Spirit is distinctively named charity."[80] The one unity of God "coincides with love."[81]

Augustine confesses that knowledge beyond this is too wonderful

78. See, for example: "The doctrine of the three hypostases or Persons of the Trinity is dangerous too, because it applies one and the same concept to the Father, the Son and the Holy Spirit. This suggests that they are homogeneous and equal, namely hypostases, persons or modes of being. But the heading hypostasis, person or mode of being blurs the specific differences between the Father, the Son and the Holy Spirit. This became particularly clear to us from the difficulty of understanding the Holy Spirit as 'Person' and as 'third Person' at that—that is to say, the difficulty of understanding him in the same way as the Son and the Father. The 'three Persons' are different, not merely in their relations to one another, but also in respect to their character as Persons, even if the person is to be understood in his relations, and not apart from them. If we wanted to remain specific, we should have to use a different concept in each case when applying the word 'person' to the Father, the Son and the Spirit. The Holy Spirit is not a person in the same, identical sense as the Son; and neither of them is a person in the same, identical sense as the Father." Moltmann, *Trinity and the Kingdom*, 189.

79. Gioia, *Theological Epistemology*, 127. Gioia argues that the dispute with the so-called Arians moved Augustine to overemphasize the essential unity rather than risk offering a unity of will that would support, rather than reform, the Arian position. Thus, Augustine's primary use of the unity of substance serves a polemical, rather than constructive, purpose. Ibid., 130–31.

80. Augustine, *De Trinitate*, 15.29.

81. Gioia, *Theological Epistemology*, 129.

and too mighty for him.[82] *De Trinitate* does not move much further into the mystery of how love reconciles these lines of theological predication in the living God, save for its continuing exploration of our salvation—that is to say, Augustine is not to be distracted from his ultimate goal by searching for an answer to a question that is conditioned by the limitations of signification. For while not exhaustive of its content, the question of salvation—and specifically its mediation—still looms large over *De Trinitate.* Augustine sets before himself the task of exploring our reception of the gift of love and our graced formation to the image of God. Whatever else it may be, *De Trinitate* is fundamentally saturated with soteriological concerns, offering a linguistic and conceptual structure that invites (in and through its admitted limitation) the reader to a humble awareness of the distance between the saving God and the creation in need of salvation. At the same time, this structure orients and opens us to the reception of the healing and formation effected by the saving gift of love.

Significantly, Ayres observes that Augustine's articulation of relation is predicative and *not* strictly ontological.[83] In one sense, this is clearly obvious: Augustine contrasts relation with substance. However, the tension apparently obstructing Augustine's movement forward into a deeper formulation of Trinitarian relations stems not simply from the terms themselves but from the fact that they represent differing approaches to theological language toward God. Relational predication is, in a sense, not attempting to say anything at all about God. Anything said about God is said substantially. What his predicative structure does, then, is condition our language in naming Father, Son, and Spirit by regulating how we can speak of each as God, particularly how the Son and Spirit are "God from God." It guides our understanding and usage of "from," preserving *missio* as an affirmation of divine identity and not inequality, and allowing us to trust in the mediation of this revelation as precisely God's being present in the

82. Augustine, *De Trinitate,* 15.50.
83. Ayres, *Augustine and the Trinity,* 225.

world with us. "The medium of God's revelation, therefore," writes David Bentley Hart, "is God himself; and the site—the matter—of that revelation is the living soul."[84] Such language opens to a theological approach to God through the gift of love.

Moreover, substantial predication never escapes its own linguistic predicative lineage. As linguistic, it is inescapably relational. In as much as Augustine is straining to both describe and name the one whose very being ought to serve as the context for our own created being, so our only context for understanding this prototypical divine being is through its significantly tarnished image. The complication that sits at the end of an analysis (like Teske's) of divine substance is that we are attempting to discern the trace and contours of the being of God (that is, the only being truly deserving of the word) from human being—we are trying to define the prototype from the created and fallen type, from a type that itself derives its meaning from the prototype.

The attempt to bring an end to this tension through either reconciliation or conquest itself is always already a forfeiture of the ultimacy of divine love. That neither substance nor relation stands as an exclusive and exhaustive foundation for theological language toward God is anticipated by an attentive reading of *De Trinitate*. But how these two methods of predication shape theology through their respective strengths and inadequacies serves as a means for recognizing the limitations of theological discourse. Moreover, the limitation turns us from the search for language equal to the task of signifying God and to a way of proceeding based upon our conformity to the end so restlessly sought—conformity to love, through love. This love comes to us as something always already present as the constituent element of our humanity made to the image of God. But this image, unlike the Son's being the image of the Father, is not one of equality but of approach, whereby we come to God "by likeness or similarity, as one moves away from dissimilarity or unlikeness."[85] It is

84. David Bentley Hart, "The Hidden and the Manifest: Metaphysics after Nicaea," in Demacopoulos and Papanikolaou, *Orthodox Readings of Augustine*, 215.
85. Augustine, *De Trinitate*, 7.12.

an approach, "not proximity of place but of imitation"[86] of that which is eternal love.

Only God, Augustine writes, as "that which not only does not but also cannot change deserves without qualification to be said really and truly to be."[87] Ayres observes that Augustine's use of *idipsum*, being immutable and everlasting, as a name of God in Godself is not only unparalleled among the bishop's predecessors[88] but marks the deep mystery of God's relationship with creation. An ostensibly philosophical term, *idipsum* is, in this context, profoundly theological, measuring the infinite distance between God and creation and establishing therein the method of relationship.[89] Crucially, creation's finitude and mutability are not defects but defining characteristics of the ability to receive form.[90] Complementing the gift of the Holy Spirit as eternally givable, it is this receptivity that defines the so-called substance of human being(s). In the truest sense, therefore, only God is essence or substance, and all other beings *are* only insofar as they are in relation to God. All created substance, therefore, is dependent first upon relation. In a particularity that defines the rule, human beings made to the image of God are rendered who we are by this directional "to" (*ad*)—our essence is conditioned by our relation.[91] However, it is not just relation generally speaking but one marked by the gift of love that so constitutes us.

Book 7 concludes with a reiteration of the healing transformative significance of love through the words of the Pauline epistles: "*Be refashioned in the newness of your mind* (Rom 12:2), and elsewhere he says, *Be therefore imitators of God as most dear sons* (Eph 5:1) for it is with reference to the new man that it says, *Who is being renewed for the recognition of God according to the image of him who created him* (Col 3:10)."[92] Augustine is here concerned with the salvation of the human

86. Ibid.
87. Ibid., 5.3.
88. Ayres, *Augustine and the Trinity*, 204.
89. Ibid., 205.
90. Ibid., 207.
91. As in, for example, Augustine, *De Trinitate*, 7.12, 12.12, and 14.6.
92. Ibid., 7.12.

being through a renewal of that which is most central to that being. But to discuss a soteriological or economic intent as operative behind the composition of *De Trinitate* can be both helpful and misleading. It is helpful to recognize that the healing of the Christian and the formation of that person to the image of our creation is a central theme of the work and ought not be overlooked while focused on the tension between substance and person or the so-called "mental analogies" of the Trinity. Augustine uses these approaches, to whatever limited degrees they are valid, to serve the movement of the soul to God. Yet such language can prove misleading if it leads to a belief that Augustine is examining such distinctions as the one between the immanent and economic trinities—between the discussion of who God is in Godself and who God is for us in salvation history. For these dichotomies force upon Augustine a structure that is both foreign to him and frames his thought in a context unsuitable for it. Gioia significantly states that an "identification between the form and content of revelation and the identity of the revealer developed through the theology of missions . . . constitutes the foundation of Augustine's Trinitarian theology."[93] Who God is and what God does in saving us, while possibly articulated distinctly, are inseparable realities—the latter, for Augustine, necessarily dependent upon the former. In fact, what God does to save us is to reveal the Trinity—that is, to give us the gift of love. In particular, that the Son reveals his sonship and that the Spirit is the gift of the Father and Son means that what is given to creation is precisely the love of the Father and Son, a love that is the Trinitarian life of God. God's salvation is the revelation of the Trinity through the Trinity. "This point is crucial," Gioia writes, "*the goal and end of the knowledge of God is the Father*. In other words, it is not as if the Trinity were the object of salvific knowledge in an undifferentiated way. Knowledge of the Trinity means that *God can only be known in a Trinitarian way*, i.e. under the form of knowledge *of* the Father *through* the Son *in* the Holy Spirit."[94] Relational predication serves to tie language about God

93. Gioia, *Theological Epistemology*, 142.
94. Ibid., 164; emphasis in original.

to God's self-revelation to us. Books 5–7 present the reader with a careful analysis of the limits of theological language about God (and thus of our knowledge about God). How love affects this revealed knowledge—specifically how the gift of the Spirit opens us to see Jesus Christ as Son, that is, as God from God—occupies Augustine in book 8 and is operative throughout the rest of *De Trinitate.*

4

Books 8–15: The Gift of Love to the Image of God

To be sure, this renewal does not happen in one moment of conversion.
—Augustine, *De Trinitate*, 14.23

"Words have force only to the extent that they remind us to look for things," Augustine instructs his son, "they don't display them for us to know."[1] How then can theological language remind us to look for the Trinity—and not simply any trinity but "the Trinity that God is"?[2] Book 8 marks a transition from the historical accounts of the divine missions and the rules of theological language by which we might speak of God to a more inward path,[3] which is, for the Doctor of Grace, also the possibility of a path upward to God. Precisely how we might discern a point of contact between our own minds and the reality of God despite (or perhaps by means of) the limitations of finite creation and distorted love occupies Augustine's thought for the remainder of *De Trinitate*. Augustine, of course, has not abandoned his intellectual

1. Augustine, *De Magistro*, 11.36.
2. Augustine, *De Trinitate*, 1.7: "de trinitate quae deus est."
3. Ibid., 8.1.

pilgrimage toward the Trinity. Nor has he abandoned his defense of Nicene orthodoxy and its subsequent tradition, affirming three relationally named divine persons with no diversity of being, each equal to the others, each fully and truly God. But the relational naming of the one God as Father, Son, and Holy Spirit, read through the bedazzling prism of the gift of love, does not yet, as book 8 draws to a close, present the Trinity to our gaze. Concluding with a Sabbath-like moment of rest, book 8 finds its author hopeful that in love he has found, if not yet the fullness of the vision sought, at the very least where the Trinity "has to be looked for. It has not yet been found, but we have found where to look for it."[4] This is a place where love offers itself to be seen and understood as a sign—a sign that is at the same time the gift of the signified. It is a place where this gift effects the formation of the receiver into a living image of itself. Much of the second half of *De Trinitate* is a mapping of this sharpening and quickening of love and its movement of the human being to image of God.

This chapter will begin with a study of the Trinitarian hermeneutic of love established in book 8, particularly how love assists in signification. Then we will turn to the so-called mental analogies of the Trinity that occupy much of *De Trinitate*'s second half, with attention to how these dynamic, tripart illustrations function and particularly to what Augustine is not claiming to achieve through them. Finally, we will examine how these illustrations, read in the context of the revelation of love in Christ through the Spirit, assist the overall movement of the text through limited created being toward the "Trinity that God is."

Nothing by Way of Signs Alone

Always aware of the limitations of a nature both finite and fallen, Augustine exercises due diligence warning his readers—and one might think himself, too—of the dangers of presumed knowledge won by

4. Ibid., 8.14.

ascribing to God any material reality whatsoever. "Indeed," he writes, "any and every bodily conception is to be rejected."[5] So too, we are not to ascribe to God any spiritual conception that is changeable. Already, even before his first mention of the dynamism of the human mind as a possible step toward a deepening appreciation for the divine inseparability of operation among the distinct Father, Son, and Holy Spirit, Augustine vigilantly guards against the direct application of created being as a model for the Trinity. At the same time, he sees in this very vigilance a glimpse of the wisdom he seeks: "For it is no small part of knowledge, when we emerge from the depths to breathe in that sublime atmosphere, if before we can know what God is, we are at least able to know what he is not."[6] Assessing how and where creation—be it material or spiritual—reaches its limits in attempted signification of its Creator is the first step toward wisdom and the one Augustine eventually takes in book 8.

At the heart of all of our desires, then, lies neither material good nor created spiritual good but a fundamental desire for the unchangeable good itself.[7] Embraced as that which leads us to our proper end, this love can bring us to the fullness of the vision of God. To see God requires that we love God. But what do we love when we love our God?[8] The deepest foundation of Augustine's hermeneutic of love is marked by this question. The inability of the sign to be fully identified with the *res* and theology's related never-firm-enough grasp of its object both haunt his theology. As neither material good nor created spirit are what God is, knowledge of them cannot lead directly to God. And yet they together serve as the medium of intelligible experience (and the vehicle of God's activity and the context of revelation) and open our only path to God. Augustine seeks a form of knowledge that is sufficient for directing our love to its proper object, asking, "Who can love what he does not know?"[9] Moreover, where knowledge reaches

5. Ibid., 8.3.
6. Ibid.
7. Ibid., 8.4–5.
8. Augustine, *Confessions*, 10.6.8, 10.7.11.
9. Augustine, *De Trinitate*, 8.6.

its limit, faith cannot provide an easy solution but rather defers the unknown to a more exalted status. As we cannot love what we do not know, so we cannot have faith in something that remains fully outside of our experience in inaccessible mystery. If the Trinity is alien to our understanding, such that we know nothing of it so that no sign directs us to it, then we can neither love it nor have faith in it.

In his formulation of this challenge, Augustine acknowledges those things that that we do, in fact, know. Christian faith is possible because, although later generations do not know Jesus, Mary, or any of the figures prominent in the two testaments as their contemporaries would have known them, we do know what it is to be a man or woman. Although we may have no experience of virgin births or resurrections, we do know what virginity, birth, death, and life (although perhaps not in its glorified form) are. From our own experience we know enough so as to begin to understand the claims of the Christian faith. We can form judgments about the claims and our disposition toward them based upon our knowledge. But while we know what *three* is and what *one* is, this knowledge is not sufficient for directing our faith to the Trinity. A general knowledge of all things triune cannot simply bridge the infinite gap between sign and God. "Perhaps then what we love is not what any trinity is," Augustine writes, "but the trinity that God is. So what we love in the trinity is what God is."[10] Augustine's struggle is with his apparent incapacity to discover a standard of likeness—a knowledge—by which he might believe in the Trinity and "love the as yet unknown God."[11]

That the bishop does not approach this question by means of the scriptures is a significant characteristic of his argument. Perhaps it is the case that although we know both three and one, we do not know the Trinity that God is. But the Christian faith asserts that through God's self-disclosing revelation, we do know something of who the Father is, who the Son is, and who the Holy Spirit is. While this knowledge is not as effortlessly discoverable as that of virginity and

10. Ibid., 8.8.
11. Ibid.

birth, it is narrated and discussed in the scriptures. What Augustine does not do is attempt to come to a deep knowledge of the Trinity through the historical development of doctrine and the movement from the witness of the scriptures to the canonical statements of the councils and church leaders. Despite his focus in books 1–4 on the divine missions revealing who God is through a multileveled and complex symphony of scriptural texts, his question here squarely engages our reception of such revelation and how we might achieve a true understanding of this revelation, effecting a (relatively) adequate translation of the texts into knowledge not of the texts themselves, nor even ultimately of a doctrine, but of God. Immersed in questions both epistemological and spiritual, fitting to the inward turn he proposes as book 8 begins, Augustine is in search of the needed element to bridge the gap between any knowledge gleaned from the analogical language of the scriptures and the Trinity who God is. Augustine offers love as the means by which we "concretize or existentialize"[12] this standard of both comparison (of our knowledge to its object) and unity (by which our knowledge is conformed to its object). Love promises to effect this translation of *signa* to *res* in both our hearts and minds.

Progressing interiorly, Augustine approaches his driving question of how we are to love God through analogy: he suggests the example of knowing and loving the "just man" to further develop his idea of knowing and loving God. Though it is just to love the just man, how are we to love the just man if we do not yet know what *justice* is?[13] Can only the just love the just? (More to our point, can only the saint love God?) Augustine's response finds its roots in his faith in human beings as created by and for the God of love, whose call to us is a constituting element of our epistemological make-up, always illuminating in our minds those things that we know not and are not but to which we are called. In what he calls a "wonderfully surprising" discovery of illumination—that is, precisely something that we cannot simply work toward, building knowledge upon knowledge, but something that we

12. Edmund Hill, "Introductory Essay on Book VIII," in *The Trinity*, 239.
13. Augustine, *De Trinitate*, 8.9.

come upon as always already there—we find that the mind can "see in itself what it has seen nowhere else, and see something true."[14] In this way, the just man and the unjust man both perceive "just" within themselves even if one rejects it as a standard of behavior—an act that does not require one to be just but a judgment shaped by an "immoveable eternity" that "sheds its light on our mind."[15] Such illumination is not a magical imbuing of the mind with supernatural clarity, arbitrarily granted to some people at some times. Rather, it is grounded in a faith in creation as intelligible and in a human mind that is created to know not only creation but also God. In book 12, Augustine writes of this intelligibility:

> The conclusion we should rather draw is that the nature of the intellectual mind has been so established by the disposition of its creator that it is subjoined to intelligible things in the order of nature, and so it sees such truth in a kind of non-bodily light that is *sui generis*, just as our eyes of flesh see all these things that lie around us in this bodily light, a light they were created to be receptive of and to match.[16]

An outcome of the concordance of the intelligibility of creation and the dynamism of the human mind, the resulting illumination is the light by which judgment is made. We can have within us a vision of that which we are not, that which is other than us but to which we find ourselves drawn nevertheless. We can find within us that which is other than ourselves.

As an appetite cannot be for the unknown thing itself, as "absolutely no one can love a thing that is quite unknown,"[17] it must be for knowledge itself.[18] But where unaided knowledge cannot traverse the distance between who we are and that otherness that we long to know, it can, with the help of love, be formed by, and toward, that otherness it recognizes inside. In what still requires further analysis and reflection, Augustine offers love as the bridge between our knowledge and that

14. Ibid.
15. Gioia, *Theological Epistemology*, 195.
16. Augustine, *De Trinitate*, 12.24.
17. Ibid., 10.1.
18. Ibid., 10.4.

not-completely-unknown otherness that we discover within ourselves as not yet who we are and not yet what we truly know. Love is that which allows us to cleave to the form of this otherness that we behold in order to be formed by it.[19] This is what love does: lead knowledge yearning for vision by quickening our desire for it. Love is the movement that opens to that which is other than us, to that within that "has not yet 'formed' us, which does not yet belong to us."[20]

Here the line between love and knowledge is further strained and hints at an unsatisfying circular path of argumentation. Augustine claims that the unjust man may find justice intelligible through the illuminating power of his working mind, wherein he comes to know creation because, simply, that is what the mind is created to do. That the unjust man recognizes justice according to the form of justice within can lead to the further question: how does he recognize the form precisely as justice? The answer, well summarized by Gioia, speaks to the significance of the transformative power of love:

> One of Augustine's crucial epistemological principles is suggested here which must be carefully understood: justice seen in truth itself is called a form (*forma*). It is not simply an idea or a knowledge which could be envisaged from a uniquely intellectual viewpoint. A form is something with an inherent teleological thrust: its dynamism is not simply fulfilled in the act of making itself known to us, but especially in the act of "forming" (*formare*) us.[21]

Love forms us by conforming us to that which we long to know so that we may know it. Thus, most properly put, we, if primarily unjust, only know justice to the degree that we are just and are just only in loving justice. This is possible only insofar as we are just, or see within ourselves a trace of justice, or desire justice, or feel within ourselves a void outlined by hints of forgotten memories of what little justice still remains in us. Only one who has completely obliterated all fragments and echoes of justice within is without hope of knowing it and is left to the impossibility of knowing justice and therefore to the hell of the

19. Ibid., 8.9.
20. Gioia, *Theological Epistemology*, 179.
21. Ibid., 179–80.

impossibility of knowing the God who *is* justice (save, as always, for ineffable mercy on the part of God, for whom nothing is impossible).

For what Augustine seeks here is not knowledge of the created world, something that can be discovered through observation, but knowledge of the as of yet unknown God. In his analysis of this relationship of love and knowledge, Gioia is careful to maintain this "radical difference between love for the 'God-whom-we-do-not-know-though-believing-in-him' and any other form of knowledge."[22] And while it is good and fitting to ensure that we do not directly apply empirical methodology as a means of exploring who God is, it is not necessary that we close the path of influence moving in the opposite direction. That the means of attaining knowledge of the created world are not sufficient for responding to questions regarding the nature of the Trinity does not necessitate that our understanding of creation be severed from knowledge of God. Augustine is always aware of the radical difference between knowledge of the created order and knowledge of God, always on guard against the direct application of created categories to the Creator. Yet this does not mean that his speculation on the Trinity does not shape his understanding of the linguistically framed meaning of all of our thought. As discussed previously, love impacts all levels of our appreciation of meaning and value, all those forms of knowledge beyond those purely empirical.[23] This love is not without its connection with God.

How, then, does love negotiate knowledge of the unknown? Continuing along his interior way, Augustine presents love as shepherding our knowledge of the unknown God because, and only because, God is love.[24] To know God requires us to know love, and such knowledge is identical with loving. In what might strike readers as a strange formulation, Augustine maintains that when we love our neighbor, we not only love the beloved but, above all, we love love itself; that is, we love the love with which we love.[25] It is not of little

22. Ibid., 180.
23. Moreover, one might even say with Bernard Lonergan (*Insight*, 376) that even the most empirical knowledge is won through a "detached, disinterested, *desire to know*."
24. See Ayres, *Augustine and the Trinity*, 283.

significance that Augustine arrives at this point by means of scriptural reflection on the great commandments to love God and love neighbor. This love of neighbor is bound to love of God, together giving Augustine the foundation for his conclusion. In "a passage . . . not to be dismissed as an example of Augustine's rhetorical fervour,"[26] Augustine concludes that as the love of neighbor is at the same time love of God, and "God is love and whoever abides in love abides in God,"[27] so when we love, we love love itself. Of such love we are intimately familiar, Augustine reminds his readers, even more so than we are with the neighbor we love. We have an intimate knowledge of our love that we can only hope to have with our neighbor. A further development of Augustine's description of God from *Confessions*—"More interior than my inmost part and higher than my highest part"[28]—here, that intimacy provides the ground upon which both love of neighbor and any knowledge of God is possible. "There now," Augustine writes of the one who loves, "he can already have God better known to him than his brother, certainly better known because more present, better known because more inward to him, better known because more sure. Embrace love which is God, and embrace God with love."[29] Knowledge of God is therefore possible through the complementary love of God and love of neighbor because our love—familiar as it is all-consuming, all-powerful, and still mysterious—is the presence of God. This first trinity—"love means someone loving and something loved with love"[30]—is not yet a clear analog for Trinitarian God but is the place where God can be found.[31] Love is the place and means of search in and by which Augustine hopes to come to know the Trinity.

This method by which the bishop suggests we might come to knowledge of God can disconcertingly appear to echo of the love of

25. Augustine, *De Trinitate*, 8.10.
26. Burnaby, *Amor Dei*, 161.
27. 1 John 4:16.
28. Augustine, *Confessions*, 3.6.11.
29. Augustine, *De Trinitate*, 8.11.
30. Ibid., 8.13.
31. Ibid.

love marking Augustine's student days in the "cauldron of illicit loves" of Carthage.[32] Nascent but not explicit in these two different accounts is the significant distinction of love's object, the "something loved." "Love is by definition always loving something," Gioia notes.[33] Never a static form, love only *is* as it is loving something.[34] As the soul's weight, love always moves the lover toward the beloved. Spiritually contextualized, this movement is not through a distance of measurable space but from who we are to the person we become in so loving a particular thing. The love moves us toward the object of love by conforming us to it. The distinction made by love's object can serve to illuminate further Augustine's way of proceeding through the rest of *De Trinitate*. On one hand, he suggests love as the means—apparently the only means—by which we might come to know an otherwise unknowable God. Only love can enable us to cling to the Trinity who God is, the Trinity who has no direct analog in creation. This love is a desirous search for an object, a grasping for that which promises fulfillment. On the other hand, it would appear that love, always a love for something, can never be simply a desire unordered toward a particular object. Not an always already present impulse seeking an object, love develops from the lover's engagement with—or knowledge of—the beloved. This love, necessarily related to the concrete neighbor, is at the same time an embrace of this beloved and of the God of love who is always already active within us—it is a love of love.[35] Love is fundamentally responsive in nature.

It would be misleading to echo Anders Nygren and directly ascribe the terms *eros* and *agape* to this distinction.[36] In part because Augustine

32. "As yet I had never been in love and I longed to love; and from a subconscious poverty of mind I hated the thought of being less inwardly destitute. I sought an object for my love; I was in love with love, and I hated safety and a path free of snares. My hunger was internal, deprived of inward food, that is of you yourself, my God. But that was not the kind of hunger I felt. I was without any desire for incorruptible nourishment, not because I was replete with it, but the emptier I was, the more unappetizing such food became. So my soul was in rotten health. . . . To me it was sweet to love and be loved, the more so if I could enjoy the body of the beloved. . . . I rushed headlong into love, by which I was longing to be captured." Augustine, *Confessions*, 3.1.1.
33. Gioia, *Theological Epistemology*, 184.
34. Augustine, *De Trinitate*, 8.11.
35. Ibid., 8.10.
36. Anders Nygren, *Agape and Eros: The Christian Idea of Love*, trans. Philip S. Watson (Chicago: University of Chicago Press, 1982).

himself never held fast to any such distinction, but more significantly, this dichotomy does not serve in our reading of Augustine because both lover and love are shaped by that which is loved. We are not simply desirous but desirous of something or someone. We are not simply restless but restless for the God who made us. While certainly the love that consumed the young student was shaped by its materiality, particularly in the form of sexual desire,[37] Augustine is far from decrying the material world as evil. For the battle with pride ever haunts *Confessions*—indeed, all of his work—signifying that the true tension within the heart of the young Augustine was not a conflict of desire between bodily and spiritual objects, nor between his desire of being loved and his desire to give love, but between maintaining his own ways and being converted to the way of God.[38]

Not a matter of erotic desire versus kenotic charity, the rich distinction everywhere quickening Augustine's theology is between *caritas*—love ordered to God and therefore the only love deserving of the name—and *cupiditas*—that is, disordered desire. By turning inward and looking to our experience of our own love, Augustine is not inviting his readers to reflect on a desire that selects, as it were, through some "motiveless choosing of motives,"[39] from among spiritually neutral possibilities, each good inasmuch as it is chosen and therefore deemed "good" by the selecting will. Such a choice between options, if it has a place in Augustine's thought, is not an instance of liberty or of love at all but a deterioration of a will that ought to order us to God. The youthful longing for love that Augustine describes in *Confessions* is, at its heart, a longing for God but is twisted away from its object toward an empty promise of fulfillment.

Not an innate natural desire for the beautiful or good in itself in

37. Augustine, *Confessions*, 3.1.1–3.4.7. It is interesting to note that along with the uncontrolled sexual desire well commented upon by readers, Augustine also mentions that his love of love also found him immersing himself in the less referenced, tragic spectacle of the theater and in friendship with those known for their relentless bullying of younger students.

38. See *Confessions*: "O my God, my great mercy, my refuge (Ps. 58:18, 143:2) from the terrible dangers in which I was wandering. My stiff neck took me further and further away from you. I loved my own ways, not yours. The liberty I loved was merely that of a runaway." Augustine, *Confessions*, 3.3.6.

39. Hanby, *Augustine and Modernity*, 103.

a matter that brackets our status as having been lovingly created by and for God, love is first and foremost responsive. Therefore, coming to know God in love is a matter of coming to recognize that God is ceaselessly more intimately present to me than I am to myself, there within always already loving me. In turn, this very recognition is at the same time an acceptance of our being created by God, a restoration of our relationship with God, and therefore (almost by definition) salvific. It remains to be explored just how love accomplishes this. But the knowledge of God that Augustine seeks is nothing less than the open and accepting response to the gift of salvation—that is, the gift of remembering, understanding, and loving God. In this way, the reception of salvation is tied to our love of love and our openness to love's part is conditioning our interpretation of ourselves, our neighbor, and of all of creation. "Augustine is," Kolbet writes, "perhaps, at his most innovative in his creative interweaving of hermeneutics and soteriology."[40] The understanding of God's revelation of Godself to us necessitates a love for God, which in turn is founded upon a closeness to God. Our true knowledge of God is inseparable from a recognition of God's saving presence in our lives. Any and all knowledge of God comes from a love that responds to God's love already given, for "there is nothing that invites love more than to be loved first."[41] We can discover in ourselves a *caritas* that resists being reduced to our own weakened desires, a love of neighbor that we can, in turn, embrace as something received. That we love as we do is more than a sign of God's presence, it is the receiving of the gift of the Holy Spirit.

How Augustine's Analogies Mean

"It is probably not necessary to emphasise just how complex the *intellectus fidei* is in these final texts of *De Trinitate*," Basil Studer observes.[42] Rowan Williams seems to concur: "The later books of *De trin.*

40. Kolbet, *Cure of Souls*, 208.

41. Augustine, *Instructing Beginners in Faith*, trans. Raymond Canning, ed. Boniface Ramsey, The Works of St. Augustine: A Translation for the 21st Century (Hyde Park, NY: New City Press, 2006), 4.7. All English translations throughout are from this version.

are so laboured and so diffuse in their structure that it is extremely difficult to see how they form a single argument."[43] The so-called "mental analogies" of the second half of *De Trinitate* (often understood as "philosophically the most exciting part of the work" by modern interpreters[44]) threaten at all moments to lead the reader astray, either lost in Augustine's explication of trinity after trinity, comparing and contrasting the relationships inherent in each triad and among them, or concluding that Augustine is the legitimate father of the modern self-substantiating, self-possessed, self-thought self and therefore (so goes the argument) the scandalous and idolatrous prototype of which the Trinity is merely an image.[45] Studer continues, however, noting, "As is the case in so many other of his texts, here Augustine intimates that the more we love, the more we know, and that the more we know, the more we love the *Trinitas quae unus est Deus*."[46] The philosophical and purely epistemological content of these books are of less importance to this project than *how* these triads direct the reader to respond to the gift of love with a deepening understanding and love of God, and *why* Augustine might approach these books as he does[47]—that is, of *how* Augustine *means*.[48] Thus, this chapter focuses more on the Trinitarian and soteriological (and soteriological because Trinitarian) movements of love than on explicitly philosophical reflections on the nature of the human mind (although these two lines of thought, like most of Augustine's, cannot be cleanly separated).

Augustine has already warned his readers against a direct

42. Basil Studer, OSB, "History and Faith in Augustine's *De Trinitate*," *Augustinian Studies* 28 (1997): 26–27.
43. Williams, "*Sapientia* and the Trinity," 324.
44. Gareth B. Matthews, introduction to *On the Trinity, Books 8–15*, by Augustine (New York: Cambridge University Press, 2002), ix.
45. See Hanby, "Chapter 1: A Grim Paternity?," in *Augustine and Modernity*, 6–26.
46. Studer, "History and Faith," 26–27.
47. See Gioia: "From this moment onwards, it becomes evident that the aim of the patient and sustained unfolding of triadic structures or patterns in the human mind and in its activity of will and knowledge, is not only nor primarily the detection of the most perfect triad from a formal viewpoint, but the exploration of the situation of created beings with regards to their creator and of its epistemological consequences. Augustine does not look for *an* image of God, but *the* image of God." Gioia, *Theological Epistemology*, 227.
48. This phrasing is borrowed from Orson Scott Card, "How Tolkien Means," in *Meditations on Middle Earth*, ed. Karen Haber (New York: St. Martin's Press), 2001.

application of analogy. Books 6–7 lay out an explicit repudiation of any form of analogy relying upon the pairing of the divine persons and particular functions of created trinities. The very challenge at the heart of these books is how to discuss the divine persons in a way that ensures each as fully divine, avoiding ascribing any divine attribute to any particular person—his primary example being wisdom to the Son—thereby resulting in the absurdity that the other persons are not also wisdom itself by virtue of being God. Such an ascribing of specific functions to each of the divine persons is a woefully inadequate approach to the Trinity. Therefore, whether in an early sketch of a trinity—a drink of wine, water, and honey[49]—or in a more often referenced later one—the one mind's remembering, understanding, and willing itself[50]—Augustine is not laying out a one-to-one analogy of any three things to the Trinitarian life of God, saying that the Father can be compared to self-remembering, the Son to self-understanding, and the Spirit to self-willing. "Simply put," Ayres notes while excavating the foundation of Augustine's Trinitarian language, "Augustine *never* directly uses *analogia* or *proportio* to describe the relationship between God and any aspect of the creation (and interestingly neither term ever appears in [*De Trinitate*])."[51] The bishop not only does not use the terms to describe his work, but forbids such a use of analogy as an inappropriate and therefore dangerous formulation.[52]

What, then, is Augustine doing? Looking to the bishop's letters for insight into his approach, Ayres argues that the unity Augustine seeks to articulate is a very specific form of unity, not that of the one divine essence that renders superfluous and inconsequential any subsequent distinction of persons,[53] but that of the inseparable operation of the

49. Augustine, *De Trinitate*, 9.7.
50. Ibid., 10.18.
51. Lewis Ayres, "'Remember That You Are Catholic' (serm. 52.2): Augustine on the Unity of the Triune God," *Journal of Early Christian Studies* 8 (2000): 61.
52. Augustine, *De Trinitate*, 7.2.
53. Ayres cites John Zizioulas as a notable recent adherent of the textbook thesis that the Western theological tradition is shaped by beginning with the unity of God and then moving to the persons, while the Eastern begins with the three divine persons and moves to unity. Ayres, "Remember That You Are Catholic," 39–40. Importantly, Ayres reminds his readers that

divine persons. In epistle 11,[54] a letter Augustine wrote to his friend Nebridius around the year 389, the bishop of Hippo responds to the latter's question as to why it was the Son who became incarnate rather than the Father or the Holy Spirit. By maintaining the unity of inseparable operations, Augustine refines his friend's question to "ask not why the Son in particular becomes incarnate, but why we must speak *as if* the Son alone works in the Incarnation."[55] This distinction is significant in *De Trinitate* for three not unrelated reasons.

First, the roots of Augustine's analogies of Trinitarian unity point to inseparable operations rather than the fixed and hardened unity of essence, an accomplishment so often laid in its final form, rightly or wrongly, at the feet of neo-scholastics. As discussed in the previous chapter, Augustine certainly maintains that Father, Son, and Holy Spirit each are fully God, the essence of each being identical with the divine essence, distinctly referenced only in relationship with each other. But preceding and contextualizing this discussion in books 5–7, Augustine looks to the accounts of both the sending of the Son and Spirit in the New Testament and the other theophanic events recounted in the scriptures. To see in either case a particular divine person acting alone is precisely to miss the revelation as such, to miss God therein. The missions of the Son and Spirit are to reveal themselves as themselves, that is, as God from God, light from light, true God from true God. This doctrine of inseparable operations moves toward securing the Nicene faith that it is truly God we encounter in Jesus Christ and the Holy Spirit.

Second, this distinction is one between theological and spiritual language and the reality toward which that language is directed—that is, between *signa* and divine *res*. Caught in the impossibility of an unmediated access to a particular *res*, Augustine recognizes that

discussions of such a beginning point may lead readers "to envisage the existence of a body of theological works written in a physical order resembling some modern systematic theologies, or perhaps some styles of medieval treatise, from which it would supposedly be evident that a discussion of *De Deo Uno* physically *and* logically precedes *De Deo Trino*." Ibid., 42.

54. Augustine, "Letter 11" in *Letters: Vol. 1, No. 1-99*, trans. Roland Teske, ed. Boniface Ramsey, The Works of St. Augustine: A Translation of the 21st Century, vol. 2, no. 1 (Hyde Park, NY: New City Press, 2001). All English translations throughout are from this version.
55. Ayres, "Remember That You Are Catholic," 50.

revelation itself is a mediation of the divine life to the human, true to its source but eschatologically deferred in its fullness. Revelation is not a face-to-face encounter with the divine Trinity but one mediated in the incarnate Son, visible in Jesus Christ and the working of the Spirit in scriptural and communal witness.

Third, not so much despite this limit to language as because of it, Augustine maintains that it is only through such revelation that we might come to have our vision healed so that we can see God. Not only does such an approach speak from our limited human perspective, but it is also done for it. Our language about God, groping along in the dark is as dark does, serves our formation toward God. Ayres writes, "These separate operations are 'shaped' as separate and in a certain order or dispensation to educate and *move* our fallen human minds towards a perception of the inseparable Trinitarian action."[56] Seeing the Son and Spirit as God from God—and, as Augustine established, "from" does not necessitate any inequality[57]—means recognizing that the relational distinctions among Father, Son, and Holy Spirit embraced in this "from" are not simply the result of a limited human perspective but truly reveal God to us, thereby offering a path of healing through realigning our vision and reordering our love toward God. God and language about God—and the idea of God and the Trinity that God is—cannot be clearly separated for us who use this language to come to name God so as to call upon God by that name. Any modalistic tendencies here—and certainly a doctrine of inseparable operation can tend toward reduction of the divine persons to one monolithic agent—are tempered by *De Trinitate*'s first seven books, wherein Augustine works to establish the full divinity of the sent Son and Spirit through a sophisticated symphonic composition establishing the missions as revelatory of *God from God.*

Moreover, the ascending trinities that structure the second half of *De Trinitate* further serve this healing. Augustine is not merely searching for an adequate analogy through which our being created to the image

56. Ibid., 54; emphasis in original.
57. Augustine, *De Trinitate*, 4.25–32.

of God might be further understood, discarding each as a better is discovered. "Once again," Ayres writes, "the *exercitatio* of reading the mind as an image depends as much on a knowledge of that which we seek to understand as it does on a knowledge of the analogical site within which our minds are exercised."[58] It is the activity of the Son and Spirit—that is, the one activity of the one God—that makes present within us that which we seek to understand, forming and healing us in a process by which we grow to know the *res* that we would otherwise vainly hope to signify. Gioia observes:

> Comparisons in Augustine have a fluid character which sometimes make attempts to summarize them analytically very difficult. The reason for this is very simple: examples for him are not simply illustrations of a point, nor do they aim at grasping an ineffable reality by assimilating it to objects within our grasp. On the contrary, they reflect the constant attitude our mind must adopt in the presence of realities which infinitely surpass it, that is a constant availability to redefine parameters in order to cling as closely as possible to those imposed by the object.[59]

These comparisons serve to illuminate our memory, understanding, and love as they are and realign them more closely with the Trinity. Augustine is not seeking to discover or even restore in us a functioning nature or image by which we can then move toward God. We do not, cannot, come to God as first healed but are only healed in moving toward God. By the movement, we are healed. The only restoration possible, because the only one there is, is to be restored in the ordering of our love toward God. We are restored to our proper nature only as we are healed to the image of God.

The analogies explored are therefore analogies only metaphorically understood and are understandable only in light of the gift of love already present within us. They can serve us as a structure by which we might come to appreciate a play of distinction and unity. They can encourage us to look at memory, understanding, and love and endeavor to transcend the materiality that conditions the very activity of the mind. They can even invite reflection on reflexivity and direct

58. Ayres, *Augustine and the Trinity*, 288.
59. Gioia, *Theological Epistemology*, 177–78.

us to a deeper appreciation of what we might mean by a *sui generis* essence. But the relationships brought into relationship with each other through analogy cannot overcome the infinite distance marked by the analogical "as." For it is not in the illumination of the unified, three-part functioning of the human mind that we find a one-to-one analogy of the life of the Trinity. An analogy, in the technical sense, "implies to Augustine the possibility of our grasping the proportion between the terms involved,"[60] and unfortunately for all those putting all their theological stock in analogical *vestigia*, our grasping of such proportion requires both a sufficient understanding of the human mind and the life of God. Rather, the missions of the Son and Spirit are to reveal God as love (and in doing so, also love's being the foundation of creation) and to strengthen our faith in this love

Through Healed Creation to Healing Creator

This revelation also illuminates two interrelated, but distinct, "distances": the distance between our love as it should be and as it is (or between *caritas* and *cupiditas*, "the acquisitive compulsion we sometimes call love"[61]) and the distance between the reality of the divine life of love and our limited understanding of this life (between the divine Trinity and our understanding of the Trinity by means of various models of triunities). Augustine offers the incarnation itself as the key to an approach that recognizes both the insufficiency and the necessity (and perhaps the necessary insufficiency) of analogies from creation and the relationship between these two distinct distances. Ayres writes:

> Comprehending this doctrine is interwoven with comprehending the function of the Incarnation and the nature and purpose of Scripture. Augustine argues that understanding why we speak about the Incarnation as we do is only possible when we see *what* the Incarnation must accomplish and *how* it manages to accomplish that task. We need to see that the Incarnation is adapted to our need for differentiated speech and to our need for a form of life that will enable us to grow in knowledge and

60. Ayres, *Augustine and the Trinity*, 286.
61. Williams, "*Sapientia* and the Trinity," 323.

> love of God. Only by participating in this process of reformation will we be able to appreciate both the form of the Incarnation and hence the God who is therein revealed.[62]

As previously established,[63] it is only through the excessive sufficiency of *caritas* that we can come to see creation as lovingly created by God—that is, to relate each thing to its source and end and thus see each thing truly. This true vision is also the only means to see clearly our fallen sinfulness, the only way by which we can begin to comprehend the depth and breadth of our failures to love.

How do we, then, mark the distance between our love as it should be and our love as it is? Augustine's often repeated question, "Who can love what he does not know?" takes on a more ominous timbre in book 13 in his discussion of humankind's shared "will to obtain and retain happiness."[64] Here, there is both a desire—created in us as ordered toward God—and a thing desired—a happiness only to be found in God. But the restless desire for God in each person is distorted by a lack of faith, resulting in a conflict of desire and a perceived insubstantiality of the divine promise of peace. We can arrive at a fulfilled rest only by both having everything we want and wanting rightly. But such rest requires both faith in what we ought to desire and a steadfast love by which to cling to it and only it. Without such faith and love (and, it ought to be added, hope of reaching—or being reached by—such an end), we abandon our devotion to this end for which we are created and favor instead more immediately gratifying but ultimately unfulfilling goods.[65]

This lack of faith, this privation of the good, whispers to us and encourages us to seek fulfillment in the various and sundry goods we can acquire and retain. A weakened faith yields to impatience for fulfillment, twisting our desire toward an attempted full enjoyment of creation, rather than appreciating creation as ordering us toward God. This attempt seeks in creation a guaranteed happiness that is

62. Ayres, "Remember That You Are Catholic," 55; emphasis in original.
63. See chapter 1.
64. Augustine, *De Trinitate*, 13.7.
65. Ibid., 13.9.

not there. The fundamental activity of sin is not a simple attempted enjoyment of those things we ought to use but the disorder of use toward something other than God and the seeking of our proper end elsewhere than with our Creator. That is to say, it is a lack of devotion to our proper end that leads to the search for ultimate happiness within creation. The desire for God at the heart of each person as made to the image of God is corrupted through seeking its end in finite goods. Disordered love is always also disorientated love.[66]

Insofar as it is ungrounded in *caritas*, this happiness remains an abstraction, inaccessible because it is not a real *res* at all. As love is always a "love of," a "love of happiness" falls prey to the very distortion that marked Augustine's youthful "love of love"—a pursuit of happiness through the acquisition and consumption of good things within a context bracketing, or severed from, God. Free from the measure such a context affords, we hope to find an infinite fulfillment in the goodness of things while ignoring the Good itself. We hope to acquire happiness abstracted from its source. The good things are consumed in an appetite for happiness, leaving the soul all the more restless, all the more twisted in its seeking yet more happiness. Adam Kotsko offers a helpful description of this process:

> In its attempt at possession, [the mind] misses the things themselves and derives its pleasure instead from images of them that have been formed out of "its own substance" (10.7). In this way the mind becomes infinitely impoverished, losing not only God but also the beautiful things that it initially desired to have apart from God—though it never loses itself. The preservation of the mind itself, even in the situation of *cupiditas*, testifies to the fact that what is at stake here is not the destruction of the mind but a perversion of the mind's proper state.[67]

Not fully destroyed, we continue to seek yet another taste of fulfillment, always trying in vain to possess and hold those things whose nature is to direct us onward toward God, to hold tightly to the expectation that peace and fulfillment can be won through the

66. "An alternative form of desire . . . is also an alternative truth." Hanby, *Augustine and Modernity*, 178.
67. Adam Kotsko, "Gift and *Communio*: The Holy Spirit in Augustine's *De Trinitate*," *Scottish Journal of Theology* 64, no. 1 (2011): 9.

ownership and consumption of those things that ought to direct our attention toward the love of God and love of neighbor.

Sin, as Augustine presents it in *De Trinitate*, is a distortion of received goods into possessed goods, of goods that ought to serve love into the object of love: "That is why greed is called the root of all evils."[68] But in the context of book 12's elaboration of the distinction between wisdom and knowledge, he goes a step further. Indeed, at the heart of our spiritual sickness is the lust to possess, to have in reserve, to control as ours, those things given to us as means of signifying love. Like the hermeneutic that guides the Christian reading of the scriptures, the interpretation of each created thing must be done in light of the call to *caritas*. But the sickness tormenting us is not fundamentally misreading of the temporal order—it is not merely mistaken or insufficient knowledge. It is the rejection of a shared truth, of a common possession of the higher things.[69] It is not any particular good thing, material or spiritual, that in itself is endemic of our sickness, but the severing of the good from its context and the refusal to see it as a sign of God's extravagant love. Seeing what is given to us as *ours* as exclusively *mine* and directing it toward my own pleasure is a rejection of the truth of creation as much as a selfish and avaricious act.

Not simply the breaking of a moral rule or religious standard, such self-interested possession effects a change within us, perpetuating our sickness and quickening the decay of our love. For as it clings, such love loses its nature and is increasingly hollowed into *cupiditas*. What both *caritas* and *cupiditas* seem to have in common is that they both serve as the soul's weight, directing the soul toward that which is desired. But as such direction is not material but spiritual, the attracted movement of the soul is one of transformation—the direction is not incidental to the movement. As we draw closer to that which we desire (here, through either *caritas* or *cupiditas*), our memory, understanding, and love increasingly resemble that which we most desire. This love makes us in the image of that which we love. Augustine writes, "Yet such is

68. Augustine, *De Trinitate*, 12.14.
69. Ibid., 12.14.

the force of love that when the mind has been thinking about things with love for a long time and has got stuck to them with the glue of care, it drags them along with itself even when it returns after a fashion to thinking about itself. . . . So it wraps up their images and clutches them to itself, images made in itself out of itself."[70] *Cupiditas*, though directional like *caritas*, is only disguised as love.

To love in the true sense of the word—that is to love at all—requires that we attend to our having been created to the image of God. Love in any other context threatens our own spiritual disfigurement through self-indulgent lust to possess. Seemingly trivial grasping, followed by an easily rationalized possession and attempted enjoyment, masks a spiritual autoerotism that, despite its promises, leads to an exhausted and unfulfilled parody of happiness. Comparing such a lust for possession to sexual sin, Augustine writes:

> But when the soul, greedy for experience or for superiority or for the pleasure of physical contact, does something to obtain the things that are sensed through the body to the extent of setting its end and its proper good in them, then whatever it does it does basely and *commits fornication, sinning against its own body* (1 Cor 6:18). It drags the deceptive semblances of bodily things inside, and plays about with them in idle meditation until it cannot even think of anything divine except as being such, and so in its private avarice it is loaded with error and in its private prodigality it is emptied of strength. Nor would it come down at a single jump to such a base and wretched fornication, but as it is written, *He who despises trifles will fall away little by little* (Sir 19:1).[71]

Though consummated through a series of ostensibly small actions, this *cupiditas* exhausts and empties us of our orientation to our proper end and in doing so, imprisons us in the very creation intended to signify our being made for God.

But why do we not recognize this lie in the form of a promise, this wolf in sheep's clothing that devours us even as vowing our

70. Ibid., 10.7.

71. Ibid., 12.15. Although in his retractions (Augustine, *The Retractions*, trans Sister M. Inez Bogan, RSM [Washington, DC: Catholic University of America Press, 1999], 147), Augustine will back away from such a figurative interpretation of Paul, the point of the passage nevertheless remains the same. Such a lust for possession is akin to the self-indulgence of idle fornication and just as empty.

fulfillment? In the substitution of abstract happiness for a loving relationship with God, we replace a received *caritas* with supposed happiness found elsewhere than in our relationship with God and neighbor. Unmoored from loving relationship—often disturbed by the sacrifices required of such relationship—this happiness is sought in the only place left: the self.[72] But a "self" without its constituting orientation toward God is a contradiction in nature. Like a nightmarish mythical torture for the gluttonous in Hades, wherein each taste promising fulfillment leaves the consumer hungrier than before, the never fully destroyed soul becomes an ever increasingly misshapen idol. Of such self-worship, Cavadini writes:

> The soul aware of itself in this way is *an inverted image* because its remembering, understanding and loving are so formed that it knows, understands and loves *God*, in effect, as the image, and *itself* as the reality. . . . If the phrase 'the self' has any warrant for use in Augustine, it would be for this prideful soul which has reified itself as the ultimate *res* for which even God has become a signifier. If "The Self" corresponds to anything in Augustine, it is this reified structure of pride, an attractive illusion, but ultimately a self-contradiction, doomed to eternal incoherence.[73]

This inversion is delineated not by the turn inward (as for Augustine, the inward turn initiates an upward movement to God) but by refusal to recognize and respond with openness to the already present otherness within—that is, to refuse that which is received in preference to that which is merited, controlled, or possessed. It is a rejection of "something that is present to me, and it is present to me even if I am not what I perceive"[74] in favor of the perverse worship of the self.

The only alternative is faith in Jesus Christ as God from God, as a revelation of God as love, and as the mediator of all meaning and

72. For a contextualizing study as to what degree the word "self," with its complex philosophical history, might be an accurate translation of the proximate object of Augustine's inward contemplation, see Brian Stock, "Self, Soliloquy, and Spiritual Exercises in Augustine and Some Later Authors," *The Journal of Religion* 91, no. 1 (2011): 5–23.
73. Cavadini, "The Darkest Enigma," 127.
74. Augustine, *De Trinitate*, 8.4.

value in creation. "Nothing was more needed," Augustine writes, "than a demonstration of how much value God put on us and how much he loved us,"[75] and God revealed that love—that is, God revealed Godself—in the sending of the Son. That the only way to truly love each good thing—whether one's own self, another, or any material object—is to order our use of it toward strengthening our love of God, requires of us that we have faith enough for the ordering of our love. Such faith in the potency, pervasiveness, and significance of love is faith in Christ as the omnipotent, omniscient, and creator God.

In his most explicitly soteriological section of *De Trinitate*,[76] Augustine exhibits some tendencies of his time, grounding the efficacy of Christ's saving sacrifice in a double enactment of justice. In turning away from God, we were deservingly held captive by our sins, lawfully imprisoned by the devil. But in overreaching his rights and in killing the one without sin, the devil forfeited his custody of us and was overcome not by power but by divine justice.[77] Christ's divinity is revealed in his obedience to God, going to death on the cross as an innocent man and shattering the devil's chains.[78]

But Augustine's conventional soteriological structure does not exhaust its significance. Christ's justification of sinners comes not through his appeasement of a God seeking just retribution from human beings but is an act of God—an inseparable operation of the divine persons—of which we speak as if only the Son were directly involved. The Doctor of Grace is clear that salvation is the gift of God: "Would the Father have not spared his own Son but handed him over for us, if he had not already been reconciled?" He continues, "I observe that the Father loved us not merely before the Son died for us, but before he founded the world."[79] The sending of the Son was the initiation of a salvation brought about through justice. However, this justice,

75. Ibid., 13.13.
76. Ibid., 13.13–23; this section is an echo of the christological discussion in book 4, ordered to the explication of the distinction between wisdom and knowledge, unlike the earlier defense of the sent Son's equality with the sending Father.
77. Especially ibid., 13.21.
78. Ibid., 13.18.
79. Ibid., 13.15.

Augustine's context makes clear, is not an abstract structure imposed on the world but is grounded in Christ's right will—that is, God's always already active love of sinners.[80] The power to save follows upon the just will of Jesus Christ because both salvation and power proceed from God's love. Here is the measure of the distance between our fallen love and *caritas*: our conformity to the image to which we are made—through, with, and in whom we receive the gift of love that has the power to overcome such distance. "For man's true honor is God's image and likeness in him," Augustine writes, "but it can only be preserved when facing him from whom its impression is received."[81] Kolbet adds, "The treatment prescribed for our souls is one that Christ the physician endured himself before our very eyes."[82]

Thus it is not by the mind's self-reflection that the image of the Trinity can be found. It is not in purified self-remembering, self-understanding, and self-loving that we enact a trinity analogous to God. And the very attempt to locate the image of God in a manner free from God's gift of saving love, to "insist arrogantly on leaping over the healing process in order to begin with vision itself,"[83] not only is insufficient but is itself in direct contrast to the gift of love. That "there is such potency in this image of God in it that it is capable of cleaving to him whose image it is,"[84] directs us not to our "growing in [our] own nature, truth, and happiness,"[85] ordering and measuring the meaning and value of the world and we see fit, but toward conforming ourselves to the one whose image we bear, conforming ourselves to Jesus Christ, who is God from God.

It should be noted that the daily transferal of "love from temporal things to eternal, from visible to intelligible, from carnal to spiritual things,"[86] is not only an ongoing process of healing but is directed toward finally being healed and formed to God. Christ's ordering of

80. Ibid., 13.21.
81. Ibid., 13.16.
82. Kolbet, *Cure of Souls*, 172.
83. Ibid.
84. Augustine, *De Trinitate*, 14.20.
85. Ibid.
86. Ibid., 14.23.

his own will to the *caritas* of God—through his life, certainly, and culminating on the cross, specifically—does not find its end in death, however willingly accepted. While our knowledge of God may be "as in a mirror darkly"[87] and our formation toward wisdom a long process, the conformity to the loving life and death Christ promises a conformity in resurrection. It is only this promise that makes rational a life lived in *caritas*. On this, Augustine is clear. He concludes book 14 with a criticism of Cicero's *Hortensius*—the very book that set young Augustine on fire in a new desire for wisdom. In it, Augustine reads Cicero as impacted by the doubts of the Academicians, foolishly trusting the promise of happiness found in the "contemplation of the truth"[88]: that an expected "cheerful sunset" will conclude a life lived in pursuit of what is often called wisdom.[89] Such optimism in the potential reach of the unaided human mind is mocked by the experienced reality of death, disintegration, and decay. Wisdom is only to be found in, thus should only be sought in, the full vision of God—who, Augustine discusses, *is* wisdom.[90] Our perfection as image is received in our completed formation to the one by, for, and to whom we are created. Our knowledge of God perfectly coincides with the full vision of God—only fully given and received in becoming "immortal after the manner of Christ,"[91] that is, in resurrection.

Only resurrection liberates love from romanticism, tragedy, and nostalgia by uniting our love with its true source in God and thereby rendering it efficacious. Less a guarantee that the sacrifices of love are ultimately "worth it," assuring a heavenly reward for earthly investment, here the resurrection makes it reasonable to have faith in Christ's being *God from God*. A life lived in imitation of Christ's is revealed to be the life by which our being made to the image of God is realized. The resurrection makes love into something far more charitable than kindness, something stronger than passion, and

87. 1 Cor 13:12 referenced in Augustine, *De Trinitate*, 14.23.
88. Augustine, *De Trinitate*, 14.26.
89. Ibid.
90. Ibid., book 6.
91. Ibid., 14.24–25.

unfetters it from vain self-destruction. It is not an overstatement to say that the resurrection frees love from idolatry. "The image of God will achieve its full likeness of him when it attains to the full vision of him,"[92] Augustine writes, uniting our formative devotion to the God of love to the reality of who God is. Our proper understanding of love, then, finds its beginning and end in the mystery of God and in nowhere else. The resurrection reveals a real and fundamental relationship between the love revealed in Christ and the truth about who God is and thereby proclaims the ultimate incompatibility of such revealed love and of death as the end of possibility and meaning. The distance of love, between where we are and the image to which we are made, when measured by the resurrected Christ in and through our sharing in his resurrection, is transformed into the very means of salvation. It is only in the resurrection that the gift of love is made complete.

Caritas and *cupiditas*, while both "weights" moving the soul, differ in their direction. *Caritas* is responsive to the anteceded gift of Jesus Christ and therefore brings us into relation with him. While the fulfillment of this relationship is eschatologically deferred, we are nevertheless brought to love God and neighbor here and now. *Cupiditas* breaks our understanding of creation (both material and conceptual) from the guiding hermeneutic given in and through Christ, reducing what is given to us to something that I hold to be exclusively mine. This lust for possession disallows deferral and thereby disavows signification, leaving me only with, and to, myself.

Along with the distance between *caritas* and *cupiditas*, there is a second interruptive distance between the God of love and our understanding of that God—an understanding that only comes through creation. Augustine begins book 15 assuring his readers that the time and effort spent in study and contemplation of the first fourteen books have not been fruitless. The slow, step-by-step journey through "various trinities of different sorts until we eventually arrive at the mind of man" is not a vain intellectual exercise. Looking at creation serves as a means for coming to know the Creator, significantly here

92. Ibid., 14.24.

in the manner in which creation's analogical limits are marked by the transcendence of the gift of love. Seemingly against this, he insists that the reception of this gift, by which we lessen our greed and bind ourselves with charity to God, "depends on divine assistance"[93] and is only received through the power of the gift itself. Kolbet observes:

> It is important to note that scripture is no *deus ex machina* in this process of renewal, as if it could mechanistically cure the soul as a kind of efficient cause. . . . Augustine preached to his congregation, "We cannot love God except through the Holy Spirit." "Since the Holy Spirit is God, let us love God with God." He explained, "To love God is even a gift of God. . . . Through this Spirit we love both the Father and the Son, and this Spirit we love together with the Father and the Son." The only unforgivable sin was to resist the Spirit's persuasion, to reject this love.[94]

But just as the scriptures are no *deus ex machina*, neither is the Holy Spirit. Taken on their own, statements about the necessity of the Spirit can lead to an interpretation of this graced activity as precisely a mechanical cause—that as we cannot be saved without God, grace is therefore a foreign force imposing itself through a violent reconfiguration of our hearts. However, such divine assistance is not unrelated to the continued movement of the soul toward God. The process of movement toward God is the salvific activity of God, present fundamentally through the formation of our love. Love and only love opens us to knowledge of the Trinity—an entrance first appearing clearly in book 8—because God is love.[95] For the way toward remembrance, understanding, and loving the Trinity who God is, is itself the always already presence of God. We are only formed to the image of God in the continuing reception of the gift of love. It is not, finally, in a triune nature of the human mind that we come to see the image the triune nature of God, because love is not part of who God is, as it is for human beings—God, each divine person, is love.[96]

Thus the distance between how we love and the *caritas* that is God

93. Ibid., 14.23.
94. Kolbet, *Cure of Souls*, 192.
95. Augustine, *De Trinitate*, 15.10.
96. Ibid., 15.11–12.

is redoubled in the distance between the God of love and our understanding and love of that love. As Augustine suggests that knowledge of God is knowledge of our love, so the ways in which the fullness of love is well beyond our comprehension echo the ineffability of God. Each distance is itself incomprehensible for three reasons, which in turn can be reduced to one.

Augustine's own narrative questions the wisdom of claiming to understand the depths of one's own motivations and decisions, to claim to therefore be able to live in utter consistency with one's desired good. Having become a mystery to himself,[97] both finitude and sin weighed heavily upon him, the latter perverting the former, each then turning his heart toward those things that imprisoned him even while promising freedom.[98] An understanding of God seems all the more distant when we consider that even wrapping our mind around our own love is, itself, a daunting task: Augustine asks, "How, I say, can any man comprehend this wisdom, which is simultaneously prudence, simultaneously knowledge, seeing that we cannot even comprehend our own?"[99] Made toward the image of God but with movement impeded by the weight of distorted desire, we find that the point of reference by which we might begin to understand ourselves is obscured by that distortion leaving us lost in the self.

Second, infinitely complicating the matter is the mystery of God. It should be no surprise that even at this late point in the text, we return to its raison d'être, as seeking knowledge of that in whom "knowing and being are the same"[100] is the experience from, and for, which Augustine composed *De Trinitate*. Yet, as Augustine holds to the scriptural distinctions of Father, Son, and Spirit, while at the same time maintaining a unity by which "the Son is powerfully unable to do anything but what the Father does,"[101] the significance of this repeated

97. Augustine, *Confessions*, 6.6.9, 10.33.50.
98. For an insightful Heideggerian analysis of the relationship between the weight of the burden of finite life and that of the sinful life, see Emmanuel Falque, "Saint Augustine: The Weight of Life—Sin and Finitude" (paper presented at "Phenomenology and Theology in Contemporary French Thought: Lectures and Colloquium," University of California, Santa Barbara, May 3–6, 2011).
99. Augustine, *De Trinitate*, 15.13.
100. Ibid., 15.23.

proclamation has added to it the authority that only an arduous and rigorous climb confers. This authority Augustine now shares with readers who have committed themselves to the pursuit of a deeper understanding of the transcendence on display in the text's Trinitarian ascent. The Augustinian maxim holds true even at the heights of *De Trinitate*: to come to know the God who is more intimate to me than I am to myself and higher than my highest height requires that I turn into myself with the precision, clarity, and searing purity of love. But this turn inward gains such precision, clarity, and purity only as it is empowered by the love of God—here such "love of God" acts as both a subjective and an objective genitive with the former conditioning and allowing the latter.

Third, the transcendence of God renders the distance between either our love and divine *caritas*, or our understanding and the Trinity who God is ultimately incomprehensible (although not utterly inaccessible). There is no neutral place at which we might stand to come to see either where we stand or the reality of God. There is no place from which to observe, comment, and analyze without commitment and the corresponding openness to conversion. We can only see by means of our own gaze, but there is nowhere from which we might see that gaze.[102] We are freed from such feigned neutrality by the gift of love so that we might turn to God. Augustine cannot get beyond or beneath his own mind; he is unable to see his own mind with a reflexive gaze that is not already the activity of the mind. Augustine observes: "And what makes the enigma all the more puzzling is that we should be unable to see what we cannot not see. Who fails to see his own thoughts? And on the other hand who does see his own thoughts—and I do not mean with the eyes of flesh but with the inner gaze? Who fails to see them and who does see them?"[103] But in seeing this enigma, the bishop does not thereby end his Trinitarian pursuit in failure. For failure to achieve complete and perfect knowledge of the Trinity—like such a failure of self-knowledge—is a means, and here the only means, by which the

101. Ibid.
102. See Ayres, *Augustine and the Trinity*, 306.
103. Augustine, *De Trinitate*, 15.16.

reality of the love of God might actually take hold within us as it reveals to us the reality of who we are. Cavadini concludes:

> The content of self-awareness, for those truly self-aware, is much more disturbing and mysterious, more exciting and hopeful, more treacherous and full of risk. Someone who is self-aware is aware not of "a self" but of a struggle, a brokenness, a gift, a process of healing, a resistance to healing, an emptiness, a reference that impels one not to concentrate on oneself, in the end, but on that which one's self-awareness propels on, to God.[104]

Such a self-awareness—defined in terms of limit—is, for Augustine, a wonder and relief:

> It is a relief in this kind of difficulty and frustration to cry out to the living God, "*Your knowledge is too wonderful for me; it is might and I cannot attain it* (Ps 139:6) From myself indeed I understand how wonderful and incomprehensible is your knowledge with which you have made me, seeing that I am not even able to comprehend myself whom you have made, and yet *a fire burns up in my meditation* (Ps 39:3), causing me to seek your face always.[105]

The only way forward, because the only way there is, is to be conformed in love to the image to which we are made. Who we are is found only in the one to whom we are going.

Thus, in *De Trinitate*'s final book, Augustine returns to the gift of the Holy Spirit, now with significantly more structure in place by which to contextualize and reveal—always only with relative adequacy—the true nature of this gift. It is of no little significance that he concludes *De Trinitate* with this reflection on the gift of love and its effect on our coming to know God by being formed to the image of God. For in the end, the inadequacy of knowledge of the Trinity does not ultimately

104. Cavadini, "The Darkest Enigma," 123. See also Augustine's articulation of this in his sermons: "We are not now discussing, brothers and sisters, possible ways of understand the text. . . . It can only be understood in ways beyond words; human words cannot suffice for understanding the Word of God. . . . But in any case, it wasn't read in order to be understood, but in order to make us mere human beings grieve because we don't understand it, and make us try to discover what prevents our understanding, and so move it out of the way, and hunger to grasp the unchangeable Word, ourselves thereby being changed from worse to better." Augustine, "Sermon 117," in *Sermons 94A–147A*, trans. Edmund Hill, OP, ed. John E. Rotelle, The Works of St. Augustine: A Translation for the 21st Century, vol. 3, no. 4 (Hyde Park, NY: New City Press, 1992).

105. Augustine, *De Trinitate*, 15.13.

frustrate Augustine's desire to love God. Rather, when approached through faith and contextualized by his analysis of the weight of love, the mystery of God fosters and quickens love. "We can embrace more than we know"[106]—in fact, in this approach to God, the only embrace possible lies beyond that which we know. The possibility of such an embrace turns upon the gift of the Holy Spirit: "In order that faith might work through love, *the charity of God has been poured into our hearts through the Holy Spirit which has been given to us* (Rom. 5:5)."[107] This gift of love is illuminated both in examination of its being a gift and as precisely a gift of love—while in the end, each points directly to the other.

It is the gift's being love that defines it specifically as gift. While the gift is the "common charity by which the Father and the Son love each other"[108]—here a distinctive mark of it being the Holy Spirit[109]—Augustine maintains, too, that "God is charity."[110] The ontological inseparability of the Trinity, the related inseparability of Trinitarian activity, and the irreducibility of any name of God to one particular person (save, of course, Father and Son and related names) support the status of the Holy Spirit as revelatory of God. In revealing itself as love, it reveals both itself to be God and God to be love. Christian faith is a belief and trust in love as "God from God."[111] It is for this reason that "even faith is only rendered of any use for the purpose by charity,"[112] not for any weakness on the part of faith, but by the very nature of a faith in the God who is love and, therefore, in love as the only way to God, for "this form and truth cannot be loved and appreciated according to the standard of anything else."[113] It is this

106. Foster, "Augustine's *De Trinitate*," 268.
107. Augustine, *De Trinitate*, 13.14.
108. Ibid., 15.27.
109. Ibid., 15.29.
110. Ibid., 15.27.
111. Ibid., 15.31.
112. Ibid., 15.32.
113. Ibid., 8.9. See also: "So the love which is from God and is God is distinctively the Holy Spirit; through him the charity of God is poured out in our hearts, and through it the whole triad dwells in us. This is the reason why it is most apposite that the Holy Spirit, while being God, should also be called the gift of God. And this gift, surely, is distinctively to be understood as being the charity which bring us through to God, without which no other gift of God at all can being us through to God." Ibid., 15.32.

love that cannot be taken, commanded, or compelled; this love that by its very nature can only be given. The giver, what is given, why it is given, and the act of giving are revealed to be different articulations of the one love that the Trinity is. So unified, too, is the formative effect of the gift: "So it is the Holy Spirit of which he has given us that makes us abide in God and him in us. But this is precisely what love does. He then is the gift of God who is love."[114]

We can never achieve knowledge of this formative mystery abstracted from the received gift given and revealed in and through the Son and Spirit, for this knowledge is not informative but performative.[115] This knowledge cannot be received without effecting a change upon the receiver, cannot be anticipated in full before it is given, and cannot be longed for without its already being present.

114. Ibid., 15.31.
115. Cf. Benedict XVI, *Spe Salvi* (encyclical letter, Rome, November 30, 2007), http://tinyurl.com/jntob2v.

Conclusion to Part One

It is my intention that part 1 presents *De Trinitate* in light of two primarily complementary contexts. First, contemporary scholarship on *De Trinitate* (and that on Augustine in general) has shed the cumbersome weight of the long-standing dominant interpretation of the text as one burdened by the presentation of the Trinity made in the image of the three faculties of the one human mind. Instead, the text can be read as an illuminating study of "how we come to knowledge of God, how we become wise."[1] In this way, *De Trinitate* offers rational inquiry into the God's healing and saving activity in our lives—an activity that plays out in our theological concepts, certainly, but also, and more fundamentally, within our hearts. Second, reason's inability to present the Trinity does not, as such, indicate a theological failure but rather an opening to God's self-revelation in and through the missions of the Son and Holy Spirit. If the Trinity cannot be signified without our already in some way knowing it, then to know it depends first upon its already being present within us, upon its already being given to us through the gift of love that is poured into our hearts. It is this openness before mystery that the more properly conceptual journey illuminates. It is my hope that part 1 brings together the insights of these fresh readings of *De Trinitate* under the banner of the gift of love, highlighting how this gift is everywhere present in the text's argument and argumentation, and underlies the structure

1. Gioia, *Theological Epistemology*, 289.

of *De Trinitate* itself. It is my conviction that *De Trinitate* is in this way soteriological in its pedagogical and pastoral concerns, examining as it does the gift of love, which itself is a matter of God's always already working out our salvation amidst (and despite) our fear and trembling.

However, as I observed, to speak of this gift as simply solving the problem of signification, giving to us what we otherwise cannot achieve (as one might be given the answer to a question that he or she could not have possibly known) is to see it as a *deus ex machina*. Knowledge of the Trinity is not given as other data are given, taught as a brute fact to be categorized and memorized, or even given as a beautiful vision to be cherished as it takes our breath away in wonder. Rather, if the Trinity is revealed to us in and through this gift, it must be done so in a way that forms us, in a way that makes love present in a way that it was not previously present, making us into people that we previously were not—it must make us in the image to which we are created. It must be given in a way so as to make love incarnate within us, to be given so indelibly and intimately to us so as to become determinative of who we are.

Bridging (Rather than Abridging) Distance

Why turn now to Marion for an investigation into love's incarnation? In hindsight, perhaps, this question might sound unnecessary. The question of the "postmodern Augustine" has been discussed for decades now (we might mention the notable conferences "Religion and Postmodernism 3: Confessions" at Villanova University in 2001 and "Augustine and Postmodern Thought: A New Alliance Against Modernity" at Leuven in 2006), and, even granting legitimacy to the criticisms of his phenomenology, Marion is part of the postmodern philosophical conversation (at least, in most of the ways that that terribly ambiguous term, "postmodern," might be understood). And with Marion's publishing of *Au lieu de soi* in 2008, the movement here from a fourth-century North African bishop to a twenty-first-century French philosopher appears to be not so much a leap as an almost calm and sensible crossing. But this crossing would not have necessarily appeared as the next logical step before Jacques Derrida's 1989 composition of *Circumfession*, "a journal he kept as his mother lay dying in Nice, like Monica in Ostia, creating an odd and beautiful dialogue with Augustine."[2] Soon, other postmodern engagements with Augustine would be published, some, perhaps, inspired by Derrida, others perhaps the result of a happy coincidence of interest.[3] This postmodern revival of Augustine may explain why Marion might have had Augustine on his mind as he prepared for the 2004 lectures he gave at the Institute Catholique de Paris, lectures that would inspire *Au lieu de soi*.

Alongside and intertwined with this attention to Augustine is a curious interest in the possibility of the gift—again energized by Derrida and this time directly engaged by Marion.[4] But where the revived interest in Augustine needs little help to attract the attention of theologians, an analysis of the gift, particularly arising from an anthropological study of gift exchange in so-called archaic cultures,[5] may not immediately entice theological consideration. Derrida's early significant writing on the gift came with *Donner le temps* (1991) and *Donner la mort* (1992). And while Marion had long investigated the concepts of givenness and gift at the porous border of philosophy and theology—notably in *L'Idole et la Distance* (1977) and *Dieu sans l'être* (1982)—John Milbank brought the question of the gift into an explicitly theological context with "Can a Gift Be Given? Prolegomena to a Future Metaphysic" (1995).[6]

Milbank's analysis of the possibility of the gift moves from a study of the work of Derrida and Marion to the Christian concept of *agape*,

2. John D. Caputo and Michael J. Scanlon, eds., introduction to *Augustine and Postmodernism: Confessions and Circumfession* (Bloomington: Indiana University Press, 2005), 3.
3. Caputo and Scanlon mention as significant: the publishing of Heidegger's 1921 course "Augustine and Neoplatonism" (1995); the English translation of Hannah Arendt's doctoral dissertation, *Love and Saint Augustine* (1996); Jean-François Lyotard's *The Confession of Augustine* (1998); and Augustine's influence on Paul Ricoeur. One might speculate that this revived interest is supported theologically as well, particularly in the work and prominence of Joseph Ratzinger.
4. See chapter 7.
5. Marcel Mauss, *The Gift: The Form and Reason for Exchange in Archaic Societies*, trans. W. D. Halls (New York: W.W. Norton, 1990). *Essai sur le Don* was first published in 1950.
6. John Milbank, "Can a Gift Be Given? Prolegomena to a Future Trinitarian Metaphysic," *Modern Theology* 11, no. 1 (1995): 119–61.

via Heidegger's "immanentist parody of the Augustinian account of the participation of temporal relationality in the relations of the Trinity,"[7] and the perceived influence of this parody upon *L'Idole et la Distance.* While I will briefly consider Milbank's criticism of Marion in chapter 8, here it is helpful to note that Milbank explicitly takes up the question of the place of the philosophically articulated gift within Trinitarian theology. He traces the appearance of the gift through the scriptures, observing that gift exchange (paradigmatically given in the covenant between God and the Hebrews[8]) serves to unite God's people across distinctions, differences, and distances into a community marked by the "full realization of the covenanted fiction of 'one blood.'"[9] This gift exchange occurs within the church, wherein each person "receives gift *as* the gift of an always preceding gift-exchange."[10] In so doing, gift exchange creates the church:

> We are . . . given the *possibility* to love because we are given the true shape of love in the form of a love that is always already repeated, in a double sense—both within the series of Christ's continuous and coherent actions, and in the series of exchanges between him and his followers. To be a Christian is *not*, as piety supposes, spontaneously and freely to love, or one's own originality and without necessarily seeking any communion. On the Contrary, it is to *repeat differently*, in order to repeat, *exactly*, the content of Christ's life, and to wait, by a necessary *delay*, the answering repetition of the other that will fold temporal linearity back into the eternal circle of the triune life.[11]

Although I will take issue with Milbank's emphasis on the purified exchange of gifts and his reading of Marion, I will gratefully ride the momentum of his analysis that leads him to understand the gift as always already received within the church—that is, received in and as an interpersonal or communal event. If it is not to lead to nihilism, the gift cannot be separated from love and, theologically understood, love always receives itself from the Trinitarian God who is love.

7. Ibid., 139.
8. Ibid., 145.
9. Ibid., 149.
10. Ibid., 150; emphasis in original.
11. Ibid.; emphases in original.

Yet, if we are to see the Trinity in and through love,[12] we must yet see love. There must be something given to us, something present to us, that we might embrace as love. Love must be concretized and existentialized.[13] Augustine powerfully and masterfully argues that God is revealed to us through, with, and in this gift of love. Yet how the phenomenon of love appears (and appears and is known to us *as mystery*) is far from clear. What Paul van Geest observed about Augustine's apophatic approach to the healing relationship between God and human beings in *De Trinitate* might be specifically focused on the gift of love: if "Augustine indicates that God's activity has a curative effect, but that he does not know exactly how this activity is best described,"[14] so, too, we might say that Augustine does not exactly know how best to describe how this gift of love is made incarnate in our lives. We might observe that we "catch fire"[15] with a love that moves us, but indeed we hope to be able to name that love, to praise that love, to love that love. It is for this reason, ultimately, that I turn now to Marion. Not, to be sure, because he and Augustine both discuss "gift," (to whatever degree Augustine's concept might be echoed in Marion's) but because Marion's phenomenology of gift grows from, and leads to, his analysis of the phenomenon of love. It is my hope that an investigation into *how love appears as given to us* might further Augustine's insight and illuminate what is perhaps inchoate in both *De Trinitate* and in the Christian faith in the Trinitarian God of love. Therefore, if it is the God of love we wish to know, then it is love that we must come to know, and know not as an object but as that which is incarnated within our flesh, within the very transformation of ourselves into lovers.

12. Augustine, *De Trinitate*, 8.12.
13. Cf. Hill, *The Trinity*, 239.
14. Paul van Geest, *The Incomprehensibility of God: Augustine as a Negative Theologian* (Walpole, MA: Peeters, 2011), 154.
15. Augustine, *De Trinitate*, 8.13.

PART II

Jean-Luc Marion and the Question of the Unconditioned God

5

[For]giving Theology its Groundlessness

God's action is antecedent to ours.
—The Society of Jesus, General Congregation 34

"One must obtain forgiveness for every essay in theology. In all senses."[1] This, because Marion understands theology to be a responsive discipline, demands that we speak beyond our means, speak another's words, and speak for another (and even to speak against ourselves if necessary).[2] The end of theology to which each essay is ordered demands that the theologian abandon all pretense of speaking both authentically (of speaking for oneself and of oneself) and about the divine (as though God were an object of study). To the degree that such so-called authentic discourse marks one's theology—that I speak *for* myself, *as* myself, *about* God—it is not theology at all but, at best, an exercise in spiritual anthropology or, at worst, an impatient stand at the foot of another Mount Sinai, melting down our treasures to be poured into the awaiting cast.[3] Rather, Marion's understanding of

1. Jean-Luc Marion, *God Without Being*, trans. Thomas A. Carlson (Chicago: University of Chicago Press, 1991), 2.
2. Ibid.
3. Marion notes the difference between these two general types of discourse in various ways: At times, he speaks of ontotheology (the subjugation of theology in and through the terms of being)

theology requires the theologian to relinquish any claim to such so-called authentic language and instead open themselves to the message and claim of the revealed word of God.

To hear the word of God as it is given and not as I want to receive it: this is a formidable, if not impossible, process indeed, seemingly ignoring the insights of hermeneutics and pursuing a pure uninterpreted message.[4] However, Marion claims to speak not of purely unmediated phenomena but of phenomena that appear in excess of antecedent mediating structures. The stakes of the success of Marion's theological turn, and of any subsequent theological appropriation of his work, are therefore high (one might even say excessive), speaking as they do to and of the very heart of theology itself: what it is, what it hopes to say, and whom it hopes to praise—that is, a response to the word of God, to denominate God, to speak (to) God. In such speech, in such naming, it falls to theology—or more exactly to each theologian—not to speak for themselves but to allow the word of God to be seen and heard. The theologian's words—written starkly as black ink against white paper or spoken against silence—assert themselves not from their own authenticity but as signs and icons ordered to draw the reader's/hearer's attention always through themselves to revelation. Like John the Baptist responding to a word that first came to him,[5] leaning on an authority that is never strictly speaking his, and directing his disciples to "behold the Lamb of God,"[6] the theologian offers words that are responsively orientated (so as to orient) toward God.

"Theology," Marion writes, "always writes starting from an other than itself,"[7] and this commencement from elsewhere offers itself as

and revealed theology (which is the only discipline that can make any true claim to the title "theology"). At other times, he marks the difference in written text by italicizing the controlling element of the term, distinguishing between our response to the word of God—*theo*logy—and the human preoccupation with words about God—theo*logy*.

4. "When there is only one absolute interpretation," John Caputo warns, "there are no more 'interpretations,' but only the special delivery of The Secret courtesy of God, or Being, or the Absolute Spirit. . . . An absolute hermeneutic is the end of hermeneutics, which is why it is too good to be true." John D. Caputo, *More Radical Hermeneutics: On Not Knowing Who We Are* (Bloomington: Indiana University Press, 2000), 203.
5. Luke 3:2.
6. John 1:29.

both precarious and liberating. Precarious, in part, because the promise to transcend the limits of my own preconditioning of divine revelation threatens to be simply another bedazzling mirror in which we see nothing but ourselves. For at some point in time, at some place, I choose to (or am called/invited/compelled to) put into words a response to revelation I hope to be not of myself but of God. Such activity, however, is unsettled by the ambiguities of hope: I hope I am responding to revelation and not, in the end, asserting my own will. I hope, but I cannot be certain. In standing upon hope, theology both risks idolatry and opens to liberation. This liberation arises from the possibility that it is only in the risk of opening to an other—the risk of a vulnerability that unsettles my certitude—that we can come to understand and love this other. It is only in opening to God—opening to the ordeal that our conversion and formation may necessitate—that we might begin to remember, understand, and love God. With a promise to free us from our idols—or perhaps, with a demand to so free us—this particular "liberation theology,"[8] following the promises of its many cousins, hopes for much. But like other forms of liberation theology, danger arises from its susceptibility to being co-opted by another concern—be it social, political, or personal. And here, at the limits of human possibility that mark the territory of theology, no danger is more threatening than the chance assertion of my own understanding and will under the banner of the divine, the assertion of a God made in my own image.

Whether Marion's approach leads to liberation or idolatry depends significantly on two factors. The first of which will occupy most of my attention in the following chapters: What is Marion offering as a path

7. Marion, *God Without Being*, 1.

8. In applying this term to Marion, Thomas A. Carlson speaks of the liberation of God from "the alienation in which he would have been placed by the reign of the human sciences (which would understand revelation in terms of everything but its own unconditional self-showing) and by metaphysics (especially modern metaphysics) that would undergird the human sciences and culminate in the nihilism of our time." Thomas A. Carlson, "Blindness and the Decision to See: On Revelation and Reception in Jean-Luc Marion," in *Counter-Experiences: Reading Jean-Luc Marion*, ed. Kevin Hart (Notre Dame: University of Notre Dame Press, 2007), 153. I have adjusted the context from the liberation of God from human knowledge to our liberation from idolatry to the worship of God—that is, to a freedom to follow the first commandment.

toward this liberation? Or, how is this path a responsive address *to* God rather than language *about* God? As Marion discusses particularly in the case of Augustine, the words with which the theologian refers to God are not even theirs to begin with.[9] The language of theology is—at its roots, certainly, but also in its approach and aim—the language of the scriptures (and indeed the ensuing tradition) and thus the foundational language that is given to us from God. It is a language that is not ours, not mine to hold or direct, but a discourse given to us, operating through us, that forms us toward God. "To do theology," Marion writes, "is not to speak the language of gods or of 'God,' but to let the Word speak us (or make us speak) in the way that it speaks of and to Gxd ."[10] Thus the theologian never speaks authentically, never speaks his or her own words, because the language of theology is a language first received through revelation. Such a specific understanding of theology—for which, perhaps, *Confessions* is paradigmatic[11]—has significant implications for both the discipline's methodology and its *telos*, and illuminates its capacity and limitations (a capacity, as I will demonstrate, that is a result of a particular understanding of its limitations). Thus Marion's articulation of the nature of theology is not incidental to this exploration of *De Trinitate*

9. Marion, *In the Self's Place*, 21.
10. Marion, *God Without Being*, 143. The crossing out of "God," marked in this text with the crossing of the letter "o," signifies, for Marion, the transgressing of being and turning instead to the "unthinkable" as the opening to God: "The unthinkable marks the gap, a fault ever open, between God and the idol, or, better, between God and the pretension of all possible idolatry. The unthinkable forces us to substitute the idolatrous quotation marks around 'God' with the very God that no mark of knowledge can demarcate; and, in order to say it, let us cross our Gxd, with a cross, provisionally of St. Andrew, which demonstrates the limit of the temptation, conscious or naïve, to blaspheme the unthinkable in an idol." Ibid., 46.
11. See Marion, *In the Self's Place*, 291. It is worth noting that *Confessions* is the only theological text to which Marion devotes an entire monograph. Joeri Schrijvers observes that Augustine's apparent influence on Marion's thought had, until this text, been "at best negligible—which makes it all the more surprising to find Marion writing a work of this stature, at this moment in time, where Augustine plays such a prominent role." Joeri Schrijvers, "In (the) Place of the Self: A Critical Study of Jean-Luc Marion's *Au lieu de soi: L'Approche de saint Augustin*," *Modern Theology* 25, no. 4 (2009): 662. Marion maintains that "Augustine did not . . . play a part" in his "sketching a phenomenology of givenness, phenomena as given, particularly saturated phenomena, including even the erotic phenomenon." Marion, *In the Self's Place*, xiii. However, despite the paucity of early references to Augustine, and Marion's own words, it remains striking that Augustine would not have had a greater influence on Marion, particularly in light of the similarities marked by *In the Self's Place* (similarities, it remains important to note, with which not all readers of Augustine would agree).

and its articulation of a language that orients its readers toward God. This theological appropriation of Marion's work will be shaped by his emphasis on the prohibition of idolatry and the hope in the possibility that God can make Godself known to us in and through creation, and will rest on faith in revelation having been (and continuing to be) given. When brought to bear on *De Trinitate*, Marion's work can serve as a lens through which we can focus on the particular pattern of responsive formation present in the treatise. Most importantly, and consistent with Augustine's primary concern, by bringing these two thinkers together on the question of the gift of love, it is my hope that they might together better illuminate what it is that animates and quickens the theological endeavor to come, in some manner, to know and love the Trinity who God is.

Engaging the second factor that marks theology as liberating or idolatrous, however, is to open a question that pervades many of Marion's texts and occupies much discussion in the secondary literature on his thought. It is this question that I will explore first, before more thoroughly examining Marion's phenomenology. Speaking of a theological appropriation rather than of the theology in Marion's work is to acknowledge the far-from-settled debate about whether Marion is "just a philosopher," writing within clearly demarcated limits or whether he is, despite his protestations, "doing theology."[12] While the theologian must obtain forgiveness for every essay in theology, must also the philosopher—more exactly this philosopher (in the lineage of Heidegger and Derrida, of all people[13])—be forgiven for venturing into theological concerns, analyses, all in the name of the "unconditioned"? Certainly he himself does not seek to obtain such forgiveness for (perhaps) essaying into theological realms, but ought he seek forgiveness of his colleagues

12. Mark Dooley, for instance, describes Marion as having earned "his reputation as the leading Catholic theologian of his generation." Mark Dooley, "Marion's Ambition of Transcendence," in *Givenness and God: Questions of Jean-Luc Marion*, ed. Ian Leask and Eoin Cassidy (New York: Fordham University Press, 2005), 190.

13. Derrida's own relationship with theology and particularly with Augustine is significantly marked in his *Circumfession* (as part of *Jacques Derrida*, by Geoffrey Bennington and Jacques Derrida [Chicago: University of Chicago Press, 1993]). The text is the result of a friendly bet with Geoffrey Bennington as to whether or not the latter could systematize the former's thought.

(both theologically and philosophically inclined) for his foray into theology (if, in fact, he has actually done so)? Ought he do so of God? And should I (here, not an anonymous author but one particular person peddling the words of Marion, Augustine, and the scriptures), then, be the one to apologize for him, in both senses of the word—to seek forgiveness *in* defending him theologically and to seek forgiveness *for* defending him?[14]

The Paradoxes at the End of Metaphysics

Sufficiently patrolled or not, the border in question between theology and philosophy is, for Marion, more specifically one between theology as a response to the given revelation of God and the particular philosophical discipline of phenomenology and its response to the so-called end of metaphysics. Whether the responses are celebratory, mournful, or incredulous, much has been made of the "end of metaphysics." My concern here is not to enter into the debate but to explore Marion's use of this controversial idea and its impact on his own thought. Its definition itself can be problematic, both in its lineage and possibility, and attention to Marion's use of the term can clarify how it came to be unexpectedly fertile soil for Marion's philosophy, nourishing his work even after he became more cautious about its articulation.[15] In his typical use of it, "metaphysics" refers to a particularly modern attempt to ground all thought on a single universal or structure of universals. He highlights three traditions of prominence in this endeavor to locate and define an underlying

14. This shift from the general first person plural pronoun, *we*, that I used in part 1 to the first person singular pronoun, *I*, in part 2 is not unintentional on my part. In beginning his essay into love, Marion notes, "I will say *I* starting from and in view of the erotic phenomenon within me and for me—*my* own. . . . But, dear reader, know this: I will say *I* in your name. Do not pretend to be unaware of the erotic phenomenon, or to know more about it than I. We don't know the same thing about the erotic phenomenon, yet we know as much; we remain in front of it with an equality that is as perfect as our solitude. Thus you are going to allow me to speak in your name, because I am paying the price here of speaking in my own name." Jean-Luc Marion, *The Erotic Phenomenon*, trans. Stephen E. Lewis (Chicago: University of Chicago Press, 2007), 9–10. In part 2, I will write as the *I* in whose name Marion speaks, the *I* that arises from the intimate conscious experience of receiving love and of loving.
15. Robyn Horner, *Jean-Luc Marion: A Theo-logical Introduction* (Hants, England: Ashgate, 2005), 49.

structure upon which all subsequent philosophy rests—that is, a "first philosophy."

Following the first category of use as the science of immutable essence, metaphysics attempts to ground thought in what is ostensibly (but ultimately not) the Aristotelian *ousia*, universal and given.[16] But Marion observes that the translation of *ousia* into the Latin as both *substantia* and *essentia* would eventually lead to the modern division of what for Aristotle was a unity: of that which assumes attributes—marking the "fundamental distinction between things that bear or 'stand under' (*substare*) properties, and the properties they bear"[17]—and that which retains identity through changes.[18] Particularly after René Descartes, substance would come to delineate that which "cannot be conceived without its attributes."[19] But as only the attributes "are knowable by us directly (here, extension and thought) . . . substance, as such '. . . does not affect us.' Substance remains unknown as such, except according to its epistemological dependence on its attributes and its accidents."[20] This unknown, hovering behind its attributes without any possible reference as such, would eventually be proclaimed a phantom concept by Nietzsche and his disciples, a concept without any discernable meaning or value, one idol among many that would collapse with the fall of metaphysics and death of God.[21] The concept of essence would fair no better, achieving

16. Jean-Luc Marion, *In Excess: Studies of the Saturated Phenomena*, trans. Robyn Horner and Vincent Berraud (New York: Fordham University Press, 2002), 4.
17. Summarized succinctly, albeit in a different intellectual context, in Alston, "Substance and the Trinity," 181.
18. Ibid.
19. Marion, *In Excess*, 5.
20. Ibid.; also: "As such, no substance affects us immediately: In short, none appears to us in the highest degree as a phenomenon." Jean-Luc Marion, "The Phenomenality of the Sacrament," trans. Bruce Ellis Benson, in *Words of Life: New Theological Turns in French Phenomenology*, ed. Bruce Ellis Benson and Norman Wirzba (New York: Fordham University Press, 2010), 93.
21. For example, "It is true, there could be a metaphysical world; the absolute possibility of it is hardly to be disputed. We behold all things through the human head and cannot cut off this head; while the question nonetheless remains what of the world would still be there if one had cut it off. This is a purely scientific problem and one not very well calculated to bother people overmuch; but all that has hitherto made metaphysical assumptions *valuable, terrible, delightful* to them, all that has begotten these assumptions, is passion, error and self-deception; the worst of all methods of acquiring knowledge, not the best of all, have taught belief in them. When one has disclosed these methods as the foundation of all extant religions and metaphysical systems one has refuted them! Then that possibility still remains over; but one can do absolutely nothing with it, not to speak of

significance only through the assertion of certain permanent presence, further separating it from that which is knowable to us through the contingencies of properties.[22] Essence, like substance, has been abstracted away into irrelevance.

Second, Marion notes the distinction in the work of Thomas Aquinas between metaphysics as primary science, metaphysics of being (which one might refer to, anachronistically but for clarity's sake, as ontology), and metaphysics as cause. Having adjusted his earlier position,[23] Marion recognizes Thomas's insistence on the incompatibility of ontology as first philosophy and the primacy of the divine over all created being—God is not subject to being.[24] Nor is God, as uncaused, subject to the metaphysics of causality. However, in Marion's reading of the Angelic Doctor, causality, as more fundamental than being, would still stand as the universal ground for thinking about creation—first and foremost *caused* as creation *qua* creation. But such a ground would, too, prove to be both abstracted into irrelevance and unstable. Irrelevant because, withdrawn as it must be from the things themselves, it assumes an illegitimate "transcendent usage beyond the limits of possible experience, concretely beyond the limits of sensible intuition."[25] And unstable insofar as any ultimate statement of cause is

letting happiness, salvation and life depend on the gossamer of such a possibility.—For one could assert nothing at all of the metaphysical world except that it was a being-other, an inaccessible, incomprehensible being-other; it would be a thing with negative qualities.—Even if the existence of such a world were never so well demonstrated, it is certain that knowledge of it would be the most useless of all knowledge: more useless even than knowledge of the chemical composition of water must be to the sailor in danger of shipwreck." Friedrich Nietzsche, *Human, All too Human*, in *A Nietzsche Reader*, ed. R. J. Hollingdale (New York: Penguin, 1997), 54–55.

22. Marion, *In Excess*, 6.
23. How Marion's critique of metaphysics relates to the metaphysics in the work of Thomas Aquinas is a disputed question. *God Without Being* focuses much attention on Thomas's privileging of *esse* over the good (as is prioritized in Pseudo-Dionysius's *On Divine Names*). In his preface to the English edition (1991), published nine years after the original (1982), Marion shows signs of reconsidering implicating Thomas in his critique of "being." As Horner writes, "Marion had already, in fact, softened the blow for scholars of Aquinas with the preface to the English edition, rereading Thomas in such a way that he is implicated neither in 'chaining' God to 'Being' nor in simply perpetuating a metaphysical concept of God. . . . But Marion still claims that even if it is freed from its metaphysical overlay, 'Being' is not the most appropriate name form God." Horner, *Jean-Luc Marion*, 10. Horner also distinguishes between Thomas's metaphysics and that of Francisco Suarez and points out that the tradition following the latter is much more apt to trap God within metaphysics through identifying God as the "highest being." Horner, *Jean-Luc Marion*, 20.
24. Marion, *In Excess*, 7.
25. Ibid., 8.

itself an endeavor fraught with difficulty. The history of either of these two universal foundations—metaphysics as ontology or as the science of cause—has proven them not so much irrational or (for whatever the word might mean) incorrect but irrelevant. These two grounds cannot contend with the realization that "the self-evidence of the question, Why? can—and undoubtedly must—always become blurred when faced with the violence of the question that asks, Why ask why?"[26] These phantom concepts struggle in vain to reverberate in our particular lived (that is, for Marion, phenomenological) conscious experience. To guarantee universal ultimacy, abstraction has sacrificed relevance—and with it, meaning—in the human context. Nihilism relentlessly haunts the abstraction of the universal ground.

The third examined universal is "the science of the knowledge of being in general, insofar as it is reduced to what is intelligible, that is to say the *cogitabile* [conceivable], such that it responds to the *a priori* conditions of its appearance to an *ego cogito*."[27] It is this sense of "metaphysics" that is most often the focus of Marion's attention, establishing as it does the transcendental *ego* as the foundation of all further thought and experience, as that which sets the conditions for what I can know and experience. Reduced only to the conditioning *ego*, I sever the transcendental *I* from the empirically experienced *me*, untethering that which structures the inexorable conditions and possibilities of experience from the actual experiencing of that which is other than *me*.[28] But rather than escaping the threat of nihilism, the establishment of the *ego* as the measure of all things—whose conditions of possibility, whose limitations universalized in advance, determine the appearance of truth—merely confirms the "end of metaphysics" as "in no way an optional opinion; it is a fact of reason."[29]

26. Jean-Luc Marion, "Metaphysics and Phenomenology: A Relief for Theology," trans. Thomas A. Carlson, *Critical Inquiry* 20 (1991): 578.
27. Marion, *In Excess*, 11.
28. Of this split, Marion writes, "This dichotomy will never be surpassed by modern (post-Cartesian) metaphysics, not even with Husserl, because it will initially be defined by it. Further still: just as this truly first *I*, because transcendental, is not known to me, it leaves me universal; it is not sufficiently able to individualize me (in space and time or otherwise); this, in stripping me of my individuality, it renders me unfit for any access to another person—except in reducing the other in the rank of an object, in the manner of my empirical me." Ibid.

However, an end does not necessarily necessitate an abolishment. Turning this possible nihilism into an opening for phenomenology, Marion suggests that beyond ending in its own collapse and death, metaphysics actually accomplishes its goal, having "managed to make the best hand possible with the cards at [its] disposal. From one winning hand to the next, metaphysics has placed all of its cards and has finally fulfilled its contract."[30] Having exhausted all possibilities for a universal *a priori* condition of rationality—notably "being," "cause," and "the subject"—metaphysics marks the limits of its own possibilities and ushers us toward paradoxes of the impossible.[31] Paradoxes "because they do not give themselves in a univocal display, available and mastered, according to a *doxa*,"[32] that is, according to the accepted metaphysical thinking. Impossible because Marion, following and furthering Heidegger,[33] finds at the end of metaphysics an opening both for a phenomenology of the unconditioned (precisely that which is metaphysically impossible) and for the possibility of theological reflection on the unconditioned God[34] (the one who is master of all that is impossible for us[35]). After metaphysics, and marked against the limits of its measure and judgment (beyond, and therefore impossible for, metaphysics), Marion suggests the primacy of phenomenological reduction to givenness (and the particular phenomenon of the gift).

29. Marion, "Metaphysics and Phenomenology," 578.
30. Jean-Luc Marion, "The 'End of Metaphysics' as a Possibility," in *Religion After Metaphysics*, ed. Mark A. Wrathall (Cambridge: Cambridge University Press, 2003), 167.
31. Metaphysics, here, is defined by *what is possible* according to *a priori* structures: "Thus, there emerges a science [i.e., phenomenology] that is more comprehensive than metaphysics, since the latter limits itself to the region of that which is or can be (the possible), by excluding the impossible." Jean-Luc Marion, *The Reason of the Gift*, trans. Stephen E. Lewis (Charlottesville: University of Virginia Press, 2011), 31.
32. Marion, *In Excess*, 112.
33. For Marion, Heidegger's "being" is one more idol separating us from givenness: "And that requires making appear what cannot be shown as beings, what is phenomenalizable without assuming the forms of beings. It is always still a phenomenology, but this 'phenomenology is a phenomenology of the inapparent' ('Zähringen Seminar,' in *Gesamtausgabe*, vol. 15: *Seminare* [Frankfurt-on-Mein: Klostermann, 1986], 399)." Marion, "'End of Metaphysics,'" 174.
34. This God being infinitely distant from the dead God who collapses with our other idols: "Now it is this simple possibility that suffices to recognize, in the 'end of metaphysics,' the 'death of God.' For the divinity of God should not be capable of lacking. If therefore it is lacking, if only imperceptibly, then God is already no longer at issue—but rather 'God,' who by this quotation marks is stigmatized as an idol." Marion, "Metaphysics and Phenomenology," 579.
35. Luke 1:34–37.

As the philosophy of conscious experience, phenomenology affirms "that every act of consciousness we perform, every experience that we have, is intentional: it is, essentially 'consciousness of' or an 'experience of' something or other."[36] There is an inescapable relationship between my intuition of a thing (that is, my conscious experience of that which is present before me or given to me) and the thing as such, between the *appearing* and *that which appears.* Phenomenology stands aside of any simple separation of subject thinking and object thought and any reduction of focus to either a subjective *ego* constituting reality or an extrinsic empiricism to which we must simply conform. Rather, it maintains that the impact made upon my consciousness by phenomena is not incidental to my awareness and knowledge of them. I am not abstractly and inattentively conscious in a vacuum only to subsequently turn my consciousness to something, but insofar as I am conscious, I am always conscious *of* something or someone. Phenomenology tries to mark the impact of a phenomenon upon my intentional consciousness—that is, to describe the mode of the phenomenon's own self-presentation as not conditioned and defined by my own mind but appearing there nevertheless. The phenomenon is not so constrained by the philosophical and epistemological borders established by a dichotomy of subject and object. Instead of being constituted in such a one-directional manner, the phenomenon always shapes my consciousness simply by appearing to me, by my being conscious of it. It "simply presents itself"[37]—maintaining its appearance to me (and thereby my intentionality) in and through (not despite) our distinction from one another.

Following, albeit briefly, the philosophical momentum behind Marion's phenomenology can help clarify his turn to the phenomenon of the unconditioned and the reduction to givenness. It is not my concern here to interpret the validity of Marion's understanding and

36. Robert Sokolowski, *Introduction to Phenomenology* (Cambridge: Cambridge University Press, 2000), 8.

37. Robyn Horner, *Rethinking God as Gift: Marion, Derrida, and the Limits of Phenomenology* (New York: Fordham University Press, 2001), 3.

criticism of Husserl and Heidegger, nor trace their (and, subsequently and significantly, Derrida's and Levinas's) influence upon his thought. I am content to leave these phenomenological questions in the hands of my philosophical betters. Here, I am interested in what Marion understands these thinkers to be saying and how this understanding shapes his own thought.

Marion's general narrative of this phenomenological momentum (recounted in detail in *Being Given* but ever present in his work) begins with Edmund Husserl and Husserl's taking into account the givenness of an object as an essential aspect of its being made known to us, "the correlation between reduction and givenness" that "determines the essence of the phenomenon itself."[38] By means of *reduction*—by bracketing all that is transcendentally posited, all *a priori* definitions and systems, assumptions, and beliefs I have about something—phenomenology seeks a vision or understanding of the phenomenon as it is given. It was Husserl's hope that by means of such a reduction—by bracketing all that I think I know about something so as to open myself to see the phenomenon as such—I might achieve a type of objectivity.[39] Such phenomenological reduction makes possible the appearance of the object not in a predetermined way that fits an abstract or theoretical definition of it but as it is given; it makes it possible for me to see it *as such*.

Yet for all this bracketing of *a priori* definition, Marion observes that Husserl's phenomenology is limited by its primary focus on objects.[40] Here, Marion follows Martin Heidegger's criticism and expansion of Husserl's work and emphasizes that such privileging of objects does not, in fact, liberate us to see the phenomenon as such; rather, this "phenomenality of objectness can only constitute the phenomenon of the basis of the *ego* of a consciousness that intends it as its noema."[41]

38. Jean-Luc Marion, *Being Given: Toward a Phenomenology of Givenness*, trans. Jeffrey L. Kosky (Stanford, CA: Stanford University Press, 2002), 21.
39. Horner, *Rethinking God as Gift*, 21.
40. This does not mean that Marion accuses Husserl of focusing only on objects or on reducing everything to the object. Marion notes that Husserl (along with Descartes and Kant), "knew perfectly well that the object constitutes only a species, and not even the most usual, of what appears." Jean-Luc Marion, "The Banality of Saturation," trans. Jeffrey L. Kosky, in Hart, *Counter-Experiences*, 400.

The object is determined by the subject. It is precisely what the subject intends it to be: a means defined by a specific end. And as is the very nature of the object to be defined and used by the subject, the object is further reducible to the subjective *ego*; it is defined by the subject as a means to the attainment of another end. And while this is easily seen in manufactured production (e.g., the computer upon which I type this is fully knowable [by me], fully understood [indeed, by someone quite other than me], can therefore be mass produced, and in the end, is precisely what it is deemed to be by the one who uses it [here an object to be used for the purpose of composing a theological text]), it is no less the case in an objectifying gaze, whereby I see the phenomenon not as an other but as an object that is only a means to an already established end. I see only what I already am prepared to see, acknowledging only what I already know and love, and thus conforming the other to my own horizon.

Overlooked in the first reduction is the very being by and in which objects appear to us—the *how* of their appearing. Phenomena appear not as merely brute objective facts, but as *beings*. In doing so, they hint at that which is never here present, *being* itself. Turning his focus from objects to being and given beings, Heidegger seeks to overcome the forgetfulness of being and recognize the ontological difference between beings and being itself by working back from individual beings to that which gives both the beings and their horizon.[42] For Heidegger, phenomenology allows us to see beings not as objects but as givens of being itself, not as things whose meaning can be constituted by my use of them but as givens always already in the world that precedes me. As being itself can never be conceived within the horizon of being, it can never appear because it *is* the perpetually withdrawing horizon, it can never appear as such but can only be "seen" in the

41. Marion, *Being Given*, 32.
42. Heidegger's turn to being relies significantly on the German locution *es gibt*. While commonly translated into French as "*il y a*" and English as "there is," Heidegger builds upon the more dynamic roots of the German, transforming what is often construed as a simple factual statement about the object into the being's *giving* of being. Instead of French "*il y a*," Marion therefore prefers the "*cela donne*"; likewise, English commentators following Marion often prefer (when they translate it at all) "it gives."

withdrawal that allows beings to appear, as the fold in which beings become phenomena. By their visibility, beings allow the horizon of being to be thought. "As a result," Marion writes, "it is no longer a question of thinking Being directly as such (in the fashion of a being), but rather its withdrawal as such, since this withdrawal is given as Being."[43]

As much as Heidegger might further phenomenological analysis through a liberating reduction to being, Marion concludes that he is as trapped as Husserl. In the end, a reduction to being no more grants me access to the phenomenon than does a reduction to the object. This is because, Marion argues, this second reduction still assigns "in advance conditions of possibility to the given—nothing gives itself except as object or being—imposing in advance on the phenomenal given that it give itself only according to two particular modes of manifestation."[44] The phenomenon can only appear according to the *a priori* definitions and conditions of the object or of being. The conditions of possibility of the appearance of beings are as demanding as those of an object and perhaps all the more insidiously powerful because of their claims to grant access to deeper purity—to reality as such. However, Marion observes that the conditions of possibility of being itself do not allow, by their very definition, the appearance of anything not constrained by being, or, for that matter, that which is unconditioned. And it is his understanding of the limits of these reductions that provokes Marion to bracket even the conditions of being (although not to abandon them, which is impossible) and to attempt a phenomenology of the unconditioned through a reduction to givenness.

By this proposed reduction, Marion does not offer givenness as an answer to the question of metaphysical limitations of being, cause, and the subject. At the very least, it does not continue the metaphysical search for a universal *a priori*. Rather, he suggests givenness appears as a principle of non-presupposition—a principle that requires no principles, tautological but "nevertheless meaningful."[45] This

43. Marion, *Being Given*, 36.
44. Ibid., 38.
45. Marion, "Metaphysics and Phenomenology," 580.

reduction to givenness attempts to overcome *a priori* conditions by turning to the phenomenon and allowing it to show itself, rather than requiring it to *be* according to the terms of being, a caused effect or my own subjective conditions. "The principle here is there is not any principle at all," he writes, "if at least by principle we mean that which precedes, 'that starting from which.'"[46] Or, it might be said that the only principle starting point is the givenness of the phenomenon itself and not a conceptual presupposition.

If a phenomenon is defined as that which appears to my consciousness (as that which I consciously experience), then the mode under which it appears—as neither being nor effect nor a result of my own subjectivity—is its own givenness. And the phenomenon only appears according to givenness and only because it appears to me precisely as that which is not constructed and conditioned by me. Rather than seeing in the being before me a confirmation of what I already know and already believe possible—that is, not seeing the phenomenon itself but only what is possible and understandable according to my limited *a priori* conditions—the phenomenon appears to me as other than me, as given:

> Now, this datum gives itself to me, because it imposes itself on me, calls me, and determines me—in short, because I am not the author of it. The datum merits its name by its being a *fait accompli*, such that it happens to me, and in which it is distinguished from all foreseen, synthesized, and constituted objects, since it happens to me as an event. This unforeseen happening marks it as a given and attests in it to givenness. Givenness does not indicate so much here the origin of the given as its phenomenological status. . . . Givenness does not submit the given to a transcendent condition, but rather frees it from that condition.[47]

Marion distinguishes between an objective given that is presented to me by someone and the phenomenological given as that which appears. Such an object would, in a colloquial sense, be "given" to me, but it does not thereby appear according to the phenomenological reduction to givenness. There remains behind this "given" object

46. Ibid., 582.
47. Marion, *In Excess*, 24–25.

questions of its facticity, of the one who (generously or not) presents it to me, and of the presentation itself. While such an object may invite a reduction of some sort, it does not appear as given, precisely because as object it invites a reduction to a further use, meaning, and value as defined by me. Whereas the phenomenological given is not the result of another's decision to give but simply arrives *as a given.* To the question of the presence of a giver—divine or otherwise—which seems to be the cause of much criticism directed at him, Marion does not so much actively deny the possibility as deems it irrelevant to the strictly phenomenological question. "We must not infer from this any transcendence, any addition of givenness of top of the given," Marion writes, "for givenness belongs to the very definition of the given *as* given."[48] There is nothing further behind this givenness that can stand as its foundation. There is no further reason for its being given. The phenomenon gives itself—in this way, it is given.

As that which is free from *a priori* conditions, the given's appearing to my consciousness—my intuition of it—stands as the *a posteriori* principle of phenomenology. Paradoxically, phenomenology's foundation is always already secondary and contingent; its only principle is a givenness that arises only from, and according to, the phenomenon that gives itself. Thus, the intuiting *I* does not ground the appearing of the given but itself appears only in response to the given. *I* am that to which a phenomenon is given; *I* am that which intuits givenness. As such intuition is not a conditioning *a priori* but an "originary *a posteriori*,"[49] phenomenology is not so much a method, but a "counter method" of the last principle.[50]

But does this *a posteriori* not restrict the *I* to pure passivity, as that which becomes a malleable object before the advance of the given?[51]

48. Marion, *Being Given*, 65.
49. Marion, "Metaphysics and Phenomenology," 581.
50. Marion, *Being Given*, 7.
51. This general criticism appears in a variety of specific enumerations throughout the secondary literature on Marion, and it is one that I will take up in the final chapter of part 2. Moreover, the (supposed?) vulnerability of Marion on this account serves as a setting of correspondence between Marion and Augustine. For each has been accused of the securing the passivity of the human being before the phenomenon—whether a banal given or graced event—and the evacuation of the *I*—or at least, the freedom of the *I*—before that which arrives to me. Augustine,

Would not this reinscribe the "priority of the 'given'" as "that which is spatially and measurable over-against us," and instead of "humbling our modernity, only repeat its essence"?[52] Such a move to passivity seems to invite a violent "gnosticism" and evasion of hermeneutics,[53] resulting in a phenomenon only accessible through the submission of the self to the discriminatory terms of givenness—terms most likely articulated by the powerful elite of a particular community or tradition.[54] Here, I would know a phenomenon only when such extrinsic terms have been met. The most forceful articulation of Marion's response to such a criticism falls to the saturated phenomenon and its overcoming of the subject by way of the *adonné*, which I will take up in pages to follow. For the moment, this paradox of an originary *a posteriori* will rest upon the phenomenological reduction to givenness—the method of bracketing all *a priori* conditions of appearance before the givenness of the phenomenon.

"As much reduction, as much givenness."[55] This principle of phenomenology marks the direct correspondence between reduction and givenness. This reduction is the phenomenological counter-method by which I suspend antecedent judgment of the phenomenon by bracketing my natural attitude, metaphysical assumptions, and all that which is transcendently signified so as to see the fact before me. Marion notes, "Phenomenology agrees with empiricism in privileging recourse to the fact, even if it stands apart from it in refusing to limit the facts solely to empirical sensibility."[56] In eliminating all that is

for instance, can be read through a Freudian lens, revealing a man who replaces a relationship with an overbearing mother with that of an overbearing church; in each case subsuming his own desires into that of another more powerful presence.

52. Milbank, "Can a Gift Be Given?," 141–42.
53. Graham Ward, "The Theological Project of Jean-Luc Marion," in *Post Secular Philosophy: Between Philosophy and Theology*, ed. Phillip Blond (New York: Routledge, 1998), particularly 232, 234.
54. See ibid., 230: "Marion-as-Conservative-Catholic" turns to "the explicit espousal of an authoritative given and an explicit commitment to . . . an imaginary community" and ecclesiastical authority.
55. I share Robyn Horner's preference for this translation of the refrain, "*Autant de reduction, autant de donation*" rather than the often chosen, "So much reduction, so much givenness," which is also, "perfectly legitimate. Nevertheless, I prefer 'as much' for *autant*, since it underlines the proportionality of the formula: the more strictly the reduction is applied, givenness increases." Robyn Horner, translator's introduction to *In Excess: Studies of the Saturated Phenomenon*, by Jean-Luc Marion (New York: Fordham University Press, 2002), x–xin4.
56. Marion, *Being Given*, 119.

not part of my conscious intuition of the phenomenological fact, I can analyze this givenness without deferring ultimately to structures of being, cause, or the *a priori* conditions of my own subjective experience.

But the appearing of the phenomenon, although dependent upon its being given, does not arise directly and necessarily from its givenness. While what appears to me is certainly given, that which is given may not actually appear to me. The phenomenon gives itself, but I receive this givenness in proportion to my reduction, to the degree that I get myself sufficiently out of the way so as to see what is the case.[57] "Set in its terminal form," Marion writes, "the phenomenon no longer appears as soon as I open my eyes to it, like an object summoned to the gaze that produces it; rather, it arises when my gaze has satisfied the demands of the perspective."[58] Marion uses the term *anamorphosis* for this appearing. The word is borrowed from the visual arts, where it names a procedure by which the viewer is presented an image without discernable form that directs the viewer's gaze to adjust itself to "a precise and unique point from which it will see the de-formed surface trans-form itself in one fell swoop into a magnificent new form."[59] For Marion, then, the phenomenon only appears to me when I have accepted the terms of its givenness, when I have reduced my intentional gaze to see it as it gives itself, as it demands to be seen.

Lest he be accused of advocating a principle of an empty head, whereby knowledge is delivered directly and without sensual or hermeneutic mediation into the mind, Marion maintains that such anamorphosis does not eliminate the need for rigorous reflection on how I receive the given. It does not simply supersede the need for interpretive theory nor shatter the conditions of possibility—in fact, it highlights both their functioning and their limits. This reduction gives rise to two related questions, each associated with the *truth* of my intuition of the phenomenon. First, what of hermeneutics? While the analysis of interpretation might seem to be superseded by the impact

57. I here borrow from the summary definition of the goal of asceticism offered in Michael Himes, *Doing the Truth in Love* (New York: Paulist Press, 1995), 139.
58. Marion, *Being Given*, 124.
59. Ibid., 123.

of this givenness, it may very well be that reduction to givenness actually demands that I take into account how I might come to rest assured (whatever that may look like) in having allowed the phenomenon to show itself. If mistakes in my understanding of the phenomenon are the result of a lack of reduction,[60] this phenomenology would need to somehow assume some tenets of a hermeneutic of suspicion as a way of judging the sufficiency of a reduction to givenness.[61]

Second, what of the subject? It can be argued that I can have no conscious experience of a phenomenon should *I* not have the experience—that while all this talk of the phenomenon giving itself might attract or fascinate, there is no way of ultimately escaping subjectivity. Or, to come at the problem from the opposite direction, does not Marion overpower the subject beneath the force of the appearing phenomenon, reducing the *ego* to nothing but a reflection of the phenomenon, without substance, freedom, or autonomous identity? He himself recognizes that this cannot be a matter of "annulling or overcoming the conditions for the possibility of experience" but rather of "examining if certain phenomena contradict or exceed those conditions and if they nevertheless appear."[62] Sufficient response to these criticisms requires one further significant move, from the phenomenon, as such, to that which exceeds and contradicts the conditions of possibility, to that which Marion calls the "saturated phenomenon" (which is the subject of the next chapter).

Thinking the Unconditioned and Opening to Theology

Returning to the heart of the question: how can I speak of/to that which exceeds my horizon? Such language is, indeed, impossible. But if, as Marion writes, this impossibility is "no longer what cannot be thought, but whose fact has to be thought," I must then ask, "how is it possible to remain rational and to have a discourse dealing with

60. Marion, *In Excess*, 20.
61. See David Tracy, "Jean-Luc Marion: Phenomenology, Hermeneutics, Theology," in Hart, *Counter-Experiences*, 63.
62. Marion, "Banality of Saturation," 398.

the impossible?"[63] Crucially, Marion does not suggest that the philosophically impossible might fall completely under the horizon of a theology where we might speculate about a reality that has no phenomenality. Theology is not a specific way of engaging certain cosmic structures and events about which phenomenology maintains a disciplinary agnosticism. Moreover, as groundless writing starting from another, theology cannot presume that the truth of God's revelation might be delivered to us without needing to be mediated by language and concepts (and therefore without rational consideration of how such mediation might occur). If the phenomenology of the unconditioned and a responsive theology are to converse and support one another, they must do so in another way. Marion's work offers at least one way of proceeding toward this discourse: exploring the relationship of philosophy (the study of rational conditions and possibilities) to theology (the openness of reason to that which is unconditioned and impossible for us) embraced under the banner of "Christian philosophy."

In his essay "Christian Philosophy: Hermeneutic or Heuristic?,"[64] Marion explores the possibility and potential of Christian philosophy through Étienne Gilson's defense of the discipline in light of the early- to mid-twentieth-century dismissal of it as an absurd juxtaposition —akin to "Protestant Mathematics." For Gilson, Marion writes, "Christian philosophy" might exist "whenever revelation makes suggestions to reason, without substituting itself for reason or modifying reason's requirements, in order to broach themes rationally that reason could not handle by itself or even suspect."[65] Marion presents Gilson defending Christian philosophy as a discipline determined not by the theme of study (e.g., the Eucharist or epistemology) but by its "radically original interpretation" of theme.[66] *Philosophy* insofar as it considers things of this world and not the nature

63. Marion, in Richard Kearney, "On the Gift: A Discussion between Jacques Derrida and Jean-Luc Marion," in Caputo and Scanlon, *God, the Gift, and Postmodernism*, 74.
64. Jean-Luc Marion, "Christian Philosophy: Hermeneutic or Heuristic?" in *The Visible and the Revealed*, trans. Christina M. Gschwandtner (New York: Fordham University Press, 2008).
65. Ibid., 67.
66. Ibid.

of God, and *Christian* in the interpretation of creation as relatable to God.[67] In such an approach, Christian revelation becomes "an indispensible auxiliary to reason,"[68] not a necessary interpretation but a possible one[69] (and, one might conclude, the preferred one in a Christian context). Such a "Christian philosophy" is thus, first and foremost, a hermeneutic, and as a hermeneutic, it can make no authoritative claim to its definitive nature.[70] "Christian philosophy," then—as one of many interpretive choices, the legitimacy of each self-established—is not philosophy at all but "merely Christian interpretation of philosophy," which leads, in the end, to "branding it as arbitrary."[71] As strictly a hermeneutic, Christian philosophy establishes itself as one interpretation of truth among many.

Marion maintains that the contrasting alternative to an arbitrary hermeneutic of Christian philosophy—that which sheds a certain slant of Christian light on the phenomena of the world[72]—is the "radical

67. Here, one can see Karl Rahner's *Foundations of Christian Faith* as an example of the question of *being* leading to the question of God or Paul Tillich's *Systematic Theology* as an example of the movement from the experience of existential anxiety to faith in God. Furthermore, in this essay, Marion cites as paradigmatic of this approach Augustine's *De Trinitate*: "St. Augustine built his entire doctrine of the images of the Trinity within us on the possibility of interpreting the faculties of the soul, *memoria/intellectus/amor*, as Trinitarian indications." Marion, *Visible and the Revealed*, 68. He does not, however, elaborate on this reference. It would seem fairly reasonable to argue, as I will, in light of his more recent work and the contemporary reevaluation of *De Trinitate* that I explored in part 1, that he would no longer so quickly abandon *De Trinitate* to such a simple interpretation. Rather than a possible Christian interpretation of the three faculties of the soul, Marion emphasizes the ultimate reference of meaning for the human being made in the image is the mystery of God: "But these triadic analogies disclosing an image of the Trinity do not display it in themselves as their stable content, but solely in the degree to which they refer this content to God himself." Marion, *In the Self's Place*, 257.

68. Marion, *Visible and the Revealed*, 69.

69. Ibid., 68.

70. As recent example of such an approach, Marion offers: de Lubac, Rahner, Gilson, Blondel, Lonergan, Moltmann, Mascall, Tracy, and "even" Ricoeur. Ibid., 69.

71. Ibid., 70.

72.

> There's a certain Slant of light
> On winter afternoons
> That oppresses, like the weight
> Of cathedral tunes.
> Heavenly hurt it gives us;
> We can find no scar,
> But internal difference
> Where the meanings are

Emily Dickinson, "There's a certain Slant of light," in *The Complete Poems of Emily Dickinson*, ed. Thomas H. Johnson (Boston: Little, Brown, 1960), 118–19, #258.

newness" and "unsurpassable innovation" of Jesus Christ.[73] What Christ offers is not, first and foremost, an interpretive lens (although it is that) but revelation of the Trinitarian God of love.[74] This love—or, to name it more solidly in the Christian tradition, *caritas*—serves as an "indispensable auxiliary of reason,"[75] not only as a hermeneutic through which we might begin to interpret a given, but foundationally as a phenomenon made visible only in the radically new event of revelation.

"In consequence," Marion writes, "'Christian philosophy' would remain acceptable only so long as it invents—in the sense of both discovering and constructing—heretofore unseen phenomena"[76] and insofar as it serves heuristically by offering to reason these phenomena for analysis. It would need to offer something new, something more than unheard of by reason but impossible according to reason (and therefore according instead to a Pascalean reason of which reason knows nothing). Once offered, Marion insists, such phenomena can "function philosophically even without the Christian convictions of their user."[77] Thus, if Christian philosophy *is* at all (and Marion has concluded that the term itself is not particularly helpful),[78] it is a discipline that receives what is given to it in revelation and abandons this gift of new phenomena (without expectation of reciprocation) to philosophy—it is the unnecessary intellectual middleman between theology and philosophy. What is important here is not the statutes of Christian philosophy but Marion's insight regarding the relationship between the disciplines of philosophy and theology. Philosophy—here meaning phenomenology—can provide theology with the language that can (1) transcend the metaphysical methodology ordered toward the determination of objects, being, cause, or the subject, (2) bracket claims to *a priori* knowledge, and (3) make it possible to see those

73. Marion, *Visible and the Revealed*, 71.
74. Ibid.
75. Ibid., 72.
76. Ibid., 74.
77. Ibid., 76.
78. Ibid., xvi; reiterated in formal conversation with the Department of Philosophy, Georgetown University, April 8, 2011.

phenomena as they give themselves. Marion suggests that philosophy can receive and analyze phenomena that theology can then receive back again, this time described with more clarity, precision, and critical suspicion. This is the technical expertise that phenomenology can offer.

Theological reflection on revelation, then, interacts with phenomenology at two overlapping, co-determining moments. First, revelation becomes the medium (such that it is) by which certain phenomena offer themselves—or better, revelation is the offering of phenomena that cannot be adequately conceived as objects or in terms of the metaphysics (i.e., the reduction to the object, to being, or to the subject). Second, phenomenological description can then serve a proper theological understanding of an event believed in faith to be revelatory of God by sharpening the description of how such an event impacts the beholder. "The heuristic of charity itself is charitable," Marion concludes, "what it finds, it gives without reserve."[79] What it receives, this heuristic gives unconditionally to phenomenology. Significantly for Marion, the fundamental gift received by theology is the distinct christologically given revelation: God is love[80]—the further significance of which is the topic of part 3.

The chapters to come in part 2 explore this saturated phenomenon of the gift of love by building Marion's argument piece by piece. After attending to the concept of phenomenological saturation itself, chapters 7 and 8 will present both Marion's understanding of the gift and his reduction to love. The final chapter will consider important and illuminating concerns and criticisms directed at Marion's project.

79. Ibid., 76.
80. 1 John 4:8.

6

Marking Excess: The Saturated Phenomenon

Only if there are angels in your head will you ever, possibly, see one.

—Mary Oliver[1]

To have a discourse dealing with the impossible—what can justify this privilege? What can justify Marion's turn to the unconditioned, away from the *as such* by which individual instances appear under a horizon of possibility, conditioned and defined in advance by what we conceptualize their essence to be, by what we understand they can be? By what criteria might we justify impossibility so we might pass judgment on the veracity of discourse—to deem such discourse meaningful amidst the possibility of vanity? Indeed, such questions do not remain obediently restrained in phenomenological circles but reach as well (or perhaps paradigmatically) to the very heart of theology—the discipline that attempts (or presumes?) to speak of, or to, the impossible God. This way of proceeding is marked by a phenomenological overflowing of our own finite concepts and

1. "The World I Live In," *Felicity* (New York: Penguin Press, 2016), 11.

possibilities by those phenomena that appear through the counterexperience of that excess. This chapter will mark—as much as it can—this excess in four parts, presenting Marion's concept of the saturated phenomenon, through its manifestations as event, flesh, and (occupying the preponderance of my analysis) as idol and icon.[2]

The Event

If phenomenology claims to allow a return to the things themselves, the validity of such a claim rests upon how such a return illuminates the truth of things. Significantly recontextualizing Pilate's question, I can ask Marion, "What is the given truth so illuminated?"[3] As it is customarily understood, Marion notes, truth is either "accomplished in perfect evidence, when intuition completely fills the concept, thereby validating it without remainder"[4] or achieved through "the partial validation of a concept by an intuition that does not fulfill it totally, but is enough to certify it or verify it."[5] The former case is exemplified by mathematics, the latter by the common experience of collecting data until all relevant questions have been answered and making a wager on the veracity of my judgment. Thus, my conscious experience of a phenomenon can be equal to my concept or it can fall short of the clarity and completeness of my conceptualization of it. In and of themselves, these definitions are adequate—provided they extend only to their proper limits and lay no claim to a universal definition of truth. But beyond these common (as in supposedly paradigmatic, not necessarily the most frequent) and poor (lacking in intuition equal the concept) phenomena, there lies a third possibility—precisely an impossibility according to the principle of sufficient reason and Kantian conditions of possibility. What if, Marion asks, "the ideal norm of evidence (equality between intuition and the

2. Marion usually presents these in a slightly different order, with the flesh and the idol in reverse positions. This order reflects my focus upon the idol/icon relationship and its significance for reading *De Trinitate*.

3. Cf. John 18:38.

4. Marion, "The Banality of Saturation," 384.

5. Ibid.

concept) is no longer threatened only and as usual by a shortage of intuition, but indeed by its excess"?[6] Everywhere his work bears the mark of this excess (*le surcroît*, the addition, increase, extra)[7] and his attempt to trace its impact upon truth, designated by a saturation of the concept with more intuition than it can absorb and impossible insofar as in excess of the conditions of the possibility of experience and knowledge. That what appears is given, that the phenomenon is our conscious intuition of a particular mode of givenness, is the foundation of Marion's phenomenology. But he maintains that what is given is not necessarily phenomenalized—or can be inadequately phenomenalized—as a result of our inability to bear witness to that which is in excess of our conceptualization. Beyond the common and poor phenomena, Marion proposes the saturated phenomenon.

Such saturation gives rise to a series of related questions: How can I experience and know this saturation that is impossible to experience or know? How do I have a discourse about a truth that transcends my horizon? How can I mark excess? Marion responds to this line of questioning not by focusing on how a lack of intuition challenges the equation of intuition and concept (and also, then, how to increase that intuition of which we have too little), but by turning to saturated phenomena as a way to describe the process of phenomenalization in general. This is not insignificant. Saturation is, for Marion, the paradigmatic form of the phenomenon.[8]

Ranging from the shared phenomena that occupy the attention of historians (say, the First World War or the French Revolution[9]), to

6. Ibid.

7. Marion, *In Excess*, xxi.

8. The marking of this given excess is inescapably and liberatingly paradoxical, defined as it is through and against (but not without) the modern subjective conditions that it saturates (which is the subject of Marion's concern): the Kantian categories of quantity, relation, quality, and modality.

9. In six and a half entertainingly exhausting pages of *Plurality and Ambiguity*, David Tracy offers a list, incomplete to be sure, of possible answers to the question, "What was the French Revolution?" The list ranges from discussions of historical causes, to historical effects, texts, symbols, movements, individuals, rituals, discourses, structures, and *mentalités*. Tracy, *Plurality and Ambiguity*, 1–7. As an opening to his study of hermeneutics and the importance of interpretation, these pages succeed—at least in the eyes of this particular interpreter—in conveying the overwhelmingly overdetermined nature of the event and a helpful description of the communal form of the phenomenon Marion discusses here.

the those that concern just a small number (the lecture at which he delivers a paper on saturation, Marion likes to uses as an example), to those intimate phenomena bearing on just us or solely me (perhaps my falling in unrequited love), the *event* rises to my attention unpredicted, unprovoked, and uncreated—that is, in the "absence of definite reason."[10] Such events cannot be produced in the manner of an object. For example, an event like a wedding, despite it often being labeled a "production" and occurring on a scheduled day and in a chosen place, relies upon the experience and attention of any number of individuals (from the presiding official to cleaning staff), is attended and shaped by family and friends (each with his or her own perspective on, and experience of, the celebration), and depends absolutely on the relationship of two people, each with a lifetime of accumulated history and influences. The event—as it actually arrives—cannot be fully anticipated as such.

The event arises to be seen as a *fait accompli*, having happened in a manner that could not have been predicted and therefore could not have been fully expected. It arises from a site other than my own mind and will. Absent the predictability of a cause leading to an effect (as opposed to the objectively trustworthy predicative hypotheses resulting from, and further impelling, the scientific methodology of the natural sciences), the event arises without definite reason. In fact, it incites a phenomenological, if not logical, reversal of cause and effect, wherein the causes are delineated and explored after the fact so as to appear precisely not as causes but as effects of the event. The event reverses cause and effect, establishing the cause, such that it is, as a phenomenological *a posteriori*.

Marion enumerates three features of the event,[11] each tied to the fundamental absence of a clear discernable cause. First, the event is identically unrepeatable, and as such, is unique. It cannot be reproduced like the mass produced object. The latter is a result of a known formula and process, with each product identical to the others,

10. Marion, *Being Given*, 160.
11. See, for example, Marion, *In Excess*, 36–37.

each replaceable by the others. In the case of the object, adequate knowledge can very well predict the outcome—in fact, mass production relies upon it. The event appears because such knowledge will always be insufficient for exhaustive understanding of the given phenomenon. Second, the event is without discernable finite reason. Thus it demands a hermeneutic "deployed without end and in an indefinite network" in which "no constitution of an object, exhaustive and repeatable, would be able to take place."[12] This endless hermeneutic relentlessly reminds that phenomenology is fundamentally a countermethod that begins with an acknowledgement of its always finite vision. It is a countermethod that begins *a posteriori* with what is given and is thus dedicated to tracing its own borders against that which it cannot fully understand and interpret, a method of confronting the never fully apparent event. In opening myself to the possibility that the phenomenon before me is not reducible to an object, to its being defined solely by me and by its use to me, I also make it possible for me to see it in ways unexpected and all together new. Third, the event cannot be ultimately foreseen. It cannot be seen in advance of its appearing because it arrives absent a discernable and definite reason. The unforeseeable event is distinguishable from the accident, in that the latter is metaphysically understood as deficient in discernable cause and therefore as against precisely the philosophical conceit of the universal conditions of metaphysics. That which is the exception for metaphysics as lacking in discernable cause becomes the foundation of phenomenology, demanding as it does an endless hermeneutic of the unapparent:[13] "The accident, or more exactly the incident, therefore gives rise to an obvious dilemma: noetically, the incident remains impractical, degree almost zero . . . of knowledge, but it nevertheless offer a privileged figure (the only real one) of phenomenality, since it gives itself without preliminary,

12. Ibid., 33.
13. Marion, *Being Given*, 160.

presupposition, or foresight."[14] Where the accident appears deficiently, the event is defined by this gratuitous givenness.

Finally, the event does not stand on only the privileged ground of the exception, dallying only in revolutions, celebrations, and other dramatic occasions of human life. For its arising, like that of the flesh, the idol, and the icon, is not the unique province of a "confused and out of the ordinary ravishing"[15] (like death and birth),[16] nor does the lack of discernable reason render the event unintelligible. Instead, Marion suggests that saturation can appear (insofar as excess "appears" at all) in the most banal phenomena, and therefore "the less they let themselves be inscribed in causality, the more they show themselves and render themselves intelligible as such."[17] By renouncing the reduction to causality, the given is allowed to appear and might begin to be understood. By way of example, he offers the lecture hall in which he delivered an early form of the chapter "The Event of the Happening Phenomenon," in *In Excess*,[18] noting that even at its most objective (as permanent, subsistent, and waiting-to-be-used), the hall can still saturate my concept of it. It can appear in awaiting the arrival of occupants who enter that which they did not, themselves, produce but rather that comes from the past of foggy memory (Who built it? Why? How did it impact their lives?) and is not only defined by my being in the hall (What else had happened in this room? To whom?). In the present, there can be no measure of why each person comes to such a room on such a day to hear such words, nor would, on another day,

14. Ibid., 152. It is worth nothing that Marion turns to Thomas Aquinas (Ibid., 154–56) for the definitive defense of his own interpretation, noting that for Thomas, being itself arises according to the incident and without necessity. This arises as given from the outside (*adveniens ad extra*) of being, also thus necessarily entailing a lack of cause. "As soon as it imposes its figure on Being itself (it too *adveniens*), the incident becomes the ultimate norm for the entire field, whose margins alone it was supposed to occupy. Being should henceforth be thought according to the determinations of the incident, far from the incident being ontically devalued into a marginal accident. The exception becomes the rule—no one understood this better than Thomas Aquinas." Ibid., 156.
15. Marion, "Banality of Saturation," 389.
16. Marion, *In Excess*, 39 and 41, respectively.
17. Marion, *Being Given*, 162.
18. Reproduced (or, to be specific, the read text was reproduced) as Jean-Luc Marion, "The Event, the Phenomenon, and the Revealed," in *Transcendence in Philosophy and Religion*, ed. James E. Faulconer (Bloomington: Indiana University Press, 2003). The paper was then resituated in Marion's *In Excess*.

with even the same people in attendance, hearing the same words lead to an exactly reproduced evening. Finally, even in reading the text read that day (adding eyewitness accounts from the audience), no one in the future could describe fully what happened that evening in that hall, nor could they take into full account the audience's reception (both immediate and long-term) to Marion's words. The endless hermeneutic required of any who would begin to describe that night in no way leads to its unintelligibility but illuminates precisely how such an event, in all of its excess, might be seen as intelligible. It is the attempted descriptions and explanations of that night that select causes and effects (choosing some over and against others), determine what or who was there and why they were there (selecting reasons according to some *a priori* criteria), or explain what Marion said that night that lead to unintelligibility of the event. This selection that defines *what happened* through only my interpretation of what happened as ordered by my own priorities and criteria for judgment certainly can lead to an intelligible description. But such description speaks to my own thought and not of the event (now veiled beneath my own conditioned interpretation). Such analysis suggests the banality of saturation —*banal* not because *frequent* like the mass produced objects but following its strict political and legal sense as concerning "all and is accessible to all."[19]

Furthering Marion's argument that while what appears is necessarily given, not all phenomena that give themselves appear (or appear as they give themselves), and that even the banal might open to that which is not visible under the common natural attitude suggests that rather than an exception to phenomenology in general, the saturated phenomena opens us to its excessive and never fully apparent heart. "The *majority of phenomena, if not all*," he writes, "can undergo saturation by the excess in them of intuition over the concept of signification."[20] If all that shows itself gives itself but not all that gives itself shows itself, then the decisive factor allowing for the

19. Marion, "Banality of Saturation," 390.
20. Ibid.; emphasis in original.

appearance of the phenomenon is—for the lack of a better term at the moment—the subject. But Marion's phenomenology takes seriously the limits of the subject to whom the phenomenon appears—limits in memory, understanding, conceptuality, and perspective, certainly, but also limits of will and desire. Whether as common, poor, or saturated, the phenomenon only appears to me as I allow. If all I see is an object, then this being-object is a result of the limits that I have drawn around the phenomenon. I allow it to appear to me "only" as an object to be controlled and proscribe the saturation that, by definition, defies my mastery. "The poor phenomenon, in the sense of the denigrated phenomenon, is what I see without wanting to see," Anthony Steinbock observes. "I see in ordinary terms without receiving; I 'merely' constitute it. I master it before I could receive it or 'want' to receive it. The problem is not on the 'side' of phenomenal givenness, but the said of the 'subject.'"[21] Thus, the manner of appearance of the phenomenon is a measure of the one who enacts the reduction; it is *my* reduction that determines how the phenomenon appears *to me*.[22]

Against his critics who argue that he is trafficking in irreal abstraction, Marion replies, "The fact of not comprehending and seeing nothing should not always or even most often disqualify what it is a question of comprehending and seeing, but rather the one who understands nothing and sees only a ruse."[23] Fortunate is the instructor, for example, who has never had a student, although present in the classroom, conclude that "nothing" happened during the lecture or discussion on a given day. To hear only the droning on of the lecture and the all too eager responses of other students, to see nothing but the clock's slow progress—these hinder the possibility of understanding the course material and thus inhibit the appearance of the event. No matter how much intriguing material is offered by the instructor (and

21. Anthony J. Steinbock, "The Poor Phenomenon: Marion and the Problem of Givenness," in Benson and Wirzba, *Words of Life*, 129.
22. See also: "In the knowledge of the object, it is the *ego* more than this object who objectifies it, constitutes it, and literally certifies it. Yes, the object shines with certainty, but this certainty would have no meaning if it did not refer to the *ego*, who alone sees and above all founds it. The object owes its certainty—its certificate—to the *ego* that certifies it." Marion, *Erotic Phenomenon*, 12.
23. Marion, "Banality of Saturation," 388.

we all do hope it is quite a bit), nothing new or interesting can appear to the student if he or she is unwilling to see it. The saturated phenomenon appears if I am open to its appearance as contrasting and in excess of what I already know and can control.

Three observations are warranted here. First, Marion maintains that this *apparent* return to the subject is not a move back to the conditions of possibility of experience and knowledge, a move back to the *ego* that determine what I can see, experience, and know by marking those conditions in advance. Such a subject only appears as a complement to the appearance of the object. That is, the reduction to the object not only hinders the appearance of saturation but also establishes me as a subject. Or, as Horner notes, "What is reduced also becomes the measure of the one who so reduces."[24] Echoing the reversal of causality by which the cause is regarded only after the effect and thereby becomes a phenomenological effect of the effect, here my appearing as a subject (that is, the one who constitutes the objective world) is a result of my measuring objects. It should be noted that such objectification can serve a real and pragmatic need. Certain phenomena, although reducible to saturated givenness, might aid in other reductions if reduced to common objects. Objects allow us to both go on with our daily business (whereas, for example, too much attention to givenness to the world around me while driving a car would certainly be a risk to my well-being). They also allow us the time and space wherein other saturated phenomena might appear. The pure givenness of an actual book, *In Excess* for example, (the colors of the cover, the feel of its pages, and the scent of its print) might well be sacrificed for what I can read inside. Saturation does not eradicate the subject any more than it eliminates *a priori* conditions. But it does depose these conditions from their dominion over the phenomenon by revealing their limitations in light of the excess of intuition. The *a priori* conditions and antecedent concepts simply cannot fully circumscribe what is given.

While never proposing that I might do away with some

24. Horner, *Rethinking God as Gift*, 92.

epistemological or metaphysical conditions of possibility by which I, as subject, come to experience and understand phenomena (and this is important—Marion never supposes that I might operate void of all conceptual structure), Marion contends that the saturated phenomenon appears as a counterexperience—as that which contradicts or exceeds those very conditions of possibility. It arises precisely in contradiction to a phenomenon interpreted as an object—its excessive intuition pushes back against such limited reduction. There is more trying to appear, more to be understood. In so doing, the counterexperience of the saturated phenomenon calls all the more for a recognition of my limitations and all the ways I try to resist opening myself to that which is in excess of my understanding and control. As observed by Merold Westphal, Marion's phenomenology invites a certain hermeneutics of suspicion turned toward the subject and not a dismissal of the subject as such; it calls for "not an 'experience without subject' but experience without a *certain kind* of subject"[25]—one that receives itself in the limits that appear in the overwhelming light of saturation. This phenomenology abandons the pretense of neutrality, as though "phenomenological vision is to be the view from nowhere in particular,"[26] and accepts the always active conditioned and conditioning self. But in doing so, it also maintains the "possibility of an experience in which alterity precedes intentionality,"[27] an alterity that appears in the counterexperience of my own resistance to it and in the force I receive by the impact of this otherness. To mark that which comes after the subject—that is, he or she who opens to excess and by what means this is accomplished—requires further investigation into saturation, given later in part 2. For now, it is sufficient to see this instability in the subject and to imagine the way forward through saturation.

As a second point to observe about saturation, Marion argues that the tautological structure of this argument is rooted in the

25. Merold Westphal, "Vision and Voice: Phenomenology and Theology in the Work of Jean-Luc Marion," *International Journal for Philosophy of Religion* 60 (2006): 125; emphasis added.
26. Ibid., 126.
27. Ibid., 130.

phenomenological countermethod itself. If the reduction allows givenness to rise to phenomenality—if *how* something is seen influences *what* is seen—then the phenomenon whose arising saturates my consciousness with more intuition than my concept can handle signifies in me an insufficient concept and an incomplete reduction. Such limitations, however, are not necessarily a sign of intellectual or moral weakness, or of the absence of something that "ought" to be there. The appearance of the saturated phenomenon does not carry with it any grounds for such judgments—be they metaphysical or theological. Phenomenologically speaking, such insufficiency and incompletion is purely descriptive.

Third, the saturated phenomenon itself resists—in and through its excessive givenness—its being reduced to an object. In fact, as arises as a counterexperience against and in excess of conditions of possibility, its appearing impacts me with a force that counteracts, contradicts, and accuses my finite understanding of truth. When faced with saturating givenness, "I undergo the obscure obligation of letting myself conform to (and by) the excess of intuition over every intention that my gaze could oppose to it."[28] In giving more than I can grasp, the saturated phenomenon demands of me more than a recognition of equal measure of my concept to an objective phenomenon—not, of course, through a moral imperative, but by the structure of phenomenality itself. It invites an anamorphosis by which I conform to it in the only way I can conform to that which is beyond what is possible for me: that I be (trans)formed[29] by it by opening myself to accept all that it gives and all that the given does to me.

Of course, I can refuse. But before the given excess, I cannot remain neutral. In this way, "more essentially than a judgment about things (true or false), more essentially even than the manifestation of the phenomenon by itself, the truth produces a verdict about myself,

28. Marion, "Banality of Saturation," 405.
29. In setting "trans" in parentheses, I hope to signify Marion's insistence that the transcendental *I* is not established prior to encounters with saturated phenomena and that it is not always already there. It is not transformed from one stable form to another but is always in the middle of being formed by the appearance of such phenomena.

according as I can accept it or can only reject it."[30] Again, Horner's words: "What is reduced also becomes the measure of the one who so reduces."[31] I can hate that which is given in excess of my own possibility—I can resent it for resisting my attempt to render it an object. Or I can open myself to it and risk being devastated and reformed by what it gives. Unpredictable and without discernable cause, the event gives itself, and gives itself to me. Paradoxically and in excess of my possibility, it surges toward appearance—an appearance possible only on its own terms and terms to which I, to see it, must make myself vulnerable. That which gives itself in excess of my possibility appears to me only in and through my conversion to it.

My Flesh

Whatever the context in which a phenomenon (whether saturated or not) might appear to me and however it might appear, Marion observes that the phenomenalization of a given nevertheless necessitates that it appears *to me* (or you, him, her, them). The conversion of the given into the phenomenon—into that which appears to me—requires a mode of apparition. Yet such an appearing is never simply a matter of my directly absorbing the given, imprinting upon my consciousness an intuition of the given free from my already being involved in such an encounter. The given phenomenon does not appear to me unmediated and relieved of hermeneutical concerns. As the phenomenon appears, so too does my flesh appear as that medium wherein this appearance occurs; it is where and how I receive givenness. My phenomenological flesh marks not just that which touches (my fingers) but also the act of touching; not just that which sees (my eyes) but also the seeing. I do not just touch and come in contact with someone or something but am conscious of myself as touching and of being touched. It is not just that I experience a phenomenon (acquiring data about what appears) but that I experience myself experiencing it—that is, I experience that which

30. Marion, *In the Self's Place*, 110.
31. Horner, *Rethinking God as Gift*, 92.

is not me *as* that which is not me. My flesh is what allows my body to differ from the many other material bodies in the world. Where these bodies may well "act upon one another . . . they cannot touch themselves, or destroy themselves, or engender themselves, because none of them feels any other."[32] My flesh is not just an epistemological condition of possibility of experience but the site of my intuition of that which is other than me. "In short," Marion concludes (with the help of Michel Henry), the flesh is the identity "of the affected with the affecting."[33]

By the term "flesh," Marion both marks a necessary element of all phenomenology and delineates a phenomenon that appears, itself, only as saturated. Without flesh, "nothing of the world would ever appear" (as the world must appear to something that feels it—my flesh), but itself remains, importantly, "not of the world."[34] Distinguished from my body, which is always visible to my eyes (my body: my nose, ears, tongue, skin, eyes, and all these things as they function together—this includes, too, the concepts by which I understand smells, sounds, feelings, tastes, and sights processed through my functioning nervous system), the flesh alone remains invisible all the while marking the phenomenological translation of the given to my intuition. It "renders visible the bodies of the world that would remain, without it, in the night of the unseen"—without my flesh the givens of the world would never appear to me. In this way, the flesh "provokes and demands [the] solipsism"[35] by which phenomenology operates, making possible the appearance (always *to me*) of that which gives itself. Flesh marks the possibility of my being conscious of a given, the foundational receptivity that allows for the appearance of anything at all. In doing so, the flesh cannot be understood as something I *have* (as one often says about the body) but as that which I *am*.[36] I do not exist prior to my flesh and operate it as

32. Marion, *Erotic Phenomenon*, 113.
33. Marion, *Being Given*, 231.
34. Marion, *In Excess*, 87.
35. Marion, *Being Given*, 232.
36. Marion, *In Excess*, 92.

one would the tools of excavation, slowly exploring the world around me. It is not me who has flesh but the flesh that gives me myself in making me conscious of touching and being touched by that which is not me.

Importantly, this receptivity is also a saturated phenomenon in its own right. It is inescapably always invisible itself, "because this intuition [of the flesh] precedes and renders possible all intentionality, therefore all signification intentionally aimed at."[37] By making intentionality possible, this receptive flesh can never appear as intuition. It appears only against and in excess of my concepts and understanding. Marion offers by way of example of this saturated phenomenon both suffering and pleasure.

My suffering is a matter of not just pain receptors registering an unpleasant feeling (in this way, I do not say that I "suffer" from a paper cut) but of the phenomenalization of a particular type of given—that is, of the appearance within my consciousness of that which causes me pain (be it physical, emotional, psychological, or spiritual) and from which I cannot detach myself.[38] In this way, it is not just the pain but the fact that the fundamental receptivity that gives me myself is now inescapably saturated with pain. While that which makes intentionality possible is always invisible to my intuition, here it "appears" not as a visible phenomenon but precisely as that phenomenon from which I flee. Suffering "imposes itself on me like a destiny—undergone, managed"—but remains that which I "never probably wanted for itself."[39] Thus, suffering "appears" as that excess which I try unsuccessfully to evade—it appears in my resistance to its inexorable appearance in the foundational receptivity of my flesh.

In a similar but opposite manner, the phenomenon of pleasure is not a matter of my nervous system indicating an agreeable touch (be it physical, emotional, psychological, or spiritual). Where the excess of suffering appears only through my resistance to it, pleasure appears in my openness to the ultimate receptivity of flesh, here manifest "for

37. Ibid., 99.
38. Ibid., 92–93.
39. Ibid., 99–100.

the first time without restriction . . . or exception."[40] If the saturated phenomenon of flesh appears through suffering through my resistance to it, it appears in pleasure through my submission to it. The excess of the flesh cannot appear here any more than in suffering. For here, my passivity to that which is given guarantees that the phenomenon cannot be measured or conceived—for it appears only as I abandon all mastery of it and abandon myself to it.

In this way, it is the flesh and only the flesh that gives me myself—that individualizes me. Understanding alone—the dexterous application of my conceptualizing—cannot do so, "for, to the contrary of flesh, not only can another understanding also think what my understanding thinks, but rational commerce demands that any understanding can do it."[41] Moreover, it is precisely its receptivity that allows me not only to feel but to feel myself—it not only allows the phenomenon to appear and to appear *to me* but for me *to appear* as the one to whom the phenomenon is given.[42] My flesh, then, is the phenomenon that gives me myself in individualizing me through marking the distinction between that which I experience and that which experiences those people and things. "In receiving my flesh," Marion notes, "I receive my myself—I am in this way gifted [*adonné*, given over] to it."[43] In his privileging of the flesh as that which makes possible phenomenology in general, Marion reverses cause and effect and determines that phenomenology emerges from saturation.

The Idol

> When the people saw that Moses was delayed in coming down from the mountain, they gathered around Aaron and said to him, "Come, make us a god who will go before us; as for that man Moses who brought us out of the land of Egypt, we do not know what has happened to him." Aaron replied, "Take off the golden earrings that your wives, your sons, and your daughters are wearing, and bring them to me." So all the people took off their earrings and brought them to Aaron. He received their offering,

40. Ibid., 94.
41. Ibid., 97.
42. Ibid., 87.
43. Ibid., 98.

> and fashioning it with a tool, made a molten calf. Then they cried out, "These are your gods, Israel, who brought you up from the land of Egypt." On seeing this, Aaron built an altar in front of the calf and proclaimed, "Tomorrow is a feast of the LORD."[44]
>
> From this it is clear that the golden calf was intended as an image, not of a fake god, but of the Lord himself, his strength being symbolized by the strength of a young bull. The Israelites, however, had been forbidden to represent the Lord under any visible form. Cf. 20:4.[45]

First, a distinction: the term "idol" is saturated with a religious significance that can never be easily disregarded even in its most phenomenological context. Marion's two primary early studies of the idol—*L'idole et la distance* (1977) and *Dieu sans l'être: Hors-texte* (1982)[46]—are expressly theologically oriented and, perhaps in the case of the final three chapters of *God Without Being*, explicit exercises in theology. But his use of the term extends well beyond primarily religious contexts. In subsequent years, with the notable exception of the second half of *La croisée du visible* (1996),[47] the idol often assumes, for Marion, an essentially phenomenological role, which he often explores in the context of art. It is not my desire to here test the strength of the concept of the idol when severed from its religious role (if even such a removal is possible) nor to judge it as a helpful or valid concept for the disciplines of art criticism or art history. This section, like the complementary one on the icon, will not flee from theology. For it is the idol theologically understood (which is not contrary to its phenomenological mode, but a specific, if paradigmatic, instance of it) that will resonate in general with Augustine's work and, more specifically and fundamentally, with *De Trinitate*.

The idol, like the event and the flesh, is a saturated phenomenon.

44. Exodus 32:1–5 NAB.

45. Jean Marie Hiesberger, ed., *The Catholic Bible: Personal Study Edition* (New York: Oxford University Press, 1995), note to Exod 32:5.

46. Jean-Luc Marion, *L'idole et la distance. Cinq etudes* (Paris: Grasset, 1977) and Jean-Luc Marion *Dieu sans l'être: Hors-texte* (Paris: Arthème Fayard, 1982), published in English as Jean-Luc Marion, *The Idol and Distance: Five Studies*, trans. Thomas A. Carlson (New York: Fordham University Press, 2001) and *God Without Being* (1991), respectively.

47. Jean-Luc Marion, *La croisée du visible*, rev. ed. (Paris: Èditions de la Différence, 1996), published in English as Jean-Luc Marion, *The Crossing of the Visible*, trans. James K. A. Smith (Stanford, CA: Stanford University Press, 2004).

It gives more than can be conceived, conceptualized, or grasped. But the idol does not delineate a definitive being or type of being. Not an idol because it is in the form of a golden calf or any other thing—the idol is a *manner* of being. More specifically, it is a way of being seen. Unlike the event, which appears precisely as saturated when I accept its paradoxical appearance and open myself to a phenomenon that arrives unpredictably and without discernable reason, the idol, as the "low water mark" of saturation,[48] appears only negatively and only as I frame the phenomenon. The idol is marked by the limit I place upon my intuition of saturation, the point beyond which I dare not venture. It delineates the border between what appears to me and that which I ignore, reject, or to which I am indifferent. For while the idol follows the foundational logic of the saturated phenomenon whereby saturation arrives in excess of the conditions of possibility of my experiencing it, it is defined as that phenomenon I perceive only by allowing a fixed part of it to appear to me. Faced with the saturated phenomenon, I allow it to appear "in fixing references to it, as one founds strongholds in the too vast, undefined plain, where everything would otherwise be merged, in short, in taking a stand in order not to be lost there."[49] I frame it so something might appear to me rather than being swept away in the relentless current of excess. Thus the idol is not something other than what is given—it is not a replacement of one phenomenon with another. It is a fixing, a reifying, an enclosing of the phenomenon so I might understand it—I frame it clearly so "the very fact of seeing it suffices to know it."[50] I conceptualize it, I define it as a concept that is no less the possible idol than the golden calf (indeed, the latter only becomes an idol under the horizon of the former, as the statue without the idolatrous concept is merely decoration).

Such a vision attracts and does so in two ways. First, it serves as a point of reference. When faced with an I-know-not-what (when I await a Moses delayed in returning from the mountaintop), I seek some foothold by which I might reasonably go on. The idol promises

48. Marion, *God Without Being*, 27.
49. Marion, *In Excess*, 56.
50. Marion, *God Without Being*, 9.

to delineate and explicate where I stand. Second, such a frame offers the pleasure of seeing—a "*libido vivendi*" by which I might grasp the phenomenon, "especially what I do not have the right or the strength to see; the pleasure also of seeing without being seen—that is, of mastering by the view [*vue*] what does not return to me without exposing me to the gaze of another."[51] It promises that I might see without risk to myself, my understanding, or my desire.

It is significant that Marion's concept of the idol carries with it this doubled attraction. In both cases, the foothold and the mastery, I am drawn to frame the idol so I might be free from the excess of the given phenomenon. Each case is a concept measured by my own desire—be it certainty of knowledge or mitigation of risk. For here, the framed image of the phenomenon "must make itself the idol of its viewer. With the image, the viewer sees the satisfaction of his desire, thus of himself."[52] But while sharing in their manner of appearance, these two ways of attraction are marked by a distinction. The foothold allowing me to go on—or just as well, not be lost—functions similarly to the pragmatic reduction to the object, as discussed in the previous section. While Marion establishes saturation as paradigmatic of phenomenology—and as "banal" it is open to all—he recognizes that it is not the most frequently appearing form of phenomenality. If applied to each phenomenon, the reduction to pure excessive givenness creates a vast and undefined plain wherein I would most certainly find myself unable to attend to the daily activity of my life. In appearing "proportionate to the experience of desire," and thus fulfilling "(sometimes to a degree more than expected) the anticipation,"[53] the idol, as the measure of my desire, allows my desire to rest, satiated. The idol allows me to go on to other things that might occupy or demand my attention.

But it is the second form of desire—that of mastery without risk—that more clearly illuminates the idol and all that it veils. For while the reduction of the phenomenon to object, cause, or being can

51. Marion, *Crossing of the Visible*, 50.
52. Ibid., 51.
53. Ibid., 33.

occasion idolatry, it is the conceptual idol that ultimately governs idolatry, and therefore it is the subject who measures—and thus masters—the phenomenon as idol. Such a subjectivity—seeing only that which can be aimed at in advance and prohibiting the appearance of anything in excess of this *a priori* condition—reveals the idol (again, not a thing in itself but a manner of being seen) to be nothing more than a fixed point that reflects the desire of the subject—that is, to be nothing more than a mirror of sorts. As a mirror, the idol "reflects the gaze's image, or more exactly, the image of its aim and of the scope of that aim."[54] It attracts because it perfectly satisfies my desire to see. However, what is shown is not the phenomenon as such but the fullness of my desire as fixed by the frame. Because I approach the edge of what I can anticipate and foresee, this fullness—precisely as the fullness of my limited desire—veils the mirror function of the idol in its intense bedazzling light. I rest, exhausted, by the complete fulfillment of my own expectations—expectations that are never at risk of being overwhelmed because I accept only what I can expect and allow to appear. The idol is the limit I place upon my desire. It appears as my refusal to desire according to the saturated givenness of the phenomenon and instead pursue only what I can fully conceptualize. This idol is the desire for what I already know, have, and am.

It is in this way that Marion can say that nothing is lacking in the idol, nothing is absent, negated, or invisible. With its mirror function veiled, the idol shows all that can be seen and only what can be seen. To recognize the mirror would be to become aware of the conditions I have placed on phenomenality—it is to become aware that there is more given than I can see. The givenness of the phenomenon is truly visible in the idol, but only a fraction—or better, because of its separation and not just distinction from saturation, a fragment—of that givenness is visible; it is the fragment that fully confirms and satiates my desire to see. The idol, then, as a result of my own measuring, becomes my own measure. "In short, it denudes my desire and hope,"

54. Marion, *God Without Being*, 12.

Marion writes. "What I look at that is visible decides who I am. I am what I can look at. What I admire judges me."[55]

Marion's philosophical description of the idol often assumes the context of visual art—more specifically of painting, "the visible par excellence."[56] A first inclination, he notes, might lead me to approach the painting as precisely that which prevents me from seeing it as an idol, insofar as its appearance seems to rest on a resemblance to an original.[57] Such a claim to resemblance ought to remind me of the original and thereby make me aware of the frame I have placed around it. But Marion suggests that the resemblance of the painting-as-idol takes a particular form such that, framing as it does a fragment of the phenomenon (thus by definition veiling the saturation), the painting violates its resemblance to the original, adding "presence to presence, where nature preserves space and thus absence."[58] The painting-as-idol appears because I find in the image more satisfaction that I have found in the original. Where the latter is a constant reminder of my limited understanding and knowledge, the former holds my gaze upon only itself, captivating my admiring gaze that "is therefore concentrated on the resemblance, precisely because it no longer resembles anything, but, drawing onto itself all the glory and confiscating it from everything else, it enters along into pure semblance."[59] In pretending to regard equality with the original as within its grasp, the painting-as-idol presents a fullness that, as limited, satisfies my limited desire. The givenness of the original is reduced to "the pure and simple plane-ness of the surface," and "must end inevitably in the façade" that "cancels all depth."[60]

This can be true for visual art in general—even, or perhaps particularly, in celebrated and extraordinary paintings. "In art—in great art—nothing is lost when something does not make itself seen"[61]

55. Marion, *In Excess*, 61.
56. Marion, *Crossing of the Visible*, ix.
57. I will explore what this original "is" later. Suffice to say that adding a more substantive presence (e.g., "an original *thing*") unnecessarily limits what for Marion is an all-pervasive possibility.
58. Marion, *In Excess*, 66.
59. Ibid., 58.
60. Ibid., 76.
61. Ibid., 66.

because it presumes sufficiency in itself. The ostensible self-sufficiency of the idol disrupts external referentiality and results in the absence of any origin. The idol marks the absence of absence—there is nothing missing, nothing further to be seen. Here, what is at issue is not so much that the category of the original is something that ought to be there but is noticeably absent, but that the image-as-idol blinds us—as a mirror reflecting the light of a flashlight back into our eyes—to any absence at all. On television or in the National Gallery of Art, an image becomes an idol when nothing else will appear and we are content with that—again, the idol appears to me not as a particular *thing* but as a result of my *way* of seeing.

The religious idol functions no differently than the purely phenomenological idol—it is, in fact, an instance of the conceptual idol. The idol is the expression of the desire to "fix in stone, strictly to solidify, an ultimate visible,"[62] some point where my gaze rested in full satisfaction. The idol is not an object that stands directly contrary to God, a counter-god to be worshiped "instead of." The idol appears not in proclaiming itself to be other than God but in framing a genuine—although limited, and sometimes cripplingly so—experience of the divine. Marion observes, "What renders the idol problematic does not stem from a failure (e.g., that it offers only an "illusion") but, on the contrary, from the conditions of its validity—its radical immanence to the one who experiences it, and experiences it rightly so, as impassable."[63] It is the limit that marks the idol, not inauthenticity. In being so marked, the saturated phenomenon can become an idol precisely because it is saturated, because the more the divine mystery is given, the greater is my exhausted desire to step away from the revelatory whirlwind.

The larger and more comprehensive the frame, the more I might become convinced of the sufficiency of my image. This particular form of the idol also manifests the double attraction of foothold and mastery. I can only be bathed in the relentless waves of excess for so

62. Marion, *God Without Being*, 14.
63. Ibid., 28.

long before I retreat from the mountaintop. The need arises to reflect upon—to describe in woefully inadequate words—what I have seen. I frame and define the space as a sign of the (supposed) unbearable excess, but in doing so I signify only what I already know and embrace. In so far as I decrease my vulnerability to that which is unbearable, I fix the advent of the divine and open "the site of a temple" wherein "that god whose space of manifestation is measured by what portion of it a gaze can bear."[64] The decision for some certain foundation from which I might go on—go on with my daily life, certainly, but also go on with my study of God—becomes also the measure of my own God.

The pattern continues, too, in the image's pretension to resemblance of the original, such that the concept of God that shines brightly while framed by my intentionality claims to "reproduce its original according to degrees of similitude"[65]—or rather (because it is the *subject* who governs the appearance of the idol), *I* claim the similitude between this image (visual or otherwise) of divinity that I have framed and the original. Marion writes:

> The idol always marks a true and genuine experience of the divine, but for this very reason announces its limit: as an experience of the divine, starting in this way with the one who aims at it, in view of the reflex in which, through the idolatrous figure, this aim masks and marks its defection with regard to the invisible, the idol always must be read on the basis on the one whose experience of the divine takes shape there.[66]

It is the decided sufficiency of the similitude that renders it idolatrous—too tired to continue, too overwhelmed by excess to make myself vulnerable to more, I have decided that the similitude of this particular image to the original will serve me better than the invisible original itself. The idol becomes more God to me than God. Or, more accurately, the idol is the God sufficient for me.

64. Ibid., 14.

65. Marion, *Crossing of the Visible*, 70. Augustine, too, notes the relationship between similarity and idolatry: "So the soul fornicates (Ps. 72:27) when it is turned away from you and seeks outside you the pure and clear intentions which are not to be found except by returning to you. In their perverted way all humanity imitates you. Yet they put themselves at a distance from you and exalt themselves against you." Augustine, *Confessions*, 2.6.14.

66. Marion, *God Without Being*, 27–28.

At least two questions invite further reflection. First, is there something unique about the double attraction of the specifically religious idol? For while Marion seems to speak of the idol as both something we turn to amidst relentless saturation so that we might focus on something rather than everything, it is important to remember that Marion's concept of the idol is, itself, one form of the saturated phenomenon and not simply the reduction of a given to an objective status. The idol resists objectivity in that it marks a true experience of the divine such that my desire is satiated. The distinction between the attraction of a foothold and that of mastery, which seems helpful when speaking of the saturated phenomenon of the idol, thus begins to show itself as a superficial one when contextualized by religion. For, theologically speaking, the prohibition against idols ought to hold my continual attention.[67] While a lesser need might submit to a greater, opening the space for a reduction of a visible phenomenon to an idol (I might, for instance, cut short my analysis of great art to be attentive to my wife), to rest amidst the whirlwind of divine excess (even as such satiation is a result of a genuine experience of God) violates the first and foundational commandment. That my desire for God is satiated is an indictment of my limited desire and my inability (or unwillingness? Is this possibility grounded fully in the will, i.e., in love?) to remain vulnerable to all that is given. Here, the attraction to a foothold always risks becoming a mask of that mastery—it can become a place of permanent rest (that is, of spiritual death), rather than a temporary place of rest from which to continue. But to continue, I require liberation from the desire for a similitude that only the icon can deliver.

Second, to what degree is Marion's concept of the idol defined by his theology? Or, to ask in a less polemical way: what is this "original" to which Marion refers? To Marion's critics who are on the lookout for traces of Platonism in his work, such a term might be cause for alarm. So too, and more to the point when the idol is contextualized

67. See Exodus 20:1–6, and for further examples, but less forceful in their proclamation: 1 John 5:21; Acts 15:19–21.

by the icon, it can be interpreted as a convenient euphemism by which theology can enter into the discussion, particularly after Marion's statement that "the formula that Saint Paul applies to Christ . . . icon of the invisible God (Col. 1:15), must serve as our norm."[68] Do you see? His critics can cry out, "Marion's 'original' is God!"—for although Marion offers a phenomenology of the idol inscribed in the language of art (and by extension through Rothko via Levinas, even into ethics[69]), his readers need not look too far afield to see that such a discussion easily, although not necessarily inevitably, leads back to theology. *The Idol and Distance* reaches a high point with Marion's study of Denys the Areopagite, the so-called Pseudo-Dionysius.[70] *God Without Being* moves quickly from idolatry to Christ as icon, never looking back to a phenomenology done in non-Christian language, following non-Christian concepts. *The Crossing of the Visible*, for all its attention to the conditions of appearance in general and to the phenomenology (and history) of art, ends with an essay on the Second Council of Nicaea and the status of the cross as an icon of God. *In Excess* does not deviate from the pattern, concluding with Marion's essay on the pragmatic language of prayer as that which might allow the icon to appear amidst threats of idolatry (indeed, even his essay on the idol leaves his readers with a glimpse at the Rothko Chapel in Houston, Texas, a nondenominational building that is "empty of a look that it desires to death"[71]).

When contextualized in the language of art criticism, Marion's phenomenological description of the idol seems to need no theology for its justification. Yet he chooses to finally justify the paradox of the icon as an aesthetic repetition of what "the hypostatic union of natures indeed accomplished in Christ, as a paradigm of the universe."[72] While this may have not been the only path of inquiry he could have chosen, Marion's phenomenology follows a religious dichotomy (idol/icon) and

68. Marion, *God Without Being*, 17.
69. Marion, *In Excess*, 75–79.
70. Tamsin Jones makes a compelling argument that despite Marion's common references to Denys, Marion's thought relies much more heavily upon that of Gregory of Nyssa, and much of what Marion attributes to Denys is actually derived from Gregory. Tamsin Jones, *A Genealogy of Marion's Philosophy of Religion: Apparent Darkness* (Bloomington: Indiana University Press, 2011).
71. Marion, *In Excess*, 81.
72. Marion, *Crossing of the Visible*, 84.

comes to a crescendo in an analysis of explicitly Christian theological doctrine. While Marion directs the interweaving of phenomenology and theology like a virtuoso conductor, he may not, in the end, convince his cultured critics that his phenomenology can stand pure of the influence of his theology. But, then again, he may not ever intend to do so. To the degree that Westphal is correct and Marion's phenomenology can also be understood as an exercise in hermeneutics, taking into account the fact that our subjectivity is not originary in itself but always already relational, involved, and responsive, then it may not be too much of a risk to say that Marion does not feel the need to apologize for having a discourse dealing with precisely that which is deemed *impossible* for those who do not believe. That phenomenology might open to theology is not, itself, a theological claim except to those who forbid all language of God in philosophy. Should it be a surprise that if, in the end and against his own assertion, Marion fails to maintain so-called phenomenological purity, it may be not because his faith is tainting his thought but because his drive to think the unconditioned necessarily leads him to consider the unconditioned *par excellence*—God?

The Icon

"The icon does not result from a vision but provokes one"[73]—this, the difference between the idol and the icon, marks a response the icon initiates within me that depends not upon the icon's adherence to the conditions of experience and knowledge that I have set in advance (such that this phenomenon might appear according to my expectation and measure) but solely upon my anamorphic formation to see it as it gives itself to be seen. The icon is the phenomenological inverse of the idol. Where the latter appears only as framed—as an attempt to mark the limits of what is given in excess of my ability to grasp it and to only allow a fragment to appear so I might actually hold and understand it—the former appears only when I have given up my

73. Marion, *God Without Being*, 17.

desire to so frame the saturated phenomenon and instead allow what is given to determine how it is to be seen. In this way, as saturation becomes the paradigmatic mode of all phenomenology for Marion, so the icon is saturation's "terminal form" wherein "the phenomenon no longer appears as soon as I open my eyes to it, like an object summoned to the gaze that produces it; rather, it arises when my gaze has satisfied the demands of the perspective."[74] After analyzing Marion's use of the concepts of counterexperience and the invisible, I will attempt to outline Marion's iconic hermeneutic.

Counterexperience

Marion's concept of the icon, like that of the idol, is significantly shaped by his phenomenology of the painted image. While this is certainly in large part a result of the religious history of iconography, it is not strictly an imposition of the spirituality of iconography upon the phenomenology of the image. Or, perhaps better, Marion seeks to develop a phenomenological analysis mirroring this spirituality insofar as the religious practice of devotion to icons effectively resists the reduction of the given saturated phenomenon to either physical or conceptual object. The icon both maintains a phenomenological way of receiving the other in excess of my concept and opens the possibility of a theological appropriation of this phenomenology in the tradition of icon veneration.

In the visual arts, icons serve as examples of what Marion loosely terms "authentic" painting. This authenticity is a process of making visible the unforeseen (*imprévu*)—not of rendering an already seen or conceived image upon canvas, but in allowing what defies anticipation and expectation to arise from beyond conceptualization and impose itself upon the canvas.[75] This is why the artist continually steps back from the canvas to survey the whole piece (such that it is). This is why an artist never really knows what they "have" until the work is complete (or, as it has been said, an interesting stopping place is

74. Marion, *Being Given*, 124.
75. Marion, *Crossing of the Visible*, 28.

found). Here, Marion draws a distinction between the "authentic painting"—as that which resists objectification[76]—and what might be understood as imposing upon the canvas an already fully conceived and anticipated image. The latter is a matter of conquering virgin territory and imposing upon it a visual image of what exists already in my mind. The former allows the unseen—the unanticipated—to arise from the depth of the painter, from a part of him or her that defies conceptualization. Such a painting has a complementary effect on the viewer as well. Arriving upon the painting—coming around the corner of a corridor in an art museum into the gallery, perhaps—I am struck by two "contradictory attractions":

> First, of course, the fascination of the gaze by the irresistible attraction of its weight of glory. But also terror in the face of the power that it exerts in the name of the darkness from which it arises. The picture has transgressed the most forbidden border: it comes to us from the unseen, by forced entry, illegally, heroic and threatening; it has seen what cannot be seen—namely the unseen; it still bears the marks of the forbidden, despite having renounced it. The authentic painting defies us, provokes us, sometimes with the mischievous arrogance of some upstart who has reached visibility, more rarely with the royal and sacerdotal holiness of a master of appearance. To think about it properly, it would be necessary to be purified before entering into its presence. For glory threatens, even when it saves.[77]

Such an authentic painting (like truth itself[78]) is marked by the saturating appearance of the previously unseen and unanticipated and imposes a decision of intentionality upon all to whom it gives itself, a decision that delineates how it will appear. I can resist its provocation, its challenge to my concepts, its invitation to form myself and my gaze so as to see what is given, or I can allow myself to be vulnerable to

76. Ibid., 41.

77. Ibid., 31. In this text, Marion first uses the term "glory" (*la gloire*) in the context of the Cyril of Alexandria's christological paradox of "divine glory (δόξα) within the structures of the human." Ibid., 1–2. Glory, then, is the phenomenological name for that which marks an encounter in visibility of "that which one should not have encountered there . . . the paradox . . . born from the intervention of the invisible in the visible." Ibid., 2. Glory serves Marion in a similar way, as do "saturation" and "excess," signifying the appearing of that which is more than I can conceive but with an added emphasis on my attraction to this phenomenological blinding. Glory is the excess that draws me toward it because it overwhelms me.

78. See chapter 10.

its challenge of (trans)formation. To be sure, such a decision does not occur in a temporal moment after the phenomenon's appearance, in a neutral space and time where and when I might decide if and how I will subsequently accept such phenomenality. Rather, my response to its givenness determines how it might appear to me—intentionality marks the line between the idol and the icon.[79]

If I resist and instead choose to remain content with all that appears to me and only that which appears to me, rather than face the "darkness from which it arises," I stand before it as a spectator before an idol. Because of exhaustion before the threatening excess or the self-assertion of a longed-for mastery, I see what I desire to see and nothing more. But in choosing vulnerability to the given phenomenon, I abandon not the desire to see but my "very meager desire—prudent and restricted—to see only what [I] have foreseen."[80] I have made it possible for the phenomenon to appear as it gives itself, according to its terms to which I transform myself. "The icon definitively exceeds the scope of expectation, terrifying the desire, annulling the anticipation," Marion writes. "It is neither willing nor able to undertake to correct this gap; the icon inverts it while substituting its own aim—its aim toward us—in place of ours toward it."[81]

Marion describes this inversion of aim, or gaze, as a "counterexperience." Again, by this term, he signifies not an experience that somehow occurs without subjective conditions of the possibility of experience (however one might choose to define them) but one that directly contradicts or exceeds that possibility. It is the subject's own conditions of possibility that mark the appearance of the excessive phenomenon, not in that they condition it, but that they absorb the impact of that which runs counter to them. Excess "appears" insofar as it challenges and reforms possibility in ways unforeseen and unimaginable by the subject. In fact, Marion accepts this paradox as the heart of the saturated phenomenon: "the more its own evidence increases, the more its reception depends on the possible

79. Marion, *God Without Being*, 20.
80. Marion, *Crossing of the Visible*, 32–33.
81. Ibid., 33.

myopic gaze of the spectator (who is squinting, to say the least)."[82] Before the icon, the word "subject" (to the degree that such a term still applies here; one might just as easily refer to "one who comes after the subject") signifies not that whose *a priori* structures determine the possibility and impossibility of all that falls before its gaze but rather an active receptivity to what is given.

Marion often offers two examples of the phenomenon of the icon: the painted (religious) icon and the face of the other. Unlike representative art, the painted icon—here, strictly speaking, the religious image of Christ or the saint that bears the traditional iconic style and name—"offers itself to be seen by the gaze without the mobilization of perspective."[83] Its gives itself in a manner that defies spatial and temporal structures of appearance and attempts to precisely and accurately reconstruct a realistic image, inverting many of the principle qualities of the portrait. What is shown in an icon is not, strictly speaking, the directly representative image of such-and-such a person in a particular context but rather the paradox of phenomena that "can well escape the look (*intuitus*) and nevertheless appear, but they are unable to be looked at."[84] The icon does not simply respond to my own intentionality but exceeds and/or contradicts it (contradiction being a species, perhaps, of excess), prohibiting its reduction to an object or a framed idol of perfect fulfillment (which, in the end, function similarly for me, the latter veiling my reduction of it to the rank of the idol by permitting some "limited saturation" to, in fact, appear). Before the infinite depth of the icon (infinite because I cannot measure it, infinite because the icon only shows itself in showing the excess that gives rise to it), I am conscious not of an object but of the limits of my intentionality. The icon appears as a counterexperience: Instead of my seeing only the painted image, I open to the excess of the invisible to which the painted image directs my gaze and allow myself to be seen by it. Instead of my envisaging it (in a manner always conditioned by my perspective), I allow it to

82. Ibid., 43.
83. Ibid., 20.
84. Marion, *In Excess*, 115.

envisage me. "Through the merely painted icon," Marion writes, "I discover myself visible and seen by a gaze that, though present in the sensible, remains invisible to me. How do the visible and the invisible coincide? We have already indicated the answer: intentionality."[85] This coincidence (the appearing of the icon to me and thereby delineating me by the saturation of my limits) is precisely my allowing the invisible to determine the terms of its appearance in the visible to me and my allowing myself to be seen by that which I cannot see, that which I do not define and control. The icon is the image wherein and by which I open to excess.

Lest one too soon dismiss this concept of the icon simply as a heavy imposition of the theology of the painted icon upon phenomenology, Marion offers a second, and perhaps more convincing, description of the icon in a context adopted from Levinas: the face of the other. For Levinas, the face is "the way in which the other presents himself, exceeding *the idea of the other in me*" and serves as the means by which I "*receive* from the Other beyond the capacity of the I."[86] The face marks all that I cannot define and serves to remind me that the person before me is more than my concept of them. In so doing, the face opens me to that which is not me and is beyond my control. As Marion presents it, the face—precisely as "face" and not an object to be defined or a mere façade to be seen—"obliges me to situate myself in relation to it. I do not adapt it to my visual devices, as I would do with an animal or tool. I do not approach it following my intention, but following its intentionality, because it is the face that asks me not to kill it, to renounce any mastery over it, and to distance myself from it."[87] The face appears when I renounce mastery over it, relinquish my definition of it, and abandon my own conditions of possibility by which I would allow it to appear to me. A saturated phenomenon where intuition is in excess of my intuition (precisely because I have allowed the phenomenon to appear on its excessive terms rather than my own),

85. Marion, *Crossing of the Visible*, 83.
86. Emmanuel Levinas, *Totality and Infinity: An Essay on Exteriority*, trans. Alphonso Lingis (Pittsburgh: Duquesne University Press, 1969), 50–51; emphasis in original.
87. Marion, *In Excess*, 117.

the face effects a call upon me. The saturation of the face "subverts and therefore precedes every intention that it exceeds and decenters,"[88] opening me to receive myself in my response to its givenness. With my intentionality decentered, I am invited into excess, invited into that which is not me and cannot be defined in advance by me. The object, in my defining it, remains mute—it does not draw me beyond myself. The face (rather than the façade) appears as the phenomenon that calls me into excess.

The Invisible

"Whatever is or pretends to be will have to appear at the end"[89] or else it is not a phenomenon. Accordingly, it is not in vain that one might ask, "What does the counter-gaze of the icon actually show?" That is, whether in the case of the painted religious icon or that of the face, if what appears before me is not only the sensible physical object—paint upon canvas or skin upon the skull—then what else appears? What gazes upon me and calls me to see it, and see it as it gives itself, full of radiant excess? Here the heart of Marion's phenomenology begins to come into focus. The intention to think the unconditioned is, itself, a more generalized articulation of a deeper phenomenological goal: to allow what gives itself to show itself as it gives itself. But giving itself in excess of my conditions of possibility means not only that what appears will necessarily appear *as event* (without my anticipating or justifying it) and as giving myself to me through the fundamental receptivity of *my flesh* (that which appears does so only in open response to the phenomenon's givenness and thereby allows the phenomenon to appear to me in my response to it), but if it is not to be reduced to the status of an idol in my refusal to admit precisely its saturation, it can only appear to me *as invisible*. Marion's phenomenology of the icon is a matter of, first and foremost, the paradox of the "visible image of the invisible *as invisible*."[90]

88. Marion, *Being Given*, 267.
89. Marion, "Phenomenality of the Sacrament," 90.
90. Marion, *Crossing of the Visible*, 58.

In the appearance of the saturated face-as-icon, the phenomenon shows precisely nothing—no thing that can be conceptualized as an object. That which appears to me does so not as something visible (either to the physical eye or as a concept before the mind's eye) but "appears" in its transformation of my attention from one concerned with looking at objects to one that can respect the phenomenological distance[91] between myself and the phenomenon by accepting its excess. I become one who opens to accept all that remains invisible to me. Although related to it, this invisible is not governed by the qualities of the unseen (*l'invu*, "invisible by default"[92]). For the latter is that which can appear but does not—perhaps it will, perhaps it will not, perhaps because of the particularities of the context, it cannot appear here and now but will perhaps appear in another context. The invisible, however, "remains forever as such"[93]—never visible, as it appears only against or in excess of the conditions of possibility of my experience or knowledge. Thus, while any image can show objective phenomena, the icon "shows" the invisible.

The Hermeneutic of the Icon

As is the case of each individual saturated phenomenon, Marion's concept of the icon requires a specific hermeneutic so as to be seen. This hermeneutic of the icon has three interrelated characteristics. First, the icon is that before which I find myself not envisioning it but being envisioned *by* it. Second, such a phenomenon only appears to me if I can confess it as such. Third, it appears not according to any similitude with its original but rather in the mode of fidelity to

91. The term "distance" marks the opening to "the separation that unites only on the basis of a term that is discovered there, or better that discovers there its own horizon: distance is discovered only like a path is cleared, starting from a site, but not like one reads an itinerary on a map, in the elsewhere of a neutralized representation." Marion, *Idol and Distance*, 199–200. As such, its appearance requires both my antecedent involvement and a maintained alterity (the otherness of the other). I cannot define the distance that has appeared to me because a definition of distance would necessitate my being able to define that which keeps me at a distance from the other, which in turn would define the other in terms of the self. Only in accepting the other as other, by understanding the self in relation to the other, and by willing this distance can I remain faithful to the other as such.

92. Marion, *In Excess*, 105.

93. Marion, *Crossing of the Visible*, 25.

it. Together, these lead to Marion's conclusion that before the icon, I am transformed into one who receives my very self from receiving the icon's excess—I become a witness, one gifted with this vision.

First, as before the face, I find myself not so much seeing the icon but being seen, and "I must feel myself thus in order for it to function effectively as an icon."[94] Even the most banal of phenomena can appear as saturated if I am willing to bear the weight of this gaze. Where the face of the other may very well seem to make this demand more efficacious, our daily interactions with people are in stark contrast to such an obligation to "welcome the distance of infinite depth."[95] It is my lack of openness to the impact of depth, and that of others who encounter me, that permits me to go on with my daily business. "Our reciprocal inauthenticity assures social relations very well," Marion notes, "which standardization and effectiveness require, which anonymity guarantees."[96] It is not the banality of the everyday that resists saturation but my desire (arising from limited time and energy, certainly, but also the willingness to accept my vulnerability) to open myself to saturation only in particular contexts.

To see the icon, I must learn to see it, to accede to its mode of givenness (that is, excess) and to be vulnerable to the demands it makes. But this is not a decision on my part—at least insofar as "to decide" means to stand aside from my options, view them from a neutral position, weigh them against some *a priori* standard, and then make a calculated choice to orient myself toward one option. "In these mountings of visibility (as one speaks of mounting vigor, fever, desire, or anger)," Marion writes, "we—the *I/me*—no longer decided the visibility of the phenomenon. Our initiative is limited to remaining ready to receive the shock of its anamorphosis, ready to take a beating from its unpredictable landing."[97] Beating, shock, impact—Marion suggests that such vulnerability to the phenomenon leads to its effecting change (sometimes painfully so) upon me. I give up control

94. Ibid., 59.
95. Marion, *God Without Being*, 23.
96. Marion, *In Excess*, 121.
97. Marion, *Being Given*, 132.

of the terms of its appearance. Such a change transforms my vision so I can recognize its appearance not by seeing the invisible (because saturated) phenomenon but by recognizing the impact of something other upon me. The phenomenon teaches me to see it as it gives itself, as my vulnerability to its impact transforms my vision so as to see it. Marion's point is not best illustrated with two people looking at the same phenomenon and seeing it and interpreting it differently. Rather, it is a matter of two people seeing two different phenomena in the same visible, where "they recognize, on the basis of different marks, different meanings, which are equally invisible even though all informed and organized by this visible."[98]

Second, I can only see the icon if I confess it as such. The icon appears to me in excess of the conditions of the possibility of my experience and knowledge of it but does so only as I accept its call upon me as antecedent to my response. The confession "does not consist only or first in an act (even of language or even a performative) but in a disposition (indeed, being put at the disposition) on the part of the one confessing to the confessed."[99] To see the icon is to have already made myself vulnerable to its gaze, to have already had my gaze transformed to see it. To confess, for Marion, is not to speak a judgment reached through deliberation (to decide that this or that image meets my definition of an icon) but to speak my starting point (to receive my reason *from* a particular phenomenon). "For what is proper to a starting point," Marion observes, "consists precisely in that it starts by starting from itself and that nothing else precedes it."[100] The recognition of a particular invisible meaning of the phenomenon is determined by whether I have conformed myself to it and received my starting point from it. To see an icon requires that I am converted to it and thus confess it as icon. I see the icon as icon—that is, as the visible of the invisible as invisible—only if I accept the relationship with the invisible that it claims and as it claims. I cannot decide (according to particular *a priori* conditions) to see the icon in advance of its

98. Marion, *Crossing of the Visible*, 72.
99. Marion, *In the Self's Place*, 56.
100. Ibid., 12.

appearance and cannot determine what excess it will give me. I can only allow myself to be vulnerable to what it gives and to be surprised by what appears. Marion argues that this acceptance of the givenness of the phenomenon—to stand under the gaze of the icon—leads to the possibility of its making itself known to me. Gaining this knowledge is otherwise impossible for me as an achievement of my own labor. But in receiving the saturated phenomenon as it is given, it might appear to me as it gives itself.

Third, the icon appears under the mode of fidelity to the invisible. Marion's most comprehensive articulation of this mode describes the fidelity of Jesus Christ to the invisible God, offering the mission of Jesus Christ as the paradigmatic icon. In a move that is far from the patterns and ends of historical-critical exegesis and is characterized by a philosophy with a heavy theological accent, Marion turns to, and interprets, the canons of the Second Council of Nicaea, convened in the eighth century to engage the iconoclasm controversy and to decide the orthopraxy and orthodoxy of the veneration of images.[101] From these canons, Marion concludes that "icons are thus opposed to idols by two qualifications," the first dependent upon the second: "First because they alone deserve and can demand the veneration of the faithful; second because they alone keep and manifest a trace of the brilliance of the holiness of the Holy."[102] The icon appears according to the mode of the trace—by being marked by that which it is not.[103] The justification for the veneration of icons is found in the icon's continued ability to bear the face of the invisible holy one while at the same time never claiming that holiness for itself—to maintain both relationship with, and distinction from, that which it shows. It is by maintaining

101. "We define with all accuracy and rigor that, concerning a manner [of] approaching to the type of the Cross . . . worthy of honor and invigoration, it is necessary to set up . . . [for God] holy and respectable icons, [made] from colors mosaics, and other suitable materials." *Actio* 7, as presented in Marion, *Crossing of the Visible*, 68; The translations of primary texts are Marion's own.

102. Ibid.

103. For more on "trace": "For if every element of the system only gets its identity in its difference from the other elements, every element is in this way marked by all those it is not: it thus bears the trace of those other elements. . . . These traces are not what a certain linguistics calls distinctive features, being nothing other than the traces of the *absence* of the other 'element.'" Geoffrey Bennington, *Derridabase*, in *Jacques Derrida*, by Geoffrey Bennington and Jacques Derrida (Chicago: University of Chicago Press, 1991), 75.

this tension that the icon becomes paradigmatic of the "appearance" of saturation and thus of phenomenology as a whole. It responds to the "inevitable dilemma" of religious piety: "Either the Holy maintains itself as such, in which case it refuses itself to every spectacle, and the holiness of God remains without with image or visage; or the image that delivers the Holy to the visible simply abandons it as a victim to the torments of its executioners—and the image, widow of all holiness, fills the role of an obscene blasphemy. Either the invisible or the imposter."[104] So, too, the icon becomes the fundamental mode of phenomenality; here, the phenomenon does not appear according to my established conditions of possibility (in which case it would not actually appear as such) but on its own terms. Yet the icon's bearing of this trace is a matter of my intentionality—that is, of my willingness to see what gives itself and not what I expect or desire to be there. The icon/idol distinction is always manifest "for me" and makes no metaphysical claim about the essence of that which appears. Thus it is never a matter of presenting the invisible (God) to be seen "as such." Rather, the mode of the icon is a matter of being formed to see it and of being converted by it, to it. The icon invites an anamorphosis by which the viewer adjusts his or her own expectation and understanding to meet the demands of what is given in the icon. I turn myself from my previous way of seeing toward seeing according to the givenness of the icon, toward seeing what it invites me to see.

But how does the icon form my intentionality so as to make visible the invisible as *invisible*? Borrowing from John of Damascus, Marion defines icons as "the types of that which has no type."[105] That the icon lays no claim to similitude with the invisible—that is, the mode of the icon is indifferent to the question of similitude or dissimilitude—is the key to iconic manifestation. It is never a matter of following a "logic of *mimesis*"[106] whereby the invisible is rendered visible through the icon's approximation of the holy. The need "to remain bound to a ruled relation to a prototype without having to obey the laws and demands

104. Marion, *Crossing of the Visible*, 67.
105. Ibid., 69.
106. Ibid., 71.

of the mimetic"[107] leads Marion to suggest that the icon follows the rule of fidelity to the invisible; this rule, in turn, depends upon the unique act of return accomplished by Jesus Christ upon the cross. The cross is the final measure of his fidelity, making visible the invisible *as invisible* through Christ's refusal to regard equality with God as something to be grasped. For Christ makes no claim to render visible the invisible God as such but instead always directs all veneration, and returns all holiness, to God—for Christ, as icon, has nothing that he did not first receive. In refusing similitude with God and remaining faithful to God in returning all things to God—even unto death on a cross—Christ reveals the invisible God without measure, concept, or image. He never claims to show God but calls those who hear him to fidelity to God.[108] This faithful return of all to God is accomplished without reserve or measure. "Christ does not offer only himself to my gaze to see and be seen," Marion writes, "if he requires of me a love, it is a love not for him but for his Father; if he demands that I lift my eyes to him, this is not at all so that I see him, him only, but so that I might see also and especially the Father"[109] As such, Christ's complete giving over of himself to God—a return of fidelity, not a claim of similitude—is

107. Ibid., 71–72.

108. Of course, in John's Gospel, Jesus says, "Whoever has seen me has seen the Father." But the larger context of these words seems to reinforce, rather than contradict, Marion's understanding of Christ as icon. For Jesus insists that his words and works are not his own but are received by him from the Father. Jesus Christ shows the Father by being transparent to the Father, not by claiming equality with the Father:

> Thomas said to him, "Master, we do not know where you are going; how can we know the way?" Jesus said to him, "I am the way and the truth and the life. No one comes to the Father except through me. If you know me, then you will also know my Father. From now on you do know him and have seen him." Philip said to him, "Master, show us the Father, and that will be enough for us." Jesus said to him, "Have I been with you for so long a time and you still do not know me, Philip? Whoever has seen me has seen the Father. How can you say, 'Show us the Father'? Do you not believe that I am in the Father and the Father is in me? The words that I speak to you I do not speak on my own. The Father who dwells in me is doing his works. Believe me that I am in the Father and the Father is in me, or else, believe because of the works themselves. Amen, amen, I say to you, whoever believes in me will do the works that I do, and will do greater ones than these, because I am going to the Father. (John 14:5–12 NAB)

109. Marion, *Crossing of the Visible*, 57. The resurrection narrative at the end of John's Gospel ("Simon, son of John, do you love me more than these?" [John 21:15]) proves more difficult to reconcile with Marion's interpretation than do other passages. It might be argued that at this point in the narrative, Jesus is well on his way to establishing that his unity with the Father is more than one of obedience, but such an argument may not be strong enough to wholeheartedly support Marion's philosophical exegesis.

marked only by his "coming undone [*se défaisant*] for the sake of the Father, by making sure that henceforth, all holiness finds its fulfillment in its transfer by itself toward the invisible Holy."[110] Here, Christ performs, and establishes, the logic of the icon:

1. Christ abstains from the claim of similitude—to render visible the invisible God, *as such*. Instead, he recognizes God as the source of all that is holy and acknowledges God as a prototype without type—as the one origin without equal.
2. The fullness of Christ's fidelity leads him to a perfect return, without reserve or measure, of all that he is and receives back to the source of holiness. This return is effected by his giving over of his entire life in perfect love of, and obedience to, God's will (obedience even unto death on a cross[111]).
3. This return—not as exchange of what is his for what is God's but as return of his entire life—bear witness to the excessive gratuity of God's gifts. By virtue of his fidelity, all that he is and does is a presentation not of his own will but of the one to whom he remains faithful.
4. While the invisible God is never rendered visible, Christ's faithful witness thus allows the invisible to appear as invisible precisely because he returns everything to it while never claiming to reveal it. "The icon is ordered to holiness by never claiming it for itself."[112]

Seeing this particular phenomenon as an icon of fidelity *par excellence* follows a properly theological confession. It recognizes Jesus Christ as not only the paradigmatic icon but thereby as the icon of the invisible Trinitarian God. This complete giving over of holiness to God "displays, in the humility of time and space, the unique act of return which, accomplished on the Cross, revealed economically the original return of the Son to the Father in the Spirit."[113] The confession of the cross as

110. Marion, *Crossing of the Visible*, 76.
111. See Philippians 2:5–11; this, of course, opens the question of how we are to discern God's will through interpreted revelation.
112. Marion, *Crossing of the Visible*, 77.

icon is a statement of faith that the visible there reveals the invisible as invisible—it is a confession that Jesus Christ is the revelation of the Holy One, a revelation brought to fullness in Christ's complete giving over of himself upon the cross. It is a confession that the complete fidelity of Jesus Christ, who "did not regard equality with God something to be grasped," reveals in "the form of a slave" and "in human likeness," that "Jesus Christ is Lord."[114] To see the cross as an icon of God is the confession of Christian faith.

Marion adds that such complete fidelity is also marked by resistance to it—specifically *my* resistance to it. Paradigmatically excessive, this return to the invisible God effects a call to me, a call to open myself to what is given in this phenomenon, to allow it to make itself appear to me by forming my gaze so as to see it. But to see it as it is given to me means a relentless conversion of both mind and heart to this immeasurable excess. It is here before the call to openness to such fidelity that the invitation of the idol is perhaps most attractive. The move to frame such a phenomenon in pleasant enough images and conceptions, whether because of my desire for mastery over it or only the exhausted longing for a place upon which to rest, arises as the alternative to complete fidelity.

Thus, in response to the icon's excessive call to fidelity to the invisible God, I might attempt to mark this holiness as visible. I frame it and proclaim the bedazzling fragment as all there is to be seen—I exert myself against its fidelity and try to replace it with an idol—with a God that I can grasp and—if you will—nail down. Christ's complete fidelity is made visible in my rejection of it and marked with my rejection of him. Christ's wounds signify the depth of my resistance to my own formation to faithful openness to the invisible God who saturates his life. In veiling excess, framing the phenomenon, and marking it with

113. Ibid. 76.

114. Philippians 2:5–11; see also, Marion: "It is always necessary to recognize in *this* visible spectacle, this visage and shape, these gestures and words, the definitive and incomparable mark that the invisible holiness imposes upon common visibility, the τύπος on and as which God condescends to be made seen as well as seen poorly, allowing itself to be both known [*connaître*] and misunderstood [*méconnaître*]. The type of the Cross—the sign of the Cross—bears the mark where the invisible Holy is given with such little reservation that the immediate rupture of its glory is abandoned." Marion, *Crossing of the Visible*, 73.

visibility, the wounded idol always already bears counterwitness to excess in the very rejection of that excess. The idol *is* my rejection of saturating givenness of the phenomenon; as such, the idol always negatively signifies that which I refuse to see. The saturated phenomenon (thus, even the saturation reduced to the idol) is always given in such a way as to resist being so completely framed—it always pushes back against my idolatry and strives for visibility even in being marked with my rejection of it.

Marion insists that this mark does not indicate the Father's willful sacrifice of the Son as a necessary step toward making the Father's presence known—this is not a case of celestial child abuse and the appeasement of a divine blood lust. The visible icon receives such a mark only as a result my reducing the visible icon to a visible idol (that is, by seeing only what is visible) in my own refusal to see (and therefore to endure) the icon's fidelity to the invisible. "In this struggle," Marion writes, "the invisible remains innocent: it is thus not the invisible that will forcibly brand the visible; it is on the contrary the visible [i.e., the image now reduced to an idol] that will mark the invisible with a fatal blow."[115] Christ's wounds signify the depth of my resistance to complete fidelity to the invisible Holy and in doing so reveal all the more the saturated givenness of the icon's fidelity. This revelation by trace of excess is perhaps visible as a phenomenological characteristic of the branding of slaves. One of the reasons the practice was inhuman was that the brand attempted to counter the very freedom that the human person, by their very appearance, demands. If that call to freedom was not part of the givenness of the face, no brand would be necessary (except insofar as to distinguish my cattle, etc., from my neighbors'—an act with a significantly different meaning). The brand illuminates, through contrast, both the excess of freedom called for by the saturated phenomenon of the face of the other and the slave owner's rejection of the freedom.

Even on the cross, Christ preserved the logic of the icon in refusing claims of similitude to God and remaining faithful to the invisible as

115. Marion, *Crossing of the Visible*, 73.

invisible. Christ remains faithful in his return without measure or reservation even while being marked by my resistance. What appears, then, is this infinite fidelity, this perfect return to God, this bearing witness to the Holy One who has no type. And it is in doing so that "the corpse of Jesus bears the marks [*les stigmates*] of the living God."[116] On the cross, Christ completes the logic of the icon and reveals himself as the Son of the Father—here his sonship is defined in the fidelity with which he returns all he is given to the Father in the Spirit.

To summarize the paradox of the icon: First, to see the icon I must be taught to see it. Second, I am so taught according to my confession of the phenomenon *as an icon*. Third, the icon appears under the mode of fidelity, not similitude. And in his perfect reception and return, Christ is the normative icon. It is my own intentionality, open to excess rather than restricted by *a priori* concepts, that allows the icon, rather than the idol, to appear. But, both complementary and paradoxical to this, I am not converted to such an intentionality of confession—to fidelity to the invisible—by my own authority or will because this confession is not mine to grasp but only mine to receive. I do not claim to define and name the excess given to me but only receive it and be formed by it.

Marion maintains tension at the heart of fidelity by reinterpreting the phenomenological subject as one who is always already involved by virtue of its having received, rather than established, itself. This new subject—or the one who comes after the subject (for terminology only matters to the extent that one is tied to preexisting definitions)—marks the phenomenological *I* which is not *a priori* but a received, and thus an *a posteriori*, origin. *I* am always already involved in interpretation, always already seeing the icon or the idol. Westphal observes, "Marion's phenomenological work has *de facto* taken the hermeneutical turn and is interpretation, caught up in the hermeneutical circle, rather than pure intuition"[117] (if by pure intuition, one means that of an unoriented, disinterested, conditioning *ego*). To call this a hermeneutic (as is not Marion's standard

116. Ibid.
117. Westphal, "Vision and Voice," 127.

terminology) is to recognize that Marion's understanding of phenomenology renounces all claims to the philosophical conceit of *a priori* neutrality and instead posits an intentionality that is always already responsive to an antecedent alterity.

But phenomenology itself cannot—indeed it does not presume to—have the means by which I might judge—morally, ethically, religiously—my decision to turn my gaze to an icon or to rest in the idol. It cannot judge the goodness, justice, or holiness of my response according to antecedent criteria. That I have done one or the other can be ascertained through phenomenological analysis. What I *ought* to do is a matter for nonphenomenological judgment of that which is phenomenologically described. But even as the presumption of mastery itself betrays the phenomenological endeavor—conditioning givenness with my own frame and not allowing the phenomenon to appear as it gives itself—I can still acknowledge that I must make choices as to the orientation and focus of my intentionality. Openness to the saturation of some phenomena as they are given precludes (because of time, exhaustion, commitments, etc.) such openness to others. This idols allows some saturated phenomena to appear to me at the expense of others. I close my eyes to the saturation of a given phenomenon so as to have time to open to excess elsewhere. But how to make this (often indirect, to be sure) choice (a decision, indeed, that is not reducible to antecedent conditions)? For while the movement between the idol and the icon can be described phenomenologically and even while the icon can be defined by this method as that which allows that which gives itself to show itself and therefore as that which furthers the phenomenological pursuit, making this distinction itself does not offer guidance regarding how I might come to open myself to the excess of a particular phenomenon. Phenomenology does not provide the needed guidance for my actual and limited lived life, choosing as I must between givens. It does not guide me in my discernment of this hermeneutic over another. To open to the saturation of *this particular phenomenon* rather than *that one*—this, indeed, is not a matter only of phenomenological distinction, nor of *a priori* choice, but of a reception of the gift of love (the focus of the next two chapters). To praise this reception as *good*, to speak of it as the meaning of human life, this is the concern of theology and of part 3 of this book.

Thus, the three characteristics of the hermeneutic of the icon lead Marion to conclude that the one to whom the icon appears is given the (previously impossible) possibility to see it in its being given to be seen. In being transformed to see the saturated phenomenon, I receive *myself* from that which gives itself to me. It is to this received and devoted self—what Marion names *l'adonné*—that I now turn. Chapter 7 explores this phenomenon of the gift, by which I receive myself from antecedent alterity. Chapter 8 examines the devotion of that self (the site of my turning to either the icon or the idol) through the saturating excess of love.

7

The Impossible Gift

> Let reality return to our speech.
> That is, meaning. Impossible without an absolute point of reference.
> —Czeslaw Milosz[1]

The icon offers a paradox: it is only in my openness to excess that I might see the image as icon, but such openness is always already a received response to the excess. It is through this reception that Marion hopes to speak of the rationality of a discourse dealing with the impossible, particularly with reception in the context of the gift. This chapter will begin with a brief recapitulation and furthering of the "new subject": the one who is given themselves in receiving the phenomenon as it gives itself. It will continue with a consideration of the gift and of Marion's articulation of this paradox of receiving: I receive who I am in my response to what is given—I receive myself as a gift. That the possibility of such a gift relies upon a paradox is nevertheless "not enough to disqualify [it] . . . for paradoxes only arise if one attempts to aim at certain phenomena starting from a point of view other than that which they ask for."[2] Thus we do not need to

1. "Treatise on Theology," in *Second Space: New Poems* (New York: HarperCollins, 2004), 47.
2. Marion, *Erotic Phenomenon*, 216.

be derailed by such paradox but are invited instead to reorient our attentive inquiry to what is given. Marion turns to that which appears as a metaphysical paradox, trusting that the phenomenon of the gift might itself offer that which it requires, hoping that the phenomenon of the gift itself gives an approach to its own givenness.

Always Already in the Middle: *L'adonné*

Against a subject defined by its "obsession with permanence and self-presence displayed in its control and constitution of objects through the method of certainty"[3] and in "its insistence of autarchy leading to solipsism,"[4] Marion posits instead a self who is received from my response to that which is given to me. Rather than exercising a mastery of that which appears to me according to my own *a priori* conditions, I find myself enveloped "in an experience where I occupy only one pole of a phenomenological horizon,"[5] and a responsive (although not necessarily subservient) one at that. To say that "*I* experience *myself*," (to use the nominative pronoun), "means that the *I* . . . experiences itself as a *myself/me*,"[6] not as an object (as a thing at my own subjective deposal), but in the dative case, as the receiver of the action of another.[7] I find that I am always already in the midst of being in relation with that which is not me, impacted and shaped by its appearance.

Marion argues that contrary to the common understanding, the autarchic, self-grounded subject fails to achieve what seems to be among its fundamental purposes: to delineate my active individuality. The inefficacy of grounding myself in the *cogito* (the "I think") lies significantly in its inescapable solipsism. The self grounded in the certainty of its own thought reduces each representation to an instance of "self-representation" wherein "all *cogitatio* harbors a

3. Christina M. Gschwandtner, *Reading Jean-Luc Marion: Exceeding Metaphysics* (Bloomington: Indiana University Press, 2007), 205.
4. Ibid., 206.
5. Ibid., 208.
6. Ibid.
7. Marion, *Being Given*, 249.

cogitatio sui."[8] As each thing is fundamentally a thought-thing, then "all 'I think' implicitly develops an 'I think myself.'"[9] Inasmuch as everything I think about is grounded first in the *I* who so thinks it, there is nothing that marks the distance, distinction, difference between *me* and that which is *not me*. Thus, in reducing all things to a self that is first self-thought and therefore self-caused, this subject is forbidden the one thing that can individualize them: the finitude that preserves, and is preserved by, alterity. In contrast, Marion suggests that the individualized *I* reaches its fullest phenomenality (that is, it most appears to me as it is given) not in the *cogito* but in and through a finite *me* who is first affected by intuition of that which is given. My individuation is not secured in a solipsistic reduction of all things to my self-caused thought but received in a givenness not my own. Individuation, therefore, is not the result of rendering all intuition under the mode of the object, of seeing all things as determined first and foremost under my gaze, but of an opening of my intuition to being affected by that which is decisively not me. I can begin to speak of myself only in receiving and responding to the impact of alterity—for it is this reception alone that I receive myself who is individualized in my response. For me to say, "I," another must first address me. I receive myself in being called.

That this impact of given alterity appears as a call, Marion admits, "has sometimes been troubling."[10] For his use of such language has often incited criticism, particularly regarding a supposed unspoken source of this call: God.[11] But Marion maintains the fundamental phenomenological anonymity of the call, asserting that insofar as the investigation into the call remains a phenomenological one, the concern at hand is with the givenness of the call—visible in its impact on my intentionality—and not the search, judgment, or interpretation of its possible source(s). In fact, the anonymity of the caller is phenomenologically necessary insofar as I receive myself from the call

8. Ibid., 253.
9. Ibid.
10. Ibid., 266.
11. I will explore Derrida's and Horner's exemplary criticisms on this matter in a later chapter.

first and can only later attempt to identify the source. The discernment of a source, the naming of the caller, is not therefore forbidden. However, such an identification is not possible while exclusively under the unique auspices of phenomenology, and to name the call as the voice of God is an act of faith or an interpretation of theology. Before any discernment of its source, the call itself characterizes me as the called, the addressee, the surprised one (*l'interloqué*). The call is the mode under which the saturated phenomenon appears—excess calls me to open to what is before me and therefore more than me. Finitude permits individuation and only originary reception opens the possibility for this finitude. In coming from an *elsewhere* that cannot be established by the transcendental *I*, the call, in its surprising address, gives me to myself as *the one who is called*. In confronting such excess, I am ensured my finitude; my own borders are drawn (if at times ambiguous). Marion offers a name for this post-subject self: *l'adonné* (other related terms, like *l'interloqué*, *l'attributaire*, and *l'amant*, are variations that build to this larger theme over the course of Marion's work).[12]

Phenomenologically speaking, this call gives me my devoted self through its antecedent alterity, identifying "the I only by transforming it without delay into a *me* '*to whom*.' The passage from the nominative to the objective cases (accusative, dative) thus inverts the hierarchy of the metaphysical categories."[13] Such an inversion of the "precedence of a formal *a priori* to experience"[14] establishes relation with alterity as

12. A note on translation: In *Being Given*, Jeffrey L. Kosky translates *l'adonné* as "the gifted," choosing to emphasize the one who "receives itself entirely from what it receives" (Marion, *Being Given*, 268) and maintaining the resonances with givenness, the given, and the gift. Christina M. Gschwandtner argues, however, that *l'adonné* "means to be 'devoted,' 'given over to,' or even addicted," and, "'gifted' works neither as a translation of the French term nor as a description of Marion's use of it" (Gschwandtner, *Reading Jean-Luc Marion*, 213), and prefers the translation, "the devoted." In recognizing that the French term carries with it the characteristic of not only reception but also this giving oneself over in devotion, Robyn Horner notes: "While Marion's preference is for a translation of *l'adonné* with 'the gifted,' I prefer to leave it untranslated and so to maintain its other awkward and ambiguous resonances." Horner, *Jean-Luc Marion*, 115n41. Because both the receptive and the devotional characteristics of the *adonné* are essential to my larger task—to relate Marion's work to *De Trinitate*—I will usually maintain the French, while at times emphasizing one resonance or the other.
13. Marion, *Being Given*, 268; emphasis in original.
14. Ibid., 271.

the ground for individuality, as the source from which I receive myself. This self, "accomplished in inauthenticity, originally nonoriginary,"[15] reveals claims to self-authenticity—of being first true to myself as the constituting *ego*—to be veils covering the truth of who I am.

This correlates with Marion's description of theology as that which "always writes starting from an other than itself."[16] This particularly theological take on inauthenticity is perhaps most clear in Marion's work in his analysis on Augustine's account of human creation in *On the Literal Interpretation of Genesis*. There, he highlights the distinction in the bishop's work between those things "created according to its kind, '*secundum genus suum*,' in conformity with itself alone," and the creation of the human being, not to the resemblance of itself "but according to its resemblance to another beside itself—and moreover, to another of maximum alterity, since it is a reference to God."[17] While the particular Augustinian notes of this articulation will be a significant focus for part 3, here it is enough to note the theological resonances of this inauthenticity and to see that the phenomenological and the theological (and properly Augustinian) each have (somewhat) independent grounds for their similar conclusions. The self is first received in being addressed and called by another.

To the objection that such a call would remain vain if there were not first a self to receive it, Marion responds by pushing the *aporia* even further, arguing that while I cannot say "I" until I first receive myself as *me*—that is, the *I* does not precede the call—neither does the call precede my response to it. Marion declines to play by the modern metaphysical rules that ground the self in either a subjective *I* or an objective *me*, with an underlying dichotomy of subject and object. If I receive myself by the call, so too do I receive the call in my response to it. In fact, I can only be said to receive a call as I respond—in some way—to the given phenomenon (if I do not respond, I neither could begin to interpret the call nor even be said to have received it). The

15. Ibid., 270.
16. Marion, *God Without Being*, 1.
17. Jean-Luc Marion, "Resting, Moving, Loving: The Access to the Self According to Saint Augustine," *The Journal of Religion* 91 (2011): 25.

icon forms me to see that which is given to me through it (i.e., the invisible) by giving me myself in my response to it. The *adonné* is a received self, who, marked by the counterexperience of saturation, is visible only in its response to that which is other than it. To be first responsive to that which is given is to open the space where the phenomenon can appear and to receive its otherness in my being formed to see it.[18] The one to whom the icon appears is given the (previously impossible) possibility to see it by being opened to that which I do not condition (i.e., the impossible for me). For it is only through such gratuity that the icon maintains the double phenomenality by which the invisible, as invisible, might actually appear in the visible. I see the invisible (God) because I receive the freedom to open myself to the invisible (God).

The call is only heard—made phenomenologically visible—in my response to it.[19] And yet there is no place from which I might be free of this antecedent call. I cannot escape from having already been in relationship with those others through whom I receive myself. While I can flee to the desert, to the fringes of civilization (be it geographically or, more likely, within my own mind), I cannot undo the fact that I did not establish myself in a space of personal neutrality (having been born of parents, shaped by those with whom I grew up, addressed by name, taught to speak my native tongue, and formed to think and act within a specific culture and system of beliefs). "I am" always already in response to the call of the other. "Consequently," Marion writes, "one could not decide to respond or even to refuse it. . . . Hearing has always

18. Jean-Luc Marion, *Prolegomena to Charity*, trans. Stephen E. Lewis (New York: Fordham University Press, 2002), 166–67.

19. What of this (pre)occupation with visibility? The language of *visibility* and *invisibility*, of the seen, the appearance, the gaze so fills Marion's analysis that it is not too far afield to suspect that the structures of visibility might actually significantly shape, if not constitute, those of the saturated phenomenon. In his article arising from the conference, "In Excess: Jean-Luc Marion and the Horizon of Modern Theology," University of Notre Dame, May 2004, David Tracy invited Marion to add a phenomenology of the voice to that of the visible, to respond to what he sees as a theological need for an account of the voice of God in the whirlwind, in the prophetic proclamation, and in its incarnation in the visible face of Christ. Tracy, "Jean-Luc Marion," 64. Marion's own language of "the call" seems to call for it—to need someone to allow its own particular givenness to be heard in the manner in which it is given. But, indeed, such a need is not limited to theology. For Marion's paper "The Banality of Saturation" sets out, in a limited fashion, a phenomenology of the other four senses with, once again, saturation as paradigmatic for each.

already begun."[20] I do not first hear the saturated phenomenon of the call yearning to give myself to me and then choose my response so as to render it visible (a situation in which two people might receive the same call, subsequently choosing divergent ways of response). Rather, it is my response that shows the phenomenon to me (where two different phenomena might then appear to two people based upon their openness to being shaped by the givenness of the given). The certainty of a modern (Cartesian) self—a self grounded in thought (doubting or otherwise) and formed by the belief that certainty was to be found in a truth of full validation of a concept that is perfectly equal to my intuition[21]—slides along the surface of such deep phenomenology, searching vainly for a place to ground itself. And while I can choose to believe its foundational claims, I can only preserve such belief to the extent to which I can batten down my idolatrous frame against the waves of vanity. If the certain self is grounded in the solipsism of the self-thought self—a vain certainty, to be sure—then the *adonné*, as always already responsive to antecedent alterity, is assured of itself only as having been received and formed, and continually being received and formed, by that to which it is devoted. I am assured only of being received from, and formed by, that to which I am devoted (and not, it should be noted, necessarily that I am devoted to that which I think myself devoted, nor does it offer any extrinsic measure by which I might judge whether I ought to so devote myself). I receive this self only inasmuch as it is given to me as a gift. And as that which is an impossible result of my own making, the gift can appear only under a reduction to givenness itself.

The Gift: Impossible?

At the Religion and Postmodernism Conference at Villanova University in 1997, Marion described his interest in this question as regarding the gift's phenomenological possibility and its relationship with the reduction to givenness: "At this stage of my work, I have to emphasize

20. Marion, *Being Given*, 288.
21. Marion, "Banality of Saturation," 384.

that I am not interested in the gift and I am not interested in the religious meaning of the gift."[22] He maintained that his concern was for the *gegeben*, the given, as the "ultimate determination of the phenomenon."[23] Using his conversation that day with Jacques Derrida as an opening through which to interpret Marion's philosophy of the gift, this chapter will respond to three questions, each a variation on the theme. The first question entails the tension between the gift and the horizon of economy: *Can a gift be given?* The second explores Marion's inquiry into whether the addition of the "as such" fits the givenness of the gift: *Can the impossible gift appear?* The third investigates the relationship between the gift and givenness: *Can the gift be given according to givenness alone?*

The First Question: *Can a Gift Be Given?*

Derrida's deconstructive reading of Marcel Mauss's *The Gift: The Form and Reason for Exchange in Archaic Societies* is one of the markings of the aporia of the gift from which Marion's own work finds a fruitful space to grow and will therefore serve here as an introduction to the philosophy of the gift. In his anthropological study of gift exchange in so-called archaic societies (though Mauss is clear in his conclusion that his analysis echoes true in contemporary life as well), Mauss locates the gift in the midst of a complicated cultural-economic framework, in which, through a continuing delicate game of patronage and debt, it serves to maintain the right relations and security of social place for those involved. Societal cohesiveness rests upon a continued exchange of gifts. In binding us to perpetual exchange, the gift binds us as a society. Therefore, "a gift that does nothing to enhance solidarity is a contradiction."[24] Whole sections of business law,[25] social insurance legislation,[26] and even family assistance funds[27] all grow from, and

22. Kearney, "On the Gift," 56.
23. Ibid., 57.
24. Mary Douglas, forward to *The Gift: The Form and Reason for Exchange in Archaic Societies*, by Marcel Mauss (New York: W.W. Norton, 1990), vii.
25. Mauss, *The Gift*, 66.
26. Ibid., 67.
27. Ibid.

have the potential to further secure, a "morality of exchange-through-gift,"[28] wherein societal relationships are established and maintained through a constant exchange of gifts. Mauss argues that this process of obligatory reciprocation, securing and perhaps furthering an individual's place in the larger structure, is "one of the human foundations on which our societies are built."[29]

Such giving is often conditioned by a continual need to out-do a received gift with a new and greater (or at the very least, not a lesser) gift. We cannot "'lag behind,' as the expression still goes. We must give back more than we have received. The round of drinks is ever dearer and larger in size."[30] This institution of the gift—the *potlatch*—eliminates the threat of the unreciprocated gift, which would otherwise make the "person who has accepted it inferior, particularly when it has been accepted with no thought of returning it." Mauss continues, "Charity is still wounding for him who has accepted it, and the whole tendency of our morality is to strive to do away with the unconscious and injurious patronage of the rich almsgiver."[31] The institution of the gift, therefore, ensures that I will maintain my equal (or at least just) relations with those around me by not taking more than what I have given. In receiving from another, I am obligated to give (and if I cannot give back, I at very least must pay-it-forward, as it were).

Derrida questions the apparent univocality of terminology whereby Mauss "speak[s] of [the *potlatch*] blithely as 'gifts exchanged'" without ever asking "the question as to whether gifts can remain gifts once they are exchanged."[32] He argues that the exchange of gifts nullifies the very possibility of gift, reducing the generosity of the gift to a form of masked barter: I give so as to receive and in receiving am indebted to give, all the while I deny the obligatory nature of such exchange. This denial is marked by both extravagance and deferral. First, an essential

28. Ibid., 70.
29. Ibid., 4.
30. Ibid., 65–66.
31. Ibid., 65.
32. Jacques Derrida, *Given Time: I. Counterfeit Money*, trans. Peggy Kamuf (Chicago: University of Chicago Press, 1992), 37.

feature of the *potlatch* is its lavish nature: "a moderate measured gift would not be a gift."[33] There is a certain "madness" about this exchange, a giving urged to a point of extravagant destruction where it cannot even appear that the giver wants repayment.[34] Here, an equal exchange would betray the gift, and thus only a magnanimous giving might allow the gift to appear. The key point here being that I always give more so as to avoid even the possibility of debt—to secure my societal ledger against any red. I cannot allow the possibility that I have received more than I have given. Second, the gift exchange operates according to a temporal cadence, an "interval that separates reception from restitution,"[35] that distinguishes it from other economic exchange. As an immediate exchange would void the gift as simply economic (I give you *x* for the *y* you give me), the gift only appears to the extent that it also gives time—that it gives time between the gifts and therefore temporally distances one from the other, allowing each to still seem to be a gift.[36] In both cases—and these are not exhaustive descriptive markers of the gift but representative ones—the gift relies both upon some exchange taking place (for even the magnanimous giver receives praise, honor, or at least self-satisfaction) while at the same time distancing itself from a direct economic exchange through an escalation of the returned gift over the received gift and the temporal deferral of such a return. It is this masked distancing from economic exchange that Derrida brings to light.

To state Derrida's deconstructive move simply: if the gift always grows from, and subsequently demands, reciprocation, then the gift does not escape the cycle of economic exchange. Even the extravagance of giving more is not the result of pure generosity but is instead tied to the desire to not be indebted to the other party. I give more so as to escape my debt; I give more so as to place others in my debt. The gift masks the exchange that continues below a surface of polite interaction, kindness, and even love, problematizing the purity

33. Ibid., 38.
34. Ibid., 46.
35. Ibid., 39.
36. Ibid., 41.

usually ascribed to both these markers of social relationships and to the freedom of the gift itself. The gift is given from obligation and the given gift is an obligation to reciprocate, all the while being also a denial of these very obligations. It is both an exchange and a denial of exchange, wherein the "conditions of possibility of the gift are also its conditions of impossibility."[37] While a gift free of the (always veiled) exchange would destroy solidarity, the very appearance of the gift would suffice to nullify it. It is not for nothing that "the Latin (and Greek) *dosis*, which enters English as 'dose,' bears the meanings of both 'gift' and 'poison.'"[38]

If the appearance of the gift under the conditions of exchange by which Mauss defines the gift would nullify the gift *as gift*, then Derrida's next question regards the phenomenological possibility of the gift and asks whether the gift can actually appear precisely *as gift* and not as a marker of economic exchange. Rather than problematizing "the gift in the horizon of economy, of ontology and economy, in the circle of exchange, the way Marcel Mauss has done," requiring, therefore, that somehow "we have to free the gift from this horizon of exchange and economy," Derrida tries "to precisely displace the problematic of the gift, to take it out of the circle of economy, of exchange, but *not* to conclude, from the impossibility for the gift to appear as such and to be determined as such, to its absolute impossibility." He continues:

> I said, to be very schematic and brief, that it is impossible for the gift to appear as such. So the gift does not exist and appear as such; it is impossible for the gift to exist and appear as such. But I never concluded that there is no gift. I went on to say that if there is a gift, through this impossibility, it must be the experience of this impossibility, and it should appear as impossible.[39]

The gift, problematized under the inescapable social and economic conditions of obligation and debt, is impossible. But, as it has already been established, such impossibility does not eradicate possibility but

37. Horner, *Rethinking God as Gift*, 9.
38. Ibid.
39. Kearney, "On the Gift," 59.

instead marks a paradox that might serve to reconfigure and resituate it.

Marion does not differ significantly from Derrida regarding the particular impossibility of the gift under the horizon of economy. He, too, recognizes the irreconcilable tension between the gift as that which is freely (without taking account of any obligation and debt) given (in that it must somehow phenomenologically appear) and the "malaise" with which the gift must suffer being measured against previous and future exchanges.[40] Where they disagree is a matter of the definition of phenomenology and the possibility of impossibility. Marion holds that the impossible can appear—it appears not by my rendering it possible (that is, achievable *by me*) but by my allowing it to appear according on its own terms (that is, as impossible *for me*).

The Second Question: *Can the Impossible Gift Appear?*

In response to this problematic, Marion proposes a description of the gift "outside of the horizon of economy" where "new phenomenological rules appear."[41] This suggestion of new rules is not inconsequential to the possibility of the gift, as they modify the definition of phenomenology and open the door to the criticism that Marion has left behind the rigor of this particular science for quite something else entirely (that is, for theology).

Marion describes the gift as consisting of a giver, the gift itself (the "thing" given, although this is not always, or even primarily, an object or the object that changes hands), and the receiver. To speak of a problematic of the gift is to recognize that the gift itself does not appear as *given*—or as *a given*—if it is further reducible to an economy of exchange between the giver and the receiver. The gift would therefore not appear if it serves as a token by which the giver gives debt and the receiver receives it. Furthermore, the status of giver or receiver themselves—precisely as giver and receiver of the gift—could not likewise be given. If the gift is a token of debt exchange, then the giver

40. Horner, *Rethinking God as Gift*, 6.
41. Kearney, "On the Gift," 63.

and receiver exchange that debt. Marion suggests, however, that while the gift cannot appear with all three of these elements at the same moment, we can "describe a phenomenon with two of the elements, not with the three."[42] Bracketing one element would therefore allow the gift to appear: a gift can be given without a receiver, as in the case of a gift to an enemy (who will refuse it) or an anonymous recipient (to whom I could not have been previously attached); a gift can be given without a giver, as in the case of receiving an inheritance (from one who can never more be present or even from whom I may have never met) or in finding upon the ground something of value (which further raises the question of whether there has to have ever been a giver at all); or a gift can be given where no *thing* is given, as in the cases of giving time, life, death, or power.[43] In bracketing one of these elements, Marion hopes to raze the masked exchange of debt and clear a place for the appearance of the gift.

Within such a place, Marion maintains that it is possible to describe the gift through bracketing elements, even as it forbids the "comprehension of [the gift] as an object."[44] He admits that such a description can never fully escape the threat of economic reduction but hopes that it can still serve to indicate that "it is impossible to reduce *everything* to economic terms."[45] The bracketing is not an end in itself but signifies (albeit weakly) the possibility of the appearance of the impossible gift. Whether or not such bracketing is convincing as a foundation for the gift is not the issue here (nor is it a helpful line of inquiry). Rather it is this possibility (as opening to the gift's own terms, impossible though they may be for me) that is Marion's deeper concern. To speak to this deeper possibility, he takes his argument one step further. As such an opening beyond economy is not possible by word alone, it is accomplished not in textual philosophical argument but by the formation that comes with commitment. He adds:

42. Ibid., 65.
43. While Marion has often described such bracketing, the text from which these particular examples come is Kearney, "On the Gift," 62–63.
44. Ibid., 62.
45. Horner, *Rethinking God as Gift*, 6; emphasis added.

> If I agree with Derrida to go beyond economy, I disagree with him on another point: This description of the gift can be made, but only in a very particular way. For we cannot make this description, which brackets one or perhaps two of the elements of the so-called economical gift, if we have not previously, in pragmatic experience, enacted by ourselves a gift without a receiver, or a gift without a giver, or a gift without anything given. And indeed this is not a neutral description: We have to commit ourselves by achieving the gift by ourselves, in such a way that we become able to describe it.[46]

Here, Marion inscribes the possibility of the gift within the context of the saturated phenomenon, arguing that its appearance rests upon the discovery, and not the *a priori* conditioning, of the gift, at the same time insisting that this discovery is only possible in my commitment—my conversion—to see it in its particularity. "The gift" only appears in my committed openness to *this gift that I give* or *this gift that I receive*. In this sense, the gift, as saturated, is not something that can be conditioned in advance of its appearing, explained abstractly so that it might be predicted and repeated. Calculation, prediction, and the constitution of sufficient reason of the gift all poison the gift because it thereby becomes the result of a cause (or series of causes). As a result, it appears not as gratuitous but because it had to, because it was reasonable to appear. The gift, if it is to appear, can only appear *as event*.

Marion's challenge here continues to be, as it has been elsewhere, the articulation of an intelligible description of the event that arrives in excess of all horizons save that of givenness itself. This pursuit of this rationality of the event of the gift leads Marion to suggest doing away with the "as such" of phenomenology—a move Derrida declared to be the "first heresy in phenomenology." To this accusation, Marion replied, "Not my first, no! I said to Levinas some years ago that in fact the last step for a real phenomenology would be to give up the concept of horizon. Levinas answered me immediately: 'Without horizon there is no phenomenology.' And I boldly assume he was wrong."[47] According to Marion's thesis, the "as such," rather than return to the

46. Kearney, "On the Gift," 64.
47. Ibid., 66.

unconditioned thing itself (which is precisely the intended use of such an "as such"), would situate the phenomenon under the horizon of the object or of being and define it as an instance of an essence, therefore actually veiling the givenness of the particular phenomenon itself under the guise of more of the same.

Changing the rules of phenomenology so as to include the possibility of a description of the unconditioned leads Marion again and again to the paradigmatic example of the unconditioned: God. Some fourteen years after the Villanova conference, Marion delivered his inaugural lecture as the Andrew Thomas Greeley and Grace McNichols Greeley Professor of Catholic Studies at the University of Chicago Divinity School, entitled "The Question of the Unconditioned—God."[48] In line with Marion's earlier work, the lecture begins with a consideration of the post-Cartesian status of the object as the inheritor of the Greek-initiated tradition (a lineage beginning with Plato's ιδεα and Aristotle's ειδος, moving to *forma, Wesen,* and *quiddity*) of speaking of the appearance of a thing as an individual instance of its essence. As an instance, I transform the phenomenon "into its form, to transpose it into a topic of knowledge"[49] and reduce it to an object. Under the horizon of the object, "essence demarcates what of the appearing can be thematized with certainty, hence what can be constituted as a distinct and defined object, producible from what in it exclusively comes down to order and measure . . . so that it might be produced and reproduced in actuality."[50] But, Marion asks, does this objective understanding of essence—of the phenomenon *as* an instance of essence, or the phenomenon *as such*—manage "to say the permanent truth about the thing, which its first appearing was not yet able to make available"?[51] Likewise, the alternative reduction of the

48. Jean-Luc Marion, "The Question of the Unconditioned—God" (inaugural lecture as the Andrew Thomas Greeley and Grace McNichols Greeley Professor of Catholic Studies, University of Chicago Divinity School, Chicago, November 3, 2011); all quotations are taken from the copy of the lecture distributed at the Divinity School. The fact that Marion continues to try to think the unconditioned God outside of being (since, at the very least, the original French publication of *Dieu sans l'être: Hors-texte* in 1982) shows significant continuity in his thought despite the expected growth and transformation.
49. Ibid., section 1.
50. Ibid.

phenomenon to an instance of being itself (whence the contentious and modern term "ontology") inscribes the phenomenon within the horizon of the being. The problem is that in reducing each phenomenon to an objective instance of essence or to a being as an instance of being itself, by referring the individual phenomenon to a pure essence, the *as such* "always establishes an a priori, which precedes and determines the conditions of appearing of any thing it takes as theme (indeed as object)."[52] This leads Marion to ask, "Can the two a priori which we have seen emerge, that of essence and that of beingness, be suitable for what we call—at this moment without precaution—God?"[53]

Marion is concerned with what is established in the "as such" or the "as" when we speak of the appearance of a phenomenon "as such" or "as [its] essence": the problematic *a priori* that sets the conditions for the possibility of the phenomenon's appearing to me as an instance of its essence—problematic for any phenomenon (as I presented in the previous chapters) but particularly for that which we call God (in whatever manner God might be said to "appear" to me—which is, precisely, the question at hand). Such conditions threaten both to betray the phenomenon by defining it in advance of its appearance and to mask the limitations upon, or absence of, appearance with presumed substance. Following Robyn Horner's reminder that phenomenology is not strictly a matter of examining that which is "manifest as present, but also that which is unapparent," and that "it is because phenomena are sometimes not readily given that phenomenology is necessary,"[54] I must reiterate my inability to allow the unconditioned givenness of a saturated phenomenon to appear *as* a concept of its essence. As my phenomenological vision is finite, my approach to an awareness of the unapparent (whether unapparent because of saturating or absent givenness, we can never be sure), will inescapably dabble in conditions. Thus, I can encounter excessive (or perhaps privative) givenness in

51. Ibid.
52. Ibid.
53. Ibid.
54. Horner, *Rethinking God as Gift*, 85–86.

two contrary ways. First, I can compare the phenomenon as it appears to that essence of which I know it to be an instance, filling in the gaps in appearance as we go with the substance of the known essence. Second, I can endeavor to acknowledge limitations (both known and unknown) on the appearance of the phenomenon, particularly those assumptions, beliefs, and judgments that I bring to the examination, and thereby give time and space within my consciousness for the phenomenon to present itself. The phenomenological approach acknowledges the less than clearly marked path between the phenomenon and my description of it, putting into question my attempt to articulate that which is unapparent to me. The impossibility of my having an unconditioned concept marks the saturation and invites my further openness to the given excess.

Central to Marion's phenomenology is the expectation that there will be obstacles to the appearance of a phenomenon, hence the need for a reduction that aims to bracket all that hinders appearance, even the *a priori* horizon in which I inscribe the phenomenon. This prompts two distinct though not unrelated questions for Marion, each relating to the way in which this phenomenological search for the unconditioned might lead me to God. First, the question that will occupy much of the remainder of this book and is at its heart: what does it mean to speak of the God as the unconditioned? To name God as *impossible for us*? This question, which I will only begin to enter into here, points to the foundation of Marion's philosophy of religion (the disciplinary category he often applies to his own work) and to any theological appropriation of his thought. Second, and the question that concerns much of the rest of this chapter, does the advent of God into Marion's thought tie givenness to a transcendental giver and so betray it as theology masquerading as philosophy?

"Does God have anything to gain by being?"[55] Marion provocatively asks as he begins *God Without Being*. Some three decades later he asks, almost repetitively, "whether there is only one single manner of existing and a single concept of being, and especially whether God

55. Marion, *God Without Being*, 2.

must submit to this ontico-ontological univocity, indeed whether God even has to be."[56] Inscribed in a horizon of objectivity or of being, God becomes an "instance of," *par excellence* to be sure, but nevertheless determined by the conditions of possibility of the object or of being, just like each of us. "God *as such*," wherein the existence of God becomes an instance of the essence of God, an essence submitted to the conditions of possibility and possible appearance, defined *a priori*.[57] The horizon under which the "as such" allows appearance "leads to a transcendental idolatry—submitting God to the conditions of the possibility of experience, such as a finite spirit like ours would define it a priori."[58] Against this dictatorship of measure, it is Marion's goal to illuminate a path of exodus from the *a priori* conditions that we place upon God's mediated appearance.

However, Marion asserts that such a path cannot be defined before the event of exodus occurs. The way beyond the horizon of the conditions of possibility is not delineated in advance precisely because the exodus from such conditions stands as impossible for us. A path of exodus outlined in advance would adhere to the conditions of possibility material to the very horizon we seek to overcome. Rather than an already established map of access to God—referenced from a neutral position where we might see perfectly both where we stand

56. Marion, "Question of the Unconditioned," section 3.

57. In his lecture, Marion is contending, in part, with both Anselm's so-called ontological argument and Kant's response to it. He continues: "Thus in order for God to reach an essence suitable to his dignity, he must surpass the simple thought of this essence though the fact of his existence, which nevertheless remains unrepresentable in thought. God is only God by transgressing his proper concept (his thinkable essence) precisely though his existence. What is such that nothing greater (no essence) can be though, would only be thus, if it were to appear greater than anything that can be thought by a concept." Ibid. The conventional Catholic theological tradition speaks against such a separation in God, maintaining with Thomas Aquinas that the essence of God *is* the existence of God and the existence of God *is* the essence of God. Marion's original engagement with Thomas in *Dieu sans l'être* drew significant attention and criticism (for a partial list of the sources of these criticisms, see Marion, *God Without Being*, xxii n5), prompting him to note, in his preface to the English edition (written nine years after the initial French publication) that Thomas "does not chain God to Being because the divine *esse* immeasurably surpasses (and hardly maintains an *analogia* with) the *ens commune* of creatures, which are characterized by the real distinction between *esse* and their essence, whereas God, and He alone, absolutely merges essence with *esse*: God is expressed as *esse*, but this *esse* is expressed only of God, not of the beings of metaphysics." Marion, *God Without Being*, xxiii. Although what such a merging might mean in Marion's interpretation of Thomas is far from clear.

58. Marion, "Question of the Unconditioned," section 4.

and where we hope to be (as though God could be so placed)—Marion suggests an approach *quoad nos*—regarding us, relative to us. Not, to be sure, a path defined in terms of our own expectations, understanding, and desires, but *quoad nos*,

> at least in the sense where this "regarding us" is opposed to the metaphysical *as such*, would be characterized by the transgression of the a priori limits imposed on possibility, in other words, by the overcoming of the boundary between the possible and the impossible—by the exodus toward the impossible. Access to the question of God *for us* must henceforth begin from what characterizes us and *us alone*, the boundary between the possible and the impossible, toward what characterizes it *for us*, the impossible *for us*.[59]

It is this boundary marking the limits of what is possible for us and our relationship with that which is impossible for us that characterizes the principle focus of philosophy of religion and distinguishes it from the study of precisely that which is impossible for us—that is, distinguishes it from theology.[60] But at the same time, Marion is tying the appearance of the unconditioned to our relationship with it. Not only is the impossible characterized by us alone (as that which is impossible *for us*) but also and because of this, it only appears as we open ourselves to that which has already been given, recognizing that we are already in the midst of givenness. The gift appears only insofar as it is free from an "as such" (thus free to show itself as it gives itself) and inasmuch as it appears *quoad nos* (free to gives itself *to us, to me*—that is, free to appear at all).

The Third Question: *Can the Gift Be Given According to Givenness Alone?*

To say that seeing the unconditioned requires an anamorphic conversion of my position and vision to the demands of that which

59. Ibid.; emphasis in original.
60. See, for presentation of God's being impossible *for us*, Jean-Luc Marion, "The Impossible for Man—God" in *Transcendence and Beyond: A Postmodern Inquiry*, ed. John D. Caputo and Michael J. Scanlon (Bloomington: Indiana University Press, 2007). A later version of this text appears as Jean-Luc Marion, "The Impossible, or What is Proper to God," chap. 2 in *Negative Certainties*, trans. Stephen E. Lewis (Chicago: University of Chicago Press, 2015).

is given to me can perhaps begin to sound too much like theology for some—like the insistence that to see God requires a conversion of understanding and love. There is a concern from many fronts that Marion, in attempting to think precisely the unconditioned, has abandoned phenomenology in favor of a veiled theology—opening the back door of the study of appearances *as such* for a transcendental signified to sneak in within the belly of the Trojan Horse of the unconditioned and inviting the destruction of phenomenology. The Villanova conference afforded Derrida—one of the most significant voices of this criticism—the opportunity to clarify his own concern centered on Marion's joining of the phenomenological given (*Gegebenheit*) with the gift:

> My hypothesis concerns the fact that you use or credit the word *Gegebenheit* with gift, with the meaning of gift, and this had to do with—I will not call this theological or religious—the deepest ambition of your thought. For you, everything that is given in the phenomenological sense, *gegeben, donné, Gegebenheit*, everything that is given to us in perception, in memory, in a phenomenological perception, is finally a gift to a finite creature, and is finally a gift of God. That is the condition for you to redefine *Gegebenheit* as a gift.[61]

Whatever distinction Derrida intended by not calling the deep meaning of Marion's understanding of the gift "theological or religious," he does state that this understanding finally, despite Marion's protestations, links gift with God, thereby rendering all givenness as divine gift. Such a correlation overdetermines givenness, renouncing the ambiguity and undecidability of its phenomenality. Derrida warns that for Marion, givenness risks becoming gift, and gift, despite Marion's best efforts, seems to be always already a gift given by God (thereby reducing Marion's philosophy to his faith in Christian revelation).

Robyn Horner offers an alternative insight into this matter. She suggests that "Marion sees phenomenology as a sort of prolegomena for theology" wherein he "seeks the enlargement of phenomenology

61. Kearney, "On the Gift," 66.

to include the possibility, rather than the actuality, of something like theology, based on the point that revelatory phenomena cannot simply be excluded from the limits of phenomenological investigation."[62] This, in and of itself, would not be problematic if Marion would remain comfortably within the accepted boundaries of what his predecessors understood phenomenology to be. But the examples Marion often chooses in order to explore the unconditioned are religious—specifically those of Christianity (for example, annunciation,[63] the Eucharist,[64] the crucifixion,[65] and the ascension[66]). While this is not so much the case in *Being Given*, even *The Erotic Phenomenon* reaches its climax with the suggestion that true love (or, to put it better, love) is only possible in the sight of the eternity of God. Although he insists that faith in these examples as revelatory is not a necessary requirement for a phenomenological analysis of them as given phenomena in the scriptures or the Christian tradition, Horner argues that in being "confronted with a saturated phenomenon such as Marion describes, I would have to be able to put to one side the question of whether or not it was a phenomenon of revelation in order to preserve its very quality of saturation."[67] In suggesting that these phenomena might be understood as saturated without the act of faith in them as revelatory, it seems that Marion seeks to establish the very dispassionate observer that he forbids. A phenomenology that seeks to return to not only the things themselves but to the unconditioned itself cannot be so easily separated from the interpretive activity of the one who seeks to return. Horner concludes that as "it could be argued in response that phenomenology always involves such a leap, for as Derrida has shown, there is no phenomenology without a tacit

62. Horner, *Rethinking God as Gift*, 156–57. The question of the relationship between phenomenology and revelation would be the topic for Marion's Gifford lectures, delivered at the University of Glasgow in 2014 and published as Jean-Luc Marion, *Givenness and Revelation*, trans. Stephen E. Lewis (Oxford: Oxford University Press, 2016). It is my hope that this book follows one of the possible directions indicated by Marion at the end of these lectures.
63. Marion, "Impossible for Man," 33–35.
64. Marion, "Of the Eucharistic Site of Theology" and "The Present and the Gift," chaps. 5–6 in *God Without Being*.
65. Marion, "The Last Rigor," chap. 7 in *God Without Being*.
66. Marion, "The Gift of Presence," chap. 6 in *Prolegomena to Charity*.
67. Horner, *Rethinking God as Gift*, 157.

hermeneutics,"[68] the difficulty with Marion's work occurs not in asserting such a leap of faith but "when the judgment is passed off as pure description."[69]

Both Derrida and Horner allude to an apparent leap at the heart of Marion's work, whether as reestablishment of a transcendental signified or the express denial of such a move. Yet Marion maintains that givenness is always first phenomenologically undetermined. He argues that it is not the case that all givens are reduced to the gift (and thus implying the transcendental giver) but that all gifts are reducible to givenness. Therefore, rather than an assertion that every phenomenon is ultimately from God, Marion hopes to offer a phenomenological description of gifts as *given phenomena that have been recognized precisely as given.* This is not even to say, with Horner, that the gift relies upon the given and is manifest when a particular hermeneutic is brought to bear upon the given—in this case, the interpretive lens of the Christian faith. While a Christian interpretation of givenness would not necessarily contradict phenomenology, and indeed may very well be welcomed by it, Marion insists that the relationship between givenness and the gift can both be thought without reference to either a transcendental signified or a Christian hermeneutic and offers the concept of *sacrifice* as a lens through which to see the phenomenological gift.

In "Sketch of a Phenomenological Concept of Sacrifice,"[70] originally delivered as part of the James W. Richard Lectures at the University of Virginia in 2008, Marion explores the concept of sacrifice as a way to deeper understanding of the gift and by the gift, to come to a true vision of sacrifice. The common sense of sacrifice—"destroying what should not be destroyed, at least according to the normal practices of daily life, namely, the useful and the functional"[71]—leads to an aporia (disconcerting for any whose approach to life's meaning and value

68. Ibid., 158.
69. Ibid., 159.
70. Marion, *Reason of the Gift*, ch. 4. Marion would return to this question of sacrifice in "The Unconditioned and the Variations of the Gift," chapter 4 of *Negative Certainties*, where he maintains that "sacrifice supposes a gift already given" (126).
71. Marion, *Reason of the Gift*, 70.

includes some sense of sacrifice): destroying something is not sufficient to make it sacred. Moreover, sacrifice according to the mode of exchange establishes another aporia—echoing Derrida's description of the impossibility of the gift. For a renunciation of some good in hope of receiving a counter gift (delayed perhaps, but in the end "worth" the sacrifice) annuls the sacrifice, making it instead an investment in future return. A third way, sacrifice as a gift whereby "the giver allows his gift to separate itself from him, and assert itself as such, autonomous and thus available to the recipient, who appropriates it,"[72] results in the exclusion of the giver. Here, the gift would only be truly given if the giver is effaced so as to allow the receiver to lay full claim of the gift. But in so doing, the gift manages to not only efface the giver but also itself *as gift*. It becomes a "found object"[73]—which in the end is nothing more than a possession of the receiver, who, in turn, is no longer a receiver but the one to whom the object belongs. To eradicate the giver is to poison the gift, to betray the sacrifice. Thus, when Marion suggests (as he often does) that the gift might appear if one or two of the three elements (giver, gift, receiver) is bracketed, he does not intend by this bracketing an effacement. Rather, something else entirely is going on. The giver withdraws but is not thereby removed from the gift.

The possibility of the gift is tied to its relationship with givenness. However, Marion maintains that givenness is not to be reduced to the gift (a maneuver in which each given is given by someone or something) but that the gift is to be reduced to givenness:

> The question thus does not consist in reverting from the given to the giver, but in letting appear even in the gift ultimately given (in a being arrived in its arrival [*arrivage, Ankunft*] the advancing process of its coming-over, which delivers its visibility by giving it to the gift, or, more generally, the very coming-over that delivers the gift phenomenally. . . . At issue would be the suspending of the gift given, so that it would allow the process of its givenness, namely, the given character of the gift . . . to appear in its own mode, instead of crushing it in the fall from the given into a pure and simple found object. So it is not a question of

72. Ibid., 77.
73. Ibid., 78.

> suppressing the gift given, for the benefit of the giver, but of making this gift transparent anew in its own process of givenness by letting its giver eventually appear there, and, first and always, by allowing to appear the coming-over that delivers the gift into the visible. At stake here is the phenomenality of this very return: to return to the gift given the phenomenality of its return of the return that inscribes it through givenness in its visibility as a gift coming from somewhere other than itself.[74]

Givenness is the "not from me" or the "from elsewhere" from which the phenomenon arrives—it is the indetermination that allows precisely the phenomenon to appear as itself and not be reduced to an object or instance of essence. As given, the phenomenon demands that I see it as something other than what I might decide it to be, something in excess of my conditions for its appearance, something unconditioned by my expectations, understandings, and desires. In short, the key to Marion's concept of givenness is the appearance *from elsewhere*. It is a matter not of what such an elsewhere might subsequently come to signify but that here it does not signify anything other than a "not me." Not an object or an instance of essence, the phenomenon is strictly given.

The gift allows the given phenomenon to be given *to me* while nevertheless retaining its arrival from elsewhere. To sacrifice, then, is to acknowledge the origin of the gift (here, as of yet, only an underdetermined elsewhere) and to thereby return the received gift to this elsewhere. Sacrifice serves a signifying function, making appear the "referral from which [the gift] proceeds, by reversing it (by making it return) toward the elsewhere, whose intrinsic irrevocable, and permanent mark it bears insofar as it is a gift given."[75] By presuming the gift as given, the sacrifice allows the gift to appear in its return to the elsewhere whence it came; in so doing it signifies this whence as truly *elsewhere*, as saturated. The gift appears to me when I receive a given as gift. It appears as I receive a given not by claiming it as *mine* but in recognizing that it arrives from elsewhere and responding

74. Ibid., 82–83.
75. Ibid., 83.

accordingly to that arrival. It appears as I sacrifice it, recognizing that it is not mine to determine, to do with as I please, but mine to receive according to its own givenness. Thus "sacrifice does not separate itself from the gift but dwells in it totally,"[76] always attempting a return by recognition of the gift character of the phenomenon, never presuming that such a return of a received gift could ever pass for an exchange (precisely because it is first and foremost recognized as a return of what was never mine to begin with). The point of sacrifice, Marion concludes, "is the recognition of the gift as such,"[77] the gift itself being a recognition of the given phenomenon as from elsewhere than me. To say that something is a received gift is the sacrifice that recognizes its arrival from elsewhere. Thus, while the gift does, in fact, veil the giver (as the giver must withdraw so the gift might appear—or better, the withdrawal of the giver allows the gift to be given to me and not remain the giver's), it is in the recognition of this process that "the giver eventually becomes visible again as well."[78] Such sacrifice makes visible the withdrawn giver *as invisible* through my praising the given as gift. I praise the one who withdraws so I might receive.

Marion's description of the gift in terms of sacrifice carries over much of the pattern of thought from the icon. As the icon is bound to the invisible original without type, the gift only appears when the phenomenon can maintain its reference to the origin of its givenness. The phenomenon that veils such an origin is an idol. The gift that denies that it is given from elsewhere is simply not a gift. Marion offers by way of an (again, religious) example Isaac's clear status as a miracle from God whose givenness is erased insofar as Abraham claims him as his son (in what is likely a stretched interpretation of Genesis 21:3: "Abraham called the name of his son who was born to him, whom Sarah bore to him, Isaac"), thus requiring that Abraham acknowledge the gift of his son in sacrificing Isaac to God.[79] That this sacrifice did not necessitate Isaac's destruction confirms for Marion that it is the

76. Ibid.
77. Ibid., 84.
78. Ibid., 85.
79. Ibid., 84–89.

acknowledgement of the phenomenon *as given* that defines the sacrifice. Likewise, where the icon appears in its returning my gaze to the invisible as invisible, the gift appears in my willingness to sacrifice it, an acknowledgement that returns it to the elsewhere whence it came and maintains its status *as gift*. The giver can thus appear as withdrawn—that is, as invisible. To sacrifice is to recognize that the giver has withdrawn from visibility and must remain as such so the gift might appear. It is not even so much that to sacrifice we must name a giver—as though we might scour the world for some trace, some *vestigia*, and then subsequently proclaim those things marked with that trace to be gifts. Rather, the very act of recognizing givenness is itself a "sacrifice in truth,"[80] acknowledging the gift. To so sacrifice is to return the gift to an "I know not where."

But in acknowledging this *elsewhere*, a significant question remains. Can I ever name the giver? As far as a theological appropriation of this work is concerned, such a question might be rephrased: How does the underdetermined elsewhere of givenness relate to the (far too often overdetermined) divine giver? Marion may very well be able to maintain a phenomenology of givenness that falls prey to neither a necessary transcendental signified nor an active, but hidden, Christian hermeneutic. I may well be able to recognize the givenness of "the dearest freshness deep down things,"[81] to recognize that it arrives as gift, freely given. But can I name this elsewhere? And if I cannot name it, then I cannot call it by a particularizing (that is, proper) name. While Marion's concept of saturation sufficiently warns against an overdetermined elsewhere (that is, one that I determine and therefore not an elsewhere), and certainly an elsewhere named in advance, it is necessary to show how the sacrifice of the gift not only allows it to appear and allows the signification of a withdrawn giver but also that this signification might make possible the particularizing of this giver through some signification. For Abraham, however we might read Genesis, sacrificed his son not to an unnamed elsewhere

80. Ibid., 89.
81. Gerard Manley Hopkins, "God's Grandeur," in *Poems of Gerard Manley Hopkins* (London: Oxford University Press, 1949), 70.

but to a particular one with whom Abraham had a covenant, to whose call Abraham responded, "Here I am."[82] It is my hypothesis that this givenness might be ascribed to God by theology, such that the origin of the gift might be found in, and thus returned to, God. At the very least, I hope to mark how the phenomenology of the unconditioned might open to a theology (not as a possible fulfillment of phenomenology but as the possibility of phenomenological impossibility), wherein "God" and "gift" might signify each other. Although to arrive at such a naming, or to allow this name to arrive, requires one final step: one of and in love.

82. Genesis 22:1.

8

A Love that Bears All Things

> Nothing supports the lover, thus it is necessary that he bear everything.
>
> —Jean-Luc Marion[1]

If the *adonné* is a gifted self, in what sense is it devoted? This discourse on the impossible rests significantly upon a phenomenology of saturation rooted in an openness to otherness appearing in excess of my finitude and perspective and allowing the other to show themselves or Godself, truly. To allow the other to appear to me as particular and "unsubstitutable"[2]—to appear just as the other gives themselves—rather than appear as an instance of essence, a manifestation of some further reality; to allow the other to impact me, appear in me, and thereby form me from a depth more intimate to me than I am to myself—this, indeed, can be named by a single word: love.

There is no denying that Marion claims that love does much in its own appearing, which serves always and only as an end in itself. I love, for Marion, to love—both in the sense that I love *so* I can love (that is, love is and has its own reason) and I love *loving* (that is,

1. *Erotic Phenomenon*, 86.
2. Marion, *Prolegomena to Charity*, 164.

being a lover). Or better, I love because I desire to be one who loves for no other reason than to be a lover of *this particular beloved* (as I never love generally, but always particularly). And although Marion discusses the reason of love throughout his corpus (wherein all books "bear the mark, explicit or hidden, of this concern"[3]) there is no place that it receives a more intense focus than in the text that "obsessed"[4] him since his publication of *The Idol and Distance* in 1977: *The Erotic Phenomenon*.[5] Therefore, while not ignoring his presentation of love elsewhere, I will focus my attention on an explication of this text toward its application to the question at hand: God's appearing in and through love.

First, a note on the univocality of love. Marion contends that "every border traced upon the heart of love"—particularly the common distinction between *eros* and *agape* (and, although less-frequently included, *philia*)—rather than furthering understanding, "wounds [love] definitively."[6] Whether defined in terms of passionate love versus disinterested love, need love versus gift love, or pagan love versus Christian love, this distinction serves to obfuscate the truth of love, tear it to pieces, and to prevent love's unity with itself.[7] An understanding of love is additionally frustrated by the prostitution of its name wherein one "'makes' love like one makes war or makes deals, and all that remains to be determined is with which 'partners,' at what price, for what profit, at what interval, and for how long."[8] If, for

3. Marion, *Erotic Phenomenon*, 10.
4. Ibid.
5. Ibid.; published originally as Jean-Luc Marion, *Prolégomènes à la charité* (Paris: Éditions de la Différence, 1986; 2nd ed., 1991). It was published in English in 2007.
6. Marion, *Prolegomena to Charity*, 160.
7. Ibid. For an example of the distinction between "need love" and "gift love," see C. S. Lewis, *The Four Loves* (New York: Harcourt, 1960). To be fair to Lewis, he begins to transform this distinction at the end of the chapter on *eros*, when he sees *agape* as the end of erotic desire. Nietzsche's praise of the pagan *eros* carries with it a criticism of Christian love (in selections scattered throughout his corpus), which dismisses it as a weak and effeminate renunciation of one's own rights and a submission to a slave mentality. In extolling the inability for hatred as a virtue, such love makes one prey to all those whose will is strong enough to embrace their own desires. In this way, Christian love is proven to be weak and stands against life itself (as described, for instance, in the conclusion of *The Anti-Christ*). It has become standard in discussions of this distinction to reference Andres Nygren's *Agape and Eros*. In this text, Nygren maintains the distinction between *agape* and *eros* as one between Christian and pagan loves, a distinction that amounts to two contrary understandings about the ultimate meaning of human life. But where Nietzsche condemns Christian love, Nygren seeks to purify Christian *agape* of *eros*.

the ostensible goal of deepening knowledge, the distinctions between *eros*, *agape*, and *philia* reduce love to something insufficient to itself, its prostitution indicates a desire for something less than love, for something that never attains love's powerful vulnerability and instead shrouds the assertion of the *ego*. Central to Marion's task in *The Erotic Phenomenon* is the healing of the wounds that have been delivered to love—such wounding, in the end, being for each person an act of self-mutilation. If the seriousness of a concept of love "distinguishes itself by its unity, or rather by its power to keep together significations that nonerotic thought cuts apart, stretches, and tears according to the measure of its prejudices,"[9] then such a concept must both unify its differences and repair its derogations (like one repairing/repatriating oneself by returning home) by allowing love to appear as itself—to speak for itself—in the erotic reduction.

The Erotic Reduction

The Erotic Phenomenon is Marion's most attentive and thorough presentation of his phenomenology of love, describing—by the bracketing of commonly accepted understandings of love and observing the conscious experience of love in this reduced state—love as it gives itself to be seen. Yet the text begins not with love at all but with the Cartesian question of certainty and the desire to know. This epistemological certainty is grounded in knowledge of the object as that which can be "reduced to permanence (by models and parameters, reproduction and production)."[10] At the same time, certainty grounds that very knowledge by delineating the boundary of the object—that is, by defining it. In this way it is both a function of the *ego* and determinative of the *ego*, for it is precisely the subject that defines the object; in such defining, the object, in turn, becomes determinative of the subject. The object becomes that which I define sufficiently, and in defining it as sufficient to my knowledge, the object confers certainty.

8. Marion, *Erotic Phenomenon*, 3.
9. Ibid., 5.
10. Ibid., 12.

The subject *is* that which defines the certain object and therefore is defined by its relationship with objects. But putting "certainty into doubt,"[11] Marion contends: "Certainty attests its failure in the very instant of success: I indeed acquire a certainty, but, like that of beings of the world certified by my efforts, it sends me back to my initiative, and this to me, the arbitrary operative of every certainty, even my own."[12] Certainty rests in objective phenomena (that is, in phenomena that I have defined as objective), but such phenomena appear only as I allow. And, try as I might, I cannot include among those things that are certain—certified by me—that which resists this objectification: the answer to the question, "What's the use? [*A quoi bon?*]"[13]

Marion begins *The Erotic Phenomenon* with this problematizing of certainty—an opening that should not surprise his readers, Marion being so steeped in the work of Descartes. Certainty itself leads to vanity, in both of the interdependent senses of uselessness and egoism, in the subjective *ego*'s founding assertion of itself through certainty and its assertion of the certain through itself. "To produce my certainty myself does not reassure me at all," Marion concludes, "but rather maddens me in front of vanity in person. What is the good of my certainty, if it still depends upon me, if I only am [certain] through myself?"[14] This problematizing is consistent with his constructions of the *adonné*, the gift, and the saturated phenomenon, each further applicable as a way to temper the assertive yearning of the *ego*, this *libido dominandi* that characterizes for Marion the thrust of modern metaphysics. The answer to the question "What's the use?" cannot be found in my own framing of the world under *a priori* conditions of meaning. To assert with certainty that *this* particular thing (whatever it may be) can be sufficiently understood in *my* particular way is not enough to save me from nihilistic vanity. For such salvation, Marion offers an erotic reduction through which he hopes to trace the three

11. Ibid., 13.
12. Ibid., 19.
13. Ibid., 16.
14. Ibid., 19.

step movement from this vanity toward the full description of his answer to the fundamental question, "What's the use?"

Marion's first movement begins in recognizing the solipsistic vanity of this certainty and turns instead to love, asking, "Does anybody love me? [*m'aime-t-on?*]"[15] In a metaphysical context (whether accented by ontology, causation, or epistemology), such a question would necessitate an antecedent investigation into the permanency, possibility, and definition of the *ego* in question prior to establishing relational identity, ultimately reinstating me upon the throne of vanity. But the erotic reduction, abdicating claims to the establishment of a clearly defined self prior to reception of relation, turns instead to *erotic* certainty—the assurance of love. Where certainty, for Marion, rests in the *ego*, I receive assurance, as I do the gift, from elsewhere (*d'ailleurs*).[16] I turn to assurance to overcome vanity because it is a gift that I do not establish in myself. I turn to assurance, because the answer to the question "Does anybody love me?" can never be certified by me but only offered to me from elsewhere. Under the erotic reduction, I am not first subject to any other horizon, I am not a result of my first being, of my being able to acquire accidental description. Here, "loved" is not an attribute that can be applied to an existent substantive but is itself what is given when I am given myself. It becomes determinative of both subject and the act of predication—"loved" governs the "I" and the "to be" in "I am loved." I am introduced "into a horizon in which my status as loved . . . or in short my status as lovable, no longer refers to anything but itself."[17]

Moreover, Marion emphasizes here the importance of the antecedent anonymity of the response I seek, which comes "upon me without announcing itself or giving warning, and thus without allowing me to foresee anything."[18] This *given* response to my question, should it come, arrives as an event. As an event, it arrives in overcoming the vain limits of self-certainty and in excess of my

15. Ibid., 20.
16. Ibid., 23.
17. Ibid., 28.
18. Ibid., 24.

conditions. It arrives in a way I could not have predicted, by means that I cannot fully enumerate. As an event, the arrival of the assurance of love cannot be measured and defined (whether in anticipation of its arrival or even after the fact), because the very thing that arrives cannot, by definition, be objectively measured, as "the measure of this love requires loving without measure"[19] (that is, without my ever reducing this event to something I can fully conceptualize). There is no standard against which such an event can be measured save its own givenness. Precisely in excess of my measure, such assurance calls for "an exteriority that is not provisional"[20] but infinite (at the very least in promise and possibility).

I can, of course, try to sidestep this exteriority through the hope that I can assure myself, through the hope that I can love myself. Such self-love understood as self-care is a fine thing but sufficient only "in a nominal form, abstract and empty of personal content."[21] Self-care cannot quell the question that haunts me. The preservation and healthy flourishing of my being—the focus of the care of myself—are an insufficient response to the question at hand. For self-love to assure me that I am loved, my unity would have to be split into a subjective *I* assuring an objective *me*, rendering it necessary "for me to precede myself,"[22] whereby I might assure myself amidst turmoil. The subjective *I* would stand apart from the objective *me* in need, even as it is the need of objective *me* that necessitates such precedence. Such ill-fated and misnamed self-love attempts both to recognize my desire for certainty and to secure that certainty myself through the infinite assurance of a transcendental *I*. However instead of assurance, I am left only with the internal contradiction of perpetually asserting to myself and all who can hear that I am sufficient to my need—a need whose existence betrays my inability to grant myself this assurance. I cannot answer the question with the very thing that poses it.

I can proceed in such contradiction only insofar as I can maintain

19. Ibid., 46.
20. Ibid.
21. Ibid., 44.
22. Ibid., 45.

the self-deception that I am not in internal schism—that I am not struggling to sustain this self-assurance by acting the part of the schismatic, splitting myself so that I might receive from myself that which I already most need. As a schismatic, I operate under the illusion that I can, by such a split, assure myself against solipsistic vanity through self-assuring self-love. I can rest here only in frenetically maintaining the lie to myself that such infinite self-assurance (that I am sufficient for myself) is possible.[23] But the denial of this schismatic self can only be maintained for so long. Cracks in my façade begin to show both in hatred directed at others (for not loving me) and in hatred directed at myself (for being insufficient to myself). I will hate others because my need for them reminds me that I am insufficient to myself. Marion powerfully illustrates the failed promise of such self-assurance in an earlier work on love, *Prolegomena to Charity*. There, he names the source of this promise, of this betrayal: Satan. Marion's image of the mythological figure is both theologically rooted and phenomenologically consistent. The person of Satan (and here Marion relies upon the flexibility of the French *personne* to mean both "a person" [*une personne*] and "nobody" [simply *personne* without an article or as a negation *ne . . . personne*]) appears only in his absence. For hell is specifically characterized by this "missing betrayer," who marks not the deception of the soul by another (whether evil force or fallen angel, it matters little) but the leasing "of the role of the betrayer to the very one who finds himself betrayed."[24] Satan's person *is* only the deceptive "ungraspable flight"[25] upon which I try to assure myself that I am sufficient for myself. Satan is the name of the voice through which

23. Ibid., 56.
24. Marion, *Prolegomena to Charity*, 20. Charles Williams illustrates well this damning self-betrayal in the conclusion of his novel *Decent into Hell*, which describes the moment when Lawrence Wentworth finds himself, having climbed down a long rope, inescapably condemned by his own lies to himself: "he knew he was lost. . . . He wanted desperately to hold on to the rope. The rope was not there. He had believed that there would be for him a companion at the bottom of the rope who would satisfy him for ever, and now he was there at the bottom, and there was nothing but noises and visions which meant nothing. The rope was not there." Charles Williams, *Decent into Hell* (Grand Rapids: Eerdmans, 1949), 220.
25. Marion, *Prolegomena to Charity*, 23.

I deceptively say to myself that I am sufficient for myself, that I do not need assurance from elsewhere, that I am as God.[26]

In contrast to this hellish hatred of my finite self, the arrival of the *adonné* from elsewhere begins to be all the more strikingly visible (but is as of yet not fully given). If the question "Does anyone love me?" is not sufficient to free myself from solipsistic self-hatred, it can be rearticulated as "Does anyone *out there* love me? [*m'aime-t-on—d'ailleurs?*]"[27] This change turns from the attempted assurance of self-love (which is, in the end, just a mask for the quest for the metaphysical certainty that reduces me to an object) toward accepting that the answer to the question "What's the use?" cannot come from myself but can only be given to me from another. However, in turning elsewhere for assurance, I cannot simply mask a desperate groping for love by which I only take "the risk of the erotic reduction under the threat of vanity."[28] If refraining from giving love until I have first received it and found it to be sufficient to so assure me, I am merely seeking love according to the measure of my need for assurance. I do not, then, ever really escape from the solipsistic vanity by which I see this elsewhere only according to my need for it. An elsewhere defined by my need is not *elsewhere* at all but simply another route to securing metaphysical certainty. Following in the pattern of the gift, Marion finds that the specific gift of love given only in exchange for services rendered suffices to nullify the love and replace in its stead a measured exchange wherein I can be certain that my openness to this elsewhere is only as much as I think I need. Therefore, if I hope to receive love from elsewhere, to receive an answer to the question "What's the use?" that is not a mask for that which I am already certain (which, again, does not actually respond to the question), I must venture love that is not dealt according to what I first receive.

Marion initiates the second movement of his erotic reduction in recognizing this threat of love reduced to reciprocity. The rejection of a mercantile definition of love invites a renewal of the reduction by

26. Interpreting Genesis 3:5.
27. Marion, *Erotic Phenomenon*, 40.
28. Ibid., 68.

means of a new question: "Can I love first [*puis-je aimer, moi le premier*]?" Here, the lover's response to the haunting "What's the use?" is rooted not in certainty of my being, nor in self-love, nor even in acquiring the assurance that I am loved (insofar as I reduce love to a means of acquiring certainty). Rather, in initiating the love—in "advancing as lover," in Marion's terminology—I receive only the assurance that I love. Thus, while the beloved may love me (although they very well may not), my love is not dependent upon such reciprocation (for love *as reciprocated*—insofar as such reciprocation is in exchange for my initial investment of time, care, attention, etc.—is not love at all). But my giving love without consideration of necessary exchange is not therefore written off as loss. For "love itself is never lost," Marion writes, "because it is accomplished in loss."[29] The question of whether or not I receive love from the other bears no influence upon my advance. Echoing Marion's familiar transgression of the terms of metaphysical being,[30] his concept of love proceeds in excess of any terms and conditions other than its own: love is always given to the beloved without concern for anything other than its being given to the beloved. For the lover—precisely in not playing by the rules of being, of certainty, or of exchange—is always free to give. "Love consists sometimes in not being—in not being loved, or at least in accepting being able not to be loved. Nothing, nether being nor nothingness, can limit, hold back, or offend love, from the moment that loving implies, by principle, the risk of not being loved. To love without being loved—this defines *love without being*."[31] In excess of being's horizon, love includes, too, victory over nothingness. Love assures the lover of their love, an assurance grounded in nothing at all but love. "In the erotic reduction," Marion writes, "the lover who loses himself gains himself all the more as lover."[32] To be sure, this self gives not the permanence or security of my being but my status as one who loves first (that is, not only after being loved), my status as a lover.

29. Ibid., 71.
30. See, for example, Marion, *God Without Being*, especially chap. 3, "The Crossing of Being," 53–107.
31. Marion, *Erotic Phenomenon*, 72; emphasis in original.
32. Ibid., 73.

Marion builds upon his concept of the saturated phenomenon through a gift of love that appears only according to its own terms, "without reason . . . counter to the principle of sufficient reason"[33] —that is, as an event. If the saturated phenomenon is visible as a counterexperience of excess whereby I experience the transgression of my conditions of possibility and my limited horizon by that which does not appear according to my antecedent understanding, so love appears only as that which is irreducible to any calculable reason, motivation, or measure other than the desiring love of this particular other. Marion describes this reasonless love:

> The issue is not an inability of the lover to find reasons, or a lack of reasoning or of good sense, but rather a failure of reason itself to give reasons for the initiative to love. The lover does not scorn reason: quite simply, reason itself goes lacking as soon as love is at issue. Love lacks reason, because reason gives way before it, like ground gives way beneath our feet. Love lacks reason, like one lacks air the higher one climbs a mountain. Love does not reject reason, but reason refuses to go where the lover goes. Reason indeed refuses nothing to the lover—but, quite simply, when love is at issue reason can do nothing, it can do no more, it is worn out. When loving is at issue, reason is not sufficient: reason appears from this point forward as a principle of *insufficient reason* [*raison insuffisante*].[34]

Marion continually maintains that reason exhausts itself before love but also that love has its own reason (or better, that love *is* its own reason). This equivocal use of the single word hides a significant distinction for Marion between reason understood metaphysically (that is, according to an *a priori* standard against which the givenness of phenomena is measured and judged) and the reason of love (revealed in the erotic reduction as "what love does"). Both uses of the word speak to a method by which I come to hopefully understand that which is before me. And "what love does" is allow the phenomenon to appear as an other— as a beloved—for no other reason than the phenomenon's own givenness. The beloved appears only when they do not appear for

33. Ibid., 79.
34. Ibid.; emphasis in original.

any other reason than that of love, appears by no other reduction than the erotic. No reason, save love's own, can go where love goes.

And it is absolutely crucial to this description that the assurance of love can only come from the "elsewhere" of this particular other. I love for no reason other than the saturating givenness of this other. Without this reduction, love would become the pure initiative of the lover and betray love even more insidiously than does exchange, installing the *ego* as that which allows the beloved to appear. Such an interpretation of "Can I love first?" establishes an antecedent *ego* and replaces the givenness of *this* particular beloved with an idealized beloved. An idealized and generalized beloved *as such* prohibits the appearance of the particular beloved other as given, instead establishing parameters that define the appearance of an object. The question "Can I love first?" does not escape solipsism if my love appears first in the abstract, as a substance ready to be turned toward a target chosen by my initiative and criteria.[35] In such "love," I would choose a target for my affections according to other reasons, dreamt possibilities, and orienting concerns. But in turning to phenomenology, Marion maintains that the lover loves *this other* for no other reason than *this other*, who "occupies by virtue of her role as focal point, the function of the reason that the lover has for loving her."[36] I do not advance in love generally, but only toward *this particular other*; to advance generally is phenomenologically incoherent. Marion continues: "The lover has no reason to love the one that he loves other than, precisely, the one that he loves, insofar as he, the lover, makes this one visible by loving him or her first."[37] The elsewhere that assures me of my advance comes through *this particular other* whose arrival appears to me as *an event* (that is, not as a result of my own independent antecedent initiative). I am assured that I love not as I initiate love on my own but in my open response to the unpredictable and uncontrollable event of this other's givenness.

35. One form of such solipsism is seduction, where the lover wants to be loved "without, in the end, loving." Ibid., 83.
36. Ibid., 81.
37. Ibid., 82.

The Reduction to Love

While love may resist its being defined according to the metaphysical rationalities of being, cause, or subjectivity (which subsumes that of objectivity), Marion posits that love's appearance does not preclude understanding it according to its own reason. What, then, do I do when I love?

Marion devotes the largest portion of *The Erotic Phenomenon* to the description of love's reason, summarized here through five characteristics significant to my further study. First, love insists upon the continued increase of the insufficiency of the self to the self. In my advance as lover, "I start off out of balance and I only avoid the fall by lengthening my stride, by going faster, in other words by adding to my lack of balance. The more I do to avoid falling, the more I advance without any hope of return."[38] I have abandoned any hope of returning to a self without this love, to an "I" which is not preceded first by the "me" received in loving this particular other. Increasingly re-centered on this other, my status as lover is always in advance of certainty and grows increasingly dependent upon the other (although not necessarily upon the other's response of love).

Second, although I can only love in advance of all other reason, and only without reciprocal measure, I still love as if my beloved could, too, advance in love. To receive myself as increasingly balanced toward this other is to be vulnerable emotionally, psychologically, socially, economically, physically, and so on. This vulnerability is marked by a principle of insufficient reason, that which requires abandoning all antecedent and justifying reasons for love. But for Marion, "love is a phenomenon that is rational through and through"[39]; it just happens to follow only its own reason. And love's rationality holds together both that it is my love that allows the beloved to appear to me and that I love only by postulating that the beloved is, in fact, one who can love and receive love. I love *as if* my beloved were an other and

38. Ibid., 83.
39. Claude Romano, "Love in Its Concept: Jean-Luc Marion's *The Erotic Phenomenon*," trans. Stephen E. Lewis, in Hart, *Counter-Experiences*, 327.

not an object (for I can only possess, and not love, an object), thereby allowing them to appear so to me. In this *as if*, "the love does not ask for reciprocity or anticipate it" but presupposes that the other can "enter into erotic reduction" and love.[40] But while I presuppose that the other can love (indeed, I hope it so), the beloved does not have to love *me* at all. The lover allows the beloved to appear, yes. But as lover, I so allow only in being formed by my orientation to them. As lover, I am vulnerable. "To love at all is to be vulnerable," C. S. Lewis observes. "Love anything and your heart will be wrung and possibly broken."[41] I love *this* other without guarantees of the future, without certainty of my fate. But in the erotic reduction, I am assured that I love, without regard to questions of certainty or safety. Love bears the burden of granting me assurance only insofar as I abandon all attempts to construct any other foundation, to seek any other reason. In this way, love bears all things.[42]

Third, while bearing all things without certainty of any reciprocity for their advance, the lover still hopes for "the assurance that someone loves him and defends him from vanity, and thus also from the hatred of each for himself."[43] The line between the hope of the erotic reduction and the expectation of exchange is both fine and sharp, and one upon which Marion entrusts much. The hope of love specifically renounces all claims to possession, distinguishing itself from the certainty of that which is controllable by the *ego*—that is, what is *mine*—and instead advances along its "forward-tending disequilibrium"[44] *as if* the beloved might be able to receive and give love. Such an advance differs from exchange in that the love is given without guaranteeing anything for me except that I love this particular other. My love advances in my attentiveness to the beloved as *other* and not by fixation upon an object. Love presupposes love, even as it does not demand it. I can love only insofar as I embrace this hope—through my

40. Marion, *Erotic Phenomenon*, 86.
41. Lewis, *Four Loves*, 121.
42. Marion, *Erotic Phenomenon*, 85, building upon 1 Corinthians 13:7.
43. Ibid., 88.
44. Ibid., 112.

advance (and not waiting to secure an exchange), I allow this other (and not an object) to appear as saturated (thus beyond my certainty). As the lover loves in advance, so loving this other opens the possibility that they might, too, love in advance of my own love. I love in advance of certainty and I hope that this other might love in advance as well. Hope allows me to love not in spite of the lack of certainty but because of it. Hope is the embrace of love's freedom from being beholden to any reason save its own.

In this way, love "becomes thinkable only according to the mode of the hoped for," making the beloved's appearance possible for me by advancing in a love that is without certainty.[45] Paradoxically, love both makes possible the appearance of the beloved (I see this particular person rather than an object reducible to the needs and demands of my *ego* only if I love in advance of what they might "bring to the table") and advances only by hoping that the one I love might, too, be a lover (and not an object reducible to me). For, strictly speaking, "hope does not and cannot have an object."[46] I cannot hope to possess this other (for I can only possess objects), but I can hope that this other might accede to the status of lover. I can love only as I hope: without certainty, without control, and vulnerable to the other because I have opened myself to them. I stand before the other as I do before the icon, exposed to a gaze that weighs upon me, the gaze that "has become the constituting moment of my life."[47] If I am loved by the one whom I love, it is not because I have purchased or merited it. In this way, I can receive love not because I can lay claim to it but because, and only because, I make no such claim to it and instead only hope to receive it. "Love is a bet," Octavio Paz writes in *The Double Flame*, "a wild one, placed on freedom. Not my own; the freedom of the other."[48] And bets are made in opening to the event, both without certainty and in hope. I cannot force the love of the other; I cannot demand it even in loving

45. Ibid., 89.
46. Ibid., 88.
47. Marion, *Prolegomena to Charity*, 165.
48. Octavio Paz, *The Double Flame*, trans. Helen Lane (New York: Harcourt Brace, 1995), 67.

first. If I am loved (as I hope I am), it is for no reason other than my lover's response to my own givenness to them.

Fourth, anticipating the criticism that such an advance (without knowledge of the other, to be sure, but also without clarity as to either what love "is" or who I am in thus being so vulnerable to the other) lacks "judgment and prudence,"[49] Marion emphasizes the freedom of love from the principle of sufficient reason (that is, the freedom of love to be itself). Standing boldly in the paradox, he insists that love is that which translates the givenness of the phenomenon to its appearance as beloved while giving me to myself in and through my response to this given. My response *is* the appearing of the beloved. This appearing is not, to be sure, the idea of the beloved standing in dichotomous contrast to the beloved standing before me, but my intuition of the beloved whereby I allow their givenness to determine their appearance to me. I do not decide to love from a neutral position, having weighed the pros and cons, comparing potential beloveds against an ideal or set of requirements. I always advance in response to the givenness of this particular other. While I very well might reason while loving (searching for a justifying reason that I ought to love as I have already begun to), love cannot be prompted by reason. Should I discover a reason subsequent to my love, it would in no way determine "the *decision* to advance without reason."[50] Reason always arrives late to love, justifying the decision to love (and by "decision," Marion signifies the attentive participation in the erotic reduction, not the selection of a beloved according to antecedent criteria) and perhaps even assuaging anxiety about the decision but never initiating the advance. For precisely to advance in love is to love without first reasoning according to any rules but those of the erotic reduction (which Marion maintains is only a countermethod of stripping away all else so as to see love and describe love as it gives itself). Disconcertingly however, I cannot therefore be certain whether I am continually advancing in love or am justifying a rational choice under the veil of love. I can

49. Marion, *Erotic Phenomenon*, 90.
50. Ibid., 91; emphasis in original.

never be certain (judged by criteria extrinsic to love's own) whether or not I love. "To claim to love first and effectively is . . . meaningless," Marion writes. "At the instant of his initiative, the lover does not know if he acts of his own accord or under an influence, nor under what influences nor does he know any better what he is truly undertaking, or how far he will succeed."[51] In fact, Marion insists, "Whoever is assured that he actually and correctly loves either does not know what he is saying or is lying (to himself)."[52] The lover is never certain of their full reduction to love and can, therefore, only proceed in hope.

This is precisely what affords the lover the freedom to follow only love's own reason. The advance in love must be continually decided. I love as if I had no desire for possession, no antecedent reason, no expectation of reciprocation, no reason at all save my love for the beloved. Yet, even while I may fail to maintain this love (in fact, as I will later illustrate, I cannot but fail in this way), Marion holds that the decision to continually love in advance is not dependent upon its outcome. Neither hidden motivations (that is, hidden to myself; motivations hidden to the one I supposedly love and not to me make me not a lover but a seducer) nor a possible inability to maintain my love can deny the fact that the decision to love is, itself, a "loving to love (*amare amare*)."[53] In choosing to proceed *as if* I can love in advance—to decide, in hope, to be vulnerable to love's terms, to the appearance of the beloved other, and to all that this one can mean for my selfhood—this love of love is sufficient for me to receive myself as a lover of this particular other. I am a lover as I desire to love this beloved in advance. In loving in advance, I throw myself into love without a safety net of justifying reasons—I embrace love. Again, this is not an abstract decision to love that subsequently seeks a concrete other, nor a decision based upon rational calculation according to extrinsic criteria. To repeat the paradox: I consent to love the one who is given to me, thus allowing them to appear as *this particular beloved*, who, in turn, is the sole reason (here, borrowing from Pascal, the reason

51. Ibid.
52. Ibid., 93.
53. Ibid., 92.

of which reason knows nothing) of my love. The paradox according to metaphysics reveals itself to be the clearest description of the phenomenon as it actually appears. My love of love is not of "love generally speaking" but an advance in loving *this particular beloved* because they initiate my advance. By following this advance (indifferent to any cries for certainty or further reason) that this other has quickened in me, I trust and welcome this love as that which bears all things. I embrace it and allow it to transform me. In this way, I love love: I am carried by the other whose appearance is, at the same time, borne by the advance of my love.

Fifth, *this particular beloved* appears not only through my intuition (which, although is always consciousness *of* the beloved, remains interior to me), or through my promise to love the beloved in advance of any (or no) response (which Marion encapsulates in the proclamation, "Here I am!"), but also in the beloved's own "Here I am!" to me. My lover does not proclaim "Here I am!" generally (as an object is given to all to know) but to me and to me *freely*—that is, without my forceful coercion. This love, coming from elsewhere than myself and beyond my control, arrives as a gift. And although I do hope that my beloved will become, also, a lover (or even my lover), I cannot control or define this love given to me from elsewhere (and therefore accepted as saturated). Should my intuition of this gift arrive, it does so only in excess of my concept, preventing me from reducing it to an object. The continued giving of the other's love for me—their own "Here I am!"—reveals a phenomenon that is not strictly mine but one that is in excess of my own intuition inasmuch as it is shared by another.

This shared—or, as Marion prefers, "crossed"—phenomenon maintains my vulnerable disequilibrium and opens me ever more to love the other who is always in excess of my own conditions, understanding, and love. Therefore, while my own "Here I am!" allows the beloved to appear, the beloved's love for me (their own "Here I am!" to me) gives me the assurance of myself. Each "Here I am!" is said over and over, not in reciprocity or mere repetition but in persistent affirmation of the elsewhere whence the gift arrives and the promise to so persist. In promising "Here I am!" from elsewhere, not just now but for every moment, the beloved's gift comes to me in advance of my own love. I hope for but cannot force this love, and my recognition of this is precisely that which allows it to appear *as gift*. So too, my promised "Here I am!" is the advance through which I give my own love. And while my beloved could still appear in saturating excess even if they did not love me (which would not result in my love being in vain, for love is given only insofar as it abandons claims to reciprocity), the gift of love reaches its fullest phenomenality as a crossed persistence of promises (both the one I give and the one I receive) in which the other appears not only as beloved but as the one who loves me through their own advance, as the lover I hope they might be. It is by this crossing of promises—each arising in advance of the other—that *this particular other* appears to me as my beloved who advances in love for me. In this way, the "signification, which allows my intuition to make the phenomenon of the other appear to me, arises like an *oath*—or is forever lacking."[54] To promise "Here I am!" in advance is to love without placing any conditions on this gift. To be promised "Here I am!" in advance is to be loved without conditions placed upon my reception of this gift. Each lover takes the initiative of the advance; each advance is, in turn, a response to the givenness of the other and nothing else.

By this crossed oath, I receive a paradoxical response to the question "Does anyone out there love me?" First, I am saved from vanity and self-hatred only in my openness to being loved in advance from elsewhere—to receive love as gift and to thus received myself as loved. Second, this openness is possible to me only as I love in advance and hope for the other the freedom to love. Third, to love *this particular other* in advance, I do not initiate my love but am initiated by it. That is, I receive my individuation—myself—by responding in loving advance to the givenness of the other. My advance in love toward this particular other is, itself, a response to the other's givenness that appears to me in excess of my conceptuality, merit, and power.

54. Ibid., 104; emphasis in original.

Advancing in Love

In proceeding this way, Marion illustrates the lover's advance—the cadence of the erotic reduction and the attempt to speak of love in its own terms—and describes the other's appearance to me, and mine to myself, as saturated phenomena. But the advance exhausts neither the text nor its significance to an eventual theological application to *De Trinitate*. While Marion proceeds to contextualize the erotic reduction with an analysis of the flesh and the eroticization of sexual desire (many particularities of which strain a direct application to one's growth in understanding and love of God), three matters invite further exploration, each necessary for a more comprehensive picture of Marion's understanding of love: the signification of love through the play of distance and the lack of resistance, the possibility of limited or failed love, and (the third movement of the erotic reduction) the furthering of the paradox of the erotic reduction by insisting that loving in advance requires that I am loved first.

I maintain my "forward tending disequilibrium,"[55] by which I continue to move toward (but never rest in possession of) my beloved in acknowledging their saturation. In giving themselves in excess of my concept, and in my acceptance of this excess and its effect upon me, my beloved remains always in part beyond my constitution and control (and it is this "part" that I cannot name or measure that marks the excess). Excess serves to keep my beloved from being constituted under my gaze. In a way, it is analogous to the veiling of the human body, erotically preserving it from a similar constituting gaze. Here it is not simply a matter of not being able to see the body of the other that preserves their flesh (i.e., that which individualizes through the feeling of that which differs from it *as* that which differs from it), but of allowing the other to determine the terms by which they might unveil and undress and to accept that alterity demands I not reduce the other to an extension of myself. To equate knowing the other merely with seeing (or possessing) is to see only the body, which is, inescapably,

55. Ibid., 112.

an object. Stark medical nudity, for example, does not arouse desire or individualize the patient (whether from the perspective of the patient or the medical professional examining the patient) but rather annuls the "phenomenality of the flesh" by transforming "me into an object of examination, measurable under every angle."[56] Marion continues:

> Therefore, in order to remain the object of desire, the object strives maliciously not to strip itself too much, or too quickly—for the stripping nude destroys what is desirable in it, because the stripping nude transforms it into a simple object; in fact, the object can very well possess itself, consume itself, allow itself to be destroyed, but it cannot (at least not very long) make itself be desired—the object does not hold the distance of desire.[57]

My ultimate desire is not for an object (as an object cannot answer the question "What's the use?" nor can I hope in its being able to love) but for the one whose saturation calls me to love's anamorphic response. Thus, only in maintaining their distance from me—by continuing to dwell in an excess that I cannot place, measure, and name—does my beloved remain for me both given and from elsewhere. Only through distance can the other appear as a gift. The only way I can come to see my individualized beloved (that is, to see them "in the flesh") is both to receive this revelation according to their terms and to never presume that such a revelation is complete. Where reliance upon so-called "self-love" leads inevitably to hatred, only one who arrives from elsewhere can free me from vain solipsism. In remaining veiled in excess, the other maintains an elsewhere from which excess can arrive and saturate my concept. Eroticization, then, depends upon "showing that one does not show,"[58] prohibiting idolization through resisting my framing of the given phenomenon.

But, as veiling alone does not phenomenalize excess, Marion's exploration of the flesh does not end here; the aporia deepens. The object (here a body) allows itself to be reduced to my measure in its resistance to me. I can determine its shape and weight, define its

56. Ibid., 115.
57. Ibid., 116.
58. Ibid.

surface area, and observe its qualities because it stands firmly against me. "Everywhere in the world, I touch walls, limits, and borders," Marion writes of these objects, "not only am I not *in relation to* the world as an openness, but I am *in* the world as though in the midst of enclosures or private properties, or reserves that are off-limits." He continues: "The world does not receive me in a wide-open way—it always begins by stopping me."[59] In resisting me, the object prompts me to assert myself against it, to measure or control it, and to "fight for a place"[60] where I can stand in contrast to it (and in dominion over it?). Or more accurately (and especially important in light of the many ways people abuse the flesh of others, reducing given flesh to objective bodies), in asserting myself against that which is given to me, in measuring and controlling it, I reduce it to an object and subsume it under a vain solipsism that cannot individualize me nor give me to myself. In fact, it is in fighting for a place of dominion that I see only that which resists me. The object is that which I define. The objectified body appears to me because I refuse to engage the flesh of the other on their own terms.

The flesh of the other, however, appears when I enter as far as I am invited by its withdrawal that makes space for me. For the flesh of the other appears in making room for me within itself, marking the elsewhere (a place that I do not control, nor try to control) from which I receive myself. If the body participates in the erotic reduction in its resistance to my desire, the other's flesh appears only in putting up no resistance to me, withdrawing, and opening itself to me.[61] Flesh appears not in my measuring it, and thus in its resistance to me, but in my continuing movement deeper into it without meeting resistance. It is this continued invitation of the other into the veil of excess (maintaining both the veil and the uncovering according to the other's terms) that invites me to see the phenomenon as beyond my measure, that is, as saturated. In this way, I never come into contact with another flesh precisely because I come "into it as it withdraws little by

59. Ibid., 118.
60. Gschwandtner, *Reading Jean-Luc Marion*, 236.
61. Marion, *Erotic Phenomenon*, 118.

little in order to draw my flesh forward."[62] I am invited more deeply into my beloved in my recognizing their saturated depth beyond my control, by respecting the distance of the other's flesh from my own. But as a crossed phenomenon, to enter into the flesh of another without presumption of control means that I, too, withdraw to make room for the other within my own flesh. This invitation is characterized as without resistance and thus is marked with hope that my beloved, too, comes to me with respect for my own distance from them.

Both the veiling of the body and the withdrawing flesh help to maintain the distance between my beloved and me that gives me *this particular other* (and not one who meets the *a priori* qualities and conditions that I instead seek) and allows me to receive myself from the appearing of this given other from elsewhere. Moreover, this pairing of veil and withdrawal renders meaningless all attempts to define the duration and scope of the erotic reduction. The questions "When will this be enough?"[63] "For how long?"[64] and "How many times?"[65] have no place in love. Seeking to love the other "enough" establishes both my love and the other as means toward whatever answers the further question: "Enough for what?" Love, according to Marion's understanding of it, frees me from this "enough." Love has no reason for its appearance save itself; it bears its own arrival. In precluding loving "enough," in bearing its own reason against a yearning toward certainty and possession, love also bears its own possibility (deferring to no principle of sufficient reason). In so bearing its own possibility, love is free from certainty. The full phenomenality of eroticization can only occur because it is free to not occur. I love this particular other because I need not; I am loved by this particular other because I need not be. Love is possible because it is free and free because it is possible. And because love need not to happen, and if it is

62. Ibid., 181.
63. Ibid., 131.
64. Ibid., 133.
65. Ibid., 135.

to happen it must continually happen, I can ask both if I *can* sustain its happening and whether I *want* to sustain it.

As possible—as uncertain, as free to appear and free not to appear—love only appears to me in the midst of my finitude, and finitude is, by definition, inescapably ambiguous. In reviewing *The Erotic Phenomenon*, Paul J. Griffiths distinguishes between what might be theologically understood as created finitude (those limits that we have in being creatures and not the creator) and fallen finitude (the limits that are placed upon us by others and by ourselves that hinder the appearing of truth and the gift of love). He suggests that while Marion's analysis of love is sensitive to the former, it is "perhaps not attuned enough to the special incapacity that results from our fallenness."[66] Such distinction, however, mischaracterizes Marion's insight in a significant way. Certainly, I can say that the "forward tending disequilibrium"[67] of love is possible because I am not sufficient to myself. I can also speak of finitude contextualized by the *ego* and the idol, precluding the appearance of the other and subjecting all phenomena to my interpretation, understanding, and will. But further, I tend forward (by withdrawing to make space for the other) because love is possible. Phenomenologically speaking, this finitude is first the outcome of love. In loving, I make a space within myself for the other, for the gift of that which is not me and can only arrive from elsewhere.

It is perhaps more accurate to say that there are three senses of finitude operative in the text. First, there is an incapacity to love that is the result, in some manner, of my own choice. Theologically, this is the result of sin and the source of sin, and it grows from and leads to the betrayal of love. Under the erotic reduction (by which Marion attempts to refrain from passing moral, theological, or metaphysical judgment upon the phenomenon and rather strictly observe it) this incapacity to love results from, and perpetuates, the rejection of my forward tending withdrawal by which the other appears to me. Marion explores several ways in which I might betray this love: the bad faith

66. Paul J. Griffiths, "More than a Bargain," review of *The Erotic Phenomenon*, by Jean-Luc Marion, *Commonweal*, March 9, 2007, 26.
67. Marion, *Erotic Phenomenon*, 112.

of "sweet-talking,"[68] infidelity,[69] the abduction of love by "sincerity,"[70] the possessive force of perversion,[71] the betrayal of particularity for abstraction,[72] and the demands of jealousy.[73] Each section describes an approach to the other without my full openness to their givenness; each results in my reduction of the "unsubstitutable" other to the increased dominion of my *ego* and the empty promise of its self-securing certainty. Beyond these examples lies a shared fundamental rejection: each betrayal of love arises from a refusal to accept the freedom and finitude of love (and therefore goes against the momentum of phenomenology to allow the phenomenon to appear as it gives itself).

Second, Marion speaks of an "incapacity for love that we all experience because we are finite"[74]; I cannot sustain love absolutely. I tire, lose concentration, and have conflicting demands upon my attention (as, for example, the addition of a child requires that my attentive reduction turn, if even for a moment, from my spouse to the infant in my arms). Marion is clear: eroticization cannot be maintained and therefore must continually be renewed. The attention and intention of each earnest "I love you" will end. Each act lovingly performed will be completed. Each aroused desire will tire eventually. While Marion's description of this limitation is most often characterized by the language of sexual climax and the subsequent need to enter anew into the reduction, the need for renewed arousal of love is as true in general as it is within sexual intimacy: I cannot sustain the intentionality of the erotic reduction for this particular other at all times and for all time.

Third, and most crucially, Marion also asserts that there is a finitude, a limitation that is engendered by love. Under the erotic reduction, the fact that we cannot assure ourselves is not the cause of our love but

68. Ibid., 158–60.
69. Ibid., 160–62.
70. Ibid., 162–64.
71. Ibid., 164–66.
72. Ibid., 166–71.
73. Ibid., 171–75.
74. Griffiths, "More than a Bargain," 26.

results from it. I tend forward toward the other because I love. I am insufficient for myself because only the erotic reduction can answer "What's the use?" Thus, my turn to the other is not a result of an ontological lack of what ought to be there (i.e., self-sufficiency of my being) but because of the infinite love that bears all things.

Along with the "fallen" finitude and the exhaustion that comes with being a creature, I experience finitude also as the result of love (I turn forward toward the other in withdrawing myself). The line between the first two is a blurry one indeed, difficult as it is to delineate the border between the refusal to accept the finitude of love and the limits of physicality and of being. Neither is the line between the second and third clearly demarcated. For from my exhaustion arises the opportunity to recognize my forward tending withdrawal, just as that love arising from possibility cannot but contend with the possibility that I may not love. As I am loved, so too I might not have been, nor may I be certain that I will be loved tomorrow. Therefore, I must receive anew the forward tending self, my orientation toward the never possessed other. I must re-entrust myself to the erotic reduction and its consequences. "Finitude thus does not characterize eroticization as such," Marion concludes, "but rather the *automatic* eroticization of the flesh."[75] The suspension of the erotic reduction is part of the reduction—it reveals a distance between my identification of myself "with and through my flesh"[76] and the fact that I receive my flesh not through self-assertive certainty but as a gift. In this gift, the suspension and the promise coexist and allow love to appear under the mode of *the hoped for*.

For while love is not controlled or conjured, neither is it automatic. It does not continue unabated as a result of an initial decision but appears, instead, only in the continued reaffirmation of the crossing of the givenness of the other and my withdrawal before that givenness. If there is to be any truthfulness in love, it must arise through accepting my finitude (both that I receive myself only in the erotic reduction

75. Marion, *Erotic Phenomenon*, 180; emphasis in original.
76. Ibid., 156.

and that such a reduction, in not being fully under my control, is interrupted and suspended) and admitting the assurance of, but lack of certainty in, each "I love you." Dwelling in possibility, love's appearance depends always upon my promise to love again. Each betrayal of love Marion explores is a particular mode under which I refuse love by refusing its possibility. Rather than admitting the risk of my own finitude (that I may exhaust myself before fulfilling my promise, both because of my own inability to continually renew the erotic reduction and because such a reduction hopes without guarantees in the love of other), I try to secure love without risk and return once again to the vanity of self-certainty. Only in accepting that love dwells in possibility (and not certainty) do I allow for the possibility of love.

As love lives as a promise, according to the mode of hope, its assurance rests in its possibility. As possible, love can always be betrayed if it is not constantly renewed. And as possible and never automatic, love appears only in my faithfulness to my promise. Therefore, Marion contends that faithfulness—my continual withdrawal so that the given might appear—"requires nothing less than eternity"[77] for the full phenomenality of love. If at no point may I claim to have loved "enough," if I always must commit myself anew to the erotic reduction, then I must always promise to love again, to love more, to love forever. "Loving provisionally," Marion observes, is "a contradiction in terms."[78] Each love is a promise of eternity and is love only as it promises eternity. And this crossed phenomenon of our promised faithfulness unto eternity "defines the only shared present" of love.[79] This present grants each lover the assurance of the other's faithfulness and each the assurance of their own faithfulness.

The crossed phenomenon of faithful love gives to each the assurance of being loved *by* this other and of being a lover *of* this other. It is to this assurance that I speak when, in parting from those I love, I assure them

77. Ibid., 185.
78. Ibid.
79. For a more thorough presentation of the "present," see "The Present and the Gift" in Marion, *God Without Being*.

that I do know that I am loved—I assure them that they are lovers. It is this assurance that I hope to hear upon my beloved's death bed—that they know of my love, are assured by it, and can assure me of my own status as lover. It is this assurance, resting on crossed fidelity to a promise of eternity, that gives me myself as lover. It is by the crossed phenomenon of love that I receive myself (as lover and as beloved). "The lover only becomes him- or herself by being altered," Marion concludes, "and is only altered by the other, the ultimate guardian of my proper ipseity. Which, without the other, remains inaccessible to me."[80] I am given myself in being formed toward the one to whom I am devoted, the one whom I love in advance. This *adonné* is the gifted and devoted self.

Through this gifted devotion, Marion holds firmly that love's promise of eternity is not a hyperbolic exclamation, nor simply a descriptive characteristic. As love bears all things, subject to no conditions of possibility save its own and transgressing the limits of metaphysics and of being itself, its appearance is not subject even to the terms of death. As love's possibility requires no reciprocity, I can love beyond the beloved's death and I can be loved beyond mine.[81] In fact, love promises fidelity toward this *adieu* even to the point of anticipating it. This anticipation, contrary to the anticipation that precludes the event, gives space for love to appear by both promising eternity and accepting and engendering finitude. For love anticipates not that which can be predicted or produced but rather that which is definitively beyond my control. Never do I entrust myself more in love's promise than when finitude is most clear. Never is my finitude clearer than when I can love only through a promise. Death, as a "possibility of impossibility," is both the ultimate challenge to the lover (in being that which brings about the beloved's departure) and, at the same time, reveals love as the "measureless possibility" that bears all things.[82] Love, in needing not be subject to even death, appears as the possible "impossibility of impossibility" making possible the

80. Marion, *Erotic Phenomenon*, 195.
81. Ibid., 193.
82. Ibid.

promise to eternity.[83] In loving, I entrust myself to eternity. It is in this way that love's promise anticipates eternity, anticipates it or is not at all.

Marion draws *The Erotic Phenomenon* to a close by looking into the aporia to which he leads his readers. The love that anticipates eternity at the same time anticipates its own finitude. As the promise of the impossibility of impossibility must always be a promise to love again, it is also an acceptance of the limits of my ability to sustain my love. Marion suggests that carrying the "weight of the oath, like a rock that is too heavy,"[84] of the promised "continued re-creation,"[85] is aided by the arrival of a third person who might bear witness to our love while at the same time remain "unscathed by its finitude."[86] This witness, which Marion ventures to name "a child," would attest to the continued renewal of love's promise by rendering it visible. Like the icon making visible the invisible as invisible, the child makes visible that which cannot be fully phenomenalized *as* that which cannot be fully phenomenalized, bearing witness to the promise of eternity at each moment in the present. Or better, in light of Marion's hesitancy around the abstraction of the "as": this child makes visible the excess of this particular love. In not claiming a perfect mirrored resemblance to either lover, the child forbids idolization. Instead, the child "incarnates precisely" the "distance between their two fleshes,"[87] as a witness to the crossed phenomenon of the lovers' love that cannot be reduced to one or the other. The child always arrives as an event. "Despite all of the wills and all the mechanisms"[88] that lead us to speak of "making" a child, their appearance—both in the womb and at birth—is ultimately beyond our control. The child, at birth certainly, but also throughout life, "breaks down the planned course of . . . possibilities by imposing upon [the lovers] the fact of her own."[89]

83. Ibid.
84. Ibid., 196.
85. Ibid., 195.
86. Ibid., 196.
87. Ibid., 197.
88. Ibid., 199.
89. Ibid.

This third party bears witness to the fact that love's phenomenality rests upon a promise of eternity that I cannot fulfill here and now except in each renewal and the fact that I am not a lover on my own but, indeed, receive this status from my beloved. While I may certainly deviate from this phenomenalization—by seeing the child as *mine* and therefore as an idolized extension of my own *ego* or by determining the conditions through which I might allow the child to affect me (thereby not allowing them to do so)—I love only insofar as I entrust myself to those beyond myself: the beloved and the child. As witness to my love (both that I love and am loved), the child arrives from elsewhere and goes elsewhere.

But in going elsewhere, the child leaves an "obscure sorrow"[90] to the lovers, "announcing himself by his departure, precisely in order to abandon the lovers."[91] While the child's arrival signifies the givenness of the child's own life to the parents (as that which is out of their control, that is, as a gift *received*), it also marks the child's own departure from the lovers (as the life given the child cannot be returned or repaid to the parents, that is, it is a gift *given*). My status of lover, one in forward tending disequilibrium toward my beloved, is now tending even further into a future well beyond my own. But how, I might ask, can the child bear the full weight of my promise to love? In departing, not only does the child make the gift of their life appear to me (the child leaves me without repayment) but also takes their witness from me. This child's departure reiterates that I love beyond that which I can control (i.e., that in love I am vulnerable), but it also reaffirms that a departure of presence does not thereby conclude my love. In departing, my child takes the possibility of the certainty of my love with them, leaving me once again yearning for the assurance of my promise of eternity (the one crossed phenomenon of both that promise that I make and the one that is made to me).

Marion suggests that I can love into eternity by anticipating it and loving "as if each moment of [my] erotic reduction constituted the final

90. Ibid., 203.
91. Ibid., 204.

instance of [my] oath."[92] "We must love now," Marion writes, "now or never, now and forever. The instant is only given for that."[93] By loving *as if* each moment were my last, I do not "so much promise eternity as eternalize the promise by accomplishing it (by making love) *sub specie aeternitatis,* under the aspect of eternity."[94] Marion's "eternity" is not a state/place to be reached or even to be received, per se, but is the enactment of the promise by which I advance in love now, "as if this instant were to prove itself to be the final instance of making love."[95] In this way, it is never something to be possessed but is the site of the advance; it is the giving of space for the possibility of the loving advance. Phenomenologically, eternity is made possible because, and only because, love demands it for its own appearance. To bear all things is also to bear eternity's possibility. In this way, love is always excessive. Always saturated—by the excess of this beloved, of myself, of the gift of love, and by its tending toward eternity—love embraces an "endless hermeneutic,"[96] resulting in an "eschatological anticipation"[97] and the erotic reduction's opening to God. As the third party, the eternal God ("the one who never leaves and never lies"[98]) bears witness to our love as does the child, forbidding the imposition of our controllable idol upon the divine witness (that is, we can never frame and define that witness). In the same moment, God's eschatological withdrawal invites us onward (in the advent of eternity marked by

92. Ibid., 208.
93. Ibid., 211.
94. Ibid., 209.
95. Ibid., 208.
96. Ibid., 210.
97. Ibid., 211. Marion writes of this advent of eternity: "Running does not have as its goal attaining what precedes, so as to nullify the advance, but to put me too in the advance itself. To run, I must in effect constantly put myself in a disequilibrium, put myself into the advance itself. And the happiness of running the race consists in remaining permanently in the unbalanced advance, perfectly and continually free from the permanence and stability, which is illusory anyway, of a *nunc stans.*" Marion, *In the Self's Place*, 229. Tamsin Jones traces Marion's eternal advance to his retrieval of the church fathers, particularly Dionysius the Areopagite (to whom Marion himself most often refers) and Gregory of Nyssa (whose thought Jones argues is really behind Marion's own). For the latter in particular, "One 'follows' God eternally, hoping to gaze more and more lovingly at God. This is the third moment into deeper darkness, which is experienced, not as an ontological union, but as an ever-increasing movement of desire for God. Paradoxically, the eternal movement is the stasis. The final 'rest' . . . is when all creation is joined in this never-ending movement toward God." Jones, *Genealogy of Marion's Philosophy*, 50.
98. Marion, *Erotic Phenomenon*, 212.

the "*adieu*") while never departing from us. Here and only here—in eternity—does the erotic reduction find its end, insofar as eternity can be understood as the saturated end toward which love strives. "Love demands eternity," Marion writes, "because it can never finish telling itself the excess within it of the intuition over signification."[99]

Toward this eternity, by means of an endless hermeneutic, the erotic reduction initiates its third movement. To summarize the paradox of the crossed erotic phenomenon so far presented: For my beloved to appear as they give themselves, I must first withdraw and make space within me and promise to do so toward eternity. Yet, I recognize that my own advance is always already a response to the appearance of the beloved. Each lover, "in his or her own shortage of self, is revealed nevertheless as more inward to the other than this other is to him- or herself,"[100] each forming the other into that which neither can be on their own: a lover. In advancing in love—that is, in loving love—I accept myself as the *adonné*, as the one who receives who they are is from the beloved. This is who I want to be, Marion's reduction leads me to conclude, the one who advances in loving *this particular other* because of *this particular other*. That I receive myself through my forward tending advance toward the beloved, and that I advance for no reason other than this particular beloved, means that I receive *who I am* as a response to what is first given to me.

Furthermore, Marion maintains that the other "precedes me in the role of lover, which she assumes first, *contrary to what I have claimed up to this point*."[101] Now aware that "the erotic reduction was in advance even of my advance,"[102] I find that my own advancing self is received in response to the other's loving advance toward me. If I receive myself entirely from what I receive in loving, and if this received self loves love (that is, is free to advance in love), then I can reasonably say (according, at least, to love's own reason) that I receive the love of love from my being loved. If I receive myself from the one I love—receive

99. Ibid., 210.
100. Ibid., 212.
101. Ibid., 214; emphasis added.
102. Ibid.

myself as the *adonné*—and I love love, then I must have received my advance in love from the one whom I love. I receive my own advance toward my beloved from the one who advances in love toward me.

The erotic reduction ends where love begins, past self-hatred, deeper than the questions "Does anyone out there love me?" and "Can I love first?" to the one statement that assures the love's possibility and promise: "You loved me first [*Toi, tu m'as aimé le premier*]."[103] In receiving myself as lover through myself as loved—deeper and stronger than my own self-assertion (i.e., my self-hatred)—I find that loving in advance of the beloved's love, "does not belong to me and that I do not inaugurate it, but that, instead, it was expecting me, it draws me upward and supports me, like the air gives rise to a flight, or water supports swimming."[104] I can love in advance only because I am loved in advance.[105]

What remains definitive about Marion's understanding of love is that it appears *as gift* and *as icon*. The crossed phenomenon is only possible under the auspices of the advance, without waiting to secure my being loved first, without waiting to give love only according to the measure with which I first receive it. As the gift abandons all interest in reciprocity, so love turns from the anxiety about certainty toward the one assurance that I receive in loving—that I love love. Certainly, I can love—I am taught to love—"because I have believed, seen, and experienced that I too, even I, could play the lover" in my being loved.[106] But more than this, my own advance is the gift I am given through being loved first—it is *what* I receive when I receive myself. What the erotic reduction does, then, is to make me aware that

103. Ibid., 215.

104. Ibid.

105. While Marion's conclusion emphasizes my being loved in advance by my lover, he expands this to include other beloveds—friends or members of my family, for instance. For ultimately, Marion holds to the univocality of love, dismissing the oft held distinction between *eros* and *agape* and insisting that it is never "a matter of two loves, but of two names selected among an infinity of others in order to think and to say the one love." Ibid., 221. The crossed phenomena between my lover (understood in the standard sense of the one with whom I make love) and myself, my friend and myself, my parents and myself, my child and myself all operate according to the one rule of love, albeit in differing contexts. In each case, the beloved only appears insofar as I love in advance and tend toward them in my own withdrawal, a withdrawal which is the response to the beloved's appearing to me and loving me in advance.

106. Ibid., 214.

I am loved in advance, aware that my own advance is a response to that which is always already given to me and, at the same time, must remain invisible so my advance might be possible. In my withdrawing toward the other, my own advance—always in hope, never in certainty—becomes for me the sacrifice by which I acknowledge that my own love of love is itself given to me from elsewhere. I am loved first from an elsewhere; I subsequently begin the endless hermeneutic by which I continue to further understand my lover through my own advance toward them. My own status as lover begins with being given love—it is a gift. This phenomenological description of the gift of love, paradoxical according to metaphysics, "lacks neither reason nor logic,"[107] operating, as it does, according to its own reason. Love is impossible for me to create, secure, or possess, and will therefore always remain strictly impossible insofar as I demand it appear according to these conditions alien to it. Love's possibility, therefore, rests in its being given as gift.

In this way, my own advance serves as the icon by which I come to see the gift of my being loved first—I come to see my being loved only in loving. The only way for my advance to be possible (for it to be a gift to the other and not an element of measured exchange) is for my being loved first to remain invisible to me in my advance. I can love because I do not love in exchange for being loved; I can love freely because I have already been freely loved. As the icon is marked by the fidelity of its return to the invisible that which it is given by the invisible, my own advance is marked by its fidelity to the always advancing love I first received. My advance is thus the icon that reveals to me the invisible gift of the love as invisible. The one who loves me does so by always first withdrawing from visibility, withdrawing to an elsewhere, so I might, too, love first—that is, that I might, too, love. That my love marks the already received gift of love is itself only revealed to me through the erotic reduction. The erotic reduction reveals for me that my advance—the icon which makes love possible—is itself received *as gift*.

107. Ibid., 217.

But Marion does not rest there. In the final pages of the book, he returns to the question of God, this time not as the third party who eternally bears witness to my love but instead as the one who "names himself with the very name of love," through the self-revelation of the scriptures and "reveals himself through the means, the figures, the moments, the acts, and the stages of love, the one and only love, that which we also practice."[108] Love, for Marion, is univocal. While an infinitely better lover that I am,[109] God appears in the same manner as love and only in this way, according to God's own reason—that is, love. Part 3 of this book will consider the question of how God's ever advancing Trinitarian love appears to me in my own freedom to love.

But before that consideration, it is both fitting and beneficial to engage some of the most significant criticisms of Marion's philosophy. In so doing, I expect to both respond to those readings of Marion that seem to miss or misinterpret his work and to recognize the limitations (whether in range or in method) of his project. But most importantly, I hope that "criticism can . . . open a royal road to what is at stake"[110] and offer a way of proceeding not only deeper into Marion's thought but beyond it to a place where I might be forgiven the self-imposed limits to my advance and given a voice by which to call upon the invisible one who is revealed through, with, and in love.

108. Ibid., 221.
109. Ibid., 222.
110. Marion, "Banality of Saturation," 386.

9

Appraising the Gift of Love

As history shows, dead metaphors make good idols.

—Elizabeth A. Johnson[1]

If the theologian must obtain forgiveness for every essay in theology—forgiveness for speaking beginning with another, for speaking in another's words, and also for speaking these groundless words that are always haunted by the impossibility of the very unconditionality the theologian hopes to signify through them—then must Marion also do so? That is, if Marion names the unconditioned and names it God, then surely he too must seek permission for this presumptive attempt at impossible signification. It is thinking the unconditioned, the *excess*, that drives Marion's phenomenological work, but theologically considered, he is seeking not the unconditioned *as such* but God, revealed to us *as unconditioned* (that is, mediated by the saturation of my inescapable limitations and concepts). The relationship between these two modes of discourse, particularly in Marion's work, is the site of much debate, both philosophically and theologically. This chapter will explore some of

1. *Quest for the Living God: Mapping Frontiers in the Theology of God* (New York: Continuum, 2007), 20.

this debate, specifically as it pertains to the tension between the concept of the unconditioned and naming that unconditioned "God." The first section will introduce some of the accusations of the illicit crossings between Marion's phenomenology and theology. The second section will consider these crossings in light of the unfounded decision of phenomenology. Finally, the chapter will reframe the general tension between phenomenology and theology through the particular lens of Marion's concept of the unconditioned. It is my hope that the debated possibility of this "discourse on the impossible,"[2] might offer a hermeneutic by which to interpret Marion's work on the unconditioned gift of love and clarify how we might dare to name the *elsewhere* (and even, perhaps, name it "Trinity") from whom this gift arrives.

Idolizing Excess?

Marion's phenomenology of excess offers a rigorous counter-methodology that promises to speak of those saturated phenomena that give to our consciousness more than we can conceptualize and frame, those phenomena that fill and overflow our horizon. It is his hope that this way of proceeding might allow those saturated phenomena to appear to us through the very activity of transcending the concepts we so vainly struggle to apply to them. But whether or not this attempt to think excess remains within the horizon of phenomenology stubbornly persists as a matter for philosophical debate. The paradigmatic criticism of Marion comes from Dominique Janicaud's *Phenomenology and the "Theological Turn": The French Debate* and later his *Phenomenology "Wide Open": After the French Debate*: while "wanting at all costs to establish a single concept of a 'saturated phenomenon' in order to cover the extremely heterogeneous phenomenal realities," Marion "endeavors to sum up the tasks of first philosophy, all the while aiming at a disengagement from metaphysics."[3] Marion's work, Janicaud continues, hangs upon the

2. Kearney, "On the Gift," 74.

thread of his own paradoxes, by which he claims to describe a foundation that is without foundation and an elsewhere than can be both particular and unnamed. Such paradoxes, Janicaud warns, threaten to give way under the weight of the foundation and toward the naming of excess. While Marion strives to maintain the tension between phenomenology as a counter-method (bracketing all antecedent transcendence not given by the phenomenon) and the paradigm of phenomenological saturation, it is far from clear that this excess, particularly when described through the gift of love, does not establish the very *a priori* Marion seems to so strive to avoid (and, moreover, so establishing an ontotheology in naming this excess "God").

Such a concern is echoed in Graham Ward's allegation that Marion's philosophy masks an "uncritical dogmatism"[4] through which Christian faith covertly and illicitly replaces the careful philosophical method with a form of Gnosticism,[5] where only those initiated into the secret knowledge (here, the religiously faithful) might come to truly know the true phenomenon of which Marion speaks. Such a theological truth would oppose the fundamental openness of phenomenology through an *a priori* faith in the phenomenon as revelatory of God. While Marion holds that phenomenology must maintain undecidability, theology cannot. In fact, this phenomenological turn to excess is already at risk of establishing a transcendent truth even without any explicit consideration of God. Mark Dooley identifies a perhaps subtler consequence of this turn, arguing that for Marion, "excess" becomes the final or ultimate truth that phenomenology strives to show. Instead of showing themselves, all phenomena risk being subsumed into signs signifying the transcendental signified. Almost by definition, belief in a transcendence behind phenomenological appearance would imply that we need assistance to reach that which stands beyond our own horizon. And such assistance is available only as we renounce reason

3. Dominique Janicaud, *Phenomenology "Wide Open": After the French Debate*, trans. Charles N. Cabral (New York: Fordham University Press, 2005), 44.
4. Ward, "Theological Project," 229.
5. Ibid., 232, 236.

and "ignore the many useful attempts, in philosophy of language and elsewhere, to disabuse us of the belief that we can reason the unconditioned through an act of self-abnegation," which is a "self-sacrifice . . . neither possible nor desirable."[6] Dooley fears that the approach to such a saturated transcendent demanding the sacrifice of myself and my reason is a sign not of phenomenological openness at all but of a metaphysical essentialism that vainly tries to "escape a network of social practices so as to see the world in a purely disinterested fashion."[7] To approach the transcendent through a self-sacrificial commitment betrays Marion's phenomenology of the unconditioned, revealing its heart to be shaped by something other than phenomenological reduction. "The point is," Dooley concludes, "that what determines how you describe something is not a result of the degree to which that thing exceeds intention, but rather a result of the ends and purposes that you or the larger community have in mind."[8] Openness to excess would thus be little more than a concealed religious desire to abandon oneself to God.

It should not surprise, then, that this pattern of criticism draws fresh breath with Marion's engagement with Augustine, who is also often a target for those writing against the need for self-abnegation before transcendence. In his review of Marion's 2008 work, *Au lieu de soi: L'approche de Saint Augustine*, Joeri Schrijvers is perplexed by "the complete *mixture* of philosophy and theology" in the text and wonders "whether a philosopher, who, as a rule, does not love God very much (or at least too little) is able to read this work?"[9] Schrijvers concludes that Marion has finally answered his critics and has, surprisingly perhaps, shown them to be correct. For he does not shrink "back from some of the equations that this book bluntly makes,"[10] correlating the gift with grace, the plurality of things with creation, and naming God as the giver of givenness. And yet even this evaluation cannot

6. Dooley, "Marion's Ambition of Transcendence," 192.
7. Ibid., 197.
8. Ibid., 196.
9. Schrijvers, "In (the) Place of the Self," 679.
10. Ibid.

be the final word on Marion. For while it is exceedingly difficult to demarcate where in the text Augustine's thought ends and Marion's begins (indeed, if even such a line is ever possible), Marion maintains that a study of *Confessions* cannot simply sidestep the claims of the text: "Once again, the approach of Saint Augustine, by virtue of the radicality of the spiritual decisions he is trying to carry out and to theorize, forbids us from pretending to exclude them or neutralize them."[11] If one wishes to take seriously that which Augustine takes seriously, to try to ask of oneself the questions he asks, to approach truth in the matter in which Augustine does, then one cannot feign neutrality before God. And in that respect, whether the approach be categorized as philosophical or theological (defined in terms and distinctions alien to Augustine and often deconstructed by Marion[12]) seems at times to be distant from Marion's ultimate concern.[13] This grants further strength to these criticisms and renders increasingly obscure his insistence that he maintains the distinction between phenomenology and theology in his work.

To summarize the criticisms on this matter in a twofold manner: first, unable to truly maintain the distinction between the disciplines,

11. Marion, *In the Self's Place*, 4.
12. In a lecture at Georgetown University on April 7, 2011, Marion noted that both the contemporary understanding of these terms and their distinction are relatively recent constructions. For the patristic authors, for instance, "theology" referenced pagan concepts—either the poets' language about the gods, the civic worship of deities, or naturalist astronomy as an analog of the divine (see, for instance, Augustine, *City of God*, 8.1). Moreover, it was not uncommon for the patristic authors to speak of Christianity as the one true philosophy. We should not, Marion noted, take for granted that "theology" is the only word to use for the Christian rational reflection of faith. Simple definitions and distinctions of these terms are problematic on historical grounds. Furthermore, the academy's historically conditioned and often strict separation of theology and philosophy departments ought not be assumed to be the final word on the matter. We cannot simply transpose the meanings of Patristic philosophy and contemporary theology, as though the intervening fifteen hundred years of thought have done nothing to shape the approach to the current separation between disciplines. See also, Marion, *In the Self's Place*, 6–9.
13. At Villanova in 1997, he offered an insight into his chief concern: "As to the question of whether what I am doing . . . is within phenomenology or beyond, it does not seem to me very important. Let me just quote here a famous sentence of Heidegger. 'We are not interested in phenomenology, but in the things phenomenology is interested in.' Whether *Etant donné* [*Being Given*] is still phenomenology we shall see ten years later. But now it is not very important." Kearney, "On the Gift," 68.

Marion is using theology to orient and justify his phenomenology.[14] Second, he refuses to admit that he is doing this.

While the question of a veiled transcendental signified is not uncommon in the secondary literature, Marion is not without his defenders. David Tracy argues that Marion's "latter work should be read not as a theology but as a phenomenology of theological language in the Dionysian tradition."[15] He continues:

> Quite consistently from a theological viewpoint, and quite persuasively, Marion never presumes that philosophy can establish the fact, the possibility, of an actual revelation, especially the Christian Revelation that his earlier work on icon and Dionysius the Areopagite makes clear that he holds to. Here, surely, his philosophical and theological hesitation is exactly right. The phenomenological defense of "revealability" shows the condition of possibility of the "Impossible" revelation. But only the actual divine revelation itself—the saturated phenomenon *par excellence*—could ever establish it.[16]

Tracy interprets Marion as maintaining a receptivity to phenomenological givenness that must not, in advance, eliminate the possibility of divine gift, of revelation. To do so would betray the phenomenon as much as would the *a priori* decision that a phenomenon *is* a gift of God.

Similarly (although she does express concerns with the ambiguous line between disciplines in Marion's work[17]), Robyn Horner ultimately concludes that Marion does not surreptitiously (re)place God as the foundation of philosophy. Rather, she sees him (at least in his later work) as interested precisely in the limits of philosophy and how they might interact with revelation, all the while maintaining—at the very least in his properly phenomenological work—only the possibility of revelation: "Marion first tries to overcome metaphysics with theology,

14. Christina M. Gschwandtner helpfully summarizes several valuable criticisms of Marion on this point. John Caputo, Thomas Carlson, Robyn Horner, and Rund Welten all, in various ways, charge Marion with the overdetermination of the source of givenness. Gschwandtner, *Reading Jean-Luc Marion*, 160–69.
15. Tracy, "Jean-Luc Marion," 60.
16. Ibid., 62–63.
17. See chapter 7, the discussion surrounding the question: "Can the gift be given according to givenness alone?"

but subsequently attempts to do this by way of a phenomenology that is nevertheless open to the theological."[18] But even while arguing that there is neither a contradiction nor a subjugation of one discipline at the hands of the other, Horner admits that the line between Marion's philosophy and his theology is difficult to discern. Highlighting a particularly Chalcedonian description of Marion's thought, she observes: "Of *Idol and Distance*, Stanislas Breton comments: 'I see here for my part the highest 'figure' of a certain medium of thought, where what one calls 'philosophy' and 'theology' exchange their 'idioms' with neither confusion nor separation.'"[19] At best, perhaps, one might hope that the disciplines confirm and aid each other without confusion. Yet, it does not surprise that a Chalcedonian union of hypostases neither placates Marion's detractors, nor sheds significant clarity on the concern. She sharpens the concern to a point: "Claiming that Marion has a theological agenda may be accurate, but it will also be confusing unless the main game is kept in mind. In fine, can phenomenology as a methodology sustain more than can be comprehended? If yes, then the theological connections might be validly developed. If not, then it seems that Marion's work fails."[20] Even if Marion does not hope for too much in his opening to excess, and if such an opening is phenomenologically defensible, it is still not clear how his work can bear the weight of this turn to the unconditioned and justify this turn without certainty.

But for all this philosophical and methodological concern about Marion's language of unconditional giving, the threat of a Gnosticism—of a secret knowledge available to only a (for Ward, religiously faithful) few—is of further, and perhaps increased, importance under a theological horizon. Opposite and complimentary to Ward's criticism is the possibility that Marion, for all his discussion of God, reduces theology and its promised start from an other to nothing more than, at best, an exercise in phenomenology and at worst, simply another blinding yet ultimately banal form of idolatrous

18. Horner, *Jean-Luc Marion*, xi.
19. Ibid., 5.
20. Horner, *Rethinking God as Gift*, 114.

self-worship, replacing God with the idol defined by *my* horizon. Kathryn Tanner, Marion's former colleague at the University of Chicago Divinity School, suggests that Marion is unwillingly forcing revelation to conform to his philosophy—the very act that his whole system of thought intends to avoid. The "gnostic" knowledge here required to recognize and receive revelation would be the phenomenological reduction, establishing this reduction as the measure of revelation. Tanner expresses this concern well when she states:

> This possibility—this eventuality—that Revelation would exceed the bound of phenomenological description, however purified, is just what Marion's phenomenology ultimately disallows. . . . Givenness as a universal law of phenomenology permits no exceptions, not even for Revelation, not even for God's coming in advance. . . . More particularly, Revelation, in order to be entertained by phenomenology, has to be fit into the slot marked out for it in advance.[21]

It is this threat that will ever haunt a theological appropriation of Marion's work: the promised liberation from being—or more precisely in a theological context, the freedom from idolatry—is simply too good to be true. Tanner concludes that within such an approach, "the coming of Revelation in fact loses its capacity ever to disturb the discipline," thereby disallowing anything radically given to us that we do not already possess—that is, precisely anything revelatory—and instead establishes a measure for an immeasurable God.[22] If Marion does, in the end, simply reestablish the *ego* (albeit couched in differing language and concepts) as the *a priori* measure of God, then he will have failed in his most fundamental desire to think the unconditioned.

The possibility of forcing revelation to conform to human measure, rendering it anything but revelatory, leaves each theologian—and together, the intellectual activity of the church overall—engaged in a dangerous game of timing, self-reflection, and honesty with oneself. Such desired honesty elicits a flood of questions: How long do I wait for

21. Kathryn Tanner, "Theology at the Limits of Phenomenology," in Hart, *Counter-Experiences*, 203.
22. Ibid., 205.

the words with which I can speak to God? When, or at what point, can I understand my response to be a response to revelation? Can I sit at the foot of my own Mount Sinai in patient openness, gratefully reflecting on my exodus—accomplished in and for me beyond my means, expectation, and desire? Or does exhaustion lower my gaze and impatience gnaw at my faithful openness, provoking a plea, "How long do you expect me to wait before I turn your name to gold and lie prostrate before it?" To discern given excess from a hopeful, often all too comforting confirmation of what I believe God to be (especially insofar as I define God through the concept of "excess") is a notable and meaningful challenge for those who (like Marion) understand theology not as a discourse about God but as a response to God's own discourse (and not speculation at my own initiation). Precisely, how do I presume to receive and know the revealed God?

While we might try to discuss theology in the abstract, its nature (as understood by Marion) precludes anything but a committed response to revelation already received—and thus a recognition, certainly after the fact of the response, of the revelation of God. I can never know at the moment I begin to speak to what degree my words are responding to the call of God and to what degree they are merely my own. I do not know whether I am responding to a divine call or initiating a quite different conversation, and I cannot try to ground this act in the apparent revelation meeting any conditions for my belief, save the ones it establishes itself. Such a theology is necessarily rationally groundless. Thomas A. Carlson observes, "Insofar as I would seek reason or evidence in order to see, I rejoin the logic of metaphysics, whose defining trait from this perspective is, precisely, to elide faith and its unfounded decision, granting nothing without foundation or sufficient reason and this subjecting the absolute freedom of will to the authority of intellect or understanding."[23] The event of revelation—the arrival of a phenomenon revelatory of God—cannot simply meet and conform to my expectations. Such an actualizing fulfillment of what I, under my own horizon, understand as possible, will reveal to me

23. Carlson, "Blindness," 162.

only what I could anticipate and nothing that I had not already decided upon. Such an actualization could not be revelatory of God at all. Therefore, the ungrounded decision of faith in revelation cannot be understood as the actualization of what will always remain only a phenomenological possibility. Urging the conversation further toward theology's liberation from phenomenology's horizon, Emmanuel Falque asks: "to link *phenomenology* and *possibility* in this way with *theology* and *actuality*, does one not risk first submitting revelation to the simple role of fulfillment of its transcendental conditions?"[24] A theology that would take seriously Marion's concerns (phenomenologically articulated as they are) would be focused not upon specific believed actualizations of phenomenological possibility (*pace* Horner's suggestion) but upon precisely that which is not possible under the horizon of phenomenology: the possibility of the impossible. This theology would be an exercise in how this impossibility (for us) might appear to us *as impossible* through the excessive and mediating antecedent gift of love.

But does impossibility liberate? Here, a most compelling criticism arises furthering Tanner's concern. Does Marion's insistence upon the impossible excess of saturation not simply reestablish the very conditions of appearance he tries to avoid? And do such conditions, when placed upon God and upon revelation, not introduce the prospect of idolatry into Marion's attempted liberation from idolatry? In so emphasizing that revelation must come as the possibility of impossibility, might Marion be effectively tethering revelation to metaphysical possibility, defining it negatively but nevertheless still just as beholden to modern metaphysics? To repeat Marion's own question, if the impossible must be thought, "how is it possible to remain rational and to have a discourse dealing with the impossible?"[25]—how is it possible to articulate the possibility of impossibility as impossible (or the visibility of the invisible as invisible) without the rules of the discourse itself determining what can be said?

24. Emmanuel Falque, "*Larvatus pro Deo*: Jean-Luc Marion's Phenomenology and Theology," in Hart, *Counter-Experiences*, 189.
25. Kearney, "On the Gift," 74.

If the impossibility of revelation is to be possibly *revelatory to us*, it seems that such impossibility much be rendered in possible language, portending an idolatrous failure for Marion's project.

Hence there are two crucial problems facing the theological appropriation of Marion's work. First, there is the risk of the ungrounded decision of faith in *this particular revelation* as the call to which I respond. In being ungrounded, in abstaining from any *a priori* conditions of judgment, I cannot know as I begin whether the call to which I respond is from elsewhere than my own limitations and sin or whether it is a masked self-assertion. If I am always already in the middle of response, there is no way for me to judge where I am.

Second, there is the task of articulating unconditionality (i.e., that which is impossible for me) in possible language without defining impossibility through the lens of that which I deem possible (thereby making the concepts of the unconditioned and the impossible into metaphysical conditions of possibility). If Marion is wedded to thinking the unconditioned, the impossible, does this not risk struggling on a field of battle chosen by the very opponent he seeks to overcome, succumbing to terms defined in advance about what such an overcoming would have to look like? Does not unconditionality condition the phenomenon?

An Ungrounded Decision?

Joseph S. O'Leary suggests that Marion does not escape foundationalizing tendencies of metaphysics even as he explicitly moves to overcome them. Marion's phenomenology simply cannot do what he intends it to do, O'Leary argues, because the concept of givenness is too much of an essentialized metaphysical abstraction to serve as that which allows the other to appear as given. Furthermore, the saturated gift suffers a similar fate, having been so removed from the concrete phenomenon of gift giving that the former has nothing to offer our understanding of the latter.

First, O'Leary is concerned that the concept of givenness suffers from idealization by which its promise to reveal the gift gives way in the end to an emphasis on a metaphysical purity that has no real connection to phenomenality. Marion's emphasis on the invisible and impossible effaces the visible and the possible, exchanging the reality of here and now for an irreal abstraction. With such an abstract purity, the desire for epistemological certainty is not overcome but merely replaced with a certainty of givenness. One metaphysic is simply exchanged for a masked other (which in the end, is fundamentally the same as the first), leaving us to cry, indeed perhaps despite ourselves, "The king is dead. Long live the king!"

Drawing an analogy to traditional theological concepts of grace, O'Leary observes that Marion's concept of givenness promises to be a key lens through which to understand the world, but in the end it threatens to reduce all distinctions and differentiations back to its own abstract essence. O'Leary writes:

> The notions of grace and givenness share certain strengths. They are unitary notions: all the other key notions of theology and phenomenology, respectively, can be parsed and ordered in reference to them. They are critical notions: they serve to dismantle reifications and dissolve metaphysical blockages. They are charged with immediacy: led back to grace and givenness, theological and phenomenological thought is set in a fresh relationship to its theme and converged away from the merely theoretical to an existential engagement with the given in its givenness.[26]

But along with these strengths, the concept of givenness and the theological concept of grace share a significant potential weakness. For, like the danger with the theological assertion that "all is grace," the phenomenological reduction of everything to givenness courts "the danger of essentialism."[27] Such a reduction "solves" much: everything is grace; everything is given. But it does not reveal much at all. Like the reduction to the object, being, or the subject, the reduction to givenness replaces the particular appearing of each phenomenon with a comprehensive metaphysical concept, subsuming everything under its horizon.[28] To decide *a priori* to reduce everything to

26. O'Leary, "The Gift," 137.
27. Ibid., 141.

givenness—"to privilege phenomenology as the sole or even as the primary path of thinking"[29]—is to take a metaphysical stance ultimately indistinguishable from those which Marion vainly attempts to overcome. Givenness is simply one more way to describe the conditions of possibility and one that is not particularly honest about the "cryptometaphysics"[30] going on beneath its phenomenological surface. Moreover, if saturation is the paradigmatic mode of phenomenality, and if all phenomena that appear under the mode of object, being, cause, or *ego* are thereby deficient in their appearance, then Marion has established "excess" as the principle by which all phenomenality is judged. "When one starts to differentiate degrees of givenness," O'Leary writes, "recognizing that not all objects are given in the same mode, univocally, there arises the temptation to consign ordinary phenomena to a lower realm, leaving pure givenness to emerge only at the exalted level of saturated phenomena."[31] Despite Marion's attempts, this phenomenology "cannot preempt the role of judgment as a free and responsible activity of the reflective mind."[32] It inescapably remains my *ego* that judges the adequacy of the appearance of each phenomenon according to my own understanding of the abstract concept of givenness. John Milbank expresses a similar concern when he observes that in Marion's saturated phenomenon of the gift, there is "always a *leaving behind* of the phenomenal in favor of the noumenal"[33]—and this noumenal is always enmeshed in metaphysics.

As a second point, O'Leary extends his criticism to the gift, noting that the pure gift, appearing as a saturated phenomenon and free of

28. O'Leary notes that while "theologians have found in Marion a resource for the overcoming of metaphysics in Christian tradition . . . his own vision could also be seen as restoring metaphysics in the key of phenomenology. His *donation* is as comprehensive as *esse* is for St. Thomas: the analogy of being is retrieved as an analogy of donation. As in neo-scholasticism, philosophy has a rapport of mutual reinforcement with theology, with no prejudice to the autonomy of the two disciplines." Ibid., 137.
29. Ibid.
30. Ibid., 138.
31. Ibid., 139.
32. Ibid., 138.
33. John Milbank, "The Gift and the Mirror: On the Philosophy of Love," in Hart, *Counter Experiences*, 265.

reciprocity, cannot actually give much at all. Marion sacrifices the gift's possibility at an altar of purity, leaving nothing behind but "a Platonic form of the gift"[34] that bears no connection to received phenomenality. If Derrida and Marion fear that reciprocity imprisons the gift within economic exchange, O'Leary is concerned with what is left of the gift after the condition of unconditionality has been met. "If we reserve the term 'gift' for such graced phenomena," O'Leary writes, "then we can find only traces or elements of gifthood in what are commonly called gifts."[35] The term signifies a phenomenon that rarely, if ever, appears in daily life, abandoning the usual process of gift giving as mired in economic exchange and metaphysical attempts to secure the *ego*. O'Leary sees Marion as having exchanged the phenomenon of the gift for that of the abstract concept of the pure gift and notes that his focus upon the pure gift is itself the source of the paradoxes Marion expends so much effort exploring. Instead, O'Leary suggests that, "A broader and more concrete view of the culture of giving might avoid these strenuous paradoxes, and simply trust in the processes of giving and receiving, in all their unpredictability and in their occasional interaction with ordinary economic exchange."[36] In fact, he notes that even the gospel "is quite happy to accept that most giving is not purely disinterested, and even when it calls to more selfless giving, it adds that this will bring a heavenly reward. 'The gift is a boomerang.'"[37] Instead of exploring the phenomenon as it actually appears, Marion is in danger of reinscribing the phenomenon of the gift within a metaphysics of pure gift, which, in the end, is nothing more than an assertion of the *ego* through "metaphysical closure"[38] and the certainty of pure presence.

Against such pretention to purity, O'Leary reminds that the everyday common gift is, in fact, inscribed under the horizon reciprocity. We give and receive gifts according to exchange and, he

34. O'Leary, "The Gift," 152.
35. Ibid., 144.
36. Ibid.
37. Ibid., 153; interestingly quoting not the gospel but Jacques T. Godbout.
38. Ibid., 148.

argues, that there is no justifiable reason why the gift should be purified of all desire for reciprocity. To put it another way, is all reciprocity reducible to economic exchange (where I only give so I can receive), or is there a way to seek reciprocity that does not poison the gift? Even recognizing O'Leary's statement that Marion's "emphasis on the purity of the gift cuts off interest in the impure forms of giving that abound on every side"[39] is not defensible in light of Marion's repeated consideration of impure forms of giving,[40] the question itself is significant. What is wrong with reciprocity shaping the concept of the gift if it is under the horizon of reciprocity that the phenomenon of the gift usually appears? As in the case of Marion's concept of givenness, the determined escape from reciprocity can itself become an imposition of a metaphysical essence upon the fact of the phenomenon, forcing the latter to conform to a conditional *a priori*. Moreover, O'Leary warns that a "person who gave without any precautions or limits would hardly be performing the human act of giving, but would have fallen into some kind of pathology."[41] The gift becomes about *my giving it*, about my *ego* and what it can do and what it desires to do. Together, these concerns lead to the surprising conclusion that to give without reciprocity is itself an inherently self-serving establishment of the self as unilateral giver (such a conclusion would also likely have serious moral and ethical implications, along with the phenomenological concerns expressed here).

Milbank's explicitly theological criticism of Marion's account of the gift resembles O'Leary's philosophical appraisal. Milbank argues that by emphasizing a gift purified of exchange, Marion not only removes the gift of self-serving calculations but also makes the giving indifferent to reception[42] and inattentive to the receiver (and therefore to the question of what would make for a suitable gift[43]). This makes God a giver indifferent to my reception.[44] "Just as Marion's divine gift

39. Ibid., 145.
40. See, for example, the context of the gift of love in the chapter, "Concerning Lying and Truthfulness," in Marion, *Erotic Phenomenon*.
41. O'Leary, "The Gift," 150.
42. Milbank, "Can a Gift Be Given?" 134.
43. Ibid., 132.

is in this aspect a hypostatization of modern, free, post-Cartesian, capitalist and 'pure' gift, and thereby 'indifferent to content,'" Milbank writes, "so it is also (as a concomitant) relatively indifferent to counter-gift, or to relation and reciprocity."[45] Looking to Mary's *fiat* for inspiration, Milbank suggests instead that "purified gift-exchange —and *not* 'pure gift' is what Christian *agape* claims to be"[46]—a gift is only given when it is received, and attention to reception entails some element of exchange.[47] Milbank insists that the reception of the gift entails a "non-identical repetition" wherein the gift is not simply returned (a type of impure exchange that would annul the gift) but is received in a way to promise, after a delay, a reciprocal gift of some kind. Arising from Mauss's study and further contextualized biblical witness, Milbank sees a gift exchange purified through *agape* as that which opens familiar unity to those of foreign blood and thereby serves as a fundamental structure of the church. It is through a purified "give-and-take" (rather than an "absolutely free, univocal gift") that we share in "God's arrival, his for-giving, and perpetual eucharist."[48] Thus, Milbank, too, sees Marion establishing a unilateral giver indifferent to reception and therefore pointing to an "empty subjectivity, whose apparent *kenosis* is almost indistinguishable from demonic self-enclosure."[49]

To the degree that O'Leary's and Milbank's analyses are correct, Marion's phenomenology of givenness and gift would remain nothing more than a metaphysical assertion of the self through *a priori* conditions of possibility (even if those conditions demand the unconditioned). Givenness would become a metaphysical essence imposed upon phenomena. The gift would become a means to assert the *ego* upon the receiver. But also possible is that O'Leary's criticism itself imposes a metaphysical reading upon Marion's phenomenology that the latter not only does not intend but indeed intentionally avoids.

44. Ibid., 136.
45. Ibid., 134.
46. Ibid., 131.
47. Ibid., 136.
48. Ibid., 154.
49. Ibid., 137.

For just as Marion is hesitant to speak of the phenomenon *as such* (reducing what appears to an instance of an essence) and particularly of God *as such* (making *this* revelation of God to me an instance of the abstract divine essence),[50] so it seems problematic to speak of givenness *as such*. Marion's proposal of a phenomenology without an *as such* (phenomenological heresy though it might be[51]) shows him to be aware of the danger of givenness becoming a universal concept by which all things are judged.

Nothing is given "as such"; each phenomenon is given according only to itself and its own givenness. Under the reduction to givenness, the particularity of each phenomenon guides my reception of it and thereby its appearing to me. And in speaking particularly about saturated phenomena, Marion maintains a paradoxical assertion that a given phenomenon appears saturated not because it meets the antecedent conditions of such a definition but because I am confronted with more than I can conceive, understand, and explain. It is not *concepts*, per se, that Marion works to avoid (indeed, he does not advocate an empty concept-less mind) but instead their dominion over the phenomenon. Marion is not advocating an eradication of metaphysics and conceptuality but rather an attention to their limits. It helps to keep in mind Marion's statement that he is not so much interested in phenomenology, as what phenomenology is interested in.[52] He is interested not in carefully defining a phenomenology that is completely without any metaphysical reference but in the givenness of a phenomenon and how the phenomenon appears according to its own givenness (that is, appears *as itself*). He is interested in how we might receive from elsewhere. To say that since givenness emerges "only at the exalted level of saturated phenomena,"[53] all phenomena

50. See "Can the impossible gift appear?" in chapter 7.
51. Kearney, "On the Gift," 66.
52. Ibid., 68.
53. O'Leary, "The Gift," 139. O'Leary's criticism leads him to criticize phenomenology's inability to establish itself as first philosophy: "The phenomenologist's construction of the singular pure experience may illuminate many aspects of the complex reality without being accepted as the essential key to its meaning. The entire account of being or of phenomenality built on the basis of such constructions is likely to find itself enjoying the status of just one story among others." Ibid., 152. But it is because of this inability that Marion embraces the discipline.

become instances of the essence of givenness misses Marion's point: as saturation is the paradigmatic form of phenomenology, the reduction to givenness reinforces the possible excess of all phenomena. It afflicts all comfortable notions of stability and easy presence with the reminder of both my limitations and saturated possibilities of each given phenomenon. Givenness becomes what O'Leary fears only inasmuch as it is used as a concept by which I impose my order upon the world. For Marion, it is a constant reminder that the world is not *mine* to define. Marion attempts, through bracketing and reductions, to get antecedent conditions out of the way so as to see the phenomenon and to receive the way of proceeding from the phenomenon.

It is likewise with the gift. No doubt a gift free from reciprocity can become a distorted instance of the assertion of the *ego*. It can become to me a matter of what I want to give to whom, where I pay no heed to the receiver. But instead of a reduction to a pure essence of the gift that "risks short-circuiting forms of relationality that phenomenology cannot master,"[54] Marion's insistence that the gift is given without care of reciprocal exchange can also emphasize the fact that phenomenology cannot master anything at all. To define giving without precautions or limits as a "pathology" is to neglect at least two critical nuances.

First, the pathological insistence on unconditioned assertion of the *ego* (what Marion might very well label a sign of the hegemony of the metaphysical subject) is itself a result not of the unconditioned nature of the gift but of my own assertion of myself as independent of others. It is antithetical to the gift to give without consideration of receiver (to give what *I* deem to be a gift and not what the receiver needs or desires). The attempt to establish myself as *giver* without consideration of either the gift or the receiver is not to give at all but to assert *myself* over and against *objects* (that is, precisely those phenomena that I have decided to see as objects rather than particular others). There is no withdrawal of this *ego*, and without withdrawal (that is, allowing for an *elsewhere* that I do not condition) there can be no gift.

54. Ibid., 161.

Second, while O'Leary is correct when he says that an insistence upon purity can betray the gift, this betrayal occurs not in overlooking the common phenomena we often label gifts but because the refusal to receive is itself an attempt to master the gift. Quid pro quo reciprocity and the refusal to receive both, in fact, make the gift about ensuring the certainty of myself over and against the givenness of others. However, Marion's erotic reduction concludes with the understanding that I first receive the gift before I am able to give—or better, that the possibility of my giving gifts is what I first receive in being given myself. Receiving need not only be in exchange for my giving but is the originary *a posteriori* of the gift. As Milbank notes, "If there is reciprocity here, it is really the coincidence of two absolute non-reciprocities"[55] (therefore a reception that is not quid pro quo reciprocity). Thus, to say, with O'Leary, that Marion "wants the logic of the gift to be so paradoxical that the claim of logic is broken and the gift can come into view in its authentic phenomenality, like the rose that is 'without why,'"[56] is to miss the point ever-so-slightly but to do so significantly. Marion is not concerned with a gift pure of the broken logic of reciprocity. In fact, Marion is never in pursuit of a pure gift at all (a gift given without having received, even if that reception carries with it elements of exchange) but is in pursuit of a gift in excess (one that goes beyond or against) of any measure of exchange. It is not that reason (or economics or metaphysics, for the matter) is broken, or that it needs to be eliminated, but that it is insufficient for the appearing of the phenomenon at hand.

Milbank, likewise, overlooks this excess and particularly *how* Marion understands excess to appear to us. Contrary to Milbank's interpretation, Marion does not present a gift indifferent to reception. In fact, the anamorphic movement by which a given appears requires that a gift be received to appear at all. In this way, a gift never appears abstractly but always to someone. Marion focuses on *how it is* that one might actually receive (i.e., by anamorphic transformation). The gift

55. Milbank, "Gift and the Mirror," 262.
56. O'Leary, "The Gift," 163.

is given in the receiver's transformation to receive it. Milbank here offers no account of how we receive, nor of the transformation that this reception engenders. Although exchanged "in love," the giving and receiving of the gift remains extrinsic to my intuition; it is a role I play within my community so as to bind myself and others together. This concern with extrinsic order seems to arise from a metaphysical understanding of the gift that is still based on the exchange of some objective *res* that operates within a communal structure. Milbank's *agape* is defined by the exchange that is necessary to maintain correct relationships (where actually defining "correct" is another endeavor entirely). Love guarantees the church structure. For Marion, on the other hand, the gift of love is not given to serve some other purpose; it operates according to, and for, its own reason. The gift does not ensure something *else* but is received in the transformation of the receiver into one who can now give—I receive the gift of love *in* my becoming one who can now advance in love. Not a token by which I mark my participation in a community (however selflessly I may do so), the gift of love arrives in an excess through which I become a lover.

But in the midst of so much saturating excess, O'Leary's concern that there "is perhaps something mythical or even mystical about this pure phenomenological moment,"[57] speaks to a real danger that this radically unfounded decision (that is, without conditions and reason antecedent to the given excess) is itself an excessive abstraction that masks an *a priori* certainty in the particular condition of unconditionality. If unconditionality unduly conditions the gift, then Marion chances inscribing the gift under the horizon of certainty where I may be certain of it because it fits my concept of unconditioned.

Furthermore, instead of rooting his trust in love in the witness of the Christian church, as Milbank suggests, Marion seems at risk of instituting a certainty in the unconditioned gift love, co-opting love's assurance from elsewhere under a certainty in love itself. In this case, beginning his analysis with the question of Cartesian certainty, he

57. Ibid., 153.

may be defining the terms of his reduction by that very question, to the point of even framing the entire project as an overcoming of this certainty. This seems to further O'Leary's criticism that Marion's privileging of phenomenology is really a cryptometaphysical decision, here particularly recontextualized in and through the *a priori* concept of the gift of love. Marion's faith in love might entail an *a priori* decision on his part, a decision that reinscribes Marion's entire phenomenological project within the very metaphysical structures he so desires to overcome. Simply put: does Marion's faith in unconditional love mask epistemological certainty under the guise of erotic assurance? Is Marion's gift of love metaphysically grounded?

Thomas A. Carlson suggests a reading of this ungrounded decision as a response to the Cartesian metaphysical ambition to confine "the will's exercise within the scope of understanding."[58] It is Marion's concern that in so confining, this "restriction on will excludes the possibility of approaching at all the experience actually at stake" in given cases of saturation.[59] For Marion, Carlson reiterates, the decision to see—to allow a given to appear in excess of my conditions and understanding—must be made without antecedent reason.[60] He adds, significantly, that such a reasonless responsive decision "would depend on a modesty or humility, or even more a humiliation that opens me to the given."[61] Carlson proposes that privileging this decision without reason is itself an act of faith, "whose leap must be without sufficient reason or visible evidence."[62] He observes that the decision to see the phenomenon as it gives itself (or even the desire to so decide) is itself a responsive gift given by the phenomenon. Drawing an analogy to Augustinian-accented understandings of grace, Carlson writes: "If theologically speaking I am blind to the grace that sustains and saves me until grace itself turns or redirects my will to see it, so phenomenological speaking I am blind to the given that gives itself

58. Carlson, "Blindness and the Decision," 163.
59. Ibid., 164.
60. Ibid., 168.
61. Ibid.
62. Ibid., 162.

to me until I am given—by the given itself—the will that decides to see the given."[63] As the one to whom grace is given is characterized by an interplay of activity and passivity, so the *adonné* comprises this interplay in receiving its openness to receive.

But despite this interplay, Carlson argues that this charging of the *adonné* "with responsibility for all phenomenality" suggests a "decisionism or voluntarism" that maintains "a strange trace of sovereignty" of the *ego*.[64] Does not everything still depend upon my willingness to accept myself as *adonné*—to trust that love does, in fact, bear all things unconditionally (including me)? "Phenomenology," he observes, "may well be first philosophy, but philosophy is not first, for it cannot get going without faith."[65] And while this necessary leap of faith to love may be justifiable theologically, it can seem arbitrary phenomenologically. Or perhaps more to the point: what appears as phenomenologically arbitrary might very well be philosophically justifiable only under a metaphysical (or, indeed, theological) horizon, which, within the context of Marion's thought, means that it is justified only in risking the assertion of the *ego* and ultimately the vain nihilistic will to power. Whether described as theological or metaphysical, this faith in the gift of love—and importantly, not just in love but in the erotic reduction and this particular phenomenological presentation of love—seems to be, nevertheless, a result of a decision on the part of the subject. If so, this turn to this phenomenon of love as that which bears all things may not be phenomenologically justifiable.

On the Condition of Unconditionality?

It is of no less of a concern theologically than it is philosophically that the possibility that the phenomenologically unfounded decision to place my faith and hope in the gift of love establishes a cryptometaphysics according to the *a priori* condition of unconditionality. Kathryn Tanner suggests that Marion's

63. Ibid., 165.
64. Ibid., 172.
65. Ibid., 162.

phenomenology of the gift of love constrains revelation according to this condition of unconditionality (thereby smuggling in a remarkably well-hidden philosophical idol into the understanding of the revelation of God). Tanner finds this desire for unconditionality problematic both in that it hides the conditionality Marion does, in fact, place upon appearance and that it raises unconditionality into an ideal without significant theological justification. Thus, Marion's insistence on the abandonment of conditions (both antecedent and reciprocal) fundamentally distorts love into something foreign to the Christian witness. In rejecting all forms of exchange as insufficient for the gift, Marion sets up the effacement of the self before another's self-assertion as an ideal. Tanner writes: "Giving at the cost of self-evacuation is instead the demand that the world of everyday phenomena commonly puts on giving (the demand put to Christ by a sinful world in crucifying him); and it is just this demand that a theology of revelation typically refuses."[66] She is concerned that Marion's attempts to escape economic structures and the yearning for certainty (whether of being, cause, or the subject/object) have instead defined Marion's concept of the gift by those very structures and desires, albeit negatively. Against this, she offers a different reading of God's gift: "God gives unconditionally but God also does so *for the sake of a return*; and there is nothing particularly problematic about that. What is problematic is the way Marion has turned the likely eventuality of God's giving to a sinful world—its ingratitude and scorn—into an unsurpassable ideal."[67] In her reading of Marion, the humiliation and emptying of the cross, instead of being a sign of the sinful assertion of human beings upon the gift of God, becomes the very definition of the gift: exhaustive, unreciprocated, unrecognized. "Giving," she concludes of Marion's presentation, "is now conditional on the failure of a return."[68]

The criticisms of both Carlson and Tanner are rooted in fundamental questions regarding Marion's work: Does Marion describe the gift of

66. Tanner, "Theology at the Limits," 220–21.
67. Ibid., 221; emphasis added.
68. Ibid.

love correctly as that which bears all things? Can it, when received and given without conditions, form me to receive the givenness of my beloved? Or, does Marion's insistence on unconditionality itself further mask idolatry? John Caputo warns that it is precisely in allowing the unconditioned that Marion's thought is in most danger of corruption:

> It is precisely when someone claims to have reached, or been granted, God's point of view that things start getting very ungodly. It is just when someone thinks to have laid hold of the Wholly Other that we are visiting by the human, all-too-human. . . . The unconditioned corrupts; the absolutely unconditioned corrupts absolutely.[69]

The problem in sum: at the foundation of Marion's description of love is love's ability to overcome the need for certainty through its openness to the unconditioned. His faith in love, however, suggests a decision to use antecedent structures (of foundational certainty and unconditionality) to contextualize the appearing of the given. This love operates according to the terms of the concept of the saturated phenomenon and its paradigmatic form: the gift. Love therefore threatens to function as a restriction upon phenomenality, establishing a model upon an exception of unconditionality, as per the description of the gift. If Marion's phenomenological description of love according to the mode of the gift is justified, then unconditionality might therefore be normative. But if the unconditionality of the gift distorts the phenomenon of love, then he is, in fact, establishing an exception as the rule. Under this exception of the unconditioned, I mask my own intentionality with the corrupting visage of purity, hiding the phenomenon beneath my idea of its appearance, pretending to an unconditionality that betrays even as I assert it. Thus the question at hand is whether love reasons according to the concept of unconditionality (which subjects love to the antecedent questions of certainty and excess) or whether love's own reason is itself

69. John D. Caputo, "God Is Wholly Other—Almost: *Différance* and the Hyperbolic Alterity of God," in *The Otherness of God*, ed. Orrin F. Summerell (Charlottesville: University Press of Virginia, 1998), 195.

unconditioned (where the latter serves to further describe the givenness of the former).

That Marion places full faith in love is clear. Having problematized certainty and faced the question "What's the use?" he begins the erotic reduction—without further justification—with the question "Does anybody love me?"[70] noting, "To give up on asking (oneself) the question . . . or above all to give up on the possibility of a positive response implies nothing less than giving up on the human itself."[71] What it means to be human is, for Marion, inescapably tied to the question of love. If I can achieve certainty neither through the machinations of my mind nor the vain assertion of my *ego*, then I am led to turn outside of myself to others and to the beloved other. But whether or not love leads me to this *elsewhere*, indeed, depends upon whether Marion's definition of love as unconditioned gift betrays either the desired purity of his phenomenology (by introducing that which is beyond the horizon of phenomenology) or the freedom of theology (by defining the possibility of revelation according to the patterns and limits of philosophy, that is, to speak of revelation within the limits of phenomenological reason alone). Such corruption is indeed a possibility that Marion himself does not deny. The particularity of love prohibits certainty—certainty that I am, in fact, loving and loving *this particular other* and not the image I imagine or want them to be. But this specific instance of my finitude that forbids my resting confident in my love (as if I have loved *enough* and loved successfully) at the same time is the very condition that allows love to appear at all.

As saturated, love appears to me only as a counterexperience of the transgression of my finitude from and toward a particular *elsewhere*. In fact, my inability to be certain about my love—an inability that marks my finitude—is the very limit that is traversed by my loving advance, and it is this traversal that, in turn, allows my love to appear on its own terms. Crucially, as Marion is not eliminating metaphysics

70. Marion, *Erotic Phenomenon*, 20.
71. Ibid., 21.

but playing at its limits, conditionality and finitude both remain—they simply no longer hold the last word. The possibility of love's being simply an attractive rearticulation of the *ego* of modern metaphysics is also the possibility of its appearing at all. Love is only possible without certainty and at anamorphic risk to myself. I love without certainty and love as if my advance in love were possible.

While my love rests upon possibility (and not certainty), it is less clear (less certain, perhaps) whether Marion's faith in love as the meaning behind that which is fundamentally human is, itself, a faith in love or a faith in the phenomenon of unconditioned exteriority (as that which overcomes the vanity of the self-sufficient *ego*). If love is simply the concept that best and most conveniently convinces of phenomenology's effectiveness at solving its own problems, then love's reason is co-opted as part of his project toward the phenomenologically unconditioned. If love appears according to the pattern of the gift and the icon, if it serves the purpose of revelation (whether interpersonal or theological), then it becomes merely a means toward a further end. This love cannot, in final estimation, carry the gift, the icon, and the unconditioned.

An alternative to love's being a means to defend phenomenology is that unconditionality, rather than being the condition Marion places upon love's appearing, might be part of love's description as a concept that Marion uses to better describe what is revealed of the phenomenon after the erotic reduction. In this case, my love of this other is an instance not of the gift *as such* but of the paradigmatic gift. It does not only appear according to the mode of the icon but gives the icon its justification by making possible the fidelity required for making visible the invisible as invisible. The limits of certainty, the exteriority of phenomenology, and the specific instances of the gift and the icon are all partial descriptions of the one reduced phenomenon of love. In this case, while Tanner is quite correct in reminding us that Marion has not spoken the final word on the phenomenon of the unconditioned, noting that "one must be willing to allow every philosophical perspective to become merely a regional one and admit the possible provisionality of all their methods and conclusions, no matter how thoroughly worked out or apparently basic,"[72] it does not follow that his faith is proven misplaced. Rather than trusting in his understanding of phenomenology itself or in his presentation of the erotic reduction (each open to criticism according to the methods of the discipline), Marion's faith is ultimately in that which phenomenology is interested in.[73] And while *unconditionality* may very well threaten to become an idol all its own (and an idol all the more insidious because of its pretense to stand against all idolatry), it also serves as a promising way of describing the openings toward the other that allows the other to appear to me. Marion's project operates within a particular phenomenological milieu with a clear methodological goal: to think the unconditioned. But does this method shape Marion's description of the gift of love or is the method determined by the given phenomenon?

Indeed, it is consistent with Marion's own insistence to say that it is the very phenomenon in question that shapes his approach (i.e., precisely that he is still operating according to phenomenology, however he might further define it). Love appears unconditioned because it gives itself unconditionally. The concept of unconditionality would be descriptive of Marion's observation of love's givenness and not an antecedent condition of its appearance. However, Tanner interprets Marion's concept of love as acquiescing to the sinful world's demand for self-evacuation. She is concerned that there is something distorted in a love that distances itself so thoroughly from the response (even though it might be given without being dependent upon the response). Tanner's reading reveals a fundamental difference between her conception of the human being and that of Marion—a difference that, in turn, shapes their respective understanding of how one encounters phenomenological excess and what is the result of an insistence upon unconditionality. Contextualized now under the terms of theological discourse, Tanner writes:

72. Tanner, "Theology at the Limits," 227.
73. Kearney, "On the Gift," 68.

> By setting up a competitive relationship between givenness and the receiver who is to show it, between the Father and the Son who is the Father's icon, Marion tends to collapse the latter into the former in a kind of iconic return to immediate identity; all that is left of the latter is made up by the former. Giving myself over completely to what givenness demands, my will is simply that command. Since Christ is nothing of himself but a transparent point to the word of the Father, that word can be equated with the otherwise empty Christ; the word of the Father seems to push out the humanity of Christ to appear, for all intents and purposes, along in its place.[74]

By drawing attention to this transparency of the icon to the invisible that appears through it, Tanner questions the *adonné*'s unconditioned devotion to that which gives it itself. Such devotion, she warns, may be an act of self-evacuation, wherein I become nothing but a shell to be filled by the one to whom I am devoted. Likewise, an insistence upon *unconditionality* would serve to subsume me under the particularities of my beloved. The specter of legitimizing or accepting abuse (whether personal, systemic, or theological) looms large behind Tanner's concern. Here, I would lose myself to the one to whom I am devoted, allow myself to be annihilated, and be given the rational justification to defend such atrocity.[75]

74. Tanner, "Theology at the Limits," 226–27.
75. Perhaps the single most theologically controversial section of Marion's work is chapter 5 of *God Without Being*, "Of the Eucharistic Site of Theology." Drawing from the resurrection narrative from Luke 24 wherein two disciples unknowingly encounter a resurrected Jesus while traveling toward the town of Emmaus, Marion develops a theological hermeneutic derived from the Eucharistic celebration. Just as the disciples only understood their teacher's interpretation of recent events in light of his breaking of bread, so theologians only come to understand the revelation of scripture in the context of the celebration of the Eucharist. Only Jesus, as the Word of God, can provide the hermeneutic by which we might come to understand the Word of God. But the Word, Marion notes, who in the eucharistic rite is "visibly absent, makes himself recognized in the breaking of the bread, characterizes the priest as his *person*, and assimilates to himself those who assimilate him." Marion, *God Without Being*, 152. That this recognition only occurs through the priest and within the community leads Marion to assert that just as the priest only celebrates the Eucharist in communion with his bishop, so the theologian only interprets the Word of God in similar communion. "The theological teacher is not justified unless he serves charity. Otherwise he brings death," Marion (Ibid., 154) writes, and such service to charity only comes in serving the community. Such a presentation, elaborately rearticulating the patristic maxim that the theologian is the one who prays, has been no small cause of concern for those who see here a defense of complete hierarchical control over the church's theology. If in separating from the bishop, the theologian brings death, then their work threatens to become limited to what the bishop accepts and the theologian's vocation risks being evacuated to make space for ecclesial concerns (which, in turn, opens the door to significant abuses, both personal and systemic). Since *God Without Being*'s publication, Marion has further contextualized this chapter, adding "I was not, of course, taking sides in the present-day differences between, say, bishops and theologians; I

But where Tanner suggests Marion's work flattens the distance between icon and invisible (and between giver, gift, and receiver) into a univocal distance without difference,[76] Marion insists that the unconditionality of love does not run counter to phenomenality of particular individuals (where I might allow this other to appear as they give themselves to be seen) but is, in fact, the only guarantor of it. Such unconditionality leads not to an evacuation of an antecedent self but to the very reception of the self, now permitted to appear as itself and not according to any other measure. Only unconditional openness makes possible my individuation. Where Tanner warns that unconditional receptivity to excess elicits a submission to the dominion of the given phenomenon at the expense of the self, the basic assumption of Marion's phenomenology of love denies a self-presence independent of antecedent alterity and puts forward instead a self that is received from my counterexperience of this alterity. This latter concept of the self is not antecedent to a subsequent experience of the other but arises only with my intuition of my finitude in response to the excessive appearance of the other. That love is unconditioned does not, at least in Marion's *milieu*, require self-evacuation precisely because there is no already self-grounded self to evacuate, there is no established *cogito* that is only subsequently turned toward the other demanding an evacuative *kenosis*. The *adonné* appears as a response to first being loved, through a received counterexperience of those people and things to which I devote myself, for whom and which I make a space for an elsewhere that gives me myself in withdrawing toward them in love. While the reason behind Tanner's concern is

was referring back to the tradition where most of our great theologians were, at the same time, bishops in their communities." He continues, "It is difficult for us to think today about how theology was originally not supposed to be the outcome of intellectual curiosity, logical dexterity, or academic career. Theology grew out of the task of commenting on the scriptures, not because you chose to be a professional exegete of the scriptures, but because that was an essential part of the liturgy, of the Eucharistic gathering of the faithful. In this sense, theology was a communal event. The great theologians of the tradition were not writing books because they wished to get published but because they needed to address specific questions that were of importance in their communities. Their theology was built in direct relation to their pastoral service." Richard Kearney and Jean-Luc Marion, "Hermeneutics of Revelation," in *Debates in Continental Philosophy: Conversations with Contemporary Thinkers*, by Richard Kearney (New York: Fordham University Press, 2004), 21–22.

76. Tanner, "Theology at the Limits," 227.

necessary to keep in mind and the term "love" has been used to justify the annihilation of the self before the other, the very *self* in question here is carried by, rather than burdened by, its responsive appearance.

Marion's unconditionality might be best described as the concept that marks my eternal withdrawal for and toward the givenness of my beloved, the withdrawal that makes it possible for me to both receive love and advance in love (and thereby makes it possible for me to receive myself). In such a case, the unconditioned does not demand my self-evacuation or self-effacement[77] but instead gives me all the more to myself, makes me all the more visible. As my advance in love is the icon by which my being loved first is made visible as invisible, so I find that *I* am all the more visible to myself (and, indeed, I hope to others, as well) the more I open in advance to the unconditioned. For just as the invisible can only appear to the degree of the icon's visible return to it, so the unconditioned only appears in the counterexperience of that which is inescapably conditioned—that is, in the finitude of my love. Marion's insistence on the unconditionality of the gift of love does not idealize love under the auspices of the unconditioned but instead is rooted in love's being the paradigmatic way of traversing my finitude (the very finitude that is engendered by my loving turn *elsewhere* for meaning). Love as unconditioned gift does not deny my finitude; love demands it and only appears as in excess of it.

Or, at least, I hope it does. I hope that this love—my withdrawing advance in love toward (because engendered by) this particular other—is not merely (even if it is in part) another idolatrous frame by which I impose yet again my own meaning on the given phenomenon. And I so hope because love breathes only in possibility and never in certainty. Without any other antecedent reason, I hope in love's own reason. But what is far from clear, amidst the inescapable discussions surrounding the influence of theology (or what could be seen by some as, perhaps worse, Marion's own Catholic faith) upon his philosophy, is whether Marion ought to be ready to give further account to those

77. See Ward, "Theological Project," for more on the charge of effacement of the icon before the invisible.

who ask for a reason for the hope that is within him, a hope in an unconditioned gift of love. What reason can he give to hope in that which is without reason? What is missing (or at the very least underdeveloped) from Marion's account of the saturated phenomenon of the gift is a reason that might account for this hope. And of course, in a manner of speaking, it cannot but be missing, as any justifying antecedent reason would undercut the very heart of the phenomenological endeavor to allow the phenomenon to appear as it gives itself.

But still, in discussing an excess that is too much to bear, Marion may well be consorting with an excess that is too much to bear. In arriving late to the event, reason certainly struggles to understand what it cannot understand, to experience what can only appear as counterexperience. But the question inescapably remains: In the first or final moment, how do I come to hope in love, and not just love generally speaking but in this love not only as the response to the threat of vanity but as that can bear excess? How do I come to hope that I have been loved—really loved—first by this particular other? For excess, by its very nature, cannot be examined so I might know what has been offered, know what is on the table, so to speak. The counterexperience of excess may leave me blind, but what hermeneutic can distinguish between a blindness caused by a lack of light and a blindness caused by an excess of light? Caputo writes of this lack of a hermeneutic of saturation: "I find this analysis very beautiful, but if, as Marion says, the saturated phenomenon falls into confusion or bedazzlement, I do not know how to distinguish the confusion of bedazzlement or of excess from the confusion of defect. How do we know that we have been visited by a supereminent excess and not just simply invaded by *khora*?"[78] Kearney, borrowing from Derrida, summarizes the problem so:

78. Kearney, "On the Gift," 78; see also Richard Kearney, *The God Who May Be: A Hermeneutics of Religion* (Bloomington: Indiana University Press, 2001), 31–33. Marion describes *khora* as "an empty and undetermined space, where meaning . . . has disappeared. Marion, *God Without Being*, 98. It is the Heideggarian "clearing" where being occurs or the Derridean *tout autre*.

> "In order to overcome hallucination we have to listen to and closely read the other," insists Derrida. . . . "We cannot be sure that we are not hallucinating by saying simply, 'I see.' 'I see' is, after all, just what the hallucinating person says. No, in order to check that you are not hallucinating, you have to read in a certain way." In what way, we might ask? "I have no rule for that," Derrida humbly concedes. "Who can decide what counts as the end of hallucination? It is difficult."[79]

Difficult, indeed.

How might we learn to practice an Ignatian-like "discernment of spirits," Kearney asks, so we can hope in what, if anything, is given behind the appearances we witness?[80] And it is a matter not simply of being unable to discern between something and nothing but of, as described by Tamsin Jones, a "crucial ambiguity within the reception of saturated phenomena," where "Marion never discusses how one might begin to establish a mode of judging such phenomena and their intent."[81] The problem here has ramifications upon ethics, or morality, where such love without reason leaves me vulnerable to being abused and used by the one to whom I am devoted but is not yet quite formulated according to the languages of these disciplines. No doubt there is reason for real concern of the direct application of this phenomenology to ethics (no doubt there is, as well, methodological concern about such application), a concern that is furthered in Marion's insistence that while I may love into loss, such loss does not threaten my love (as love is given without counting the cost or seeking return).[82] The problem is not so much that I might love into vulnerability and loss but that I am unable to be certain that this love into loss is somehow ultimately meaningful. It is not so much that love, generally speaking, is trustworthy but that *this particular love* is, in fact, *true* (or, simply, *is* love) and that I am not, in the end, loving

79. Kearney, *God Who May Be*, 78, citing Jacques Derrida, "Hospitality, Justice, and Responsibility, (UCD Roundtable), in *Questioning Ethics*, ed. Richard Kearney and Mark Dooley (London: Routledge, 1999), 65–83.
80. Kearney, *God Who May Be*, 78.
81. Jones, *Genealogy of Marion's Philosophy*, 157.
82. For more on the application to ethics of this loving without reason, see Gerald McKenny, "(Re)placing Ethics: Jean-Luc Marion and the Horizon of Modern Morality," in K. Hart, *Counter-Experiences*, 339–55; and Andrew Staron, "Moral Action and the Pragmatic *As If*: Gerald McKenny's Critique of Jean-Luc Marion's Privileging of Love," *Quaestiones Disputatae* 1 (2010): 56–71.

this particular other as only a further manifestation of my will (leading to a love that appears through the assertion of what *I* desire or think the other ought to desire). The problem is, once again, that I am hoping in a love wherein I might not be loving this particular other at all but instead be devoting myself to an idol of my own creation.

No, I cannot be certain. Such love is always a risk—the first and last and fundamental risk of our lives, the risk that promises to give a definitive response to the threat of vanity but adds that such a response is eternally deferred. But while any ostensible certainty in this matter can be nothing more than a renewed assertion of vanity, I need not be without any hermeneutic that might guide me in my hope and guide me as a lover. It is just that Marion's phenomenology itself cannot offer an interpretive guide. Coming as it does always *a posteriori*, it cannot in this way be first philosophy. It offers no first step upon which I might begin. Phenomenology itself cannot get going without faith, Carlson reminds, and this faith is always already subsequent to what here must be understood as the foundation of this first step: the event of my falling in love with this particular other.

So it is that Claude Romano's observation that "love is not a *method* of phenomenology" but is rather an event wherein we experience that which we cannot produce on our own[83] is helpful but only half correct. While love is indeed the phenomenon that Marion hopes to explore (and not merely a methodological path toward the discovery of some subsequent meaning), it is as well the only way of proceeding toward describing and understanding this event. The event of the arrival of meaning in our lives, when phenomenologically reduced, reveals the givenness of love. But further, as love appears only in my advance (through my love of love), it is only through love that that event might appear. All the questions and responses of each movement of the reduction, from the first to the last, orient the reader toward what Marion holds to be the one phenomenon that can answer the question "What's the use?": my love that arrives from the elsewhere of this particular other (revealing this other to me and giving me myself).

83. Romano, "Love in Its Concept," 330.

Marion places his faith and hope in love. Love—that to which he turns for a response to "What's the use?" Love—that which opens the possibility that this particular other might appear as they give themselves in my respecting the limits of my finitude and my certainty before this other's excess. Love—that by which I withdraw so as to mark an *elsewhere* from where I might receive that of which I cannot be certain. He might add that the turn to love must be done in faith, with neither prior justification nor sufficient subsequent rational support. In this way, while *The Erotic Phenomenon* and all Marion's discussions of love elsewhere in his *corpus* may very well help to describe love, they cannot ultimately justify it to his reader nor to Marion himself. Love does not even finally bear its own justification in the abstract, it calls for—demands—incarnation in particularity. And for Marion, the paradigmatic incarnation of love is the incarnation of the Son in Jesus Christ. While he describes love according to a phenomenological countermethod, the event that Marion so describes is first understood theologically. The event that Marion names "the gift of love" is the giving of the invisible God in the visible Christ.

Yet holding to this a paradigmatic incarnation does not simply sidestep the questions of hermeneutics. As evident in Tanner's difference in interpretation of what the scriptures do, in fact, give to be seen, Marion's own approach to the event is conditioned by his philosophy—that is, it is shaped by what he understands and how he understands it. Marion, no less than anyone, begins speaking always already in the middle—in the middle of his life, of his faith, of his wisdom and knowledge, of his own finitude (both natural and sinful), of the conversion to his beloved that has already begun. Nothing Marion writes is sufficient to bear the justification of his own love of God in Jesus Christ, understood as responsive to the love already given to him. To begin to apologize for Marion here is to recognize that he begins always already in the middle of his faith—that is, of the saturating excess of his Catholic faith (of both the *fides qua* and *fides quae*) and his understanding of that faith. It is to acknowledge, too, that there is no other place to begin the approach to this mysterious excess than from an *elsewhere* that is already given. Likewise, nothing Marion writes is sufficient to bear *my love*'s own phenomenality, as he cannot write of *my own love of my beloved*. I can defend this, too, only in recognizing that it is grounded in nothing but itself, nothing but a love that bears all things. In the end, I place my faith not in my advance in love engendered by the beloved, abstractly described, but in the love of one whom I name and who calls me by name. Love is, I find, never a question of certainty at all.

Conclusion to Part Two

Marion's phenomenology is characterized by its attention to excessive givenness, to that which saturates our intentionality and concepts and therefore appears to us in the only way that it can—as impossible (according to the rules of metaphysics) or invisible (as that which can never be conceived by our minds or fully grasped within our hearts). Marion's exploration of the gift sharpens the impact of this excess as something always first received and to which I am called to respond sacrificially by acknowledging its arrival from an elsewhere that precedes me and is other than me. But this phenomenology of the gift is furthered and complicated by Marion's turn to love.

Love operates only according to its own reason and advances for no other reason than a love for the beloved. Yet within this call for an unconditionality save for its own conditions brews the possible deconstruction of Marion's own project in the establishment of a metaphysics that reduces all things to either a new structure offered in givenness or to being's usurper: love. I have argued that these threats do not fully manifest themselves in Marion's thought: givenness itself forbids its own universalization and the very unconditionality of love is not necessitated by Marion's imposition of a phenomenological system upon love but rather by love's own terms. In fact, the uncertainty of my love is part of its appearing as that which bears all things.

But this love, while phenomenologically presented, appears in light of Christian revelation. That Marion's search for meaning leads him to turn toward the intimate elsewhere of love itself already defines the terms of the argument. "Love" is Marion's answer to the question "What's the use?" because it is also his first step. If he finds an answer to this question in the advance of unconditional love of another, it is because his understanding of love is marked by the particularity and embodiment of the incarnation of God in Jesus Christ. While Marion might carefully avoid this theological foundation in his phenomenological reduction, he nevertheless does not fully sever his understanding of love from its appearance upon the cross. Love, therefore, appears only through incarnate particularity.

In this way, Marion is not asserting a philosophy without metaphysics, or even a theology without being, but instead a way of rationally proceeding that is not beholden to these structures but nevertheless cannot appear without them. John Caputo sees this as Marion's philosophical failure. Marion's God without being, his God of love (standing beside the God whose being is pure act of Thomas Aquinas as an alternate but complementary account of God's excess), never sufficiently liberates the phenomenological call from the particularity of its appearing—Marion's call is never purely anonymous. In his review of *In the Self's Place*, Caputo observes:

> The one thing Marion does not do is to reduce this call to its pure phenomenality by depriving it of virtual contact with being. Were that purity more ruthlessly exposed, were the call laid bare more radically as a pure call, we would find that the place of the self is a desert, not the super-sacred desert of Eckhart's Godhead, like the *agathon*, but the desert within this desert, the *khora*-like desert of which Derrida speaks. Then the incomprehensibility of God would not be a way to praise God's eminence but a confession that cuts into our hide, an incision, a "circum-fession," that we really do not know who or what is calling, or what is being called for, or what we are being called to, or to what or whom we are responding.[1]

In contrast to that, it is the faith of the Christian church that there is, in fact, something knowable about God, that something—or better, someone—has been and continues to be revealed. Marion's

1. John D. Caputo, review of *In the Self's Place: The Approach of St. Augustine*, by Jean-Luc Marion, *Notre Dame Philosophical Reviews*, January 18, 2013, http://tinyurl.com/gogrzzk.

phenomenological analysis is not of anything or of nothing in particular but of a specific given phenomenon that he (although not he alone) names "love." *This* phenomenon is love—not some abstract purity but that God loves first and sent the Son.[2]

An inviting possibility remains: Marion concludes not only in following the Christian tradition and naming God "love" but also that while God loves infinitely better than we do, God loves as we do, according to the reason of love, establishing the reason of love. The question that will guide the final pages of this book is how this descriptive account of love might be theologically situated alongside the formative journey laid out in *De Trinitate*. If, as Augustine writes, I can only know God if my memory, understanding, and will are turned to remembering, understanding, and loving not myself but God, and that this is made possible only in the gift of the Spirit, then it is my hope that Marion's description of the gift of love might serve to iconically signify the means by which we might come to know God in and through the gift of love, might come to name God, "Father, Son and Holy Spirit," and might come to call upon God by that name.

2. Cf. 1 John 4:10.

PART III

Given in Worship

10

A Beginning Given in Advance

> And I said to him: "I am the one, who when Love breathes within me, takes note, and just as he dictates within me, I set forth my meaning."
>
> —Dante, *Purgatorio*, 24:52–54

"It is a question of beginning where one is, as Derrida tells us," John Caputo observes, "not where God is, we may add."[1] To begin where we are—indeed little more can be asked of us. But to know where we are as readers of Augustine—to know where we stand when encountering a mind across the distances of time and culture, and across the personal (although for the author of *Confessions*, not private) distance between ourselves and this particular man's restless struggle to know and love the God whose call broke through his deafness and whose radiance dispelled his darkness—this is the great invitation of his *De Trinitate*. We are invited to come to where we are—not, to be sure, to receive certainty about where we stand in relation to Augustine's ideas nor, and more to the point, to receive certainty about where our understanding *about* the Trinitarian God stands in relation to the Trinity that God is. We are invited to come to where we are—to come

1. Caputo, *More Radical Hermeneutics*, 207.

to know ourselves as made to the image of God (and not to know a God made in our image) and to therefore know ourselves only as we come to know God. *De Trinitate* invites us to recognize ourselves made to the image of that "unimaginable mystery" of the "supreme trinity on which [we] are not yet capable of fixing [our] eyes in contemplation"[2] and to cleave to that upon which we cannot get a fix, so as to be formed by it and see it.[3] To begin where I am, according to Marion, is also to acknowledge that my beginning is always already responsive to that which is given and that the first step of my own love is responsive to the antecedent gift I receive. It is to begin not with epistemological, causal, or ontological certainty but with the recognition of the particularity of my love already actively opening me to be formed by that which is given, with hope only in a love that bears all things.

Augustine's early interpretive formulation still echoes true in his seeking the Trinity that God is: nothing can be taught without signs, yet nothing can be learned through signs. Reading *De Trinitate* with this in mind, we have found that the way to God is through the mediation of creation (particularly the human mind and the cultural, philosophical, and linguistic structures of meaning). But at the same time, we ever risk idolatry looking for the fullness of God precisely in this mediation (that is, by not seeing it as, precisely, mediation)—for the unconditioned God cannot be conditioned to appear without overwhelming excess. But to begin with Augustine, to begin as he begins, is to recognize this paradox is not to be rejected but can offer the path of love upon which we have already commenced,[4] where we are turned already to seek God's face always.[5] God is love and it is love that we seek to know, and we can come to know love only in loving. As naming this place from which we begin is no less impossible than naming the end we so seek, this way of proceeding is itself nothing less than marking the unconditioned impossibility that is given to us—a gift of love that both reveals and *is* God.

2. Augustine, *De Trinitate*, 15.50.
3. Ibid., 8.9.
4. Ibid., 1.4.
5. Ibid., 1.5.

The aporia of this starting place is deepened through its particularity, stretching phenomenology to its limits to describe the givenness of love. Christina Gschwandtner calls attention to the phenomenological challenge of this love, observing:

> A phenomenological analysis of love thus suffers a doubled aporia: Either it describes love "as such" in the abstract, but in that case it is "love in the void" and does not do any justice to the intensely personal and specific experience of love. Or it describes a personal experience of love, but in that case it remains autistic and self-idolatrous. Love as a figure of consciousness always ends up in self-idolatry.[6]

Either, she argues, love is an abstract essence applied to a given phenomenon, rendering the phenomenon an instance of what I conceive love to be or it is a description of my own experience of loving a specific person and therefore becomes nothing but solipsistic vanity, as it is I who declares *this phenomenon* to be the essence of love (the latter possibility would be nothing more than a further instance of the former). The gift of love is only understandable as beginning from the other, as something that is not mine but is arriving from *elsewhere*. But even in arriving from elsewhere, it must actually arrive. Should it remain always *elsewhere*, it risks remaining something I can only know abstractly. It must both arrive and yet remain from *elsewhere* or continually arrive from elsewhere. I can understand the phenomenon of love only as I receive my own advance in my love of this particular other.

But where such particularity of place threatens to strike the philosophical endeavor at its foundation and put into question the possibility of shared reason (the only reason that can claim the name) it serves theology as the discipline's received origin. For if theology, as suggested by Marion, starts from an other than itself,[7] then ever more so Christian theology starts from a *particular other*. "Especially on theological grounds," Boeve writes, "because of the Incarnation, the historical particularity . . . of Christian faith should not be conceived

6. Gschwandtner, *Reading Jean-Luc Marion*, 231.
7. Marion, *God Without Being*, 1.

as a contra-indication of its truth claim, but as its fundamental condition."[8] The particularity of theology's origin and the particularity of love are correlates (the latter resting on the revelation of the former; the former resting upon the activity of latter),[9] and this doubled particularity is the reason for hoping in love's ultimate significance (and not just to me, my beloved, and my hope for meaning in my love).

While it is certainly too much to say that the concept of the gift of love is univocal for Augustine and Marion (or, for that matter, for any two people), it is my hope that it is theologically justifiable to say that their remarkably different conceptual languages have as their goal the same referent: the promise of love (in all its particularity) to bear all things—including, to be sure, Augustine, Marion, their readers, and no less myself—made in the missions of the Son and Spirit, iconically revealed upon the cross. For although Marion does not assume a divine giver in his phenomenological analysis of givenness, he does have a particular phenomenon in mind that he names "love." He does not seek to analyze the breadth of understandings of love across times and cultures. Nor, however, does he presume to speak of his own experience of love as enclosed in his own consciousness (which would simply reestablish the Cartesian *cogito*). Instead, the momentum of his own phenomenology drives him toward the unconditioned, toward theology, toward God (no doubt at least in part because his work concerns the given phenomenon of unconditioned love). Marion tries to open to a phenomenon given to him—but not only to him—in advance of his own love. If in speaking about love, Marion is in fact naming the phenomenon whose paradigm was given upon Christ's cross (that is, to begin with the originating *a posteriori* derived from faith that God loves us first), it seems that Marion only escapes love's aporia by accepting that "in love one surrenders to and ultimately imitates God."[10] It is not so much that Marion imposes theology on phenomenology but that (consistent with his definition of the philosophy of religion as the discipline that receives and analyzes

8. Boeve, "Retrieving Augustine Today," 16.
9. Cf. Ferretter, "Trace of the Trinity," 263.
10. Gschwandtner, *Reading Jean-Luc Marion*, 249.

phenomena that it can then return to theology) it is a theologically given phenomenon that he seeks to describe and understand. It will be part of my argument in this third part that Marion's phenomenology cannot give reason for a hope in this opening to this unconditioned love. Instead, we are left with only an exhausted reduction that cannot go where the particularity of unconditioned love goes. This exhaustion marks phenomenology's impossibility and orients us to the discipline that proceeds always in the midst of impossibility: theology. For the phenomenon that Marion describes and names "love" is that which is given in Christ's fidelity to God. "Love" is the phenomenon given in Christ. I will therefore interpret both Augustine and Marion as sharing a hope that love is paradigmatically given in Christ's mediation of the Trinity.[11] As both a sign given from elsewhere and a gift always already active more intimately to me than I am to myself[12]such a given love promises the impossible: that the distinct missions of the Son and Spirit (to which the scriptures and subsequent tradition bear witness) truly reveal nothing less than the Father, perfectly mediated between God and creation; that the saving name of this one God is the Father, Son, and Holy Spirit; and that the unconditioned *Trinity that God is* might appear (as invisible) to us in our anamorphic formation to the image of God.[13]

Loosely following the three-part structure of *De Trinitate* laid out in part 1, this final part will bring Augustine and Marion into a conversation about the gift of love and the effect of that gift upon our vision of the invisible Trinity. Section 1 of this chapter will examine the mediation of the invisible God to human beings, with special attention

11. See chapter 5. I will operate under the assumption that Marion is being honest with his readers when he claims that Augustine did not play a direct part in his development of the phenomenology of givenness, the saturated phenomenon, or the erotic phenomenon (Marion, *In the Self's Place*, xiii). Therefore, any similarity between the two cannot be dismissed merely as a shift of Augustine's theology into a phenomenological key. However, this does not mean that the relationship between *De Trinitate* and Marion's phenomenology is isomorphic in nature, seeing that there is no way to completely separate what Marion understands theology to be and Augustine's own immeasurable influence upon Christianity as a whole.
12. Augustine, *Confessions*, 3.11.
13. In part 3, I return from the phenomenological *I* and reassume the first person plural, taking my place as one of the people to whom revelation is gifted and speaking theologically as part of a tradition, a community, and a church.

to the ever present risk of idolatry. Section 2 will trace the impact of the unconditioned gift of love upon Trinitarian predication, marking ultimately neither substance nor relations but our formation into those who can advance in love. Section 3 explores the relationship of love and our fidelity to the truth. The next chapter will consider the naming of the Trinitarian God in and through worship.

I have argued that *De Trinitate* is best read as rational inquiry into the soteriological formation of our minds and hearts upon the reception of God's gift of love—that we may intelligibly discuss our deepening understanding of who God is in light of the deepening of our love. Furthermore, I have offered Marion's phenomenology as insightfully descriptive of the phenomenon of the gift of love given in particularity, given so we, too, might become lovers. Marion offers here a specific instance of what he generally understands philosophy to offer theology: a technical analysis of the phenomenon given in revelation, as it is given. It is my hope that Augustine and Marion might further one another, each contributing to a deepening understanding of how love forms us to see God by receiving God. To *De Trinitate*, Marion gives phenomenological texture by which the gift of love can be received in our lived lives—that is, how the God of love might be given incarnate phenomenality. To Marion, *De Trinitate* provides what Marion's erotic reduction needs but cannot establish—the name by which I might enter into intimate relationship with the particular lover revealed in the missions of the Son and Holy Spirit. The paradox of an advance that is also responsive to particularity thereby becomes the key to understanding *what love does* when I am loved and *what* I love, which in turn allows that given gift of love to reveal itself given in particularity, given in Jesus Christ. The Holy Spirit (given as love) reveals to us (in the particular incarnation of the Son) the mystery of the one God who is Father, Son, and Holy Spirit. The question before the final part of this book is thus: if Augustine, "perhaps more than any other theologian . . . viewed Christianity as 'an aporia of the impossible,'"[14] and "the impossible now is no longer what cannot be thought, but whose fact

14. Caputo and Scanlon, introduction to *God, the Gift, and Postmodernism*, 11.

has to be thought,"[15] then how might Marion's phenomenology make it possible to remain rational and have a discourse dealing with the impossible and excessive truth of the Trinity? How might we theologically understand what is given in the gift of love?

Finitude Toward the Idol or the Icon

If language were able to speak fully of the divine with signs signifying the holy and wholly mysterious *res* with exhaustive precision, eliminating signification as such in the wake of the direct equation of abstract language and its conceptual object, we would need only to seek the perfect vocabulary and syntax.[16] Once found, theology would entail mere repetition of dogmatic formulae—as in the worst of the traditions of neo-scholasticism, dogmatism, and fundamentalism —echoing into an eternity no longer marked by the formation of our faith, hope, and love. Concepts would offer an adequate model for divine reality, truth would be "accomplished in perfect evidence,"[17] and certainty would set us free from hermeneutics and the need to be transformed. However, what Augustine offers is a path not to such certain propositional truth but to truth encountered only through the deepening of our love. That such formation is never complete while we remain pilgrims on earth—that we are bound to restless incompletion even at our most ingenious and most virtuous—does not therefore render it insignificant. The bishop instructs his readers that finding out that the thing we long for is incomprehensible does not to prohibit making progress in an inquiry into the incomprehensible, nor does it make a turn to creation to quicken that progress an exercise in vanity.[18] Instead, the way in which we engage the restless struggle and the end toward which we orient our desire are both of the utmost importance to the possibility that we might "embrace more than we know."[19] But

15. Kearney, "On the Gift," 74.
16. For a helpful description of different theological understandings of the place, necessity, and function of interpretation, see James K. A. Smith, *The Fall of Interpretation: Philosophical Foundations for a Creational Hermeneutic*, 2nd ed. (Grand Rapids: Baker Academic, 2012).
17. Marion, "Banality of Saturation," 384.
18. Augustine, *De Trinitate*, 15.2.
19. Foster, "Augustine's *De Trinitate*," 268.

as Augustine is not ultimately interested in mere appreciation of the limits of understanding before that which exceeds it (both the limits that are part of our finite reach and those limits that are further imposed upon us by sin), he does not leave his readers to the stillness of apophatic silence. Rather, he is interested in how our restless finitude might relate to—indeed, even quicken—our desire to know (conceptually, certainly, but even more so to know more intimately than we know ourselves) that which exceeds our grasp *as* that which exceeds our grasp.[20]

In this way, while it might be too much of a stretch to say that Augustine is concerned with the end of metaphysics, we can perhaps venture to say that Augustine is concerned with what Marion is concerned with and calls the end of metaphysics. The end of metaphysics that gives space for Marion's own thought is importantly not an eradication of metaphysics, conceptuality, or ontology but a recognition of their limits in the face of phenomenological excess. The conceptual idolatry that concerns Marion is defined not by the use of metaphysical concepts but in their control—their closed framing—of how the phenomenon appears. Likewise, Augustine does not presume that we might come to know the intended *res* without signification or that he can receive an unmediated truth about who God is. But it matters *how* we engage that signification in the face of our limitations.

It is a closing of our understanding of God that so concerns Augustine in *De Trinitate.* At every turn, Augustine writes under the threat of false worship, endlessly seeking liberation from his own conceptual and spiritual limits through moving beyond *his* conception and *his* desire for God to find himself knowing, understanding, and loving God as God is (and in writing *De Trinitate*, seeking this liberation for his readers as well). That Augustine grants that God is truth and

20. Cf.: "Augustine's affirmative discourse is frequently interwoven with negative discourse to such a degree that he ends up with a salutary uncertainty rather than with the knowledge to dominate God's reality and essence by identifying God with images of him, which leads to conceit and pride. Finally, in book VIII of *De Trinitate* Augustine believes that reflecting on love is less important when it comes to approaching God than performing acts based on love. But even where this love is practiced, and despite Augustine's reflections in *De Trinitate*, God still remains incomprehensible to human beings." Geest, *Incomprehensibility of God*, 174.

truth is intelligible to human beings, "leaves untouched the more difficult question of in precisely what sense God really is intelligible, despite the failure of our own attempts to comprehend him."[21] And this is all the more true of an intelligibility that is rooted in relational love and marred by sin. Aware of the tempting danger of this circumscribing of the divine with concepts native to the created world—indeed, the only concepts available to us—Augustine cries out to God, struggling to find concepts for the divine overflow beyond the limits of signification.[22] The refrain of the *Confessions*, "What then do I love when I love my God?"[23] is less a question in need of a clear answer, less a question seeking to overcome our finite minds and understand God, than the heartbeat of the theology of *De Trinitate*. As the seeking of God through an ever-deepening, never-exhaustible relationship is part of the text's theological endeavor, we are invited into its depths with our goal ever enticingly withdrawing before us. Augustine's theology is always in service of this relationship with God (and not with an idolatrous construction of divinity—grand though it may be). The idea of the Trinity (with all its conditions and limitations) that he offers and develops throughout the text serves (he hopes) to signify for us the Trinity that God is—although he recognizes that the idea alone cannot do just that.

While the entirety of *De Trinitate* engages this relationship between the Trinity and the idea of the Trinity, the specific emphasis of the text's first four books is to construct an argument against Augustine's subordinationist opponents that does not disparage created being (as though we might come to God without it) while offering a restless approach to our finite concepts that might orient us to that which is beyond the limits of what is possible for us. In examining the missions of the Son and Spirit, Augustine concludes that there is no necessary

21. David Bradshaw, "Augustine the Metaphysician," in Demacopoulos and Papanikolaou, *Orthodox Readings of Augustine*, 246. Although helpful, Bradshaw's analysis is constrained by the limited scope of its consideration of the definition and range of theological intelligibility.

22. "Do heaven and earth contain you because you have filled them? Or do you fill them and overflow them because they do not contain you? Where do you put the overflow of yourself after heaven and earth are filled? Or have you, who contain all things, no need to be contained by anything because what you will you fill by containing it?" Augustine, *Confessions*, 1.3.3.

23. Ibid., 10.7.11.

connection between *being sent* and *being subordinate.* "A word," Augustine notes in a defense of the divinity of the Word, "is absolutely the same kind of thing as the knowledge it is born from."[24] In fact, in the case of the Son and the Spirit, the connection is, in fact, exactly the opposite of the Arian accusation. To see the Son and Spirit *is* to see them as sent and proceeding, to see them as from God. It is in seeing them from God, and only in seeing them from God, that we might dare to name them "God"—indeed, to name them "God from God." To see them as "true God from God" is to see them not as less than the Father but in union with the Father.

Augustine's exegetical rule that the scriptural presentation of Jesus in the form of the servant ought to be read not as subordinating him to the Father but rather as a sign that he is the sent Son offers a deep theological insight: God's activity in sending the Son and Spirit is not extrinsic to God but intimately reveals *who God is.* It is only because of the inseparable operation of the Father, Son, and Spirit that we can trust revelation as revelation of God. Furthering his paradoxical interpretive rule that nothing can be known by signs alone but that, indeed, we can come to learn only through signs, Augustine maintains that while nothing in creation on its own may mediate God, it is only through creation *understood as a sign* that we might come to receive God's revelation.[25] It is in recognizing Jesus Christ as the sent Son—that is, as *God from God*—that we might have faith in his mediation of God; furthermore, it is the Spirit that effects this recognition. In fact, what the missions of the Son and Spirit *do* is reveal a God who can self-reveal through the mediation of creation, all the while remaining, as God, invisible. Seeing their missions *as* they are revealed is to see *what* is revealed. This temporal mediation maintains the distinction between the invisible God (that is, both Father and Son remain invisible) and the Son made visible in the form of the servant. In the form of the servant,

24. Augustine, *De Trinitate*, 15.19.

25. "We were incapable of grasping eternal things, and weighed down by the accumulated dirt of our sins, which we had collected by our love of temporal things, and which had become almost a natural growth on our mortal stock; so we needed purifying. But we could only be purified for adaptation to eternal things by temporal means." Ibid., 4.24.

the Son is made visible even while the Son remains invisible.[26] "God appears," Ayres insightfully notes, "while being hidden"[27]—and only while being hidden, we might add.

To see the Son as *from God* is to see the form of the servant as the visible mediation of the invisible God. It is never, Augustine maintains, to see God directly. We can only come to see God in coming to know the servant as the sent Son; we can only come to know the servant as the sent Son by the gift of charity that is the Spirit. The Spirit is the gift that teaches us to interpret the visible servant as the sent Son of the invisible God; it teaches us to interpret the signification of the servant toward the *res* of his origin. The Holy Spirit does not, therefore, allow unmediated access to the divine. When we receive this gift in our finitude, our love is formed toward being taught to see the signs of all of creation, and particularly the sign of the servant, as signifying the Trinity that God is. Revelation is still a mediation (we are never without mediation and thus never without interpretation), but love opens us to being taught to interpret the signs as signifying God. "The 'redemption' of interpretation," James K. A. Smith observes, "would not be a redemption *from* interpretation but a redemption of our will and a reordering of our love enabling us to construe *well*."[28] Through this hermeneutic of charity, the Spirit teaches us to see in the visible Christ the sending of the Son by the invisible God.

That the missions of the Son and Spirit working together serve as true mediation of the invisible divine to creation—that is, that they allow for God to reveal Godself to us and yet remain distinct from us—indicates that, for Augustine, love plays the crucial role of mediation between the Trinity and human beings. "To believe in Christ by the gift of the Holy Spirit"[29] is to believe "that the Son was sent to be visible by the invisible Father together with the invisible Son"[30]—it is to believe that the visible servant Christ is acting inseparably with

26. Ibid., 2.9.
27. Ayres, *Augustine and the Trinity*, 162.
28. J. Smith, *Fall of Interpretation*, 25n25.
29. Augustine, *De Trinitate*, 4.29.
30. Ibid., 2.9.

the invisible Father. It is by the gift of love that we can believe that the visible servant can at one time be visible and still be the invisible God. It is by the gift of love that is the Holy Spirit that we come to have faith in the mediation of revelation—that what is visible is at the same time revealing to us something invisible yet *remains invisible.*

This conclusion is not too far distinct—or so I propose—from Marion's own presentation of the icon as the visible image that makes visible the invisible as invisible. And such similarities should not surprise, considering that Christ serves as Marion's icon *par excellence*, giving the icon its very justification. In both cases, seeing Christ as a sign/icon requires that we be taught to see him (by the icon/sign itself), that our vision be somehow formed to recognize that the image before us serves to offer to our vision something that remains invisible. Indeed, although both Augustine and Marion share a tendency to describe knowing in visual terms,[31] neither hold to any easy and direct correlation of epistemological sight with knowledge. To know, in other words, is not simply to see but to see "what is the case." To know is to see things truly, and such vision needs to be taught. Marion's phenomenological language describes this knowing as allowing the phenomenon to appear as it gives itself, and not, to be sure, as I want it to be or as an abstract concept only subsequently applied to that which is given. And I can know this given only as I open myself to receive—through my anamorphic formation—what is given on its own terms. Knowledge is in this way not so much acquisitive but relational, and it is never certain. "To know" is to open oneself to the other so as to be formed to the other, by the other—and it therefore depends upon my receptivity to that which is given.

Marion's phenomenology of saturation—particularly that of the idol and icon—is primarily a description of *how* that which is in excess of our understanding might be mediated in a way that makes this excess somehow intelligible while it remains in excess of reason. It offers an approach to a reading of *De Trinitate* that not only insists on the iconic nature of the Son's mission and the revelatory significance of the gift

31. Barnes, "Visible Christ," 331.

of the Spirit's but describes *how* these missions might accomplish their goal of revealing the Trinity to us. To name this event that gives this unexpected breaking in of phenomenological excess "revelation" is importantly not simply an act of faith in the actualization of what must remain, phenomenologically, only a possibility. Instead, for Marion, revelation *is* the making visible of the invisible *as invisible* or the possibility of the impossible *as impossible.* To put it another way, Marion's phenomenology of excess seeks to describe in the language of a particular philosophical discipline the paradigmatic theological phenomenon of Christ's iconic revelation. What it is that Christ does in revealing God becomes paradigmatic of all excess (and it does not, therefore, surprise that Marion's project led him to the phenomenon of love). Revelation so understood is not the actualization of the phenomenological possibility that God might give Godself to be known in the same manner as any phenomenon might but is instead the event of that which is otherwise impossible, the appearing of the unconditioned invisible *as* the unconditioned invisible. But as a concept, this excess (and, for that matter, the concepts of the unconditioned, the invisible, and the impossible), too, is part of the rationality that cannot be equated to the given phenomenon's saturation. Active in phenomenology's counter-methodology, the concept of excess serves, too, to mark the limits of reason that we struggle to see—both seeing that these limits exist and at the same time not seeing them at all.[32] Therefore, it becomes a matter not of how we can transcend our finitude and our concepts (impossible, indeed) but of the possibility that they might be crossed (and never eradicated) by that which is given to us in advance of our being able to grasp it.

God reveals Godself in the missions of the Son and Spirit through the mediation of the presence of Christ and the anamorphic formation of our love, not only because of human limitations (whether as created or as fallen) or strictly because of some conceptual ineffability of the divine nature (as though that nature were strictly unintelligible to us), but because the revelation of God, as the Trinity, is given according

32. Cf. Augustine, *De Trinitate*, 15.16.

to what it is. To know the Trinity (not just any trinity, but the Trinity that God is) is to be formed to receive what it offers in love. "For it is then that the word is most like the thing known," Augustine writes, "and most its image, because the seeing which is thought springs direct from the seeing which is knowledge, and it is a word of no language, a true word from a true thing, having nothing from itself, but everything from that knowledge from which it is born."[33] Marion's phenomenological icon illustrates how such an image refers us back to that from which it is born (and particularly the paradigmatic icon of Christ, who perfectly has only what he was given from the Father) and offers a rationality by which we might describe how Augustine's missions of the Son and Spirit teach us to see and confess the servant Christ as the divine Son. As servant, Christ offers us his fidelity to God as the sign of his being sent and does not claim this equality outright. Augustine is clear: the only way to know the Trinity is to receive the sent Son as God from God, and the only way to do that is to receive the love of God from the Holy Spirit. "Love therefore is God from God,"[34] Augustine writes, and to know love is to know God.

The Overcoming of "Overcoming Metaphysics"

That a tense opposition developed at the heart of Western Trinitarian theology from what is an "arbitrary linguistic convention," offering some rules by which we might speak of the triune God "with less incoherence than would otherwise be the case,"[35] leaves commentators on *De Trinitate* with a dilemma. Augustine's analysis of the ways we might speak of the Trinitarian God is provocative and promising, but its overemphasis in the Christian tradition has aroused a rigid interpretation (both embraced and rejected) that has distorted books 5–7 and their place in the text. While the concepts of *substantia* and *persona* would become theologically canonical ways of structuring the discussion about a central mystery of the Christian faith, Augustine

33. Ibid., 15.22.
34. Ibid., 15.31.
35. Hill, "Forward to Books V, VI, and VIII," in Augustine, *The Trinity*, 188.

neither plainly defines the terms nor clearly situates them in his larger argument. This section will argue that an interpretation of this tension between modes of predication as the context for an overcoming of substance metaphysics—helpful though it may be for further delineating the tension—ultimately misreads its place and significance in the overall argument of the text. While the historical argument about what Augustine means remains significant, the question has further significance for the direction of Trinitarian thought: how, then, might we proceed to think the Trinity while taking seriously Augustine's theology and allowing his concepts to serve their heuristic purpose while refraining from dogmatizing them? I suggest a reading of the distinction between substantive and relational predication as part of, but not determining of, the overall soteriological thrust of *De Trinitate*. In so doing, I hope to find a way of proceeding that might "outplay this opposition"[36] between substantive and relational predication and perhaps even open the door to an approach to the Trinitarian name through Marion's erotic reduction.

In the most prominent tradition of Western theology (one rooted significantly, if only partially, in Augustine's thought), God is said to be three *personae*—Father, Son, and Holy Spirit—and one *substantia*—the divine substance, essence, nature, or being. Each *persona* is, at the same time, divine and, moreover, fully identifiable with the divine *substantia*. Father, Son, and Spirit are each both themselves and the one God. But such an approach, according to its critics, can lead to Trinitarian models in which "Father, Son, and Spirit appear to be full persons, but are also said to be each identical with the divine essence, thus making the *de facto* number of persons in God hard to estimate,"[37] and abandoning "real distinctness of trinitarian persons."[38] If each person is identical with the divine substance—that is, if each *persona* is also, while still *persona*, fully *substantia*—then the persons themselves become secondary to the real divinity, signified by the substance, a singular concrete "thing."[39] While the full significance of the divine

36. Bennington, *Derridabase*, 76.
37. Plantinga, "Social Trinity and Tritheism," 22.
38. Ibid.

persons might still be stressed, there is still a real risk that the result of an emphasis on the divine substance is, for all intents and purposes, a form of theological modalism in which the Trinity serves revelatory and salvific purposes but is not reflective of the truest reality of who God is. God might come to us and act for us in the three distinct modes of Father, Son, and Holy Spirit, but this personal distinction is an aspect of the revelatory process and not indicative of who God *is*. In fact, such a modalistic revelation cannot be the revelation of God, as the reality of God would therefore remain hidden behind the three modes of divine action. Here, "God" is defined first in terms of substance and the divine persons are grafted on only secondarily. The personal relations are sacrificed on the altar of the one divine substance, distorting theology and opening the door to abuses both ecclesial and political.[40]

It is because he fails to overcome this concept of *substance*, so the concern goes, that Augustine's theology is inescapably mired in *being*—a concept that in turn serves as the "medium of relation between self and other,"[41] a "narrative of relation"[42] profitable because

39. The last few decades have seen a focused interest in the Trinitarian relations and the possibility that personhood might serve as a means for escaping what is seen as the ominous threat of metaphysical substance. For examples, see Plantinga, "Social Trinity and Tritheism" and D. Brown, "Trinitarian Personhood and Individuality." Indeed, such an interest has roots in a variety of sources. Zizioulas's *Being as Communion*, for example, has served as an impetus for a renewal of attention on the Orthodox Fathers of the Church and their contribution to an understanding of God through relationality. And although much has been and can continue to be written on Augustine's relationship to the Greek Fathers (for an excellent collection of examples, see Demacopoulos and Papanikolaou, *Orthodox Readings of Augustine*), this emphasis on relationality is often seen as a contrast to Augustine's thought. The discussion of Trinitarian personhood has taken a different form under the horizon of analytic philosophy, where the focus has been (1) on the legitimacy of understanding personhood *as* relation and (2) around an attempt to understand the divine substance itself as a relation of the divine persons. These assessments of the spurious reasoning behind the claim that "persons are relations," helpful though they are, fail to achieve a fuller relevance to our examination precisely because those involved are too quick to either reconcile or dismiss the tension between reason and revelation and the way that our limitations function in our movement toward God. The importance of these tensions, and precisely why they are inescapable as structured, opens to a deeper understanding of the overall movement of *De Trinitate* and of theology. For examples of this analytic approach, see Sarah Coakley, "'Persons' in the 'Social' Doctrine of the Trinity: A Critique of Current Analytic Discussion" in *The Trinity*, ed. Stephen T. Davis, Daniel Kendall, SJ, and Gerald O'Collins, SJ (Oxford: Oxford University Press, 1999), 123–44; Harriet Harris. "Should We Say the Personhood is Relational?" *Scottish Journal of Theology* 51, no. 2 (May 1998): 214–34; and Lancaster, "Three-Personed Substance, 123–39.

40. For criticism of such political abuses, see Moltmann, *Trinity and the Kingdom* and *History and the Triune God*; also Leonardo Boff, *Holy Trinity, Perfect Community*, trans. Phillip Berryman (Maryknoll, NY: Orbis Books, 2000).

41. Oliver Davies, *A Theology of Compassion: Metaphysics of Difference and the Renewal of Tradition* (Grand Rapids: Eerdmans, 2001), 3.

shared by both. This *being*, as a source of continuity and the foundational building block of all that is, pledges itself as the key to understanding reality. Substance, therefore, becomes the manner in which being itself reifies possibility in actuality and serves as an approach to being through its presence-at-hand in the present time—its *being here now*.[43] This "metaphysics of presence" is the trust in the authenticity of interpretation of that which is thought, said, experienced, or desired.[44] It is "our deepest, most intractable, presupposition" that there is an enduring presence to such truth, a presence to be sought and attained through a correspondence of subject to object.[45] When the relationship of humanity to God is approached by defining both terms in and through being, the concept of God becomes either a being or being itself. Either case traps God in the comings and goings of being and threatens to present God as substance present here and now and therefore as defined by the necessary conditions of being present. Here, divinity is defined through ontology with the correspondence between God and present substance established *by the subject*, with God ultimately being reduced to an object-thought. The reality of such a God of substance—an *ontotheological* God whose presence is determined not by God but by the definition of divine nature in terms of its *being here* and its acting according to the rules of presence—establishes the divine existence as a determinant of God's substantial presence.

Emmanuel Falque notes that the always present possibility of the

42. D. Hart, "Hidden and the Manifest," 191.
43. Horner, *Rethinking God as Gift*, 29.
44. For more on this metaphysics of presence: "The more naive believe in a paradise lost, the more cunning restore order by claiming to think, in order, the absence of loss of order. For Derrida, as for Heidegger, in both cases (with their innumerable variations and nuances) one is constructing things on an unquestioned value: *presence*. The metaphysics of presence thinks in two (logical and often historical) moments: presence first, of the world to a gaze, of a consciousness to its own inspection, of a meaning to a mind, of life to itself, of a breast to a mouth; absence next—the world veiled, consciousness astray, non-sense death, debauchery, language, weaning. By thinking the second moment as derived with respect to the first, one returns, if only in thought, the complex to the simple, the secondary to the primary, the contingent to the necessary. This is the very order of reason and meaning, of the *logos*, and one does not escape it as easily as seem to think those who quickly invoke the unconscious or matter, madness, or even the other." Bennington, *Derridabase*, 16–18.
45. Kevin Hart, *Postmodernism: A Beginner's Guide* (Oxford: Oneworld, 2004), 22.

idolatry of ontotheology does not necessitate its full manifestation, acknowledging, "Not one author cannot be rehabilitated from the charge of ontotheology."[46] However, he adds, the recognition that the specter of betrayal has not, perhaps, ever achieved full incarnation in the classic texts of Western thought, "does not mean that it does not exist as a comportment or attitude, or as a manner of thinking one should at least try to avoid."[47] If Augustine's own thought exhibits this comportment by being "burdened with a fairly elaborate theory of being,"[48] then, as Joseph S. O'Leary argues, Augustine's God "remains nine-tenths a metaphysical construction."[49] Indeed, nowhere does this burden weigh more heavily upon those who seek to free Augustine from such a metaphysical God than in books 5–7 of *De Trinitate*, wherein the possibilities of relational predication are burdened by Augustine's instance that while the Trinitarian persons are named relationally, the term "person" itself is substantively, not relationally, predicated.

However, a univocal application of the term "substance" across the centuries is not easily justified. Marion notes that this eliding of concepts occurs (in the particular representative case of O'Leary) "without any textual precaution."[50] Likewise, Ayres warns that "modern scholarly concern for the terminology of 'person,' 'substance' and 'nature' has tended to miss the significance of the wider linguistic patterns that formed the context for these particular terms,"[51] namely the so-called Arian and Monarchian conflicts and the defense of the full equality of the Father and Son. Augustine's use of these terms should then be first and foremost tied to the particular theological concerns of the fifth century and certainly not be univocal with their use in

46. Emmanuel Falque, "Metaphysics and Theology in Tension: A Reading of Augustine's *De Trinitate*," in Boeve, Lamberigts, and Wisse, *Augustine and Postmodern Thought*, 21. By way of examples of those accused of such a crime, Falque offers Aristotle, Hegel, Aquinas, Scotus, Descartes, Pascal, and Malebranche. Ibid., 21–22.

47. Ibid., 22.

48. Joseph S. O'Leary, *Questioning Back: The Overcoming of Metaphysics in Christian Tradition* (Minneapolis: Winston Press, 1985), 173.

49. Ibid., 186.

50. "*Sans aucune precaution textuelle.*" Jean-Luc Marion, "*Substantia*: Note sur l'usage de *substantia* par St. Augustine et sure son appartenance à l'histoire de la métaphysique," in *Mots Médiévaux: Offerts à Ruedi Imbach*, ed. I. Atucha, D. Calma, C. König-Pralong, I. Zavattero (Turnhout: Brepols, 2011), 502.

51. Ayres, *Augustine and the Trinity*, 72–73.

the contemporary struggle to overcome metaphysics. Gioia, too, wisely cautions theologians against "ascribing an autonomous referential content—determined on the basis of the philosophy of their time or choice—to the Trinitarian use of substance and of any other ontological category in theology, and shape their doctrine accordingly."[52] The language and methodology of books 5–7 find their origin in particular debates with specific opponents. The bishop's response takes its definite form from the Arian theology to which he responds, resulting in a particular theological articulation that can be intellectually taxing or potentially misleading if detached from its origin.

Yet while the polemical origin of these books ought to give pause to any direct application of the terminology and structure of argument to Augustine's overall "systematic ambition,"[53] we should not join Gioia and set aside this one-fifth of *De Trinitate* as irrelevant to such ambition. Although the particularities of Augustine's polemics can threaten to overtake his larger argument, it is not necessary that they do so. That Augustine was wrestling with our particular contemporary questions is difficult to defend. But such recognition does not forbid conversation and even possible convergence of Jean-Luc Marion's and Augustine's articulations of the formative impact of the gift of love. Of concern here is expressly not a supposed univocality of "substance" as used by Augustine and in contemporary discourse but rather the theological concerns that drive such polemics: the danger of idolatry and the revelation of God through the begotten Son and given Spirit.

Meticulous attention to Augustine's tentative application of metaphysical language leads Gioia to interpret the bishop's juggling of terms and categories as a sign of a deeper resistance to any "too clear-cut definition."[54] That Augustine himself is hesitant to place too much content within his concepts serves to both warn and encourage us.

52. Gioia, *Theological Epistemology*, 148. Ayres relatedly observes, "The language for speaking of relational predication that Augustine develops here stays here" (Ayres, *Augustine and the Trinity*, 217), noting that the *ad aliquid* by which Augustine describes personal relation only appears twice outside of *De Trinitate*. Ayres attributes this paucity of references to the context and philosophical background of the discussion more than to its complexity.

53. Gioia, *Theological Epistemology*, 152.

54. Ibid., 153.

Certainly, to say definitively *what* Augustine meant by any particular use of any particular term is an exacting task at best. But his very avoidance of clearly defined philosophical language could be itself a sign that he is more concerned with signifying the *res* in question than its conceptual definition. This language, then, serves as an exercise in disciplined failure, warning readers from ascribing too much definitive content while concomitantly inviting a deeper exploration of Augustine's true concern: remembering, understanding, and loving the Trinity itself. There is absolutely no reason to move from the recognition of both a polemical origin and Augustine's straining against metaphysical categories to an assumption that neither have a larger place in the bishop's larger systematic ambition (especially in light of Augustine's lack of retractions or further contextualizing of these books). This ontological discussion, although specifically tied to polemics, remains part of *De Trinitate* and participates in its overall attempted signification of the understanding and love of the Trinity. A dismissal of its significance in the name of remaining true to the text is marked with unnecessary internal contradiction (leading, perhaps, to as significant of a distortion as reading all of *De Trinitate* through the lens of these two terms: *substantia* and *persona*). In fact, Gioia's emphasis on the manner in which love, in the form of the gift of the Holy Spirit, strains against, to the point of shattering, Augustine's ontological categories becomes all the more significant to Augustine's overall systematic articulation of the theology of the Trinity to the degree that the ontology of books 5–7 remain an integral part of the text.

Approaching books 5–7 opposite Gioia, Falque suggests that expressing the irreconcilable tension between the metaphysical (and specifically ontological) language of substance and the theological emphasis on relation is indicative of Augustine's ultimate goal in these books: to present dramatic transformation undergone by language when predicated of God.[55] Falque contends that one of Augustine's innovative contributions to Christian theology is the particular matter

55. Falque, "Metaphysics and Theology," 23.

in which he theologically engaged metaphysics in attempting to "delineate the range of this expression, certainly not to comprehend and grasp it, but rather to show it in all its ambiguity."[56] This ambiguity is born of accepting neither a separation of theology and metaphysics to their respective corners, banished from each other in the name of purity, nor a so-called unity featuring theology's inheritance of the intellectual endeavor at the point at which metaphysics finds its rationality beginning to fray. Rather, Falque proposes that in Augustine, "the tensions between metaphysics and theology are always greater than the resolutions they propose,"[57] rendering every overcoming a convulsive, but ultimately impotent, attempt at transformation. "This does not mean," he notes, "that Augustine refuses such a transcription of the philosophical into the theological—his own concern was rather to realize precisely this from within the framework of Christian orthodoxy. It means that Augustine denies the possibility of an all too immediate and univocal application of such philosophical concepts."[58] This tension is as inescapable as it is unavoidable.

Continuing, Falque observes that Augustine refuses the direct application of metaphysics to theology in book 5, escaping from the substance/accident structure by means of relational predication. "When we think about God the trinity we are aware that our thoughts are inadequate to their object, and incapable of grasping him as he is,"[59] which illuminates Augustine's reason for such a refusal: concepts and categories that are sufficient to their object in philosophical language simply cannot both retain unaltered meanings and be predicated of God—a direct translation of God into metaphysical substance would betray the Christian faith.[60] Revelation imposes demands of philosophy that cannot be met within the limits of philosophy.[61] This inadequacy

56. Ibid., 24.
57. Ibid., 25.
58. Ibid., 27.
59. Augustine, *De Trinitate*, 5.1.
60. Falque, "Metaphysics and Theology," 28.
61. For a concise and valuable account of Christianity's revision of philosophical categories, see D. Hart, "Hidden and the Manifest," particularly 203–10.

of the philosophical idiom is not an excuse for renouncing the theological endeavor but a demand for a new way of articulating meaning. Beyond a metaphysical concern for *what* is being said about God, Falque interprets Augustine as, at the same time, anxious to clarify *how* one is to understand those words and the interaction among the words said. A substance that can only be understood in a context shared with relation transforms the category into something perhaps unrecognizable, or at least unacceptable to a philosopher shaped significantly by Aristotelian thought—which Augustine was not. How the transformation is effected and just what Augustine does with this transformed category are both far from clear. This ambiguity, however, is not to be neatly circumvented nor piously fought. It is the awareness of the contours of this ambiguity, the limitations of reason, and the vector of the force transforming philosophy that more clearly reveal, through contrast, the matter at hand. The attentive use of philosophy—and specifically the apprehension of the nature and particularities of its precisions and therefore its inadequacy—allows us to receive revelation. The studied distance between our understanding of substance and what transformation is now required of the mind so as to make sense of revelation's impact traces the content of the revealed message.

Falque argues that in asking "*quid tres?*" (what three they are?), Augustine is concerned with neither substance nor accident, but prepares "the departure of theology from metaphysics' tracks, without however renouncing the path of metaphysics completely."[62] This turn to relation is first and foremost a theological one, arising from the need to make sense of the relationship among the proper names used for God in the New Testament and the way that the scriptures articulate and refer to those names. That Augustine is repositioning his philosophical terms is clear—substance is no longer the first and lone foundational term of these transformed categories.[63] But Augustine does not smoothly interchange the logical order of the categories of

62. Falque, "Metaphysics and Theology," 31–32.
63. Ibid., 33.

substance and relation, for the latter undergoes transformation as well. Falque continues, "Thus, some thing (*quid*) is a thing if and only if it is in 'relation to something' (*ad aliquid*)—'movement' of the one to the other (*esse ad*), not 'being-in' the same substance (*esse in*). Here the example (*sicut*) is paradigmatic, rather than the other way around."[64] Human relationality is not imposed on the Trinity—such categories are so woefully inadequate to the task at hand that their very definitions are strained to the point of rendering them almost unrecognizable. This relational movement, this Trinitarian "*ad aliquid*," is therefore the paradigm by which all relation is measured, despite how deficiently the human type follows the divine prototype. And it is here that Falque sees the hint of what could have been a venture into a new articulation of Trinitarian personhood. However, this promise in book 5 of "relation . . . beyond both substance and accident"[65] never achieves the conceptual velocity to escape the gravitational pull of substance. There remains a logical priority of substance over relation as there must be some *thing* to be related before it can be *related*.

But despite substance's resilience to conquest, Falque affirms not its final enthronement or the victory of theology over metaphysics (he concludes with a turn to Thomas Aquinas for a more sustainable liberation from an *a priori* ontology of substance), but an assertion almost Chalcedonian in tone, holding in unity the seemingly irreconcilable pair:

> It is not that Saint Augustine discovered just how to resolve the tension, it is rather that he brings this tension to light and dwells in the impossibility of undoing it. Theology is never more philosophical than when it imposes the obligation to surpass philosophy, or when it wants to rid itself of philosophy altogether. Philosophy, then again, is never caught more into the mazes of theology's web than when it elevates itself to the level of a necessity for theology, albeit only to be transformed by it.[66]

64. Ibid., 32.
65. Ibid., 44.
66. Ibid.

Later, he concludes,

> This transformation does not occur in the sense that theology would destroy the metaphysical concepts and lift them up to a higher order, but rather in the sense that theology attempts to alter these concepts from within in order to render them adequate, as far as possible, to the newness of the object: the triune and relational God (*ad aliquid*)."[67]

For Falque, Augustine's *De Trinitate* sharpens the point of tension between metaphysics and theology so as to shape the very edge of reason, rendering the tension "unsurpassable,"[68] while at the same time directing us to the only means of overcoming this limit.

However, while Falque is correct to say that Augustine dwells in an impossibility and is helpful in the way that he clarifies the impossibility of our coming to know God perfectly, he misnames this impossibility as a tension between theology and metaphysics, creating a theological problem from a philosophical limitation. Because Augustine never overcomes substantive predication, Falque mistakenly understands the significance of this tension as an end in itself. But *substantia*, Marion himself notes, is always already for Augustine a theological term that marks the difference and distance between God (and Marion joins the ranks of those who remind that for Augustine, "*essentia* indeed replaces *substantia* when it comes to God as Trinity"[69]) and fallen being. It is a christological term insofar as it marks, too, our redemptive returning, through Christ, to the substantive place in which and for which we are made: the place from which to praise God. Marion observes of Augustine's use of the term "*substantia*":

> Thus man, who was created substance, lost his initial stance because of his iniquity. Christ came to settle into the non-substance, into the poverty of the stance where mutable man passes life and passes away, to there restore the substances, who can now praise God. Here man loses his substance by his iniquity and recovered it so as to praise. How better to say that substance does not fall under ontology? Thus *substantia* has only a negative use for creation and of denial for the triune God, never finding

67. Ibid., 52.
68. Ibid., 23.
69. "Et finalement *essentia* remplace bel et bien *substantia* quand il s'agit de Dieu comme Trinité." Marion, "*Substantia*," 504.

> a positive and dogmatic use as a categorical determination of the being of created being, ever less of the being of uncreated being (supposing that one could be found in the case of God in the vision and the intent of Saint Augustine). Usages of *substantia* cannot therefore serve as an argument to include Saint Augustine under the horizon of metaphysics.[70]

Where such a philosophically inclined argument fails is not in its criticism of Augustine's philosophy, per se, but in understanding how philosophy serves Augustine's presentation of revelation. That Augustine does not precisely define his terms is less a philosophical failing than as a sign of his real concern.[71] Books 5–8 explore the demands of revelation upon specific elements of the philosophical tradition, a tradition with which Augustine was only passingly familiar[72] and one with which he was not ultimately interested. The missions of the Son and Holy Spirit reveal not a philosophical system nor particular descriptive terms but the Trinity that the God of love is.

The philosophical tension that is not resolved in books 5–7 acts instead as an intelligible sign, directing Augustine's readers toward a more fundamental concern, a concern to which he directly engages in book 8: love. The theological endeavor, to whatever degree it may be metaphysical, is not ultimately characterized by a pursuit of objective knowledge but by a methodology built upon revealed love and the deepening of relationship that that love offers. When the task of theology is not the ultimate adequacy of its language to its object, when incompletion and restlessness instead reveal our most exquisite words to be satisfactory signs for straw, *how* we confront this impossible signification matters a great deal. The tension between these modes of predication, like all of creation, is only understandable in light of their being ordered to the deepening of our love. Theology's way of proceeding marks that which is impossible for us, while the very subject of inquiry guaranteeing this impossibility—the God of love—conforms our knowledge to itself as gift.

This is not to say that love ought to be held over and against

70. Ibid., 511.
71. Ayres, *Augustine and the Trinity*, 218.
72. Ibid., 128.

substance as a conceptual synonym for relation. Love cannot simply replace substance without also simply taking over its position as the foundation of metaphysics and the new condition of possibility. It is possible that—like the category of relation, which Falque notes has become a banality in the way it is used in some contemporary contexts to simply abandon the tension between theology and metaphysics[73] —love is in danger of being exploited as a means by which we might simply step away from the substance of the Christian theological tradition. The concept of *love* used as a means to a philosophical end, defined and articulated in contrast to a supposed tyranny of substance does not deliver its promised liberation but simply offers us a more ostensibly comfortable prison. Under the illusion of the absence of ontology, love becomes the first and last criterion of theological meaning but at the expense of its being burdened with the responsibility for filling the structural abyss left behind in the supposed banishment of ontology. A form of love stretching to assume the role of metaphysics of substance, taking over the duty of the foundational building block of reality as such distorts love into something irreconcilable with the initial intention. Love, in trying to rid itself of metaphysics, takes on the work of metaphysics; in becoming every*thing*, it is in danger of becoming simply another name for being. The ultimate triumph of ontotheology is enshrined in its coronation of love as the ruler of all beings and even of being itself. Like all such crowns, this one weighs more than is apparent, lowering the gaze of love to apparently inescapable substance.

In *De Trinitate*, Augustine is fundamentally concerned not with the eradication of metaphysical language (as if it were possible), nor with the circumscription of God within a distorted and monstrous form of a metaphysical or ontological simplicity (although he does insist on the irreducibility of the divine persons to each other), but rather with the imposition of one's own memory, understanding, and love upon the Trinity rather than the opening of one's own reason and will to be shaped by God—to make God possible, according to my knowledge and

73. Falque, "Metaphysics and Theology," 53.

expectations, rather than the event of receiving from God precisely that which forms me into that which I cannot foresee and choose. While *what* words mean certainly changes when they are predicated of God, the further significance of Falque's argument is that *how* these words mean is also transformed, whereby both ambiguity and limitation function in the very signification of the names Father, Son, and Holy Spirit. Substantial predication and metaphysical categories are not descriptive of the inner life of the Trinity.[74] They do, however, mark the limits of what we know to be possible—and the place of opening to that which appears to us as impossible: our coming to know and love the God who loves us first. This language is not *about* God, per se, but is about our understanding of God and its relationship with our turning to God. It is not about God, *in se*, but about our salvific coming to know and love God through the missions of the Son and Spirit. The question is not so much about the tension between our idea of God and God but about how our always finite idea of God is related to our coming to know and love the Trinity that God is.

If there is a connection between a caution around a metaphysics of substance and Augustine's thought, it is in the shared concern that our thoughts toward God never fully and finally yield to our own structuring and ordering. Rather than proceeding through asking, "Lord my God, is there any room in me which can contain you?"[75] and imploring, "The house of my soul is too small for you to come to it. May it be enlarged by you,"[76] such capitulation of human thought confirms the presence-at-hand of the divine. As "at hand," this presence, while always hoped for by the religious believer, can become not only near but obtainable, comprehensible, and even malleable. The ambivalence of Marion's concept of the idol is helpful here. The phenomenological idol is a real experience of the saturated phenomenon but one marked by our recoiling before excessive givenness. That which appears is truly given, but it is only a framed fragment of that givenness and one whose conceptual luminosity bedazzles and blinds us to the possibility

74. Gioia, *Theological Epistemology*, 168.
75. Augustine, *Confessions*, 1.2.2.
76. Ibid., 1.6.

that there is anything more to be seen. Likewise, for Augustine, the goodness of creation, the dynamism of the self-reflective human mind, even the sharp pristine beauty of reason, all can serve as signs of the divine just as much as means to our own self-worship. But rather than seeing ourselves as created to the image of God, we assert of adequacy of our chosen *signa* and the divine *res*, understanding God as in our image. The specter of the *libido dominandi* always haunting him, Augustine is aware of how easily we can move from worshiping God to worshiping the idol of ourselves, often deceptively in the form of our own ideas about the divine. And it is this threat that so concerns Augustine and so animates his exploration of the predicative structure of theological language and how we may account "for the one and only and true God being a trinity, and for the rightness of saying, believing, understanding that the Father and the Son and the Holy Spirit are of one and the same substance or essence."[77]

The question of *De Trinitate*'s limitations is one of a tension not between theology and metaphysics at all but between a finite and fallen human reason and the formation of our understanding and love of God, between our desire to obtain knowledge in a manner independent of God and our openness to receiving it as gift and not as something of our own devising. Strictly speaking, the decisive tension is not even between finite human reason understood as destitute in either its created or fallen limitations (although Augustine is certainly all too aware of both of these factors). It is, rather, a matter of conforming ourselves to the way in which God is revealed based upon what is revealed. To receive love, we much conform ourselves to love. What Augustine ultimately offers is not a precisely drawn model or a set of philosophical rules, the application of which might lead to a relatively accurate image of the Trinity. He outlines the borders of Trinitarian predication and calls attention to the places where the promise of convergence of metaphysics and theology—or perhaps, because theology is always inescapably metaphysical and because Augustine's metaphysics is always already theological in its aim,[78]

77. Augustine, *De Trinitate*, 1.4.

between language toward God and the God of love—remains unfulfilled. Bringing Augustine to end *De Trinitate* not in silence but in prayer, the experience of both the impossibility of coming to a fullness of divine knowledge and the related infinite depth of divine love are given to us as grace. This is how *De Trinitate* structures the tension: between the impossibility of our signification of God and of the sign of salvation given to us in the otherwise impossible formation of our love to the gift of love.

If it is the case that *De Trinitate* dwells in impossibility, then it is precisely the impossibility of effecting a relatively adequate formation of theology to its object. In the absence of reconciliation between these two paths to God, or of theology's supplanting metaphysics as an unadulterated reflection of God, this impossibility looms large over the text. "If this cannot be grasped by understanding," Augustine writes, "let it be held by faith, until he shines in our minds who said through the prophet, *Unless you believe, you will not understand* (Is 7:9)."[79] With our minds frustrated by finitude and our language fumbling in signification, this modification of concepts requires a real and faithful appropriation of revelation. That is, it requires the faithful opening of our minds not because we must abandon reason in a pietistic devotion but because that which we long to know is inseparable from the method of knowing it: we cannot know love without loving (and specifically loving love), and we cannot advance in love without being loved first. It is not only human conceptual and linguistic finitude that hinders our articulation of *what* and *who* God is but also that knowing this God of both relation and substance marked by divine simplicity necessitates that this God make Godself known to us through the mission of Jesus Christ and the Holy Spirit and that we receive this revelation. "Knowledge of the Trinity," Gioia writes, "means that *God can only be known in a Trinitarian way*, i.e. under the form of knowledge *of* the Father *through* the Son *in* the Holy Spirit."[80] And the eloquence

78. See Ayres, *Augustine and the Trinity*, 208.

79. Augustine, *De Trinitate*, 7.12. Of course, that the scriptural passage upon which Augustine bases this statement was mistranslated has no direct and essential bearing on the content of his theological argument, only the biblical foundation of it.

of this revelation "'speaks' to us only as love actually transforms us."[81] The concise direction Augustine offers in his seventh homily on the first epistle of John—"This is what you should think if you want to see God: *God is love*"[82]—finds a furthered significance in *De Trinitate*, signifying as it does that the necessary way of knowing God is an openness to God's transforming presence—that is, a loving openness to love.[83] And it is with love, too, that Gioia concludes his investigation of *De Trinitate*. The starting point of *De Trinitate* and its goal can be summarized concisely: "*love comes first.*"[84]

The Saturation of Truth by the Gift of Love

What Marion offers to a reading of *De Trinitate* is not an overcoming of its metaphysics (however one might come to understand it) but rather a phenomenological texture and friction by which we might come to mark the transformation that love coming first effects within us. The erotic reduction traces our response to the givenness of the phenomenon of love that forms us to see it as it gives itself. In so doing, it offers a way of seeing this anamorphic formation as an icon of the unconditioned God. In being formed to that which is given, we find that we receive the very possibility of our advance, the otherwise impossible possibility of our being able to love first. It is striking that Marion describes the decision to advance in love, to become a lover, as a "loving to love [*aimer aimer*]."[85] It is an embrace of the advance (which, again, is the way that love appears) by which I turn toward this particular other. Likewise, for Augustine, this is not a love of an

80. Gioia, *Theological Epistemology*, 164.
81. Ibid., 299.
82. Augustine, *Homilies on the First Epistle of John*, ed. and trans. Boniface Ramsey, The Works of St. Augustine: A Translation for the 21st Century, vol. 3, no. 14 (Hyde Park, NY: New City Press, 2008), 111.
83. Always a gift of God's initiative, this love can bring the uneducated to a deep understanding of God. Knowledge of God is not received in the same way as is *sciencia*. Augustine's account of the vision at Ostia by his mother and himself describes a shared ascent to God, with both the educated Augustine and the relatively uneducated Monica moving in and beyond their own minds "to the region of inexhaustible abundance where you [God] feed Israel eternally with truth for food." Augustine, *Confessions*, 9.24.
84. Gioia, *Theological Epistemology*, 298.
85. Marion, *Erotic Phenomenon*, 92.

abstract, idealized love *as such*. The Doctor of Grace is insistent on this matter:

> For when we love charity, we love her loving something, precisely because she does love something. What then does charity love that makes it possible for charity herself to be so loved? She is not charity if she loves nothing; but if she loves herself, she must love something in order to love herself as charity. Just as a word indicates something and also indicates itself, but does not indicate itself as a word unless it indicates itself indicating something; so too charity certainly loves itself, but unless it loves itself loving something it does not love itself as charity.[86]

We love love not abstractly but only in loving something in particular, and it is not that we love *love* as an *object* but that we love loving. This is the opening by which we might come to know and love God, Augustine writes. In loving love, we embrace that which is more intimate to us than our knowledge of the created things we love and find; if we have not yet found the image of God, we can embrace the place where we must look for that image.[87] But this image, like love itself, is not something that can be abstractly received and embraced. The image of the Trinity by which I hope to know and love God can never be a model that presents the inter-Trinitarian life for me to see, as I might observe the inner workings of the human body or mind. In finding, with Augustine, where to look for the image, we find not a site to be excavated nor a system to be defined but a path to follow deeply within ourselves where we can come to mark the formation of ourselves into lovers—into those who love as Jesus loved, with complete fidelity to God. This gift of our advancing love serves to return us to the one to whose image we are made.

Marion, as we have observed,[88] notes the "paradoxical consequence"[89] in Augustine's thought of our being created not according to "the resemblance of the creature to itself ('secundum *suam* similitudinem'), but according to its resemblance to another

86. Augustine, *De Trinitate*, 8.11; Augustine here uses *delectio* for the act of loving and *caritas* for that which loves.
87. Ibid., 8.14.
88. See chapter 7.
89. Marion, "Resting, Moving, Loving," 26.

besides itself"[90]—that is, God. The human being "constitutes a creature par excellence, and even particularly excellent, precisely because he has neither a kind nor a species proper to him and therefore does not have a definition that would appropriate him to himself."[91] We are ourselves only to the degree that we do not stand by ourselves but instead refer faithfully and ceaselessly to the invisible original to whose image we are made. Human being functions iconically, always insofar as it is a conceptually visible sign referring to the invisible.[92] A human being, uniquely in creation but also as the interpretive paradigm by which we might understand creation, is only itself inasmuch as it refers to "an other of maximum alterity"[93]—it is only itself inasmuch as it bears the image to which it is made.

This formation into those who advance in love without antecedent reason promises to overcome our idolatrous resistance to change within us and to receiving that which is given. Certainly, this unconditioned openness to that which gives itself is a recognition of our own finitude, unable as we are to exhaustively grasp that which is given to us. Furthermore, in this response, we hope to overcome the various ways in which we might betray love, remaining faithful to its promise rather than our own conceptions of what it gives. But more fundamentally, we receive ourselves in advancing through the anamorphosis of love. We are individuated (as finite, to be sure) through our tendency to withdraw toward (that is, give phenomenological space for) the other, through our love of the one who remains both intimately constitutive of who I am and yet always in excess of who I am.

As this anamorphic love prescinds from abstraction, so *De Trinitate* is

90. Ibid., 25.
91. Ibid., 26.
92. See also: "Man is a God, like a Cézanne is a Cézanne, a Rembrandt a Rembrandt—without anything behind or beside them, that would be Cézanne of Rembrandt, yet visible as themselves as part of the painting. No, the paintings of Rembrandt or Cézanne appear as such, without any other visible mark or signature besides them, but only as paintings bearing all over the inimitable style of Cézanne or Rembrandt. In this sense, man is a God. He appears as God-made, as a God insofar as he endorses bearing God's style, and lets his own particular features be subdued, so that its provenance might appear. Man is a God only as he returns from where he comes, to his most intimate other." Ibid., 28.
93. Ibid., 25.

not focused so much on the relationship between love and knowledge abstractly understood as much as the way that my love (or lack thereof) of God relates to my understanding of God (and furthermore, the way in which these relate to my love and understanding of creation *qua* creation). With a goal of outlining neither a model of the human mind nor one of the divine Trinity, it is fitting (and not a divergence from the ultimate question at hand to an overconfident reliance upon reason) that Augustine uses the description of the mind to discuss how we might come to receive the truth of God. Marion notes that in Augustine's thought, love (and its rejection) assume "a resolutely *epistemic* (indeed phenomenological) function"[94] in opening (or closing) me to the truth of that which is given to me. In such an orientation, I do not so much formulate a concept but instead make up "*my mind*, deciding *myself*, as it were, in relation" to truth.[95] The love of love must entail, in some manner, a love of truth.

Truth appears only as a saturated phenomenon, giving itself *to me* and appearing only inasmuch as I receive it as it is given, inasmuch as I convert myself to the excessive terms of its givenness—that is, inasmuch as I love it. And in appearing, it is always mediated and thus always in danger of becoming subject to the distortions of idolatry. The idol would so appear inasmuch as I both open myself to the givenness of the phenomenon (because the idol is an intuition of a real phenomenon) and frame that givenness according to what I already know and love as possible. The idol does not so much oppose the given phenomenon with an alternative one but tempers givenness with what I am prepared to receive. It is to cling to the limited manifestation of what I already hold to be true at the expense of what is actually given to me. So Marion contends that the contrary to Augustine's understanding of truth "is not found simply in error or falsehood but in lying: wanting to keep, in addition to the true, the false, because one loves it as much, indeed more than, the true."[96] Opposing not only the incorrect but the idol, truth is iconically mediated as that which

94. Marion, *In the Self's Place*, 131.
95. Ibid.
96. Ibid., 111–12.

does not "condescend to be possessed together with falsehood"[97] but demands a fidelity than can only come through love.

Indeed, the truth about God (and therefore also the ultimate truth about all of creation *qua* creation) that we are to understand is approachable not as an object to be conceived but a formation to be borne, wherein we recognize that which is more intimate to us than we are to ourselves as what it is. And if it is by such a formation that that we come to know the Trinity that God is, then Augustine holds to a definition of truth that "that is not exhausted in its theoretic function, but can also give itself to desire as much as, indeed infinitely more than, to knowledge."[98] In so giving itself to desire, "truth does not reveal itself in a nontheoretic sense, but this is not because it would lack evidence but because its excess of evidence opens a new question—in fact, a new ordeal."[99] Again, Marion forbids neither theory nor metaphysics but instead works to mark that which appears in excess of these conditioning structures. He suggests that Augustine's understanding of the truth of God is an uncovering that opens us to the ordeal of the impossible formation of our love. Truth is not only a matter of the adequation of theory to fact, or the establishment of accurate predicative language, but also "the event of an evidence, which shows itself only inasmuch as I tolerate its excess. And I can do so only inasmuch as I love it."[100] Therefore, truth requires not only a conceptual belief in something but a fidelity to that which I believe. To say that love is the place where we might look for the image of the Trinity is also to quicken our desire to so look and to cleave to what is therein revealed. This place is not so much a theoretical possibility as it is an invitation to love.

If this epistemology rests upon love, love in turn rests only upon its own promise to traverse, while maintaining, the distance between

97. "You are the truth presiding over all things. But in my greed I was unwilling to lose you, and wanted to have you at the same time as holding on to a lie, in much the same way as no one wants to become such a liar as to lose all awareness of what the truth is. This is why I lost you: you do not condescend to be possessed together with falsehood." Augustine, *Confessions*, 10.41.66.

98. Marion, *In the Self's Place*, 104.

99. Ibid., 108.

100. Ibid., 137.

our intended signification of the Trinity and the impossibility—for us—of that very signification. This, indeed, it what love promises to do: cleave to that which we behold (while allowing it to remain what it is) in order that we might not form it but instead be formed by it.[101] Marion's erotic reduction brings this to light, showing how my love paradoxically maintains both the truth of the matter that I was loved first and that I can only come to see that I was so loved by advancing in love myself. It illustrates how this formation is also (and perhaps foremost) a mediation of the truth of what love is. To love, I must be loved first, but to understand that I was loved first, I must become one who can advance in love.

This advance in love—my willingness to go ahead and risk all else on the hope that love does, in the end, bear all things—appears to me as an event. I do not reason to this love. I do not predict this love. I do not motivelessly choose one love over another. Rather, I find that I have become one who is not only capable of advancing in love but desires to do so. Marion's philosophy of excess, marking as it does the event of my own formation into a lover of this particular other, describes *what love does.* (Or, at the very least, it attempts to do so. Criticism might certainly be directed toward his work regarding the adequacy and the precision of the reduction described therein.) This is the effect that the gift of love has upon me. This marks the distance between who I was and who I now am—the one who hopes in the promise of the gift by so advancing in love. In this way, it is my formation to the one who loves love—to the one who can advance in love without dependence upon what I will receive from my love, without my love being determined by exchange and the security of my being (at the possible expense of even my life)—that serves as the icon that signifies the invisible Trinity (even as invisible). We come to know God as we faithfully advance in love (i.e., as we love love) and only as we advance in love: this is love, not that we have loved first, but that God so loved us and therefore enabled us to advance in love.[102] In so hoping, in so advancing, we come

101. Augustine, *De Trinitate*, 8.9.
102. Cf. 1 John 4:10.

to see in ourselves the event of the irruption of love. So Augustine writes, "you do see a trinity if you see charity."[103] Love allows that which is given to us to appear to us as it is given by forming us so as to receive, and the erotic reduction teaches us to look for precisely this love.

But the Doctor of Grace crucially clarifies that it is not just any trinity that we love but the trinity that God is.[104] If love opens us to an understanding of the other that might allow an image of a trinity to so form in our mind (e.g., a lover, the beloved, and the love so given), this image is not a general model by which we might come to conceive of God. This icon of my love is not so abstractly understood but appears only in its orientation to a particular beloved. The phenomenon that Marion so seeks to understand is the gift of love offered by God through the sending of the Son and Spirit, paradigmatically given upon the cross of Christ. Even as his reduction is rigorously phenomenological, the event reduced is my formation (slow and arduous though it is) into one who hopes in the promise of that which is given upon the cross. It is the event of my becoming *a lover like Christ*—that is, *a lover of God the Father*—that serves as the phenomenon that Marion explores. This truth that I love is a saving truth, granting us ourselves now formed to the image in which we are made. In fidelity to this truth, we hope that in receiving our advance—in becoming a lover—we might open ourselves to the whole of what is given in this love that bear all things and become one who loves God the Father (and therefore all of creation) as Christ does.

This love that gives me to myself does so only as it allows *this particular other* to become more intimate to me than I am to myself, and so this love becomes that in which I hope and to which I entrust myself. I am borne by my advance toward *this particular other*, an advance that always already bears the impossibility of my receiving more than I can achieve. Love mediates that which is impossible and unconditioned and is the icon by which the impossible appears as impossible *for us.*

103. Augustine, *De Trinitate*, 8.12.
104. Ibid., 8.8.

As impossible for us is the only way in which the Trinitarian God of love might appear, it is the only way in which that given love might be received. The excessive gift of love grants me the love of love—the will to advance in love no matter what. I myself become, as the *adonné*, the measure of the distance between the revelation as given and as received—my love marks that which is given to me, a given that appears in my salvific formation to the image of God.

The speculation about the predicative metaphysics of books 5–7 serves, therefore, to illuminate both the limits of this philosophical language and how these limits might help us to understand *how* the Trinity might be revealed through such linguistic and conceptual structures, all the while stretching ever beyond them. God is revealed through, with, and in the gift of that which God *is*: love. I understand the gift of love not so much in contrast to substance but as an advance that we never seem to fully initiate, clinging (as we far too often do) to vain promises of certainty. Love appears in this way as that which is *impossible for us*, at least insofar as we cannot initiate our own love without it first being given to us. This "anterior mediation of the desired"[105] both grounds Augustine's love as weight and is the originary *a posteriori* that concludes Marion's erotic reduction: *love comes first*, not as a first philosophy, but according to its own reason and methodology. Yet arriving in excess of all antecedent structures, this gift *of the truth of who God is* invites our response. Indeed, it is given as an invitation and appears in our fidelity.

105. Hanby, *Augustine and Modernity*, 91.

11

Praising the Trinity that God Is

> I know only enough of God to want to worship him, by any means ready to hand.
>
> —Annie Dillard[1]

What reason might we have to hope in love's advance? What reason might invite progress into an "inquiry into things incomprehensible"[2] *as incomprehensible*, an inquiry that promises to make the impossible God possible, *as impossible*? Augustine concludes *De Trinitate* with an encouraging appeal to those who have begun to "comprehend the incomprehensibility of God"[3]: the Trinity is not only sought so as to be found but, indeed, is found (insofar as it is found) so that it will continually be sought. Creation, with its many unities and distinctions, generously offers to the inquirer its own limitations, not so we might rest content, but that those limits might be possible sites of saturation. The excessive givenness that draws us ever deeper invites us to see revelation not as a place to stop but as a mediating sign of the invisible unconditioned God. Even the human mind, conceived as having a

1. *Holy the Firm* (New York: Harper & Row, 1977), 55.
2. Augustine, *De Trinitate*, 15.2.
3. Ibid.

distinct memory, understanding, and will, can only suggest an image of interrelated parts of a whole, where no part can be said to be both fully itself and truly the whole, and where the whole is itself fractured and incomplete. Where we might be described as *having* memory that remembers, understanding that understands, and a will that loves, God cannot be said to so *have* parts of a whole. Augustine is clear—there is no functional psychology in God, wherein the Father is said to be uniquely God's memory, the Son God's understanding, and the Spirit God's will.[4] For the Father, Son, and Spirit are each true God, each truly being—not *having*—God's memory, understanding, and will. No, a deep inquiry into even creation's highest realization—the human mind—does not offer an image of the Trinity to be gazed upon, analyzed, and worshiped.

Concluding *De Trinitate* in book 15, Augustine does not offer an image of the Trinity to be seen but rather instructs his readers further in how this image might be sought. Although we are made to the image of God, this image is blurred.[5] It offers a clarity that we cannot quite see and fails to show us what we do not see, showing something while showing nothing clearly.[6] To know God, we must know the Trinity, and it is knowledge of the Trinity that is precisely what is impossible for us. To recognize the image of that which we are not yet capable of seeing[7] means to see in ourselves that which is in excess of our vision, to see not just that we cannot see but to see that which we cannot see *as that which we cannot see*. As God is incomprehensible for us, so the image of God must itself be incomprehensible. Yet it cannot just be incomprehensible—abandoning us to grope in the dark for what we cannot receive—but must also be revealed to us as incomprehensible and received as given.

Augustine here discusses two ways of being formed that cannot ultimately be distinguished from one another.[8] First, he describes the

4. Ibid., 15.12.
5. Ibid., 15.14.
6. Ibid., 15.16.
7. Ibid., 15.50.
8. Ibid., 15.18–20.

way in which our self-knowledge is deepened as our understanding is accommodated to that which is intimate to us—as our concept and words are formed to the inner word preceding "all signs that signify it."[9] Our outer word is conformed to the inner word, begetting knowledge of the truth of that which is given within. Augustine writes: "For it is then that the word is most like the thing known, and most its image, because the seeing which is thought springs direct from the seeing which is knowledge, and it is a word of no language, a true word from a true thing, having nothing from itself, but everything from that knowledge from which it is born."[10] To be increasingly conformed to that from which knowledge comes is to grow, too, in knowledge of the way in which the Son is eternally begotten of the Father.[11] As our self-understanding is increasingly determined by what is given within us, so too we grow in our understanding of how the Word of God can be both spoken by the Father and yet remain substantially true God. However, for whatever similarity can be found here between our own conformity to ourselves and the Word's perfect equality with the Father, the dissimilarity is so vast,[12] the unlikeness so great,[13] that the image of God simply cannot be said to be found in the human mind reflecting upon itself.

Augustine turns, then, not to the discovery of the image in our self-remembrance, self-understanding, and self-love (no matter how perfect it might be) but to the effect of the gift of the Holy Spirit. For it is only in this gift of love that we might be formed to the image of God; it is only through the impact of the love that we might open to the "Word spoken rhetorically"[14] to us. If rhetoric makes it possible for the truth to sound more like truth,[15] and if Augustine's understanding

9. Ibid., 15.20.
10. Ibid., 15.22.
11. "So the Word of God, the only-begotten Son of the Father, like the Father and equal to him in all things, God from God, light from light, wisdom from wisdom, being from being, is exactly and absolutely what the Father is, and yet is not the Father because this one is Son, that one Father. And thus he knows everything that the Father knows, but his knowing comes to him from the Father just as his being does. For here knowing and being are one and the same." Ibid., 15.23.
12. Ibid., 15.25.
13. Ibid., 15.26.
14. Kolbet, *Cure of Souls*, 11.
15. See Cole, *Origins of Rhetoric*, 140.

of the rhetoric is oriented toward not only persuasion but to teaching the Christian faith, then the truth of God is taught not as a fact to be accepted but as a formation to be born and a gift to be loved. This rhetoric invites its listeners to this truth through the Word that effects a cleaving to truth. As the Son has nothing but what is received from the Father and reveals what is given through returning it to the Father, so we grow in knowledge of the truth (indeed "no one knows false things except when he knows them to be false"[16]) only as we are formed to the loving relationship of the Father and Son, to and by the "common charity by which the Father and the Son love each other."[17] Love is the reason, and is its own reason, for our receptivity to such divine rhetoric,[18] triggering "in the heart the same spontaneity that gravity unleashes in the body"[19] and initiating our advance. It is not insignificant that the penultimate section of the final book of *De Trinitate* concerns not substance and relation, nor mental images of the Trinity, nor even strictly the Son's relationship with the Father, but the gift of love that is the Holy Spirit and love's place in naming God.

While any word predicated of God's substance may equally be predicated of the Father, Son, and Spirit, and alternatively, while any word predicated of a Trinitarian person (save Father, Son, and related relational names) can also be predicated of the divine substance, Augustine understands love's place as unique in Trinitarian language. The scriptures speak of an identity of God and love[20]—an identity that Augustine understood to mean both that God is love and that love is God[21]—leading Augustine to understand love as substantively predicated of God.[22] Father, Son, and Spirit each, therefore, may be called love. However, Augustine continues, as the Son is distinctively named "wisdom" (even as the name might apply to the Father and Spirit as well), so the Spirit is distinctively named "love."[23] As the gift

16. Augustine, *De Trinitate*, 15.17.
17. Ibid., 15.27.
18. "The gaze of thought only goes back to something by remembering, and only bothers to go back to it by loving." Ibid., 15.41.
19. Marion, *In the Self's Place*, 266.
20. 1 John 4:8, 16.
21. For a helpful analysis of this "daring inversion," see Bavel, "Double Face of Love," 169–82.
22. Augustine, *De Trinitate*, 15.29.

of the Holy Spirit is a gift of God from God, so it is a gift of love from love. "Love therefore," Augustine writes, "is God from God"[24] and turns us to love love itself. Love is nothing less than abiding fidelity to God as a result of the gift of the Spirit. When Gioia correctly writes of Augustine's theology that "knowledge of the Trinity means that *God can only be known in a Trinitarian way*, i.e. under the form of knowledge *of* the Father *through* the Son *in* the Holy Spirit,"[25] he describes how we might come to know God: through being brought into the love that is the Trinity through the Trinity, and particularly through the sending of the Son and the gift of love that is the Spirit. Alongside this deepening of love's efficacy, Augustine maintains the crucial limit to this image: that while God *is* love, we can only hope *to* love. It is love that forms us to the thing we long to know, love that so allows us to know it. For it is only in love that God is to be found. Augustine constructs an approach to the Trinity by way of the gift of love, wherein our own love responds to the activity of the Holy Spirit, cleaves to the Trinity revealed in the sending of the Son, and is formed to God. This is what love does, Augustine contends, form us in the image to which we are made, so we might know God and know ourselves.

In presenting this hope—the hope that we might adhere to God so as to be formed to God—*De Trinitate* is a soteriological text[26]; its author is attentive to how we might come to know God not as an object to perceive but as a lover to embrace because we have already been embraced. Yet as Augustine insists that this embrace opens to knowledge of God and invites his readers to consider this love, he offers only hints as to how love effects this saving embrace. For in *De Trinitate*, Augustine maintains both the impossibility of our ever coming to know the Trinity while at the same time holding to the promise that to see love is to see God. The momentum of the text—inspired by the gift

23. Ibid., 15.31.
24. Ibid.
25. Gioia, *Theological Epistemology*, 164.
26. See, for example: "Nothing is more excellent than this gift of God. This alone is what distinguishes between the sons of the eternal kingdom and the sons of eternal perdition." Augustine, *De Trinitate*, 15.32.

of love—leads Augustine to end *De Trinitate* not with an exposition of a model of the Trinity but with prayer—and not just any prayer but one that speaks of his exhaustion as much as his desire. But this man not known for abandoning his readers to apophatic heights (indeed, Augustine insists that there is a real intelligibility to God's revelation) ends *De Trinitate* not with an epideictic silence but rather by petitioning God to orient all his memory, understanding, and love to the Trinity in hopes that he might be formed to the image of God (a petition whose beauty warrants being repeated here):

> O Lord my God, my one hope, listen to me lest out of weariness I should stop wanting to seek you, but let me seek your face always, and with ardor. Do you yourself give me the strength to seek, having caused yourself to be found and having given me the hope of finding you more and more. Before you lies my strength and my weakness; preserve the one, heal the other. Before you lies my knowledge and my ignorance; where you have opened to me, receive me as I come in; where you have shut to me, open to me as I knock. Let me remember you, let me understand you, let me love you. Increase these things in me until you refashion me entirely.[27]

This prayer hopes for much, indeed. In *De Trinitate,* Augustine is concerned not with articulating an image by which we might find a similarity with God but with "*an attempt to work out what to be rational means for beings created in the image of God,* who are not simply 'like God,' but more radically coming from God, dependent on God, and destined to find their fulfillment in the knowledge of God the Trinity."[28] And because this fulfillment is not actually found so much as given, the prayer that ends the text is itself one final paradigmatic attempt to turn his readers from the desire for an objective image of God to the one hope for any rational discourse on this saving gift. It illustrates how we might hope to bring about the openness to receive that which is in excess of our own ability to find.

Here Augustine stands upon his strongest theological foundation, with his words not predicating anything of God but directly responsive *to* God, and his approach grounded upon hope in God's forming gift.

27. Ibid., 15.51.
28. Gioia, *Theological Epistemology*, 288.

Of this grounding, Gioia observes that "such talk makes sense only once [love] has become a reality already. Augustine's *De Trinitate* is not destined for people who need to be converted, to be persuaded to love God."[29] But for love to have become a reality already cannot mean that *De Trinitate* is, in fact, written for people who already love God as they ought (for indeed there are no such people). To say that the book was written only for those fully converted to God's love is to say that it is for no one. Instead, to say that the talk of love only makes sense if it is a reality already must mean that our own advance in love (and whatever understanding we may have of that advance) is only possible after we first receive the gift of love. Talk of love follows loving; loving follows being loved. In beginning with the hope that we have already received the gift of love, *De Trinitate* offers a reason for this hope that our love might still be converted to God. It offers a rational inquiry into the impossible mediation of the Trinity that God is and the hope of the possibility of that very mediation to us through the mission of the Son and Spirit. Where Augustine is standing most upon hope, he also stands closest to Marion, who hopes to speak to this rationality of the impossible and to what it means to be rational at the limits of possibility, to be rational as created to the image of God. If *De Trinitate* reasons that God is revealed in and through love, Marion illustrates how that revealed love appears: as a saturated gift. Moreover, he offers to readers of *De Trinitate* (and perhaps to all who seek an understanding of God through an understanding of this gift) a description of what this gift does to us in its appearing as given—that is, a description of its self-revelation.

On guard against a superficial mysticism ("the final recourse of the interpreter who no longer wants to understand anything"[30]) in which love banally fills conceptual gaps inaccessible by reason, Marion's phenomenology offers to the reading of Augustine an attentive and meticulous description of *how* love cleaves to that which the lover beholds so as to be anamorphically formed to it[31] through the advance

29. Ibid., 300.
30. Marion, *In the Self's Place*, 12.
31. Augustine, *De Trinitate*, 8.9.

by which love bears its own reason. This phenomenology illustrates how, amidst the inevitable yet hopeful exhaustion of memory, understanding, and will, the advance of love permits knowledge of that which is for us, by definition, impossible.

After decades of writing very little about Augustine[32] (a surprise, perhaps, for a philosopher so committed to exploring the phenomena of love and excess and whose early influences included theologians Henri de Lubac and Hans Urs von Balthasar[33]), Marion did finally turn to the Doctor of Grace and the *Confessions* in hope that he might test "the hermeneutic validity of the concepts givenness, saturated phenomenon, and the gifted, by applying them to a reference text."[34] What resulted is *In the Self's Place*, a reading of *Confessions* that both endeavors to respond to the givenness of the text (wherein the interpreter first allowed himself to be interpreted by the text,[35] anamorphically adjusting an interpretation to what it offers) and, at the same time, use Marion's own philosophical framework as a guide to interpreting the text. The hermeneutic convolutions of this undertaking should not be overlooked, nor does Marion do so. Augustine, he writes, appears to us at "one and the same time unavoidable and inaccessible,"[36] always only approachable from a particular "point of view from which the fragments would become a whole."[37] Marion himself admits his own interest in the way in which Augustine might be deeply nonmetaphysical in *Confessions*, an approach that Marion maintains should be of ultimate concern for the interpreter of the text (as opposed to the philosophical study of a particular theme or the legitimately emphasized historical point of view[38]). And amidst this lack of hermeneutic clarity, the particularity and contextuality of any approach to Augustine cannot be overemphasized. Tanner observes that Marion's phenomenology (like

32. For a very early article written by Marion on Augustine see Jean-Luc Marion, "Distance et béatitude. Sur le mot 'capacitas' chez saint Augustin," *Résurrection* 29 (1969): 58–80.
33. Horner, *Jean-Luc Marion*, 3.
34. Marion, *In the Self's Place*, xiv.
35. Ibid., 12.
36. Ibid., 1.
37. Ibid., 3.
38. Ibid.

any philosophy or theology) "is rather obviously historically circumscribed"[39]—and his interpretation of Augustine's thought is no different. By what right does Marion read the concepts of givenness, saturated phenomenon, and the gifted into the fifth century text? And to the degree that he does so, is he not falling prey to the very metaphysical concerns he so vigilantly writes against, interpreting the given in light of antecedent concepts?[40] Such a question might be approached in another way: if the interpreter is to be interpreted by the text, what, if anything, is illuminated about Marion's thought in his reading of *Confessions*?[41] What is the saturating impact of *Confessions* upon Marion's erotic phenomenology?

Marion begins *In the Self's Place* where Augustine begins *Confessions*—with praise. But where Augustine begins with praising God ("You are great, Lord, and highly to be praised."[42]), Marion begins both by asking what praise does and by defining theological language in its relationship to the language of praise. It is a furthering of an argument that Marion makes elsewhere, notably in light of Derrida's deconstructive indictment of "negative theology." As Marion recounts it,[43] Derrida interprets even radical theological apophasis as hyper-affirmation in masque, which "does not annul [*ne nie pas*] the essence, being, or truth of God but rather denies [*les dénie*] them so as to better

39. Tanner, "Theology at the Limits," 212.
40. Marion is not shy about making explicit his recontextualizing of Augustinian themes under a phenomenological horizon. The names of the chapters of *In the Self's Place* themselves marks this methodology, particularly "*Confessio* or Reduction," "Truth or the Saturated Phenomenon," and "Time, or the Advent."
41. My own particular use of *In the Self's Place* is additionally complicated by the fact that my primary concern here is not with *Confessions* at all but with *De Trinitate*. I have, at times, chosen to cite *In the Self's Place* to best elucidate particular points (the relationship of love and truth, for example) in part because in this text Marion is expressly concerned with Augustine and in part because, as a recent work, *In the Self's Place* more fully realizes his thought than do some of his earlier, perhaps more seminal, texts. While there is much in this recent text that can be used to support what Marion has said elsewhere, I am most concerned about how Marion might be said to be interpreted by *Confessions* through Marion's approach to naming God in the *confessio* of love.
42. Augustine, *Confessions*, 1.1.1.
43. It is far from clear that Derrida is saying what Marion interprets him as saying. Derrida himself states that Marion, "gave me too much as to the alleged objections to the so-called negative theology." Jacques Derrida, response to "In the Name: How to Avoid Speaking of 'Negative Theology,'" by Jean-Luc Marion, in Caputo and Scanlon, *God, the Gift, and Postmodernism*, 43. But Marion's understanding of this significantly shaped his thought as he has attempted in various ways to take such a criticism into account—a criticism that shadows that of the overdetermined gift by once again establishing the presence of a concealed theological agenda or influence.

reestablish them."[44] Such a move would reinscribe negation in a metaphysics of presence, ultimately accomplishing simply at a higher level the very thing negative theology denies and denies doing—reestablishing affirmative language about God. All theological language, even so-call apophasis, would therefore predicate something of God, would make statements *about* God.

Standing upon the shoulders of Denys the Areopagite,[45] Thomas Aquinas, and Nicholas of Cusa, Marion suggests a third way of speaking the truth that transcends the metaphysical dichotomy of true and false. This third way, Marion writes, "is no longer about saying the true of the false . . . it is precisely a matter of its not saying them."[46] This third way is not concerned with saying anything at all about God (whether true or false) but instead embraces "the strictly pragmatic function of language—namely, to refer names and their speaker to the unattainable yet inescapable interlocutor beyond every name and every denegation of names."[47] What is true about a proper name in general, consisting as it does "precisely in the fact that it never belongs properly—by and as essence—to the one who receives it,"[48] is all the more true of the name of God. Attempting no predication but only pragmatic signification, the naming of God "is no longer a question of naming [*de Le nommer*], nor by contrast of not naming [*de ne pas le nommer*], but of de-nominating God [*de le dénommer*]"[49] wherein the name is said not to predicate anything of God but instead to refer us to God. In so doing, Marion ties theology to praise, effectively designating all language *about* God that does not primarily praise God (or, at the very least, order us toward such praise) as standing upon the misguided and idolatrous presumption of a place from where we can speak about God without our own salvation and the salvation of others being at stake. "Praising," Marion writes in *In the Self's Place*, confirming his earlier position with Augustine's own approach in *Confessions*, "does

44. Marion, *In Excess*, 133.
45. For more on Marion's use of Denys, see chapter 6, note 70.
46. Marion, *In Excess*, 138.
47. Ibid., 140.
48. Ibid., 142.
49. Ibid., 139.

not designate one speech act among others, one which would be equally applicable to God and other similar targets. Praising offers the sole way, the sole royal road of access, to his presence."[50] Where Marion had already been concerned with tying theological language to praise, in *In the Self's Place* he reveals the particularity of such a confession. Augustine is engaged not simply in praise generally understood but in the doubled *confessio* admitting his own sins and limitations in light of the already given gift of God's love.

But where Marion concludes his earlier exploration by speaking of the fearful task of being called to name the one to whom God has bestowed the gift of the name above all names,[51] *In the Self's Place* begins already in the midst of a relationship with a God who is, while remaining under-determined, still named: it is the Trinitarian God of love, the God of Jesus Christ (always as understood by Augustine, certainly, but the God who Augustine names not so as to define but so as to worship). The move is subtle but significant and arcs toward theology. In the *confessio*, we begin always already at stake, ordered only to God or away from God, moving with each word in one direction or the other. Marion suggests the work of Augustine, and particularly the *Confessions*, as paradigmatic not only of theology but also of the phenomenological endeavor to think the unconditioned not by speaking *about* it but by speaking *to* it in prayer. Any neutrality of approach is not only abandoned theoretically but finds no place in his new methodology. Unlike other so-called postmodern retrievals of Augustine that emphasize "the constitutive breach otherness performs in the construction of identity, to the intricate ways in which identity is disturbed by difference,"[52] and confess alterity, per se, Marion instead follows an invitation to look for a more radical confession.[53] For Marion's approach to the *confessio* does not simply rest in an indeterminate *alterity* but instead recognizes that the constitutive breach is defined already as an intimate act of love given by the Trinity

50. Marion, *In the Self's Place*, 14.
51. Marion, *In Excess*, 162; Philippians 2:9.
52. Boeve, "Retrieving Augustine Today," 3.
53. Ibid., 13.

that God is. The gift of love that effects this breach is given not by *any other* but by this particular beloved. The particularity of Marion's phenomenology of love provokes an address to God—a naming of God that forbids determinate predication and is instead ordered only to our calling upon God.

It is a doubled *confessio* that marks the *Confessions*, Marion writes—a confession of sin and a confession of praise, wherein the latter reverses the juridical admission of the former "by constructing the sense of a glorious admission, not a shameful one, the voluntary proclamation of faith in Christ."[54] Marion notes that the language Augustine uses for this *confessio* is a language the bishop first received, through the community and tradition to be sure, but ultimately through the gift of revelation. This language is given language to which he anamorphically forms himself, becoming the one who speaks truthfully when he speaks the words of the scriptures because he speaks them faithfully. The doubled *confessio* "defines the permanent state of the Christian,"[55] wherein I am both admitting with shame my sin and admitting (that is, bearing witness to), without shame or fear (no matter where such an admission might lead me), my faith in God. This *confessio* is at its heart a confession of relationship, failed, perhaps, on my part, redeemed on God's own initiative by God's own advance into creation through the missions of the Son and Spirit. Augustine comes to know those he confesses (both himself and God, and himself only through God) only in the doubled *confessio*, which teaches him, "little by little the call from which it comes, without knowing it, as a response."[56] He comes to learn to address the one who calls to him through the formation both effected by, and revealing, this call. And in this responsive address, he too receives himself as the one called, the one gifted, the one devoted.

In contrast to Marion's reading of *Confessions* as paradigmatic of theology because its words are ordered to God, *De Trinitate* has long been interpreted as doing precisely what Marion forbids of theology,

54. Marion, *In the Self's Place*, 28.
55. Ibid., 29.
56. Ibid., 23.

of trying to "speak *of* God . . . *of* the incarnation, *of* the Holy Spirit, just as the Greek philosophers treat *of* nature, *of* the soul, *of* the world, *of* the categories, *of* the city, and even *of* the divine."[57] But it has been my argument, following recent scholarship, that *De Trinitate* has an active soteriological orientation that invites the readers, through a rational contemplation of the missions of the Son and Spirit and their equality with God, to a conversion of mind and heart to remembering, understanding, and loving God. Marion himself indicates sympathy to a possible soteriological interpretation of *De Trinitate*, observing that "it certainly will fall to saint Augustine to write as such *about* the Trinity," but "it remains to be seen if he treats [it] as one speaks *about* and *on the subject* of [it], or rather by becoming himself the subject submitted to what he evokes."[58] A rational way of proceeding by which the reader submits to and is formed to what the text evokes (and invokes), indeed, corresponds with my reading of *De Trinitate* in part 1, where God is spoken about through creation (specifically the human mind), not to display an image of the Trinity, but to offer a way of proceeding that, through the formation of our love, iconically makes possible the impossible Trinity *as* impossible *for us*.

The image of God to which we are made cannot then derive its defining characteristics from philosophical categories of substance and relation, the tri-activities of self-reflection of the human mind, or from the inescapable language of philosophical reason itself. Philosophy—whether metaphysics or phenomenology—is inadequate to the task of thinking this divine love, not because it is too human or too finite, per se, but because this gift of love that mediates revelation is impossible for us to initiate or achieve—love appears only as it is first received from an elsewhere. Certainly our natural finitude and our unnatural fallenness (both of which bind us to our limited concepts) are elements of this impossibility, but neither is the crucial determining factor. Our limitations, whether created or self-imposed, are peripheral to the only truly relevant issue at hand—the reception of this gift of love

57. Ibid., 9.
58. Ibid., 11–12.

and the demand it imposes upon us. We desire that which is other than us and excessive of us. We desire that other without condition and tending toward eternity not because we are ontologically finite (whether created or fallen) but because it is love, and only love, that bears the revelation of God. The impossible unconditionality that marks our advance toward God is not to be overcome but serves as the very way in which God's own gift of love can appear to us.

Such a reading of *De Trinitate* is not without its limitations. Just as Schrijvers wondered whether a book making the claims of *In the Self's Place* could be read by a philosopher—"who, as a rule, does not love God very much (or at least too little)"[59]—so too, we might begin to wonder whether *De Trinitate* shares the difficulty Marion attributes to *Confessions*: "If he who does not praise cannot approach God and if the *Confessiones* want to approach God, then any reader who would refuse to praise would by that very refusal be blocked from understanding and even reading the *Confessiones*. The hermeneutic obstacle would therefore stem from a properly spiritual refusal."[60] To invite the reader of *De Trinitate* to reason through our approach to the *Trinity that God is* via the doctrine of the Trinity interpreted through hope in an antecedent reception of love seems to stretch Marion's insistence on the indetermined source of the gift. How can we both praise the Father, Son, and Spirit while at the same time maintain that the gift arrives from an indetermined *elsewhere*? For even as this "proper" name is said not to define but to praise, and to praise *this beloved* as lover-who-loves-me-first, requires some way of particularizing. The implications of Marion's insistence on this *elsewhere* are threefold, each impacting the others and even the philosophical limits of Marion's own project.

First, that the giver must remain *indetermined* is crucial to Marion's insistence on the unconditionality of our receptivity to givenness. This unconditionality alone allows me to receive the phenomenon *as it is given* by being formed to meet the unique demands of its appearance. But should the giver remain completely unnamed rather than

59. Schrijvers, "In (the) Place of the Self," 679.
60. Marion, *In the Self's Place*, 14.

"denominated" (a pragmatic naming that orients us without defining the phenomenon), we are without a particularity to call by name. And while such indecision may suffice phenomenologically (although it is far from certain that it does), it must be resituated if considered theologically. How, then, might we call God by a name that orients us to receive rather than define the excessive gift of love? We might say that God can appear as given only in our prescinding from idolatrous framing and our openness to being remade as one who can receive this gift. Again, this is not to say that we can—or should—open ourselves to God in a way bereft of concepts (or without metaphysics) but that God appears to us in the ways in which those concepts are saturated. In this way, God appears as impossible for us, in excess of how we conceive God to be possible. But the love of an indetermined giver comes at a significant risk. If the given only appears as I open myself without antecedent reason and so appears only as I am converted to that which is given, then in beginning already in the process of this conversion, I am without resources (or at least have only severely depleted resources) by which I might judge whether I *ought* to love *this particular other* (whose appearing is always a matter of appearing *to me*, and thus always at risk of idolatry). There is no reason for such an "ought" within phenomenology. The only reason for my love is my loving advance toward this beloved. Phenomenology's descriptive methodology does not offer any hermeneutic that might guide our interpretation of the excess by means of interpreting its impact upon us—save whether or not it is in increasing conformity with the phenomenon we have already begun to love. This love may very well justify dangerous and (often self-)destructive behavior through a rationality that admits no need for external justification. Phenomenology's strength and its limit are both tied to its sensitivity to the given phenomenon. When the phenomenon in question is one hidden from the senses and excessive in its givenness, we become all the more vulnerable to the way in which we are guided in our interpretation of it by factors independent of its givenness—for even in praising an elsewhere, we so praise in response to what we receive as a gift. It is this gift appearing in our reduction that guides our understanding. And we are therefore always at the mercy of our own reduction and subsequent understanding of that to whom we are already devoted. The full radicality of this total devotion is often praised as martyrdom but can just as often be criticized as delusion, self-destructive behavior, and idealism. Indeed, I can interrupt my reduction to givenness and rest content with my idol, rather than open to the unconditioned excess of the icon.

Second, as Schrijvers notes, *In the Self's Place* seems to contradict the limits of Marion's own project. Derrida's concern that Marion's tying together the gift and the giver overdetermines givenness through theological faith becomes all the more justifiable in light of Marion's pursuit of phenomenological excess expressly within the pages of *Confessions*. Here, not only are the gift and giver tied together but they become, now in a Trinitarian context, one and the same. That which is given and its givenness, its manner of appearance, are one. In fact, givenness is re-rendered as gift explicitly in this text, specifically as Marion follows Augustine's theological doctrine of creation, marking, through the confession of praise, the interpretation of the plurality of things precisely as created by God.[61] *In the Self's Place* would then be the evidence of a hidden theology that many have long suspected but have been unable to clearly identify in Marion's work. This hidden theology would betray not only his phenomenology (predetermining the given) but also his theology (in defining God according to the concepts of saturation and givenness). In this way, his phenomenological failure would incite his theological failure, replacing the God who gives with a conceptual *a priori*. The other possibility is that in testing the validity of his own concepts against *Confessions*, Marion in fact reads those concepts into Augustine's text, allowing them to determine his interpretation. This, too, would lead to a doubled failure.

Third, ever at risk of idolatrous self-justification and of betraying givenness by smuggling theological assumptions into phenomenology, it is only by maintaining the indetermined elsewhere whence the gift

61. Marion, *In the Self's Place*, ch. 6.

of love arrives that I might advance at all in my own love. The erotic reduction illustrates that I can only love insofar as I love *first*, without guarantees that I am loved in return, or certainty that my loving will secure me against vanity. Moreover, I only love in loving *this particular other* for no other reason than I love loving *this particular other*. To love for another reason is not to love first at all. The lover who gives me the possibility of my own advance through loving me first must withdraw into an indetermined elsewhere so I might, too, love first. Likewise, praise, for Marion, relies upon my advance precisely as a sacrifice—as the means by which I might return what was given to me by "allowing the giver's gesture to rise again to the visible,"[62] all the while remaining invisible. I so allow this appearance of the invisible through my formed life, revealed in both actions performed in accordance with that which was given to me (making visible the invisible through my anamorphic conversion) and through a sacrifice of praise, wherein I make visible the gift by naming the withdrawn and always invisible giver. In both cases, the invisible impossible God is revealed through the phenomenological impact of the doubled confession marking the excessive gift that transforms *who I am* into *what I am given*. Augustine's statement that I know the love I love better than the beloved I love[63] (and therefore I ought to seek God in this love), reinscribed in the terms of the advance, suggests this phenomenalization of the gift of God (for this gift of love must, in some way, be given through mediation if God is to appear as the invisible mediated as invisible[64]). God is not given to be known as I know an object in creation, nor even as I come to know about another person. God is as God is given to me (and is so given through the mission of the Son and Spirit) and appears (as invisible) in the iconic fidelity of my formation to this given.

Inasmuch as I open in response the gift of my advance—inasmuch as I am formed into a lover—that which is otherwise impossible is made possible for me and offered to me: the particular naming of God as Father, Son, and Holy Spirit. The reception of the gift of love makes

62. Marion, *Reason of the Gift*, 89.
63. Augustine, *De Trinitate*, 8.12.
64. See Marion, "Phenomenality of the Sacrament," 90.

possible the naming of the *elsewhere*, just as naming it makes it possible for me to receive this love in all its particularity. Marion writes:

> The sole possibility opened to me by the pressure of the *pondus amoris* resides simply in the determination of this *elsewhere*. . . . Love weighs on myself like the sky at the horizon, not that it oppresses me with a lid of anxiety, but because it discloses to me an opening that will never be closed again: the opening onto the unshirkable, absolute, inalienable, but still always undetermined possibility of deciding to love, of *having to* love whatever comes, whatever I might want, whether I want it or not. This horizon, the never impossible possibility of loving, is never closed.[65]

In so particularizing, the pressure of my love of *this beloved* does what I otherwise cannot do: maintain the possibility that love might, indeed, bear all things. And it is only because we have named this beloved God "Father, Son, and Holy Spirit"—and, indeed, therein named God "love"—that we can join Marion and hope in this love to make this impossibility possible. For "God is either said as the master of the impossible or fails to be said."[66] While the impossible *as such* cannot be named, cannot particularize or be particularized, love makes this naming possible in grounding it in the prayer by which I call upon God by this name. The advance in love names my beloved even as I acknowledge, through sacrifice, that I name not to define but to praise this never-to-be-fully-determined *elsewhere*.

Again, with a phenomenon that is invisible to the senses and saturates intuition, those concepts, structures, communities, and traditions that guide our interpretation—that offer to us names of the given phenomenon—become all the more crucial to how the given might come to appear to us. The mediating structures of Christianity (theology and worship, indeed, but also under other cultural and symbolic forms) are unavoidable, to be sure, but they need not be merely tolerated. The particularity of the Christian faith (both *fides qua* and *fides quae*) offers the irreducibly contingent phenomenon of love by which we might address the beloved, a revealed name by which we

65. Marion, *In the Self's Place*, 271.
66. Marion, "Question of the Unconditioned," section 5.

might come to know our very advance. It provides the context wherein we might praise the one we love *as* the one who loved us first.

If Augustine wrote the *Confessions* to invite the reader's confession through the description of his own, we might say that Augustine wrote *De Trinitate* to describe the intellectual path by which we might come to know that which we confess. Augustine's transformation of classical rhetoric to language that is not only persuasive but specifically orientated to teaching *caritas* revealed in the scriptures is no less a part of what Augustine is doing here than in his sermons (although it is here refined and directed toward the minority who could engage his argument). Not even in his most speculative of works can the truth that Augustine teaches be separated from the need of his readers to love the truth so taught. What *De Trinitate* says *about* God is that God is revealed not in created tri-unities, not even the trinity of the self-reflective human mind, but in the conversion that happens to us having been given the saturated gift of love that urges us to call upon God.

The anamorphic nature of love sharpens, rather than eradicates, the need for some hermeneutic by which I might remain vigilant that I am responding, rather than defining, that which initiates my love. *De Trinitate* offers to Marion an "interpretation" of his own work—it offers him a name by which we might address the otherwise indetermined beloved and offers to Marion a needed particular phenomenon to name "love," a phenomenon in which to hope, a name to which we might be faithful. It offers a hermeneutic tradition to guide his description of this most saturated of phenomena and a name particularizing this phenomenon (the love revealed by Christ through the Holy Spirit). *De Trinitate* is a text that teaches, through its progression and limitations, that we might come to know the invisible *res* both given and signified in the sending of the Son. It teaches, in this way, against idolatry. Marion's concept of the idol is at its most unsettling insofar as it haunts most of us as all but unavoidable—except perhaps the saints, who seem to dally in excess as "connoisseurs of extravagance"[67] and advance in

67. Theresa Sanders, *Celluloid Saints: Images of Sanctity in Film* (Macon, GA: Mercer University Press, 2002), 210.

love in ways both attractive and terrifying to the rest of us and not, as Schrijvers fears, simply to the philosophers. Indeed, love appears as impossible for us, threatening idolatry if the truth of this impossibility is not somehow embraced—to be known, the truth must be loved and called upon. Marion only escapes phenomenological betrayal and theological idolatry inasmuch as what he says about God is limited to marking our anamorphic formation overcoming not metaphysics, nor conceptuality, nor even our own fallen limitation, but the impossibility of our own advance. We can only speak about God as the one to whom we call upon in a sacrifice of praise, and we can only so speak to urge and direct that praise. For this reason, the momentum of Marion's phenomenology not only prompts a theological turn but fits promisingly with *De Trinitate*'s approach to God via the mediation of the Son and Spirit in and through creation.[68] Ever in danger of idolatry, it is only in turning continually toward the revealed phenomenon that we are formed to see it as impossible—or better, the turning is only possible as a response to the given impossibility.

If *De Trinitate* offers to Marion a name by which we might call upon our particular beloved, Marion's phenomenology offers to the reading to *De Trinitate* a description of how love—through a prayerful praise that confesses—permits an encounter with that which is given to us and is otherwise impossible for us.[69] Neither a "relational trinity" wherein the substance metaphysics is overcome with a relational predication grounded in the gift of love, nor a redefinition of substance and person in phenomenological language would reveal the Trinity more than any other conceptual schema could. Such trinities would remain exercises in metaphysics, perhaps worthy endeavors in themselves but not the end of theological inquiry.

Augustine does not pretend to be able to transcend mediation or the language of metaphysics but instead illustrates the way in which

68. See also, "The Christian tradition(s) ought not in principle to be disconcerted by mediation, for Christianity has unceasingly been a religion of the Mediator, of God's icon, and hence of God's sign and supplement, of mediating, mediations and vicars, all of which concedes in principle the need to address the gap or bridge the discontinuity, between God and humankind." Caputo, *More Radical Hermeneutics*, 201.
69. Marion, *In the Self's Place*, 21.

such mediation reaches its limit. That is not to say that our language does not matter or that it (along with any part of creation) needs to be overcome. Only that we must never understand mediation as offering an image to be conceived but instead as always inviting us to an openness to receive what is given to us. Like my entrance into the flesh of another and the other's entrance into mine (the very crossed phenomenon that gives me my own flesh), *De Trinitate* describes our entrance into the space of the Trinity, into the possibility of our advance in love, as possible because the Trinity withdraws little by little in order to draw me forward.[70] The process by which we talk and think about God is inescapably part of our formation to (or deformation away from) God. "It follows," Marion writes, "that Saint Augustine's entire project aims at retrieving, behind the appearance of the word *about*, the reality of the word *to* (as response *to*, therefore *to* God)."[71] Nothing we might say *about* God is without a more fundamental orientation *to* or *away from* God. And nothing we say *about* God promises to make us more aware of this always already active *to* than how we name God. As the proper name of God "never belongs properly—by and as essence—to the one who receives it,"[72] any naming of God is inescapably also (and, indeed, more fundamentally) an address *to* God. Prayer, in being intentional about its address *to* God, is the sacrifice by which we recognize this *to* behind every *about* and accept the excessive revelation and whatever it might give to us. Prayer, Marion suggests, can serve as the intentionality by which we open ourselves to the particular saturated phenomenon given in revelation, thereby being anamorphically formed to that which is given. And in naming God, *De Trinitate* gives to Marion this directional *to* behind each of the *abouts* by which he describes love in his reduction; it gives a name for this love through, with, and in which we call upon God.

In this way, the language of prayer follows the language of love in being pragmatic and not predicative. It serves as a way of intimately

70. See Marion, *Erotic Phenomenon*, 181.
71. Marion, *In the Self's Place*, 43.
72. Marion, *In Excess*, 142.

particularizing our addressee, without intending, ultimately, to say anything definitive *about* the addressee but instead only trying to maintain our intentionality upon precisely *what is given*. That language of love offers "words for saying nothing,"[73] words that are not used "in order to describe ourselves, not to know ourselves better, nor in order to meet one another (as the beautiful soul imagines it), but uniquely in order to arouse ourselves. To speak in order to arouse—to make ourselves go out of ourselves as flesh eroticized by words, above all by words. This is what our mouths are for, when they do not give themselves to kissing."[74] But in prayer, this arousal itself is the "Here I am!" to the Father, Son, and Spirit—the name that gives me reason to hope in love (and, indeed, also an invitation to act according to this hope).

If Marion's erotic reduction teaches that our own advance in love is first received in being loved, so too it suggests that prayer—as the intentionality by which we love that particular saturated phenomenon of love given in revelation—is itself responsive to an already given gift. Especially as praise, prayer is our response to not only our being loved and saved by an unconditionality that is impossible for us, by an excess that we cannot achieve but only receive, but it is the site wherein this impossible unconditionality is made possible for us *as impossible and unconditioned*. It is also the advance by which we return what is given to us so we might become aware of the gift. Praise is a sacrifice as it marks "the process of an arrival (*une advenue*), always come from elsewhere and, for that very reason, inalienable and unavailable."[75]

That *De Trinitate* ends in prayer complements the ending of Marion's own reduction—both suggest that our own advance in love is a response to having already been loved. Where Marion's phenomenology of excess and advance gives readers of *De Trinitate* a reason for the hope in love, *De Trinitate* performs a "reduction" of its own, marking the limits of predication and conception, and opening the reader to the possibility of the graced gift of what is impossible for

73. Marion, *Erotic Phenomenon*, 143.
74. Ibid., 146.
75. Marion, *Reason of the Gift*, 90.

us. And more importantly, the end of *De Trinitate*'s reduction is the turn to prayer, by which we might call upon God by the name that is always arriving in advance of us, always in excess of our own memory, understanding, and love. "The impossibility of comprehension does not only point out a factual impossibility," Marion writes, "but also defines the field and the conditions of access to Him who, without incomprehensibility, would disappear from thought."[76] This is what *De Trinitate* can offer its readers: a way of thinking the impossibility of God that does not objectify God but invites us to call upon this God—the Father, Son, and Spirit—and hope in the love revealed in Jesus Christ.

If this impossibility appears to us not as a manifestation of the interplay between our natural or created limitations and those of our fallen condition but instead as the sign of love—signifying that we might only come to know the excessive phenomenon through an advance that is given to us as gift—then the aporia wherein we only know love through loving *this particular other* opens only in those concrete mediating structures that direct us into *this particular excessive givenness*. As long as our erotic reduction does not respond to a particular beloved—and call upon the beloved by name—we cannot open to the impossible gift of love's advance and our reduction remains within the structures of possibility. Such work remains conceptual, speculative, and even metaphysical. If the gift of love only appears as impossible and does so only in receiving the gift of our advance toward the Trinity that God is, then this gift appears only in the impossible advance toward *this particular other*, wherein we love *this* other for *this* other and for no antecedent reason. We need to name our giver—not to predicate anything *of* this giver but to particularize the advance that *this* other engenders by the gift. And we need to name this giver so we might call upon this beloved by name and open to the advance. But we need the given phenomenon to name "love" so we can in turn love this love. Revelation is that phenomenon that appears as a *fait accompli*, that makes visible the invisible as invisible, and that which gives us ourselves (all the while overcoming our urge to frame it as a

76. Marion, *In the Self's Place*, 291.

manageable fragment). Such a phenomenon can appear only as it calls us to praise this love and to praise in love.

While *De Trinitate* is not itself (whether in its composition or in its reading) an act of prayer (like the one *Confessions* illustrates and invites), it is an offer of mediation by which we are directed to the particular phenomenon reveled in the excessive givenness of the Son and opened to us by the Spirit in the received gift of our own advance. And this is what *De Trinitate* does—it offers the path of the advance toward the God whom I can name but whose name defies all structures of objective predication and invites us to call upon the Trinity by name. The text can certainly be criticized within the Christian tradition for its articulation of the path revealed in the scriptures and for the accent with which it pronounces the revealed name of God. However, *De Trinitate* ultimately offers to us not a defined image of God but rather a measure of the impact of the revelation of the God of love upon our reason and a rational exposition of the invitation to tend forward toward God. Behind each of Augustine's *abouts* is love's directional *to.* And to so tend forward in love "does not have as its goal attaining what precedes, so as to nullify the advance, but to put me too in the advance itself."[77] We are calling upon God by the name always already given, always advancing to an image of the one who loves us first.

77. Ibid., 229.

Conclusion to Part Three

To set about making an inexpressible reality inexpressibly seen[1] (or the invisible God visible *as invisible*, the impossible possible *as impossible*) in a work of theology is, itself, an impossible task and one that was never my intention. It was never my desire to try to present the Trinity to my readers, to present God *as such*. It is my hope, however, that this work might instead serve as an exercise in phenomenological theology, whereby the reception of the gift of love can be explored in the transformation it effects within us. It was never my intention to put this particular gift (given to us so we might love) on display but instead to illustrate *how* we might begin to speak of this gift, to speak of that which cannot be understood without first having received it, to speak of that which has already been given, without reserve, upon the cross. I hope to have illustrated *why* it is a matter of incarnating the revelation, of not simply verbally or conceptually confessing Jesus as God from God but of opening to the Holy Spirit that we might, from the depths of our hearts, come to remember, understand, and love the Trinity. Finally, it was never my wish to discuss *love* abstractly but rather that which is given in the incarnation of the Son and the sending of the Spirit, and thus named in the Trinity.

I have attempted to illuminate not only the how the limits of Trinitarian theology can serve to open us to the love of God but also how the limits of a particular text and those of a particular

1. Augustine, *De Trinitate*, 1.3.

phenomenology might too serve to complement each other and, through examining its incarnation, further our understanding of the gift of love. In *De Trinitate*, Augustine offer his readers a way to embrace the linguistic and conceptual limits of theology, to see in those very limits an opening to deeper understanding, yes, but more so an ever growing love. He concludes not only that the negation of whatever is expressed in a theological formula is "an essential part of the formula"[2] but that the dynamic of conceptual affirmation and negation—this play at the limits of signification—must itself be subsumed into the prayerful devotion of loving the Father, Son, and Holy Spirit. In the end, theology serves to open us to receive, and thereby give, love. But to confess faith in the Trinitarian God of love revealed in Jesus Christ is to confess faith in the incarnation of love. Therefore an understanding of *what love does to me*—concretely, phenomenologically, incarnationally—is itself the privileged way of access to understanding the one who gives love incarnate. We come to know what is given only by receiving it and by marking the formation it effects. Marion's phenomenology traces the formation of love by love, offering to Augustine's theology a description of how love appears in each of our lives. Marion gives to *De Trinitate* an analysis of the effect of love's incarnation in our lives; *De Trinitate* turns Marion to the incarnation by which this love is revealed in all its universal intimacy, given through irreducibly contingent blood[3] and named in its divine particularity.

To name God "Father, Son, and Holy Spirit" admits the impossibility of knowing God *as such* and opens the possibility of an approach to God through the iconic formation of our love of love (which we know more intimately than we know anything else) and our becoming those who can advance in love. But this advance only appears for us as impossible—certainly because we cannot maintain it, and because we are always at risk of idolatrously betraying it, but fundamentally because the advance itself is only possible inasmuch as it is a response to the always already given gift of love. We, as Augustine recognizes,

2. Geest, *Incomprehensibility of God*, 157.
3. Cavadini, "Structure and Intention," 109.

are always late to our advance in love.[4] We always advance only after having been loved, only after having already received God's name in the gift of revelation. But it is never too late to remember, understand, and love God, Michael Hanby observes, "precisely because it is always too late."[5] Our own advance is always already a response to the gift by which God offers divine love to us. Theology must therefore be forgiven its inability to justify this advance through any reason other than that of the gift already given: the mission of the Son and still active mission of the Spirit. To hope in this gift is to hope in the Spirit's continued working in creation—indeed, in our hearts—and to hope in love's bearing all things to God.

4. Augustine, *Confessions*, 10.27.38.
5. Hanby, *Augustine and Modernity*, 179.

Bibliography

Primary Sources: Augustine

Texts in Latin

Augustinus. *Confessionum*. Patrologia Latina 32. Edited by J.-P. Migne, 657–868. Paris, 1841–64.

_____. *De Catechizandis Rudibus*. Patrologia Latina 6. Edited by J.-P. Migne, 309–48. Paris, 1841–64.

_____. *De Civitate Dei*. Patrologia Latina 41. Edited by J.-P. Migne, 13–804. Paris, 1841–64.

_____. *De Doctrina Christiana*. Patrologia Latina 34. Edited by J.-P. Migne, 15–122. Paris, 1841–64.

_____. *De Magistro*. Patrologia Latina 32. Edited by J.-P. Migne, 1193–1220. Paris, 1841–64.

_____. *De Trinitate*, Libri XV, *Aurelii Augustini Opera*, pars XVI, I–II. Edited by W. J. Mountain and Fr. Glorie. Corpus Christianorum, Series Latina 50. Turnholti: Typogtaphi Brepols, 1968.

_____. *De Utilitate Credendi*. Patrologia Latina 42. Edited by J.-P. Migne, 65–92. Paris, 1841–64.

_____. *Tractatus in Epistolam Joannis ad Parthos*. In *Commento a Vangelo e alla Prima Epistola di San Giovanni, Nuova Biblioteca Agostiniana*. Opere di Sant'Agostino 24. Rome: Città Nuova Editrice, 1968.

Texts Translated into English

Augustine. *Arianism and Other Heresies.* Translated by Roland J. Teske. Edited by John E. Rotelle, OSA. The Works of St. Augustine: A Translation for the 21st Century, vol. 1, no. 18. Hyde Park, NY: New City Press, 1995.

_____. *The City of God.* Translated by Henry Bettenson. New York: Penguin, 1972.

_____. *Confessions.* Translated by Henry Chadwick. New York: Oxford University Press, 2008.

_____. *The Enchiridion on Faith, Hope, and Love.* Translated by J. B. Shaw. Chicago: Henry Regnery, 1961.

_____. *Expositions on the Book of Psalms.* London: F.&J. Rivington, 1853.

_____. *Faith and the Creed.* Translated by Michael G. Campbell. In *On Christian Belief*, edited by Boniface Ramsey. The Works of St. Augustine: A Translation for the 21st Century, vol. 1, no. 18. Hyde Park, NY: New City Press, 2005

_____. *Homilies on the First Epistle of John.* Edited and translated by Boniface Ramsey. The Works of St. Augustine: A Translation for the 21st Century, vol. 3, no. 14. Hyde Park, NY: New City Press, 2008.

_____. *Instructing Beginners in Faith.* Translated by Raymond Canning. Edited by Boniface Ramsey. The Works of St. Augustine: A Translation for the 21st Century. Hyde Park, NY: New City Press, 2006.

_____. *Letters: Vol. 1, No. 1–99.* Translated by Roland Teske, SJ. Edited by Boniface Ramsey. The Works of St. Augustine: A Translation of the 21st Century, vol. 2, no. 1. Hyde Park: NY: New City Press, 2001.

_____. *On Christian Teaching.* Translated by R. P. H. Green. New York: Oxford University Press, 2008.

_____. *On the Trinity, Books 8–15.* Edited by Gareth B. Matthews. Translated by Stephen McKenna. New York: Cambridge University Press, 2002.

_____. *Responses to Miscellaneous Questions.* Edited and translated by Boniface Ramsey. The Works of St. Augustine: A Translation for the 21st Century, vol. 1, no. 12. Hyde Park, NY: New City Press, 2008.

_____. *The Retractions.* Translated by Sister M. Inez Bogan, RSM. Washington, DC: Catholic University of America Press, 1999.

_____. *Sermons 94A–147A.* Translated by Edmund Hill, OP. Edited by John E.

Rotelle. The Works of St. Augustine: A Translation for the 21st Century, vol. 3, no. 4. Hyde Park, NY: New City Press, 1992.

_____. *Sermons 306-340A*. Translated by Edmund Hill, OP. Edited by John E. Rotelle. The Works of St. Augustine: A Translation for the 21st Century, vol. 3, no. 9. Hyde Park, NY: New City Press, 1994.

_____. *The Teacher*. In *"Against the Academicians" and "The Teacher,"* translated by Peter King. Indianapolis: Hackett, 1995.

_____. *The Trinity*. Translated by Edmund Hill, OP. Edited by John E. Rotelle. The Works of St. Augustine: A Translation of the 21st Century, vol. 3, no. 9. Hyde Park, NY: New City Press, 1991.

_____. *The Usefulness of Belief*. In *Augustine: Earlier Writings*, translated by John H. S. Burleigh, 291–323. The Library of Christian Classics 6. Philadelphia: Westminster Press, 1953.

Primary Sources: Marion

Books in French

Marion, Jean-Luc. *Au lieu de soi: L'approche de Saint Augustin*. Paris: Presses Universitaires de France, 2008.

_____. *La croisée du visible*. Rev. ed. Paris: Èditions de la Différence, 1996.

_____. *Dieu sans l'être: Hors-texte*. Paris: Arthème Fayard, 1982.

_____. *L'idole et la distance. Cinq etudes*. Paris: Grasset, 1977.

_____. *Le phénomène érotique*. Paris: Grasset, 2003.

_____. *Prolégomènes à la charité*. 2nd ed. Paris: Éditions de la Différence, 1991.

Books in English

Marion, Jean-Luc. *Being Given: Toward a Phenomenology of Givenness*. Translated by Jeffrey L. Kosky. Stanford, CA: Stanford University Press, 2002.

_____. *The Crossing of the Visible*. Translated by James K. A. Smith. Stanford, CA: Stanford University Press, 2004.

_____. *The Erotic Phenomenon*. Translated by Stephen E. Lewis. Chicago: University of Chicago Press, 2007.

_____. *Givenness and Revelation*. Translated by Stephen E. Lewis. Oxford: Oxford University Press, 2016.

_____. *God Without Being*. Translated by Thomas A. Carlson. Chicago: University of Chicago Press, 1991.

_____. *The Idol and Distance: Five Studies*. Translated by Thomas A. Carlson. New York: Fordham University Press, 2001.

_____. *In Excess: Studies of the Saturated Phenomena*. Translated by Robyn Horner and Vincent Berraud. New York: Fordham University Press, 2002.

_____. *In the Self's Place: The Approach of Saint Augustine*. Translated by Jeffrey L. Kosky. Stanford, CA: Stanford University Press, 2012.

_____. *Negative Certainties*. Translated by Stephen E. Lewis. Chicago: University of Chicago Press, 2015.

_____. *Prolegomena to Charity*. Translated by Stephen E. Lewis. New York: Fordham University Press, 2002.

_____. *The Reason of the Gift*. Translated by Stephen E. Lewis. Charlottesville: University of Virginia Press, 2011.

_____. *Reduction and Givenness: Investigations of Husserl, Heidegger, and Phenomenology*. Translated by Thomas A. Carlson. Evanston, IL: Northwestern University Press, 1998.

_____. *The Visible and the Revealed*. Translated by Christian M. Gschwandtner. New York: Fordham University Press, 2008.

Book Sections, Journal Articles, Papers Presented

Kearney, Richard and Jean-Luc Marion. "Hermeneutics of Revelation." In *Debates in Continental Philosophy: Conversations with Contemporary Thinkers*, by Richard Kearney, 15–32. New York: Fordham University Press, 2004.

Marion, Jean-Luc. "The Banality of Saturation." Translated by Jeffrey L. Kosky. In *Counter-Experiences: Reading Jean-Luc Marion*, edited by Kevin Hart, 383–418. Notre Dame: University of Notre Dame Press, 2007.

_____. "Les deux volontés du Christ selon Maxime le Confesseur." *Résurrection* 41 (1972): 48–66.

_____. "Distance et béatitude. Sur le mot 'capacitas' chez saint Augustin." *Résurrection* 29 (1969): 58–80.

_____. "The 'End of Metaphysics' as a Possibility." In *Religion After Metaphysics*, edited by Mark A. Wrathall, 166–89. Cambridge: Cambridge University Press, 2003.

_____. "The Event, the Phenomenon, and the Revealed." In *Transcendence in Philosophy and Religion*, edited by James E. Faulconer, 87–105. Bloomington: Indiana University Press, 2003.

_____. "From the Other to the Individual." Translated by Robyn Horner. In *Transcendence: Philosophy, Literature, and Theology Approach the Beyond*, edited by Regina M. Schwartz, 43–59. New York: Routledge, 2004.

_____. "*Idipsum*: The Name of God according to Augustine." In *Orthodox Readings of Augustine*, edited by George E. Demacopoulos and Aristotle Papanikolaou, 167–89. Crestwood, NY: St. Vladimir's Seminary Press, 2008.

_____. "The Impossible for Man—God." In *Transcendence and Beyond: A Postmodern Inquiry*, edited by John D. Caputo and Michael J. Scanlon, 17–43. Bloomington: Indiana University Press, 2007.

_____. "In the Name: How to Avoid Speaking of 'Negative Theology.'" In *God, the Gift, and Postmodernism*, edited by John D. Caputo and Michael J. Scanlon, 20–53. Bloomington: Indiana University Press, 1999.

_____. "Metaphysics and Phenomenology: A Relief for Theology." Translated by Thomas A. Carlson. *Critical Inquiry* 20 (1991): 572–91.

_____. "*Mihi magna quaestio factus sum*: The Privilege of Unknowing." *Journal of Religion* 85 (2005): 1–24.

_____. "The Phenomenality of the Sacrament." Translated by Bruce Ellis Benson. In *Words of Life: New Theological Turns in French Phenomenology*, edited by Bruce Ellis Benson and Norman Wirzba, 89–102. New York: Fordham University Press, 2010.

_____. "The Question of the Unconditioned—God." Inaugural lecture as the Andrew Thomas Greeley and Grace McNichols Greeley Professor of Catholic Studies, University of Chicago Divinity School, Chicago, November 3, 2011.

_____. "The Reason of the Gift." Translated by Shane Mackinlay and Nicolas de Warren. In *Givenness and God: Questions of Jean-Luc Marion*, edited by Ian Leask and Eoin Cassidy, 101–34. New York: Fordham University Press, 2005.

_____. "Resting, Moving, Loving: The Access to the Self According to Saint Augustine." *The Journal of Religion* 91 (2011): 24–42.

_____. "La saisie trinitaire selon l'Ésprit de Saint Augustine." *Résurrection* 28 (1968): 66–94.

_____. "*Substantia:* Note sur l'usage de *substantia* par St. Augustine et sure son appartenance à l'histoire de la métaphysique." In *Mots Médiévaux: Offerts à Ruedi Imbach*, edited by I. Atucha, D. Calma, C. König-Pralong, and I. Zavattero, 501–11. Turnhout: Brepols, 2011.

_____. "They Recognized Him; and He Became Invisible to Them." *Modern Theology* 18, no. 2 (April 2002): 145–52.

_____. "Thomas Aquinas and Onto-theo-logy." In *Mystics: Presence and Aporia*, edited by Michael Kessler and Christian Sheppard, 38–74. Chicago: University of Chicago Press, 2003.

Other Sources

Alston, William P. "Substance and the Trinity." In *The Trinity: An Interdisciplinary Symposium on the Trinity*, edited by Stephen T. Davis, Daniel Kendall, SJ, and Gerald O'Collins, SJ, 179–201. Oxford: Oxford University Press, 1999.

Anatolios, Khaled. "Oppositional Pairs and Christological Synthesis: Rereading Augustine's *De Trinitate*." *Theological Studies* 68, no. 2 (2007): 231–53.

Anderson, David. Introduction to *On the Holy Spirit*, by St. Basil the Great. Crestwood, NY: St. Vladimir's Seminary Press, 2001.

Ayers, Robert H. "Language Theory and Analysis in Augustine." *Scottish Journal of Theology* 29 (1976): 1–12.

Ayres, Lewis. *Augustine and the Trinity*. New York: Cambridge University Press, 2010.

_____. "Augustine on the Rule of Faith: Rhetoric, Christology, and the Foundation of Christian Thinking." *Augustinian Studies* 36 (2005): 33–49.

_____. "The Christological Content of Augustine's *De Trinitate* XIII: Toward Relocating Books VIII-XV." *Augustinian Studies* 29 (1998): 111–40.

_____. "The Fundamental Grammar of Augustine's Trinitarian Theology." In *Augustine and His Critics: Essays in Honour of Gerald Bonner*, edited by Robert Dodaro and George Lawless, 51–76. New York: Routledge, 2000.

_____. "'Giving Wings to Nicaea': Reconceiving Augustine's Earliest Trinitarian Theology." *Augustinian Studies* 38 (2007): 21–40.

_____. "Innovation and *Ressourcement* in Pro-Nicene Pneumatology." *Augustinian Studies* 39 (2008): 187–205.

_____. "'Remember That You Are Catholic' (serm. 52.2): Augustine on the Unity of the Triune God." *Journal of Early Christian Studies* 8 (2000): 39–82.

_____. "*Sempiterne Spiritus Donum*: Augustine's Pneumatology and the Metaphysics of Spirit." In *Orthodox Readings of Augustine*, edited by George E. Demacopoulos and Aristotle Papanikolaou, 127–52. Crestwood, NY: St. Vladimir's Seminary Press, 2008.

_____. "*Spiritus Amborum*: Augustine and Pro-Nicene Pneumatology." *Augustinian Studies* 39 (2008): 207–21.

Balthasar, Hans Urs von. *Love Alone Is Credible.* Translated by D. C. Schindler. San Francisco: Ignatius Press, 2004.

Barnes, Michel René. "The Arians of Book V, and the Genre of *De Trinitate*." *Journal of Theological Studies* 44, no. 1 (1993): 185–95.

_____. "Augustine in Contemporary Trinitarian Theology." *Theological Studies* 56, no. 2 (1995): 237–50.

_____. "Augustine's Last Pneumatology." *Augustinian Studies* 39, no. 2 (2008): 223–34.

_____. "The Beginning and End of Early Christian Pneumatology." *Augustinian Studies* 39, no. 2 (2008): 169–86.

_____. "De Régnon Reconsidered." *Augustinian Studies* 26, no. 2 (1995): 51–79.

_____. "*De Trinitate* VI and VII: Augustine and the Limits of Nicene Orthodoxy." *Augustinian Studies* 38, no. 1 (2007): 189–202.

_____. "Exegesis and Polemic in Augustine's *De Trinitate* I." *Augustinian Studies* 30, no. 1 (1999): 43–59.

_____. "Rereading Augustine's Theology of the Trinity." In *The Trinity: An Interdisciplinary Symposium on the Trinity*, edited Stephen T. Davis, Daniel Kendall, SJ, and Gerald O'Collins, SJ, 145–76. Oxford: Oxford University Press, 1999.

_____. "The Visible Christ and the Invisible Trinity: Mt. 5:8 in Augustine's Trinitarian Theology of 400." *Modern Theology* 19, no. 3 (July 2003): 329–55.

Barron, Robert E. "Augustine's Questions: Why the Augustinian Theology of God Matters Today." *Logos* 10, no. 4 (2007): 35–54.

Basil the Great. *On the Holy Spirit*. Crestwood, NY: St. Vladimir's Seminary Press, 2001.

Bavel, Tarcisius J. van. "The Double Face of Love in Augustine." *Augustinian Studies* 17 (1986): 169–181.

Beck, T. David. *The Holy Spirit and the Renewal of All Things: Pneumatology in Paul and Jürgen Moltmann*. Eugene, OR: Pickwick Publications, 2007.

Beeck, Frans Jozef van, SJ. "Trinitarian Theology as Participation." In *The Trinity: An Interdisciplinary Symposium on the Trinity*, edited Stephen T. Davis, Daniel Kendall, SJ, and Gerald O'Collins, SJ, 295–325. Oxford: Oxford University Press, 1999.

Behr, John. "Calling Upon God as Father: Augustine and the Legacy of Nicaea." In *Orthodox Readings of Augustine*, edited by George E. Demacopoulos and Aristotle Papanikolaou, 153–165. Crestwood, NY: St. Vladimir's Seminary Press, 2008.

Benedict XVI. *Spe Salvi*. Encyclical letter. Rome. November 30, 2007. http://tinyurl.com/jntob2v.

Bennington, Geoffrey. *Derridabase*. In *Jacques Derrida*, by Geoffrey Bennington and Jacques Derrida. Chicago: University of Chicago Press, 1993.

Blond, Phillip. Introduction to *Post Secular Philosophy: Between Philosophy and Theology*, edited by Phillip Blond. New York: Routledge, 1998.

Boeve, Lieven. "Retrieving Augustine Today: Between Neo-Augustinianist Essentialism and Radical Hermeneutics?" In *Augustine and Postmodern Thought: A New Alliance Against Modernity?*, edited by Lieven Boeve, M. Lamberigts, Maarten Wisse, 1–17. Walpole, MA: Peeters, 2009.

Boff, Leonardo. *Holy Trinity, Perfect Community*. Translated by Phillip Berryman. Maryknoll, NY: Orbis Books, 2000.

Bourke, Vernon J. *Augustine's Love of Wisdom: An Introspective Philosophy*. West Lafayette, IN: Purdue University Press, 1992.

Bradshaw, David. "Augustine the Metaphysician." In *Orthodox Readings of Augustine*, edited by George E. Demacopoulos and Aristotle Papanikolaou, 227–51. Crestwood, NY: St. Vladimir's Seminary Press, 2008.

Brown, David. "Trinitarian Personhood and Individuality." In *Trinity*,

Incarnation, and Atonement: Philosophical and Theological Essays, edited by Ronald Jay Feenstra and Cornelius Plantinga Jr., 48–78. Notre Dame: University of Notre Dame Press, 1989.

Brown, Peter. *Augustine of Hippo: A Biography*. Rev. ed. Berkeley: University of California Press, 2000.

Burnaby, John. *Amor Dei: A Study of the Religion of St. Augustine*. Eugene, OR: Wipf & Stock, 2007.

Burnell, Peter. *The Augustinian Person*. Washington, DC: Catholic University of America Press, 2005.

Burrell, David B., CSC. *Exercises in Religious Understanding*. Notre Dame: University of Notre Dame Press, 1974.

Caputo, John D. "Apostles of the Impossible: On God and the Gift in Derrida and Marion." In *God, the Gift, and Postmodernism*, edited by John D. Caputo and Michael J. Scanlon, 185–222. Bloomington: Indiana University Press, 1999.

_____. "God Is Wholly Other—Almost: *Différance* and the Hyperbolic Alterity of God." In *The Otherness of God*, edited by Orrin F. Summerell, 190–205. Charlottesville: University Press of Virginia, 1998.

_____. *More Radical Hermeneutics: On Not Knowing Who We Are*. Bloomington: Indiana University Press, 2000.

_____. Review of *In the Self's Place: The Approach of St. Augustine*, by Jean-Luc Marion. *Notre Dame Philosophical Reviews*. January 18, 2013. http://tinyurl.com/gogrzzk.

Caputo, John D., and Michael J. Scanlon, eds. Introduction to *Augustine and Postmodernism: Confessions and Circumfession*. Bloomington: Indiana University Press, 2005.

_____, eds. Introduction to *God, the Gift, and Postmodernism*. Bloomington: Indiana University Press, 1999.

Card, Orson Scott. "How Tolkien Means." In *Meditations on Middle Earth*, edited by Karen Haber, 153-73. New York: St. Martin's Press, 2001.

Carlson, Thomas A. "Blindness and the Decision to See: On Revelation and Reception in Jean-Luc Marion." In *Counter-Experiences: Reading Jean-Luc Marion*, edited by Kevin Hart, 153–79. Notre Dame: University of Notre Dame Press, 2007.

Cassidy, Eoin. "*Le phénomène érotique*: Augustinian Resonances in Marion's

Phenomenology of Love." In *Givenness and God: Questions of Jean-Luc Marion*, edited by Ian Leask and Eoin Cassidy, 201–19. New York: Fordham University Press, 2005.

Cavadini, John C., "The Darkest Enigma: Reconsidering the Self in Augustine's Thought." *Augustinian Studies* 38 (2007): 119–32.

_____. "The Quest for Truth in Augustine's *De Trinitate*." *Theological Studies* 58, no. 3 (1997): 429–40.

_____. "The Structure and Intention of Augustine's *De Trinitate*." *Augustinian Studies* 23 (1992): 103–24.

Chevalier, Irénée. *S. Augustin et la pensée grecque: les relations trinitaires*. Fribourg: Librairie de l'Université, 1940.

Clark, Mary T. "*De Trinitate*." In *The Cambridge Companion to Augustine*, edited by Eleonore Stump and Norman Kretzmann, 91–102. Cambridge: Cambridge University Press, 2001.

Clayton, Philip. "In Whom We Have Our Being: Philosophical Resources for the Doctrine of the Spirit." In *Advents of the Spirit: An Introduction to the Current Study of Pneumatology*, edited by Bradford E. Hinze and D. Lyle Dabney, 173–207. Milwaukee, WI: Marquette University Press, 2001.

Coakley, Sarah. "'Persons' in the 'Social' Doctrine of the Trinity: A Critique of Current Analytic Discussion." In *The Trinity: An Interdisciplinary Symposium on the Trinity*, edited Stephen T. Davis, Daniel Kendall, SJ, and Gerald O'Collins, SJ, 123–44. Oxford: Oxford University Press, 1999.

Coffey, David. *Deus Trinitas: The Doctrine of the Triune God*. Oxford: Oxford University Press, 1999.

_____. "The Holy Spirit as the Mutual Love of the Father and the Son." *Theological Studies* 51, no. 2 (1990): 193–229.

_____. "Spirit Christology and the Trinity." In *Advents of the Spirit: An Introduction to the Current Study of Pneumatology*, edited by Bradford E. Hinze and D. Lyle Dabney, 315–38. Milwaukee, WI: Marquette University Press, 2001.

Cole, Thomas. *The Origins of Rhetoric in Ancient Greece*. Baltimore: Johns Hopkins University Press, 1991.

Collinge, William J. "*De Trinitate* and the Understanding of Religious Language." *Augustinian Studies* 18 (1987): 125–50.

Cooke, Alexander. "What Saturates? Jean-Luc Marion's Phenomenological Theology." *Philosophy Today* 48, no. 2 (2004): 179–87.

Corrigan, Kevin. "Love of God, Love of Self, and Love of Neighbor: Augustine's Critical Dialogue with Platonism." *Augustinian Studies* 34 (2003): 97–106.

Cross, Richard. "*Quid Tres*? On What Precisely Augustine Professes Not to Understand in *De Trinitate* 5 and 7." *Harvard Theological Review* 100, no. 2 (2007): 215–32.

_____. "Two Models of the Trinity?" *The Heythrop Journal* 43, no. 3 (July 2002): 275–94.

Dabney, D. Lyle. "Why Should the Last Be First? The Priority of Pneumatology in Recent Theological Discussion." In *Advents of the Spirit: An Introduction to the Current Study of Pneumatology*, edited by Bradford E. Hinze and D. Lyle Dabney, 240–61. Milwaukee, WI: Marquette University Press, 2001.

Davies, Oliver. *A Theology of Compassion: Metaphysics of Difference and the Renewal of Tradition*. Grand Rapids: Eerdmans, 2001.

Dawson, David. "Sign Theory, Allegorical Reading and the Motions of the Soul in *De doctrina christiana*." In *De doctrina christiana: A Classic of Western Culture*, edited by Duane W. H. Arnold and Pamela Bright, 123–41. Notre Dame: University of Notre Dame Press, 1995.

Del Colle, Ralph. "A Response to Jürgen Moltmann and David Coffey." In *Advents of the Spirit: An Introduction to the Current Study of Pneumatology*, edited by Bradford E. Hinze and D. Lyle Dabney, 339–46. Milwaukee, WI: Marquette University Press, 2001.

Demacopoulos, George E. and Aristotle Papanikolaou, eds. *Orthodox Readings of Augustine*. Crestwood, NY: St. Vladimir's Seminary Press, 2008.

Derrida, Jacques. *Circumfession*. In *Jacques Derrida*, by Geoffrey Bennington and Jacques Derrida. Chicago: University of Chicago Press, 1993.

_____. *The Gift of Death*. Translated by David Wills. Chicago: University of Chicago Press, 1995.

_____. *Given Time: I. Counterfeit Money*. Translated by Peggy Kamuf. Chicago: University of Chicago Press, 1992.

_____. "Hospitality, Justice, and Responsibility, (UCD Roundtable)." In *Questioning Ethics: Contemporary Debates in Philosophy*, edited by Richard Kearney and Mark Dooley, 65–83. London: Routledge, 1999.

———. "How to Avoid Speaking: Denials." Translated by Ken Frieden. In *Derrida and Negative Theology*, edited by Harold Coward and Toby Foshay, 3–70. Albany: State University of New York Press, 1992.

———. *On the Name*. Edited by Thomas Dutoit. Stanford, CA: Stanford University Press, 1995.

———. Response to "In the Name: How to Avoid Speaking of 'Negative Theology,'" by Jean-Luc Marion. In *God, the Gift, and Postmodernism*, edited by John D. Caputo and Michael J. Scanlon, 42–46. Bloomington: Indiana University Press, 1999.

Dickinson, Emily. *The Complete Poems of Emily Dickinson*, edited by Thomas H. Johnson. Boston: Little, Brown, 1960.

Dillard, Annie. *Holy the Firm*. New York: Harper & Row, 1977.

Djodi, Jules. *Le Saint-Esprit, Don de Dieu: Une clé de comprehension de la pneumatologie de saint Augustin*. PhD diss., Université Saint-Paul, Ottawa, ON, 2003.

Dodaro, Robert. "Loose Canons: Augustine and Derrida on Their Selves." In *God, the Gift, and Postmodernism*, edited by John D. Caputo and Michael J. Scanlon, 79–111. Bloomington: Indiana University Press, 1999.

Dooley, Mark. "Marion's Ambition of Transcendence." In *Givenness and God: Questions of Jean-Luc Marion*, edited by Ian Leask and Eoin Cassidy, 190–98. New York: Fordham University Press, 2005.

Douglas, Mary. Forward to *The Gift: The Form and Reason for Exchange in Archaic Societies*, by Marcel Mauss. New York: W.W. Norton, 1990.

Drever, Matthew. "The Self Before God? Rethinking Augustine's Trinitarian Thought." *Harvard Theological Review* 100, no. 2 (2007): 233–42.

Duffy, Stephen J. *The Dynamics of Grace: Perspectives in Theological Anthropology*. Eugene, OR: Wipf & Stock, 2007.

Dupré, Louis K. *Passage to Modernity: An Essay in the Hermeneutics of Nature and Culture*. New Haven: Yale University Press, 1993.

Falque, Emmanuel. "*Larvatus pro Deo*: Jean-Luc Marion's Phenomenology and Theology." In *Counter-Experiences: Reading Jean-Luc Marion*, edited by Kevin Hart, 181–99. Notre Dame: University of Notre Dame Press, 2007.

———. "Metaphysics and Theology in Tension: A Reading of Augustine's *De Trinitate*." In *Augustine and Postmodern Thought: A New Alliance Against*

Modernity?, edited by Lieven Boeve, M. Lamberigts, Maarten Wisse, 21–55. Walpole, MA: Peeters, 2009.

_____. "Saint Augustine: The Weight of Life—Sin and Finitude." Paper presented at "Phenomenology and Theology in Contemporary French Thought: Lectures and Colloquium," University of California, Santa Barbara, May 3–6, 2011.

Ferretter, Luke. "The Trace of the Trinity: Christ and Difference in Saint Augustine's Theory of Language." *Literature and Theology* 12, no. 3 (1998): 256–67.

Fortin, Ernest L. "Augustine and the Hermeneutics of Love: Some Preliminary Considerations." In *Augustine Today*, edited by Richard John Neuhaus, 35–59. Grand Rapids: Eerdmans, 1993.

_____. "Reflections on the Proper Way to Read Augustine the Theologian." *Augustinian Studies* 2 (1971): 253–72.

Foster, David, OSB. "Augustine's *De Trinitate*: Some Methodological Enquiries." *The Downside Review* 124, no. 437 (2006): 259–276.

Geest, Paul van. *The Incomprehensibility of God: Augustine as a Negative Theologian.* Walpole, MA: Peeters, 2011.

Giles, Kevin. *The Trinity and Subordinationism: The Doctrine of God and the Contemporary Gender Debate*. Downers Grove, IL: InterVarsity Press: 2002.

Gioia, Luigi, OSB. *The Theological Epistemology of Augustine's* De Trinitate. Oxford: Oxford University Press, 2008.

Griffiths, Paul J. "More than a Bargain." Review of *The Erotic Phenomenon*, by Jean-Luc Marion. *Commonweal*, March 9, 2007.

Grillmeier, Alois, SJ. *Christ in the Christian Tradition: Vol 1, From the Apostolic Age to Chalcedon (451)*. Translated by John Bowden. Atlanta, GA: John Knox Press, 1975.

Gschwandtner, Christina M., *Reading Jean-Luc Marion: Exceeding Metaphysics.* Bloomington: Indiana University Press, 2007.

Gudmarsdottir, Sigridur. Review of *Augustine and Modernity*, by Michael Hanby. *Augustinian Studies* 35, no. 2 (2004) 327–31.

Gunton, Colin E. "Augustine, the Trinity and the Theological Crisis of the West." In *The Promise of Trinitarian Theology*, 31–57. Edinburgh: T&T Clark, 1991.

Hanby, Michael. *Augustine and Modernity*. New York: Routledge, 2003.

Hankey, Wayne John. "Re-Christianizing Augustine Postmodern Style: Readings by Jacques Derrida, Robert Dodaro, Jean-Luc Marion, Rowan Williams, Lewis Ayres and John Milbank." *Animus* 2 (1997): 1–27.

Harris, Harriet A. "Should We Say the Personhood is Relational?" *Scottish Journal of Theology* 51, no. 2 (May 1998): 214–34.

Harrison, Carol. *Augustine: Christian Truth and Fractured Humanity*. Oxford: Oxford University Press, 2000.

_____. "*De profundis:* Augustine's Reading of Orthodoxy." In *Orthodox Readings of Augustine*, edited by George E. Demacopoulos and Aristotle Papanikolaou, 253–61. Crestwood, NY: St. Vladimir's Seminary Press, 2008.

Hart, David Bentley. "The Hidden and the Manifest: Metaphysics after Nicaea." In *Orthodox Readings of Augustine*, edited by George E. Demacopoulos and Aristotle Papanikolaou, 191–226. Crestwood, NY: St. Vladimir's Seminary Press, 2008.

Hart, Kevin. "The Experience of the Kingdom of God." In *The Experience of God: A Postmodern Response*, edited by Kevin Hart and Barbara Wall, 71–86. New York: Fordham University Press, 2005.

_____. Introduction to *Counter-Experiences: Reading Jean-Luc Marion*. Notre Dame: University of Notre Dame Press, 2007.

_____. *Postmodernism: A Beginner's Guide*. Oxford: Oneworld, 2004.

Hengel, John van den, SCJ. "God with/out Being." *Method: Journal of Lonergan Studies* 12, no. 2 (1994): 251–79.

Hiesberger, Jean Marie, ed. *The Catholic Bible: Personal Study Edition*. New York: Oxford University Press, 1995.

Hilary of Poitiers. *The Trinity*. Translated by Stephen McKenna. The Fathers of the Church: A New Translation 25. New York: Fathers of the Church, 1954.

Hilberath, Bernd Jochen. "Identity through Self-Transcendence: The Holy Spirit and the Fellowship of Free Persons." In *Advents of the Spirit: An Introduction to the Current Study of Pneumatology*, edited by Bradford E. Hinze and D. Lyle Dabney, 265–94. Milwaukee, WI: Marquette University Press, 2001.

Hill, Edmund, OP. Introduction, section forwards, and notes to *The Trinity*, by

Augustine. The Works of St. Augustine: A Translation of the 21st Century, vol. 3, no. 9. Hyde Park, NY: New City Press, 1991.

Himes, Michael. *Doing the Truth in Love: Conversations about God, Relationships, and Service*. New York: Paulist Press, 1995.

Hopkins, Gerard Manley. *Poems of Gerard Manley Hopkins*. London: Oxford University Press, 1949.

Horner, Robyn. *Jean-Luc Marion: A Theo-logical Introduction*. Hants, England: Ashgate, 2005.

_____. *Rethinking God as Gift: Marion, Derrida, and the Limits of Phenomenology*. New York: Fordham University Press, 2001.

_____. Translator's introduction to *In Excess: Studies of the Saturated Phenomenon*, by Jean-Luc Marion. New York: Fordham University Press, 2002.

_____. "The Weight of Love." In *Counter-Experiences: Reading Jean-Luc Marion*, edited by Kevin Hart, 235–51. Notre Dame: University of Notre Dame Press, 2007.

Hubbard, Kyle. "The Unity of Eros and Agape: On Jean-Luc Marion's Erotic Phenomenon." *Essays in Philosophy* 12, no. 1 (2011): 130–46.

_____. "'Who Then Are You, My God?': Augustine of Hippo and Jean-Luc Marion on the Nature and Possibility of Loving God." PhD diss., Fordham University, 2009.

Jacobs, Alan. *A Theology of Reading: The Hermeneutics of Love*. Cambridge: Westview Press, 2001.

Janicaud, Dominique. *Phenomenology "Wide Open": After the French Debate*. Translated by Charles N. Cabral. New York: Fordham University Press, 2005.

_____. "The Theological Turn in French Phenomenology." Translated by Bernard G. Prusak. In *Phenomenology and the "Theological Turn": The French Debate*, by Dominique Janicaud, Jean-François Courtine, Jean-Louis Chrétien, Michel Henry, Jean-Luc Marion, and Paul Ricoeur, 16–106. New York: Fordham University Press, 2000.

Johnson, Elizabeth A. *Quest for the Living God: Mapping Frontiers in the Theology of God*. New York: Continuum, 2007.

Jones, Tamsin. *A Genealogy of Marion's Philosophy of Religion: Apparent Darkness*. Bloomington: Indiana University Press, 2011.

Kal, Victor. "Being Unable to Speak, Seen as a Period: Difference and Distance in Jean-Luc Marion." In *Flight of the Gods: Philosophical Perspectives on Negative Theology*, edited by Ilse N. Bulhof and Laurens ten Kate, 144–65. New York: Fordham University Press, 2000.

Kearney, Richard. *The God Who May Be: A Hermeneutics of Religion*. Bloomington: Indiana University Press, 2001.

———. "Hermeneutics of the Possible God." In *Givenness and God: Questions of Jean-Luc Marion*, edited by Ian Leask and Eoin Cassidy, 220–42. New York: Fordham University Press, 2005.

———. "On the Gift: A Discussion between Jacques Derrida and Jean-Luc Marion." In *God, the Gift, and Postmodernism*, edited by John D. Caputo and Michael J. Scanlon, 54–78. Bloomington: Indiana University Press, 1999.

Kenney, John Peter. "Augustine's Inner Self." *Augustinian Studies* 33 (2002): 79–90.

Kloos, Kari. "Seeing the Invisible God: Augustine's Reconfiguration of Theophany Narrative Exegesis." *Augustinian Studies* 36 (2005): 397–420.

Kolbet, Paul R. *Augustine and the Cure of Souls: Revising a Classical Ideal*. Notre Dame: University of Notre Dame Press, 2010.

Kosky, Jeffrey L. "The Human Question: Augustinian Dimensions in Jean-Luc Marion." In *Words of Life: New Theological Turns in French Phenomenology*, edited by Bruce Ellis Benson and Norman Wirzba, 103–19. New York: Fordham University Press, 2010.

Kotsko, Adam. "Gift and *Communio*: The Holy Spirit in Augustine's *De Trinitate*." *Scottish Journal of Theology* 64, no. 1 (2011): 1–12.

Kraftson-Hogue, Mike. "Predication Turning to Praise: Marion and Augustine on God and Hermeneutics—(Giver, Giving, Gift, Giving)." *Literature and Theology* 14, no. 4 (2000): 399–411.

Kuehn, Evan F. "The Johannine Logic of Augustine's Trinity: A Dogmatic Sketch." *Theological Studies* 68, no. 3 (2007): 572–94.

LaCugna, Catherine Mowry. *God for Us: The Trinity and Christian Life*. New York: HarperCollins, 1991.

———. Introduction to *The Trinity*, by Karl Rahner. New York: Crossroad, 1997.

Lancaster, Sarah Heaner. "Three-Personed Substance: The Relational Essence of the Triune God in Augustine's *De Trinitate*." *Thomist* 60, no. 1 (1996): 123–40.

Lawrence, Frederick. "*Cor ad cor loquitur*: Augustine's Influence on Heidegger and Lonergan." Paper presented at "Augustine: Theological and Philosophical Conversations—A Conference Honoring David Tracy," University of Chicago Divinity School, Chicago, May 4–6, 2008.

Leftow, Brian. "Anti Social Trinitarianism." In *The Trinity: An Interdisciplinary Symposium on the Trinity*, edited Stephen T. Davis, Daniel Kendall, SJ, and Gerald O'Collins, SJ, 203–49. Oxford: Oxford University Press, 1999.

Levinas, Emmanuel. *Totality and Infinity: An Essay on Exteriority*. Translated by Alphonso Lingis. Pittsburgh: Duquesne University Press, 1969.

Lewis, C. S. *The Four Loves*. New York: Harcourt, 1960.

Lonergan, Bernard J. F. *Insight: A Study of Human Understanding*. Toronto: University of Toronto Press, 1992. Originally published 1957 by Philosophical Library. Citations refer to the Toronto edition.

_____. *Method in Theology*. New York: Seabury, 1972.

Louth, Andrew. "Love and the Trinity: Saint Augustine and the Greek Fathers." *Augustinian Studies* 33 (2002): 1–16.

Lubac, Henri de. *The Mystery of the Supernatural*. Translated by Rosemary Sheed. New York: Herder & Herder, 1967. Originally published as *Le Mystère du surnaturel*. Paris: Aubier, 1965.

_____. *Surnaturel. Études historiques*. Paris: Aubier, 1946.

MacIntyre, Alasdair, "Aristotle and/or/against Augustine: Rival Traditions of Enquiry." In *Three Rival Versions of Moral Enquiry: Encyclopedia, Genealogy, and Tradition*, 105–48. Notre Dame: University of Notre Dame Press, 1990.

Mackinlay, Shane. "Eyes Wide Shut: A Response to Jean-Luc Marion's Account of the Journey to Emmaus." *Modern Theology* 20, no. 3 (July 2004): 447–56.

Matthews, Gareth B. Introduction to *On the Trinity, Books 8-15*, by Augustine. New York: Cambridge University Press, 2002.

Mauss, Marcel. *The Gift: The Form and Reason for Exchange in Archaic Societies*. Translated by W. D. Halls. New York: W.W. Norton, 1990.

McDonnell, Kilian, OSB. "A Response to Bernd Jochen Hilberath." In *Advents of the Spirit: An Introduction to the Current Study of Pneumatology*, edited by Bradford E. Hinze and D. Lyle Dabney, 295–301. Milwaukee, WI: Marquette University Press, 2001.

_____. "A Response to D. Lyle Dabney." In *Advents of the Spirit: An Introduction to the Current Study of Pneumatology*, edited by Bradford E. Hinze and D. Lyle Dabney, 262–64. Milwaukee, WI: Marquette University Press, 2001.

McKenny, Gerald. "(Re)placing Ethics: Jean-Luc Marion and the Horizon of Modern Morality." In *Counter-Experiences: Reading Jean-Luc Marion*, edited by Kevin Hart, 339–55. Notre Dame: University of Notre Dame Press, 2007.

Meer, Frederik van der. *Augustine the Bishop: The Life and Work of a Father of the Church.* Translated by Brian Battershaw and G. R. Lamb. New York: Sheed & Ward, 1961.

Milbank, John. "Can a Gift Be Given? Prolegomena to a Future Trinitarian Metaphysic." *Modern Theology* 11, no. 1 (1995): 119–61.

———. "The Gift and the Mirror: On the Philosophy of Love." In *Counter-Experiences: Reading Jean-Luc Marion*, edited by Kevin Hart, 253–317. Notre Dame: University of Notre Dame Press, 2007.

———. "Only Theology Overcomes Metaphysics." In *The Word Made Strange: Theology, Language, Culture*, 36–52. Cambridge, MA: Blackwell Publishers, 1997.

Miller, André. "Trinitarian Theology and the Shape of the Christian Life: The Prolegomenon to Augustine's *De Trinitate*." *Augustinian Studies* 40 (2009): 121–37.

Milosz, Czeslaw. "Treatise on Theology." In *Second Space: New Poems*. New York: HarperCollins, 2004.

Moltmann, Jürgen. *History and the Triune God: Contributions to Trinitarian Theology*. New York: Crossroad, 1991.

———. "The Trinitarian Personhood of the Spirit." In *Advents of the Spirit: An Introduction to the Current Study of Pneumatology*, edited by Bradford E. Hinze and D. Lyle Dabney, 302–14. Milwaukee, WI: Marquette University Press, 2001.

———. *The Trinity and the Kingdom: The Doctrine of God*. San Francisco: Harper & Row, 1981.

Morrow, Derek J. "The Love 'Without Being' that Opens (to) Distance Part One: Exploring the Givenness of the Erotic Phenomenon with J-L. Marion." *The Heythrop Journal* 46, no. 3 (2005): 281–98.

———. "The Love 'Without Being' that Opens (to) Distance Part Two: From the

Icon of Distance to the Distance of the Icon in Marion's Phenomenology of Love." *The Heythrop Journal* 46, no. 4 (2005): 493–511.

Muller, André. "Trinitarian Theology and the Shape of the Christian Life: The Prolegomenon to Augustine's *De Trinitate*." *Augustinian Studies* 40 (2009): 121–37.

Muller, Earl. "The Dynamic of Augustine's *De Trinitate*: A Response to a Recent Characterization." *Augustinian Studies* 26, no. 1 (1995): 65–91.

Nehring, Cristina. "Loving a Child on the Fringe." *Slate*. November 28, 2012. http://tinyurl.com/h22btex.

Niceta of Remesiana. "The Power of the Holy Spirit." In *Writings; Commonitories; Grace and Free Will*. Translated by Gerald G. Walsh, 23–42. The Fathers of the Church: A New Translation 7. New York: Fathers of the Church, 1949.

Nietzsche, Friedrich. *A Nietzsche Reader*. Edited by R. J. Hollingdale. New York: Penguin, 1997.

Nygren, Anders. *Agape and Eros: The Christian Idea of Love*. Translated by Philip S. Watson. Chicago: University of Chicago Press, 1982.

O'Connor, William Riordan. "The Concept of the Person in St. Augustine's *De Trinitate*." *Augustinian Studies* 13 (1982): 133–43.

O'Donnell, James J. *Augustine: A New Biography*. New York: HarperCollins, 2005.

_____. "Augustine's Idea of God," *Augustinian Studies* 25 (1994): 25–35.

O'Donovan, Oliver. *The Problem of Self-Love in Augustine*. New Haven: Yale University Press, 1980.

O'Leary, Joseph S. "The Gift: A Trojan Horse in the Citadel of Phenomenology?" In *Givenness and God: Questions of Jean-Luc Marion*, edited by Ian Leask and Eoin Cassidy, 135–66. New York: Fordham University Press, 2005.

_____. "Jean-Luc Marion on St. Augustine: Marginal Notes." Joseph S. O'Leary Homepage (blog). March 16, 2009. http://tinyurl.com/joyteum.

_____. *Questioning Back: The Overcoming of Metaphysics in Christian Tradition*. Minneapolis: Winston Press, 1985.

Oliver, Mary. "The World I Live In." *Felicity*. New York: Penguin Press, 2016.

Ormerod, Neil. "Augustine's *De Trinitate* and Lonergan's Realms of Meaning." *Theological Studies* 64, no. 4 (2003): 773–94.

Otten, Willemien. Review of *Au lieu de soi: L'approche de Saint Augustin*, by Jean-Luc Marion. *Continental Philosophy Review* 42, no. 4 (2010): 597–602.

Paz, Octavio. *The Double Flame.* Translated by Helen Lane. New York: Harcourt Brace, 1995.

Pecknold, C. C. "How Augustine Used the Trinity: Functionalism and the Development of Doctrine." *Anglican Theological Review* 85 (2003): 127–41.

_____. *Transforming Postliberal Theology: George Lindbeck, Pragmatism and Scripture.* New York: T&T Clark, 2005.

Pelikan, Jaroslav. "*Canonica regula*: The Trinitarian Hermeneutics of Augustine." In *Collectanea Augustiniana, Augustine: "Second Founder of the Faith,"* edited by Joseph C. Schnaubelt, OSA, and Frederick Van Fleteren, 329–43. New York: Peter Lang, 1990.

Pieper, Josef. *The Silence of St. Thomas: Three Essays.* New York: Pantheon, 1957.

Plantinga, Cornelius, Jr. "Social Trinity and Tritheism." In *Trinity, Incarnation, and Atonement: Philosophical and Theological Essays*, edited by Ronald Jay Feenstra and Cornelius Plantinga Jr., 21–47. Notre Dame: University of Notre Dame Press, 1989.

Pool, Jeff B. "No Entrance into Truth Except through Love: Contributions from Augustine of Hippo to a Contemporary Christian Hermeneutic of Love." *Review and Expositor* 101, no. 4 (2004): 629–66.

Possidius. *Sancti Augustini vita scripta a Possidio episcope.* Translated by Herbert T. Weiskotten. Princeton: Princeton University Press, 1919.

Rahner, Karl. "Theology and Anthropology." In *The Word in History: The St. Xavier Symposium*, edited by T. Patrick Burke, 1–23. New York: Sheed & Ward, 1966.

_____. *The Trinity.* Translated by Joseph Donceel. New York: Crossroad, 2005. First published 1970 by Herder & Herder.

Robinette, Brian. "A Gift to Theology? Jean-Luc Marion's 'Saturated Phenomenon' in Christological Perspective." *The Heythrop Journal* 48, no. 1 (2007): 86–108.

Romano, Claude. "Love in Its Concept: Jean-Luc Marion's *The Erotic Phenomenon.*" Translated by Stephen E. Lewis. In *Counter-Experiences: Reading Jean-Luc Marion*, edited by Kevin Hart, 319–35. Notre Dame: University of Notre Dame Press, 2007.

Rossi, Philip, SJ. "The Idiom of Spirit: Discourse, Human Nature, and Otherness; A Response to Philip Clayton and Steven Smith." In *Advents of the Spirit: An*

Introduction to the Current Study of Pneumatology, edited by Bradford E. Hinze and D. Lyle Dabney, 233–39. Milwaukee, WI: Marquette University Press, 2001.

Rudolph, Katherine. "Augustine's Picture of Language." *Augustinian Studies* 36, no. 2 (2005): 327–58

Sanders, Theresa. *Celluloid Saints: Images of Sanctity in Film*. Macon, GA: Mercer University Press, 2002.

_____. "The Otherness of God and the Bodies of Others." *The Journal of Religion* 76, no. 4 (1996): 572–87.

Scanlon, Michael J. "Augustine and Theology as Rhetoric." *Augustinian Studies* 25 (1994): 37–48.

Schrijvers, Joeri. "In (the) Place of the Self: A Critical Study of Jean-Luc Marion's *Au lieu de soi: L'Approche de saint Augustin*." *Modern Theology* 25, no. 4 (2009): 661–86.

Smith, James K. A. "Between Predication and Silence: Augustine on How (Not) to Speak of God." *The Heythrop Journal* 41, no. 1 (January 2000): 66–86.

_____. *The Fall of Interpretation: Philosophical Foundations for a Creational Hermeneutic*. 2nd Edition. Grand Rapids: Baker Academic, 2012.

Smith, Steven G. "Topics in Philosophical Pneumatology: Inspiration, Wonder, Heart." In *Advents of the Spirit: An Introduction to the Current Study of Pneumatology*, edited by Bradford E. Hinze and D. Lyle Dabney, 208–32. Milwaukee, WI: Marquette University Press, 2001.

Sokolowski, Robert. *Introduction to Phenomenology*. Cambridge: Cambridge University Press, 2000.

Staron, Andrew. "Moral Action and the Pragmatic *As If*: Gerald McKenny's Critique of Jean-Luc Marion's Privileging of Love." *Quaestiones Disputatae* 1 (2010): 56–71.

Steinbock, Anthony J. "The Poor Phenomenon: Marion and the Problem of Givenness." In *Words of Life: New Theological Turns in French Phenomenology*, edited by Bruce Ellis Benson and Norman Wirzba, 120–31. New York: Fordham University Press, 2010.

Stell, Stephen L. "Hermeneutics in Theology and the Theology of Hermeneutics: Beyond Lindbeck and Tracy." *Journal of the American Academy of Religion* 61, no. 4 (1993): 679–703.

Stock, Brian. "Self, Soliloquy, and Spiritual Exercises in Augustine and Some Later Authors." *The Journal of Religion* 91, no. 1 (2011), 5–23.

Studer, Basil, OSB. *The Grace of Christ and the Grace of God in Augustine of Hippo: Christocentrism or Theocentrism?* Translated by Matthew J. O'Connell. Collegeville, MN: Liturgical Press, 1997.

_____. "History and Faith in Augustine's *De Trinitate*." *Augustinian Studies* 28 (1997): 7–50.

Tanner, Kathryn. "Theology at the Limits of Phenomenology." In *Counter-Experiences: Reading Jean-Luc Marion*, edited by Kevin Hart, 201–31. Notre Dame: University of Notre Dame Press, 2007.

Taylor, Charles. *Sources of the Self: The Making of the Modern Identity*. Cambridge: Harvard University Press, 1989.

Tertullian. *Against Praxeas*. Translated by Peter Holmes. In *Ante-Nicene Fathers, Vol. 3*. Peabody, MA: Hendrickson Publishers, 2004.

Teske, Roland J., SJ. "Augustine's Inversion of 1 John 4:8." *Augustinian Studies* 39 (2008): 49–60.

_____. "Augustine's Use of *Substantia* in Speaking About God." In *To Know God and the Soul: Essays on the Thought of Saint Augustine*, 112–30. Washington, DC: Catholic University of America Press, 2008.

_____. "Properties of God and the Predicaments in *De Trinitate* 5," In *To Know God and the Soul: Essays on the Thought of Saint Augustine*, 93–111. Washington, DC: Catholic University of America Press, 2008.

Tolliday, Philip. "Reading—Augustine and Marion." In *St. Augustine: His Relevance and Legacy*, edited by Wayne Cristaudo and Heung Wah Wong, 263–85. Adelaide, AUS: ATF Press, 2010.

Toom, Tarmo. "Augustine on Ambiguity." *Augustinian Studies* 38 (2007): 407–33.

_____. "Was Augustine an Intentionalist? Authorial Intention in Augustine's Hermeneutics." *Studia Patristica* 54 (2012): 1–9.

Torrance, Thomas F. *The Christian Doctrine of God, One Being Three Persons*. Edinburgh: T&T Clark, 1996.

Tracy, David. *The Analogical Imagination: Christian Theology and the Culture of Pluralism*. New York: Crossroad, 1981.

_____. "Augustine's Christomorphic Theocentrism." In *Orthodox Readings of*

Augustine, edited by George E. Demacopoulos and Aristotle Papanikolaou, 263–89. Crestwood, NY: St. Vladimir's Seminary Press, 2008.

_____. "Charity, Obscurity, Clarity: Augustine's Search for a True Rhetoric." In *Morphologies of Faith: Essays in Religion and Culture in Honor of Nathan A. Scott, Jr.*, edited by Mary Gerhart and Anthony C. Yu, 123–43. Atlanta, GA: Scholars Press, 1990.

_____. "God, Dialogue and Solidarity: A Theologian's Refrain." *The Christian Century* 107 (October 10, 1990): 900–904.

_____. "Jean-Luc Marion: Phenomenology, Hermeneutics, Theology." In *Counter-Experiences: Reading Jean-Luc Marion*, edited by Kevin Hart, 57–65. Notre Dame: University of Notre Dame Press, 2007.

_____. *Plurality and Ambiguity: Hermeneutics, Religion, Hope*. Chicago: University of Chicago Press, 1987.

_____. "The Post-Modern Re-Naming of God as Incomprehensible and Hidden." *Cross Currents* 50 (2000): 240–47.

_____. "Trinitarian Speculation and the Forms of Divine Disclosure." In *The Trinity: An Interdisciplinary Symposium on the Trinity*, edited Stephen T. Davis, Daniel Kendall, SJ, and Gerald O'Collins, SJ, 273–93. Oxford: Oxford University Press, 1999.

Van Fleteren, Frederick. "Toward an Understanding of Augustine's Hermeneutic." *Augustinian Studies* 29, no. 2 (1998) 118–30.

Van Inwagen, Peter. "And Yet They Are Not Three Gods but One God." In *Philosophy and the Christian Faith*, edited by Thomas V. Morris, 241–78. Notre Dame: University of Notre Dame Press, 1988.

Ward, Graham. "The Theological Project of Jean-Luc Marion." In *Post Secular Philosophy: Between Philosophy and Theology*, edited by Phillip Blond, 229–58. New York: Routledge, 1998.

Westphal, Merold. "Vision and Voice: Phenomenology and Theology in the Work of Jean-Luc Marion." *International Journal for Philosophy of Religion* 60 (2006): 117–37.

Wilken, Robert Louis. "*Spiritus sanctus secundum scripturas sanctas*: Exegetical Considerations of Augustine on the Holy Spirit." *Augustinian Studies* 31 (2000): 1–18.

Williams, Charles. *Descent into Hell*. Grand Rapids: Eerdmans, 1949.

Williams, Rowan. *Arius: Heresy and Tradition.* Rev. ed. Grand Rapids: Eerdmans, 2001.

_____. *The Edge of Words: God and the Habits of Language.* New York: Bloomsbury, 2014.

_____. "Language, Reality and Desire in Augustine's *De Doctrina.*" *Journal of Literature and Theology* 3 (July 1989): 138–50.

_____. "*Sapientia* and the Trinity: Reflections on the *De Trinitate.*" In *Collectanea Augustiniana: Mélanges T.J. van Bavel*, edited by B. Bruning, M. Lamberigts, J. van Houtem, 317–32. Leuven: Leuven University Press, 1990.

Wills, Garry. *Augustine's Confessions: A Biography.* Princeton: Princeton University Press, 2011.

_____. *Saint Augustine.* New York: Viking, 1999.

Winquist, Charles E. "Analogy, Apology, and the Imaginative Pluralism of David Tracy." *Journal of the American Academy of Religion* 56, no. 2 (1988): 307–19.

Wyschogrod, Edith, and John D. Caputo. "Postmodernism and the Desire for God: An E-mail Exchange." In *Crossover Queries: Dwelling with Negatives, Embodying Philosophy's Others*, by Edith Wyschogrod, 298–315. New York: Fordham University Press, 2006.

Zaborowski, Holger. "*Factus eram ipse mihi magna quaestio*: Augustine, Heidegger, and Postmodern Philosophy." In *Augustine and Postmodern Thought: A New Alliance Against Modernity?*, edited by Lieven Boeve, M. Lamberigts, Maarten Wisse, 169–92. Walpole, MA: Peeters, 2009.

Zizioulas, John D. *Being as Communion: Studies in Personhood and the Church.* Crestwood, NY: St. Vladimir's Seminary Press, 1997.

Zum Brunn, Emilie. *St. Augustine: Being and Nothingness.* New York: Paragon House, 1988.

Index